MEDIA AND ENTERTAINMENT INDUSTRY MANAGEMENT

The media and entertainment industry (MEI) differs significantly from traditional industries in many respects. Accordingly, the management of strategy, marketing and other business practices in the MEI necessitates a unique approach. Sunghan Ryu offers students focused and relevant insights into critical topics, illustrated by vivid examples from the MEI.

Unlike typical introductory textbooks on business and management, this book does not overemphasize complicated layers of theory. Instead, it presents essential concepts and frameworks in a digestible manner and supplements them with opportunities to apply this knowledge to real-world cases. The textbook demonstrates how knowledge can be constructively implemented in business and management scenarios. It is structured into 12 chapters, divided into five core modules: (1) Overview of the MEI, (2) The Fundamentals of Management, (3) Marketing Management, (4) Digital Business and Management, and (5) New Business Models and Entrepreneurship. Students will gain the ability to explain key concepts and frameworks across core business and management domains and develop analytical skills through diverse real-world cases in the MEI. Based on this knowledge, they will be equipped to identify management-related issues in the MEI and arrive at practical and effective solutions.

This book is an essential guide for students who wish to understand business and management in the dynamic world of the MEI.

Sunghan Ryu is associate professor at Shanghai Jiao Tong University. His research and teaching centers on digital innovation in the MEI. He is the author of *Beauty of Crowdfunding: Blooming Creativity and Innovation in the Digital Era*, and has published in top academic journals, including the *Journal of Marketing*, *MIS Quarterly*, *New Media & Society*, and the *Harvard Business Review*.

MEDIA AND ENTERTAINMENT INDUSTRY MANAGEMENT

How to Integrate Business and Management with Creativity and Imagination

Sunghan Ryu

LONDON AND NEW YORK

Designed cover image: © Getty Images

First published 2024
by Routledge
4 Park Square, Milton Park, Abingdon, Oxon, OX14 4RN

and by Routledge
605 Third Avenue, New York, NY 10158

Routledge is an imprint of the Taylor & Francis Group, an informa business

© 2024 Sunghan Ryu

The right of Sunghan Ryu to be identified as author of this work has been asserted in accordance with sections 77 and 78 of the Copyright, Designs and Patents Act 1988.

All rights reserved. No part of this book may be reprinted or reproduced or utilized in any form or by any electronic, mechanical, or other means, now known or hereafter invented, including photocopying and recording, or in any information storage or retrieval system, without permission in writing from the publishers.

Trademark notice: Product or corporate names may be trademarks or registered trademarks, and are used only for identification and explanation without intent to infringe.

British Library Cataloguing-in-Publication Data
A catalogue record for this book is available from the British Library

Library of Congress Cataloging-in-Publication Data
Names: Ryu, Sunghan, author.
Title: Media and entertainment industry management : how to integrate business and management with creativity and imagination / Sunghan Ryu.
Description: Abingdon, Oxon ; New York, NY : Routledge, 2024. | Includes bibliographical references. |
Contents: Overview of media and entertainment industry -- Marketing management -- Digital business and management -- New business model and entrepreneurship. |
Identifiers: LCCN 2023046832 (print) | LCCN 2023046833 (ebook) | ISBN 9781032221243 (hardback) | ISBN 9781032221212 (paperback) | ISBN 9781003271222 (ebook)
Subjects: LCSH: Mass media--Management. | Internet entertainment industry--Management.
Classification: LCC P96.M34 R98 2024 (print) | LCC P96.M34 (ebook) | DDC 302.23/068--dc23/eng/20231204
LC record available at https://lccn.loc.gov/2023046832
LC ebook record available at https://lccn.loc.gov/2023046833

ISBN: 978-1-032-22124-3 (hbk)
ISBN: 978-1-032-22121-2 (pbk)
ISBN: 978-1-003-27122-2 (ebk)

DOI: 10.4324/9781003271222

Typeset in Times New Roman
by MPS Limited, Dehradun

Access the Support Material: www.routledge.com/9781032221243

CONTENTS

Preface	*vii*
Acknowledgments	*xv*

MODULE I
Overview of the Media and Entertainment Industry   **1**

  1 An Introduction to the Media and Entertainment Industry   3

  2 The Characteristics of the Media and Entertainment Industry   34

MODULE II
The Fundamentals of Management   **61**

  3 What is Management? A Media and Entertainment Industry
    Perspective   63

  4 Organizational Behavior in Media and Entertainment
    Organizations   89

  5 Strategic Management in the Media and Entertainment Industry   121

MODULE III
Marketing Management   **159**

  6 Marketing Management in the Media and Entertainment Industry   161

vi Contents

7 Customer Relationship Management in Media and Entertainment
   Organizations   202

MODULE IV
Digital Business and Management   **235**

8 The Value of Information Technology in Business and
   Management   237

9 The Digitalization of the Media and Entertainment Industry   269

10 New Technological Advancements in the Media and Entertainment
    Industry   295

MODULE V
New Business Models and Entrepreneurship   **325**

11 Business Model Planning in the Media and Entertainment Industry   327

12 Creative Entrepreneurship   350

Index   *377*

PREFACE

Outline

Media and Entertainment Industry Management: The Motivation
The Objectives of the Book
The Pedagogical Approaches of the Book
Overview of the Book
References

Media and Entertainment Industry Management: The Motivation

We all understand the importance and excitement of the media and entertainment industry (MEI). It is one of the fastest-growing and most influential domains, encompassing the production, marketing, distribution, and consumption of media and entertainment content through different media and devices. Revenues in the MEI reached $2.2 trillion in 2021[1]—comparable to the approximately $2.8 trillion generated by the automotive industry that same year.[2] More importantly, the MEI is projected to experience substantial growth in the coming years. The MEI is expected to see a 5% compound annual growth rate, potentially elevating revenues to $2.6 trillion by 2025.

It is not only the numbers that matter. The MEI is a complex and challenging sector that requires logic and creativity, and that merges the real and the imaginary. It is also a tremendously interesting, exciting, and fascinating domain. It combines multiple dimensions and extremes in order to create value. In the MEI, creativity encounters business. Imagination is realized through technology. Stories meet wealth. Different generations come together and share their fantasies.

The MEI is also a driver of change and innovation, transforming cultures and economies. The emergence of new media throughout history—from parchment paper and movable printing devices to the internet and social media—has transformed the economy, science, politics, religion, and society far beyond the MEI. There is no doubting the influential role that the MEI has played in advancing and shaping our world. There are

viii Preface

thus some essential questions to ask in this regard. Why is the MEI so important and influential? What makes it unique and distinguishes it from other industries? How do the characteristics of the MEI affect the business and management of the industry?

In principle, all businesses are managed through similar functions, such as strategic planning, financing, accounting, production, marketing, distribution, and human resources. The bare management essentials should apply across all industries; but we must also recognize that the MEI has its own unique characteristics.

Business and management practices in the MEI differ significantly from general management practices. Unlike in many other industries, activities in the MEI— particularly content creation and production—are not primarily influenced by numerical data and analytical models. Instead, the management of media and entertainment content involves a reliance on creativity, subjective judgments, and intuitive decision-making processes. The objective of maximizing profits (or shareholder value), which drives business management in most sectors, is complemented by a notable emphasis on cultural enrichment and public welfare. As a result, the MEI is regarded as a unique industry characterized by its own distinctive motivations and policy considerations.

For example, consider a television network that produces a popular drama series. The network's management team must focus on viewership ratings and advertising revenues, and must ensure the quality and artistic and cultural value of the content. They rely on the creative insights of writers, directors, and actors to deliver engaging and emotionally impactful episodes, even if the immediate financial returns are not easily quantifiable. Similarly, in the newspaper industry, editors and journalists often make editorial decisions based on their subjective judgments and intuition. They consider factors such as the importance of a news story, its potential impact on society, and the values and principles of journalistic integrity. While financial considerations are still relevant, media organizations recognize their role in shaping public opinion and fostering cultural development, leading them to balance profit-driven strategies with broader social objectives.

The unique characteristics of the MEI are outlined in Chapter 2. These characteristics impact most business and management practices and managers in the MEI. While some of these characteristics exist in other sectors, their specific combination in the MEI generates unique market structures and ecosystems.

The differences are multi-dimensional. First and foremost, media and entertainment content exhibits distinct economic characteristics, with high fixed costs and low marginal costs. Producing content is typically costly, but reproducing it is inexpensive. Similarly, the creation of distribution networks initially entails significant expenses, but their extension to additional users swiftly becomes economical. These economic traits have several management implications, including the prevalence of large firms, market concentration, incentives for mergers, opportunities for early market entry, challenges of imitation and piracy, intense price competition, unsustainable pricing that fails to cover costs, the need for price discrimination, and more practical considerations.

In addition to the economic dynamics, the management style within the MEI is noteworthy. Unlike in many other industries, where analytical approaches and motivations of management are generally unquestioned, the legitimacy of management itself is often under scrutiny in the MEI. Managers often find themselves overshadowed by 'creative' individuals with esteemed status and high public visibility. Historically, media and entertainment management relied heavily on experiential knowledge and instinct rather than numerical data and analytical formulas.

However, in today's interconnected and rapidly evolving landscape, an exclusive reliance on lifelong experience within a single segment is insufficient, and boldness alone does not guarantee success. This is where the potential value of this book emerges. Success in the MEI requires more than just creativity and imagination. While these attributes are essential, they cannot in themselves assure success. A comprehensive understanding of various facets—such as technology, markets, audience dynamics, pricing strategies, global business operations, economic principles, managerial accounting practices, and government relations—and the ability to cultivate and lead talented individuals are also needed. Proficiency in these diverse areas is essential to effectively navigate the MEI's complex and ever-evolving landscape. Indeed, recent innovation and developments make this the most dynamic period in the MEI's history. This is also the period with both the greatest opportunities and the greatest uncertainty.

Given all the excitement and expectations, this book aims to help students and professionals interested (or already working) in the MEI to develop their skills as creative managers and creatives with managerial competencies. The aim is to enhance readers' knowledge of the industry and empower them to become more efficient, productive, and responsible contributors to the field.

The Objectives of the Book

The intended readers of this book include graduate students and professionals in the MEI. Some easier, condensed texts are available for undergraduate-level courses. The foundational concepts and real cases covered in this book are universal because their significance remains consistent across different educational levels.

Business and management practices in the MEI are now being taught worldwide, with a significant number of business and communication students pursuing careers on the "business side" of media and entertainment companies. However, the curriculums they study often fail to align with this career path, for various reasons.

On the one hand, curriculums in the discipline of communications tend to focus on either theoretical or technical aspects of the MEI in general, leading to a lack of understanding of the business and management of the field. Universities typically offer broad overviews of various industries like film, music, games, and the internet.

On the other hand, business schools teach students more practical knowledge from business and management perspectives. Their programs often incorporate existing generic courses like marketing or strategy, supplemented by media-specific cases and examples; rigorous application to the MEI is usually missing.

In addition to students in these disciplines, many young professionals already active in the MEI would benefit from an in-depth understanding of management concepts. They often have risen through technical or creative positions and now find themselves in the roles of managers or executives without any formal business training. They require educational materials that can bridge the gap between their jobs and the business aspects of the MEI. However, such materials and programs are not well developed by traditional departments, schools, and disciplines—whether in management or communications schools.

x Preface

To address this gap across the educational and industrial sectors, there is a need for dedicated programs, courses, and textbooks to assist prospective and current managers in the MEI—albeit some scattered resources already exist. It is important to provide a structured collection of analytical tools to promote a holistic understanding of, and insights into, the business and management of the MEI. Over time, the need for materials to train students and professionals in the management of media and entertainment content has become more pressing, as the MEI has assumed a more prominent position within both the economy and society.

This book covers business and management principles in key disciplines and their application to the MEI. Specifically, it aims to help readers achieve the following learning outcomes:

- Explain key concepts and frameworks and their application to the MEI in diverse business/management disciplines, including strategic management, marketing management, customer relationship management, management information systems, and entrepreneurship;
- Develop logical thinking and analytical skills through real-world cases in the MEI;
- Identify management-related issues in the MEI and arrive at possible solutions; and
- Develop conceptual and practical capabilities to analyze different business models in the MEI.

The book is structured on the basis of key business disciplines, including strategic management, marketing, customer relationship management, information systems, entrepreneurship, and other aspects that shape the MEI's interdisciplinary business and management practices, such as technological advancements in this domain. It provides real cases and practices across various sub-industries—including music, film, TV, the internet, and games. These materials also cover diverse regions and cultures. I hope the book's interdisciplinary and holistic approach will be more beneficial in meeting the identified needs than the previous approaches based on disciplinary or domain-specific specialties.

The Pedagogical Approaches of the Book

The intention is that this book will be integrated into relevant programs, courses, and modules that employ outcome-based education (OBE) or outcome-based teaching and learning (OBTL) as their pedagogical approach. As a theory, the overarching objective of OBE is to ensure that each student successfully achieves the predefined outcomes of the course by the end of their educational journey.[3]

OBTL, as a pedagogical application of OBE, is an educational methodology that places the student at the center of the learning process.[4] In this approach, the intended learning outcomes (ILOs) of a program/course/module are articulated, serving as explicit targets for students. Teaching and learning activities (TLAs) are thoughtfully structured and implemented to support the achievement of ILOs. Assessment tasks (ATs) are designed to evaluate if the ILO has been achieved. The effectiveness of OBTL is contingent upon the examination of assessment outcomes and the evaluation of students' learning experiences.

ILOs are the anticipated accomplishments, encompassing knowledge, skills, and attitudes that learners are expected to acquire through active participation in purposefully designed learning activities. TLAs are in-class and out-of-class activities designed to facilitate students' achievement of the specific ILOs. Finally, when lecturers introduce an AT, guidelines are provided to students to assist them in performing the AT. These guidelines are called "assessment rubrics," and inform students of the expectations and requirements of the specific ATs.

In an ILO statement, the learning outcome is defined by utilizing an "action" verb that signifies an observable behavior exhibited by the student, which can subsequently be assessed. It is imperative that the planned TLAs and ATs effectively facilitate students' progress toward the ILOs while ensuring alignment between the instructional strategies and the assessment methods employed. This alignment serves to optimize student learning throughout the educational process.

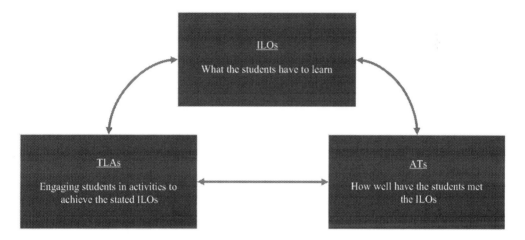

FIGURE 0 Outcome-based Learning and Teaching: Overview.

For Students

Students should know that everything lecturers ask them to do has an ILO. This means they should know what they will be expected to be able to do at the end of each class/tutorial/lecture and gives them clear directions to improve learning. To succeed in their studies and to learn effectively, students must:

- identify the ILOs of each chapter and activity;
- participate actively in TLAs; and
- evidence achievement of the outcomes through different ATs.

Students should also have an interdisciplinary perspective and an international outlook throughout the course.

xii Preface

For Lecturers

In the OBTL setting, the role of lecturers transforms into that of a trainer, facilitator, or mentor, depending on the targeted outcome. Unlike traditional approaches, OBTL does not prescribe a singular teaching style or assessment method. Instead, it emphasizes that classes, opportunities, and assessments should all align in a manner that assists students in accomplishing the predetermined ILOs. Lecturers should not provide any TLA without an ILO attached to it. One key outcome here is to "transform" students into professionals. When lecturers prepare their courses and lectures, they are expected to follow the suggestions below.

ILOs should be:

- expressed from the perspective of students;
- expressed in the form of action verbs; and
- related to criteria for assessing performance.

In suitable learning environments, students may also learn many additional things about the subject, communication skills, teamwork, and general learnings and life skills which are not necessarily included in the ILOs. These are called "unintended learning outcomes," and lecturers may also consider them when designing their courses or modules.

TLAs should be designed to help students achieve the specific ILOs. For example, if the ILO is to create a business model in the MEI, the lecturer could ask students to:

- analyze the business models of existing companies and familiarize themselves with the basic components of the business model;
- work in groups to conduct an independent study and discuss various business ideas based on the components of the business model; and
- choose and develop one business idea, and create a business model accordingly.

The types of ATs can vary according to the characteristics of ILOs and TLA. They include essay-type assignments, projects, presentations, quizzes, roleplays, written/oral tests, and so on. Lecturers should ask students to demonstrate evidence that a particular ILO has been achieved. If ILOs, TLAs and ATs are well aligned ("constructive alignment"), lecturers will know how they will assess students and students will understand how they will be assessed. For clarification, lecturers may provide students with assessment rubric criteria.

Overview of the Book

This book aims to provide a holistic, comprehensive view of business and management in the MEI. It seeks to address the limitations of traditional curriculums in business and communication-related programs, which tend to myopically apply the major dimensions of each discipline to the MEI context without making a close, systematic link between the two worlds.

This book presents media and communication students and professionals with a set of sectoral summaries across relevant business/management disciplines. Business and management students and managers will be introduced to the MEI, and will ultimately be expected to integrate the two strands of materials by applying business/management knowledge and skills within the MEI in a more organic way. In other words, this book presents key major components of a business/management program, simplifies and summarizes them, and finally applies them to the MEI.

The book is organized into five main modules:

Module I: Overview of the Media and Entertainment Industry
   Chapter 1: An Introduction to the Media and Entertainment Industry
   Chapter 2: The Characteristics of the Media and Entertainment Industry

Module II: The Fundamentals of Management
   Chapter 3: What is Management? A Media and Entertainment Industry Perspective
   Chapter 4: Organizational Behavior in Media and Entertainment Organizations
   Chapter 5: Strategic Management in the Media and Entertainment Industry

Module III: Marketing Management
   Chapter 6: Marketing Management in the Media and Entertainment Industry
   Chapter 7: Customer Relationship Management in Media and Entertainment
         Organizations

Module IV: Digital Business and Management
   Chapter 8: The Value of Information Technology in Business and Management
   Chapter 9: The Digitalization of the Media and Entertainment Industry
   Chapter 10: New Technological Advancements in the Media and Entertainment Industry

Module V: New Business Models and Entrepreneurship
   Chapter 11: Business Model Planning in the Media and Entertainment Industry
   Chapter 12: Creative Entrepreneurship

Module I introduces the concepts and scope of the MEI, including film, TV and radio, print and publishing, music and games, and emerging trends in production, distribution, marketing, and customer aspects (Chapter 1). Chapter 2 explores the key concepts and factors that shape the MEI, such as hedonic consumption, the window effect, its high-risk/high-return nature, the experience goods market, the public goods market, the importance of fans, and the concepts of cultural discount and premium.

Module II explores the fundamental concepts of management. Chapter 3 discusses the evolution of management concepts and the roles and functions of managers in organizations. It also addresses the impact of digital transformation, globalization, and ESG considerations on management. Chapter 4 aims to give students a basic understanding of organizational behavior. In addition, emerging organizational behavior themes—such as managing creativity, change, innovation, global teams, diversity, and social responsibility—are presented. Chapter 5 presents the frameworks of strategic management and provides the necessary knowledge for analyzing the process of strategy formulation and implementation.

Module III begins by presenting the paradigm of marketing management and the frameworks of marketing strategy and marketing mix (Chapter 6). Chapter 7 explains the concepts and core activities of customer relationship management: the process of building, retaining, and expanding a long-term partnership between a company and its customers based on mutual trust.

Module IV starts with a discussion of the implications of information technology and associated technologies for business and management (Chapter 8). Chapter 9 outlines the advantages of the digitalization of media and entertainment and explains how they are transforming business activities in the MEI. Chapter 10 focuses on the transformative impact of innovative technologies on the MEI, including 5G technology, artificial intelligence, blockchain, and the metaverse.

Module V presents the concepts and key components of business models, analyzing various types of business models and offering guidelines for business model planning (Chapter 11). The module then introduces the concepts of creative entrepreneurs and creative entrepreneurship (Chapter 12) as a combination of the creative and management disciplines. It also outlines the basic mindset, skills, and knowledge required to pursue a creative entrepreneurial career.

Each of these chapters covers a set of major business and management concepts and frameworks. These concepts and frameworks, and their application to the MEI, are described and analyzed. The book includes case studies, discussion questions, and further reading lists. The case studies focus on major media and entertainment companies in both the international and local contexts to supplement the chapter materials. They are presented inside text boxes. More details of each case for classroom use are also available on the book webpage at www.routledge.com/9781032221212. To facilitate the book's use in a course setting, each chapter is followed by a list of discussion questions. Sample answers for classroom discussion are available to instructors at the Instructor Hub via the book webpage. Finally, further reading lists should be helpful for those students who wish to dig deeper into a specific topic or theme.

References

1 "2022 outlook segment findings: markets and industries" (no date) *PwC*. www.pwc.com/gx/en/industries/tmt/media/outlook/segment-findings.html.
2 Carlier, M. (2023) "Automotive industry worldwide - statistics & facts," *Statista*. www.statista.com/topics/1487/automotive-industry/#:~:text=The%20automotive%20manufacturing%20industry%20generated,expected%20to%20grow%20in%202022.
3 Spady, W. G. (1994) "Outcome-based education: critical issues and answers". American Association of School Administrators. ISBN: 0876521839. https://files.eric.ed.gov/fulltext/ED380910.pdf.
4 Kennedy, K. J. (2011) "Conceptualising quality improvement in higher education: policy, theory and practice for outcomes based learning in Hong Kong." *Journal of Higher Education Policy & Management*, 33(3), pp. 205–218. doi:10.1080/1360080X.2011.564995.

ACKNOWLEDGMENTS

I have taught "Management Essentials," a core course for first-year graduate students at the USC-SJTU Institute of Cultural and Creative Industry (ICCI) of Shanghai Jiao Tong University, since the 2017/18 academic year. This textbook project was grounded on the course materials tested among multiple groups of diverse students. They were upgraded and refined based on feedback and comments from the classes over the years. I am grateful to the students and teaching assistants for their remarkable commitment and contribution to this project.

This book covers a wide range of topics and themes and owes much to the numerous authors and sources it draws upon. I owe a profound debt of gratitude to them. If any source or author has not been sufficiently acknowledged, I sincerely apologize for such oversight.

I am grateful to my friends and colleagues at Shanghai Jiao Tong University, University of Southern California, and other partner institutions worldwide for their support and inspiration. In particular, I would like to thank the Graduate School of Shanghai Jiao Tong University for providing the project funding. I would also like to thank the ICCI for providing an excellent research environment and structure.

Kendrick Loo, Chelsea Low, and their team at Routledge have been professional and encouraging throughout the process. I am thankful to them for their trust, support, and patience. Thanks also to Carolyn Boyle for her dedicated contribution to the copyediting and proofreading process.

I would also like to thank my parents for their unconditional love and support. My daughters—Jimin, Jiwon, and Jina—are my greatest source of creativity and imagination. I hope they are proud of their dad for his determination and dedication to this project.

I am most grateful to my wife, Soohee Choi, for her unlimited encouragement and advice with love. She is perfect for me and completes me.

Finally, I thank Jesus Christ for everything He has done for me and my family. I will remember His love and sacrifice and follow His word and calling forever.

MODULE I

Overview of the Media and Entertainment Industry

1

AN INTRODUCTION TO THE MEDIA AND ENTERTAINMENT INDUSTRY

Outline

1.1	The Media and Entertainment Industry: An Overview	3
1.2	The Scope of the Media and Entertainment Industry	12
1.3	Key Facts and Figures of the Media and Entertainment Industry	19
1.4	Emerging Trends in the Media and Entertainment Industry	22
Case Studies		27
Review		28
Discussion Questions		29
Further Reading		29
References		30

Intended Learning Outcomes

- Identify the basic concepts and characteristics of the business/management of the media and entertainment industry (MEI).
- Describe the scope of the MEI and major subsections of the industry.
- Analyze the growth and development trends of the MEI.
- Explain the unique aspects of the MEI in comparison to other industries.

1.1 The Media and Entertainment Industry: An Overview

1.1.1 Examples of Media and Entertainment Companies

The MEI covers various areas, including but not limited to films, broadcasting and networking, music, games, news, print and publications, and digital platforms. Each area

DOI: 10.4324/9781003271222-2

4 Overview of the Media and Entertainment Industry

has its own associated networks and infrastructure, which are interrelated to each other. Media and entertainment companies operate within these areas and offer products and services to customers ranging from individuals to large organizations.

Examples of the representative media and entertainment companies in the global market include:

- The Walt Disney Company (US)
- Apple (US)
- Netflix (US)
- Tencent (China)
- Vivendi (France)
- Comcast (US)
- HYBE (Korea)
- ByteDance (China)
- CJ ENM (Korea)
- Electronic Arts (US)
- Sony (Japan)
- Nintendo (Japan)
- NetEase (China)
- Activision Blizzard (US)
- Epic Games (US)
- Alphabet (formerly Google) (US)
- Meta (formerly Facebook) (US)

The following introductions summarize the business and operations of some of these global companies.[1]

The Walt Disney Company (Disney)

Founded in 1923, Disney is a large media and entertainment group with multiple subsidiaries.[2] In 2021, Disney generated around $67.42 billion in revenues. Disney's four segments cover the following key areas:[3]

- Media networks: This segment comprises all TV, radio, cable, and associated businesses.
- Park and resorts: This includes theme parks, hotels, resorts, sports facilities, and food enterprises.
- Studio entertainment: This includes live-action and animated films, distributed globally.
- Consumer products and interactive media: This involves the licensing and retailing of trade names, characters, and properties, as well as instructional books and magazines. In November 2019, Disney launched Disney+, an online streaming service that offers blockbuster films, original Disney shows, and vintage Disney content.

Apple

Founded in 1976, Apple had a market cap of $2.74 trillion as of October 2022.[4] In 2021, Apple recorded $365 billion in net sales.[5] After adding streaming and news media services to its portfolio, the company evolved from a tech company to a hybrid tech and media company. Its media and entertainment business line includes Apple Music, Apple TV, Apple Books, Apple News, and so on.

Netflix

Having originated as a DVD-by-mail service in 1997, Netflix swiftly transformed into a streaming giant. As of the end of 2021, Netflix boasted an impressive subscriber base of 222 million users worldwide. Its primary source of revenue is membership fees collected from its streaming customers. In 2021 alone, Netflix generated a staggering $29.52 billion in streaming revenue.[6] This exponential growth and financial success are a testament to its ability to adapt to changing consumer preferences and capitalize on the growing demand for digital streaming services.

Comcast

Established in 1963, Comcast is one of the largest global media and entertainment companies with a market cap of $213.75 billion as of October 2022;[7] it generated over $116.39 million in revenues in 2021.[8] It is also the parent company of several international media and entertainment companies, such as NBCUniversal and Sky Group. Its business is run through five segments:

- Cable service: Comcast Cable is a leading provider of broadband, video, voice, wireless, and other services to residential customers in the United States.
- Media: This encompasses NBCUniversal's television and streaming platforms.
- Studios: This encompasses NBCUniversal's film and television studio production and distribution operations.
- Theme parks: Universal theme parks are located in Orlando, Florida; Hollywood, California; Osaka, Japan; and Beijing, China.
- Sky: This is one of Europe's leading entertainment companies, which primarily includes a direct-to-consumer business and a content business.

CJ ENM

CJ ENM (CJ Entertainment and Merchandising) is a South Korean entertainment and commerce company that operates in various fields, including music, film, television, and retail. CJ ENM was established through the merger of two CJ Group subsidiaries—CJ E&M and CJ O Shopping—in July 2018. In 2021, CJ ENM recorded an annual revenue of KRW 3.55 trillion ($2.97 billion).[9]

CJ ENM has a diverse portfolio of business divisions that contribute to its success and growth:

- Media: CJ ENM operates various television channels, including its flagship channel, tvN. The company produces and broadcasts a wide range of content, including dramas, variety shows, and reality programs.
- Film: CJ ENM is known for its film production and distribution business. The company has produced and distributed numerous successful films both domestically

6 Overview of the Media and Entertainment Industry

and internationally. It has played a significant role in the "Korean Wave," also known as "*Hallyu*," by promoting Korean films globally.[10]

- Music: CJ ENM operates as a music label and distributor, managing some of the biggest names in the Korean music industry. It also involves the production and management of live performances and events, including concerts, musicals, and theater productions.
- Commerce: Originally through CJ O Shopping, CJ ENM operates different commercial and retail businesses, including TV home shopping and e-commerce.

Paramount Global

In 2019, Viacom and CBS merged to form ViacomCBS, whose name changed once again to Paramount Global in February 2022. The company operates three segments—TV entertainment, cable networks, and filmed entertainment—and reported revenues of $28.59 billion in 2021.[11] Its assets operate across radio, print, television, and advertising services. Its filmed entertainment business includes brand names like Paramount Pictures, MTV Films, and Nickelodeon. Popular TV channel brands include Nickelodeon, TeenNick, Comedy Central, and Spike TV. Paramount Global also operates gaming businesses through different online channels.

HYBE

HYBE, formerly known as Big Hit Entertainment, is a South Korean entertainment company that has gained significant prominence in the global music industry. HYBE is best known as the agency behind global K-pop sensation BTS. The company has experienced remarkable success in recent years. In 2021, it recorded annual revenues of KRW 1.2 trillion ($1 billion)—a 58% annual increase compared to 2020.[12] It is the first South Korean music agency to surpass the annual revenue of KRW 1 trillion ($838 million). HYBE has pursued business diversification to expand its reach beyond the music industry. The company has invested in diverse sectors, such as technology, gaming, and content production. For example, its social networking platform, Weverse, serves as a hub for connecting artists, content, and fans. This diversification strategy aims to capitalize on emerging trends and opportunities in the MEI, providing new avenues for growth.

Fox

After selling its entertainment business—including 20th Century Fox television and film studios and a considerable stake in Hulu and US cable channels—to Disney for $71 billion in 2017, Fox Corporation now operates as a slimmed-down media company. Its media business unit includes the Fox News Channel, Fox Business, Big Ten Networks, and Fox Broadcasting Company. In the second half of 2021, Fox reported revenues of $7.49 billion.[13]

Tencent

Tencent is a multinational conglomerate based in China and is one of the largest and most influential technology companies in the world. It recorded revenue of RMB 554.55 billion ($81 billion) in 2022.[14] Tencent's most notable platform is WeChat, a multi-purpose messaging, social media, and mobile payment app. Monthly active users of WeChat and its domestic version, Weixin, had reached 1.319 billion by the end of March 2023.[15]

Tencent is a dominant player in the online gaming industry globally. It owns and operates a vast portfolio of popular online games, including *Honor of Kings*, *League of Legends*, *PUBG Mobile*, and *Call of Duty Mobile*. The company's gaming division generates substantial revenue and has a significant impact on the global gaming market.

Tencent has invested heavily in digital content and entertainment, including music streaming, video streaming, and film production. Tencent Music Entertainment is one of the largest music streaming platforms in China, offering a vast catalog of music from domestic and international artists. Tencent Video is a leading online video platform in China, providing a wide range of licensed and original content. Tencent Pictures is involved in film production and distribution, collaborating on both domestic and international film projects.

Sony

Sony is primarily known as a leading global electronics and music business operator, but it also has other media business lines. Its key segments include games and network services (e.g., PlayStation), music (e.g., Sony Music Entertainment), pictures (e.g., Sony Pictures Entertainment), and electronics products and solutions. The pictures segment includes motion pictures, television productions, and media networks. As of the fiscal year ending March 2021, Sony had generated $9 billion in revenues across all business units.[16]

Companies in the MEI rely heavily on revenue streams generated from advertising and paid subscriptions, particularly in the business-to-consumer context. Additional sources of revenue include product sales, box-office revenue from filmed entertainment, internet services, and licensing agreements. However, the MEI is incredibly diverse. Many companies within this domain also operate businesses that extend beyond traditional media and entertainment, such as technology products, software solutions, and retail. In fact, some leading companies in the MEI have expanded their operations into this field from their original non-media-related businesses (e.g., Apple, Sony).

Furthermore, mergers and acquisitions (M&As) are commonplace within the MEI. This is largely due to the significant advantages associated with the production, distribution, and marketing of media and entertainment content on a large scale. By combining resources and expertise through M&As, companies in the MEI can enhance their competitive position and expand their reach in the market.

The MEI encompasses a wide range of businesses and revenue streams. Companies in this sector rely on various sources of income, engage in diverse operations beyond media and entertainment, and frequently engage in M&As to strengthen their market presence and capabilities.

1.1.2 Why Does the Media and Entertainment Industry Matter?

The MEI plays different essential roles in our society. Most of all, media and entertainment can provide information and education.[17] There are diverse formats through which information is made accessible. Media outlets like newspapers, news-oriented television, and radio programs disseminate global stories. Books and magazines

8 Overview of the Media and Entertainment Industry

offer comprehensive insights into a wide range of subjects. Moreover, the online encyclopedia Wikipedia provides articles on various topics. Universities can also share educational resources such as lecture notes, exams, and audio/video recordings of classes on their massive open online course platforms, enabling individuals with internet access to freely access educational content.

Media and entertainment serve as catalysts for our imaginations, offering a wellspring of fantasy and an avenue for escapism. Through the diverse array of stories they present, media and entertainment possess the remarkable ability to transport us beyond our own realities. The desire to communicate and share information and stories has been an integral part of human existence since time immemorial, and this lies at the very core of the MEI's mission. Over the decades, radio and broadcasting stations, as well as cable television networks, have been instrumental in providing a wide range of entertaining content. The emergence of the internet opened up new avenues for watching movies and other entertainment content on personal computers. More recently, the rise of smartphones and tablets has further transformed the MEI, offering us greater flexibility in terms of what we watch and the freedom to choose when and where to indulge in our preferred entertainment.

Finally, the MEI has the potential to serve as a platform for public discourse on significant matters. The internet, for instance, is a fundamentally democratic channel that enables individuals with online access to freely express their opinions through various digital platforms like blogs, social media, and podcasting. Moreover, the media plays a crucial role in overseeing the activities of government, businesses, and other institutions.

In sum, the roles of the MEI in our society include:

- providing information and education;
- entertaining and offering an outlet for the imagination; and
- serving as a public forum for important issues and monitoring authorities/institutions.

1.1.3 A Brief History of the Media and Entertainment Industry

The communication and dissemination of knowledge and stories is the primary function of the MEI, which has existed for as long as humanity itself. In this section, we discuss how the core role of the MEI in informing and influencing people has been realized from the early days to today.

Print Media

Printed materials such as scrolls and letters date back to ancient civilizations, but few of these have survived over the centuries.[18] Newspapers and magazines were introduced in the 17th and 18th centuries. *Publick Occurrences*, the first multi-page newspaper, debuted in Boston in 1690;[19] while *The Gentlemen's Magazine*, the first magazine, was launched in London in 1731.[20]

Newspapers became vital for urbanized Americans in the 19th century, offering reliable news in a changing landscape. With the Industrial Revolution, increased wealth and leisure time allowed individuals to engage with media. By the 1920s, newspapers were benefiting from improved printing methods, expanded communication networks, efficient news gathering, and rising ad revenues.[21] Newspaper companies expanded into large corporations and made enormous profits.

Radio

The radio was invented in the late 1800s by Guglielmo Marconi, who developed a wireless device capable of transmitting signals over long distances; and Nikola Tesla, who demonstrated radio frequency transmission. This innovation paved the way for the emergence of the radio industry, which was initially led by a small group of amateur broadcasters in the early 1900s. By the 1920s, radios had become commonplace in households, leading to the formation of radio networks and becoming a primary source of entertainment and news in most homes.[22] Radio quickly encroached upon the traditional domain of newspapers in news reporting. Advertisers soon recognized the potential of radio waves in expanding their reach to a broader audience.

Rich entrepreneurs less impacted by the Great Depression acquired regional radio stations and established radio network chains. Early big radio networks like the National Broadcasting Company (NBC) and Columbia Broadcasting System (CBS) were profitable even during the Great Depression.[23,24] A significant portion of radio networks' revenues came from advertisers that sponsored their shows. Radio advertising offered the advantage of reaching a large and engaged audience. During the early era of radio, advertisers had a unique opportunity to convey their sales messages to an attentive and diverse audience that was receptive, interested, enthusiastic, curious, and easily accessible from the comfort and privacy of their homes.[25]

Filmed Entertainment

Starting in the mid-1800s, numerous explorers embarked on experiments with motion picture cameras. Notable inventions in this field included William Lincoln's zoopraxiscope, Thomas Edison's Kinetoscope, and Louis and August Lumière's Cinematographe.[26] The Cinematographe was the first portable motion picture camera capable of projecting moving visuals to a crowd rather than just a single viewer.

These technological advancements in the early 1900s gave rise to the motion picture industry, marking a pivotal shift toward storytelling through film. Films such as *Life of an American Fireman* and *The Great Train Robbery*, released in 1903, showcased early examples of narrative, film editing, camera movement, and on-location shooting. As the 1900s progressed, the film industry expanded rapidly due to numerous breakthroughs and developments.

In the 1920s, Southern California—nestled beneath the San Gabriel Mountains—emerged as the world's cinema capital, famously known as Hollywood. This era witnessed the establishment of major film production studios and the introduction of sound films. The debut of "talkies" in 1927, featuring synchronized sound, drew large audiences to theaters, with approximately 110 million Americans flocking to cinemas weekly in 1930, despite the onset of the Great Depression following the stock market crash of October 1929.[27] The allure of this new technology allowed Hollywood to continue thriving financially. However, this began to change as the national economy deteriorated, leading to a decline in attendance to around 60 million by the early 1930s.

10 Overview of the Media and Entertainment Industry

TV

In the late 1920s, inventors conducted experiments with electronic television, but it wasn't until 1939 that the general public started watching television broadcasts. The turning point came with RCA's broadcast of President Franklin D. Roosevelt's speech at the New York World's Fair.[28] In 1941, CBS aired two 15-minute episodes daily, reaching a small audience. Television gained increasing popularity in the late 1940s and early 1950s, coinciding with the post-World War II rise of the American economy and increased leisure time for consumers. This period featured a variety of programming, including news, sitcoms, variety shows, and dramas. Networks such as NBC, ABC, and PBS were established during this time.

Cable television emerged in the early 1960s, initially serving remote areas and eventually expanding to broadcast regional sports team home games in New York City. In the 1970s and early 1980s, channels like HBO, CNN, and Nickelodeon were founded and grew. The proliferation of cable television in the 1980s and 1990s brought significant changes to the media landscape. Unlike the limited channel options of early television, cable companies offered customers a wide range of choices.

Unlike print media, broadcast media operates on fixed schedules, providing a sense of timeliness and transience. In the 1980s, videocassette recorders allowed viewers to record, watch, and rent movies at their convenience. The introduction of digital video recorders (DVRs) in the late 1990s enabled viewers to pause and rewind television broadcasts, offering consumers a new way to watch their favorite programs.

The television industry has been significantly impacted by changing consumer viewing habits, which have affected the value of time-sensitive advertising. This dynamic poses challenges to the TV ecosystem, while also creating opportunities for innovative solutions.

Digital Media and Entertainment

In the 1980s, consumers embraced audio compact discs (CDs) as their first digital entertainment medium, followed by DVDs in the early 1990s. Direct-to-home satellite TV providers like DirecTV and Dish Network began offering digital TV services, making satellite boxes a common feature in many households.

At the same time, the package media market experienced a renaissance, with Hollywood studios transitioning from videocassettes to digital disc media like DVDs and Blu-ray discs. Home video sales became a significant revenue source for movies and TV shows, offering consumers control over their viewing experiences through features like pause, replay, and fast-forward.

The transition from analog to digital television broadcasting posed a significant challenge for the industry, with the last analog program in the US airing in June 2009.[29] Digital terrestrial television, including high-definition video and digital audio, became the norm worldwide. However, the influence of the internet surpassed the digital television transformation in terms of its impact on the economy and people's lives. The emergence of the internet in the 1990s allowed viewers to watch TV shows and movies on their computers.

Apple's iPod, launched in 2001, revolutionized mobile technology and became an iconic symbol of the 21st century. Personal digital devices like smartphones and tablets gradually replaced specialized devices such as mobile phones, TVs, DVRs, and PCs. Consumers showed a preference for enjoying entertainment on portable devices, even with their smaller screens. These innovations expanded the options for watching shows and movies on the go, reshaping business practices.

By the early 2010s, the digital age was fully developed, bringing significant changes to the entertainment landscape. Internet connectivity has become ubiquitous through various electronic gadgets, enabling constant monitoring and personalized experiences. Online video services are available on a wide range of devices, giving consumers the flexibility to watch their favorite content at their convenience. The concept of entertainment content continues to evolve in this digital era.

Games

Electronic games or videogames have emerged as a prominent form of entertainment in the digital age, pioneering the realm of digital media. Unlike passive forms of entertainment like movies and television, videogames require active user engagement and input, fostering a deeper emotional connection.

Initially serving a niche market, the videogame industry has experienced significant growth, propelled by the success of game consoles such as the Xbox, PlayStation, and Wii. The trajectory of the industry can be traced back to early computer games like *Spacewar!* and Atari's *Pong* in the 1970s.

With the widespread availability and affordability of computers in the 1970s, games transitioned from arcades to homes; while Nintendo's Game Boy further solidified the bond between players and their games.[30] The advent of the internet and mobile technology in the 2000s saw the industry's revenues soar from tens of billions to hundreds of billions. Microsoft introduced Xbox Live in 2001, paving the way for online gaming.

The rise of mobile gaming in the late 2000s, coupled with the popularity of smartphones, resulted in significant growth and increased screen time. Games like *Angry Birds* became a sensation on the Apple App Store. Virtual reality gaming also emerged during this time, carving a path as a recognized genre. Cloud gaming, which generates substantial revenue, also became a reality.

The gaming industry has experienced fragmentation and concentration across various sectors, including consoles, computer gaming, online gaming, and cloud computing. Digital connectivity has brought success to such modern phenomena as *World of Warcraft*, a massively multiplayer online role-playing game (MMORPG). Today, gaming platforms serve as a gateway to a vast array of digital entertainment options, connecting players to online video services like Netflix, Hulu, and Disney+.

Artificial Intelligence, Blockchain, the Metaverse and More

The MEI has witnessed the emergence and growth of several new technologies, such as artificial intelligence (AI), blockchain, and the metaverse (for more details, see Chapter 10).

AI is increasingly used in the MEI to enhance the quality of content, personalize user experiences, and optimize business operations. AI-powered recommendation systems have been used by streaming services to suggest content to viewers. Streaming services like Netflix and Spotify use AI algorithms to personalize content recommendations for their users based on viewing or listening history, preferences, and behavior. AI-generated content has been used in areas such as news reporting, music composition, and visual

12 Overview of the Media and Entertainment Industry

content creation. Media and entertainment companies save time and costs and enhance the quality of their content.

Blockchain technology has been used to address copyright infringement, digital piracy, and transparent royalty payments. Blockchain-based platforms have been used to protect intellectual property (IP) rights and ensure transparent and efficient royalty payments to content creators. Blockchain-based platforms allow content creators to maintain control over their IP and receive direct compensation for their work.

As a blockchain-based application, non-fungible tokens (NFTs) are opening up a new avenue for the MEI. For example, NFTs are used to create and distribute digital content, such as music, artworks, and digital collectibles. They allow artists to monetize their work and collectors to own unique, verifiable digital assets. The sale of Beeple's NFT artwork collage, titled *Everydays: The First 5000 Days*, for $69 million in March 2021 was one significant example.[31] *NBA Top Shot*, a digital sports collectible, allows fans to buy and sell limited-edition video highlights of NBA basketball games.[32]

The metaverse blurs the boundaries between the physical and digital worlds in the MEI. Specifically, the advancement of metaverse technology has created new experiences, such as virtual concerts and immersive gaming. For example, virtual concerts allow audiences to participate from the comfort of their homes. Rapper and producer Travis Scott launched a virtual concert on the popular videogame *Fortnite* during the COVID-19 lockdown in April 2020. Over 27.7 million players participated in the in-game virtual live concert.[33]

Metaverse platforms enable players to create avatars, interact with others, and explore virtual worlds by creating their own virtual worlds and playing games on the platforms. *Roblox*, *Zepeto*, and *Minecraft* are representative metaverse platforms in this regard.

The MEI has undergone remarkable transformations and has become deeply intertwined with the traditional media and entertainment landscape and newly created digital media entertainment domains.

1.2 The Scope of the Media and Entertainment Industry

The MEI comprises businesses that produce, distribute, and offer ancillary analog and digital services and products for different media and entertainment segments, including but not limited to movies, TV shows, radio shows, news, music, newspapers, magazines, books, and games.[34] Indeed, the phenomenon of convergence has blurred the boundaries and broadened the scope of the media and entertainment segments (Figure 1.1).

There are many different approaches to classifying the segments of the MEI. For example, according to PricewaterhouseCoopers (PwC), the MEI can be categorized into filmed entertainment (e.g., motion pictures, television, streaming content); radio; music; publishing (e.g., newspapers, magazines, books in physical, digital and audio formats); videogames (e.g., physical, digital, and online games, mobile apps, virtual and augmented reality (VR/AR); and e-sports.[35] The UK government alternatively uses a broader term, "creative industry." It encompasses multiple subsectors: advertising, architecture, arts and culture, crafts, design, fashion, games, music, publishing, and TV and film.[36]

In this book, we categorize the MEI into five major domains and focus our discussion on these sectors: film, TV and radio, print and publishing, music, and videogames.

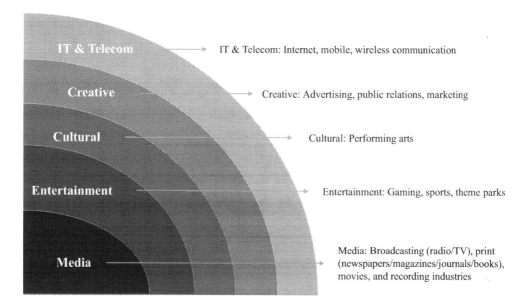

FIGURE 1.1 The Convergence of the Media and Entertainment Segments.

1.2.1 Film

The film industry comprises major studios, smaller studios, and global organizations, with notable players including Walt Disney Company, Universal, Sony/Columbia, Lionsgate, Paramount, and Warner Bros. These studios often belong to larger media conglomerates that encompass various forms of media. Within the film industry, there are subsectors such as film production, post-production, and exhibition.

Film production and distribution companies, along with movie theaters and post-production businesses, constitute the movie business. Both independent production companies (e.g., Lionsgate Films, Samuel Goldwyn Films, and Magnolia Pictures) and renowned studios (e.g., 21st Century Fox, Paramount, Universal, Sony, and Warner Bros.) exist within the industry. Independent films—which are typically more artistic and have lower budgets—are produced outside of major studios, with independent production teams responsible for securing funds.

Many prestigious film production companies also have distribution and post-production arms. For example, The Walt Disney Company owns Walt Disney Studios Motion Pictures (formerly Buena Vista Pictures Distribution) for film distribution. Post-production companies offer a range of services, such as editing, film processing, titling, animation, and special effects.

Key roles within film production studios encompass writers, editors, producers, directors, camera operators, audio technicians, lighting specialists, casting agents, animators, graphic designers, special effects artists, and costume designers and stylists.

The advent of online video platforms has had a transformative impact on the film industry, revolutionizing content creation, distribution, and consumption. Online video platforms have provided filmmakers with a global distribution reach, making it easier to showcase their work to a wide audience. The digital era has also made filmmaking

14 Overview of the Media and Entertainment Industry

more cost-effective, enabling high-quality production on smaller budgets. Platforms like YouTube and TikTok have fostered user-generated content, empowering everyday individuals to create and share videos, thereby cultivating a new generation of creators and influencers. Furthermore, online video platforms utilize data-driven insights to enhance user experience, tailoring recommendations and advertising based on user preferences.

The rise of online video platforms has significantly influenced the film industry, particularly for independent and low-budget filmmakers. These platforms offer a means for independent filmmakers to distribute their work globally, bypassing traditional channels like theaters and DVDs. Online video platforms facilitate direct interaction between filmmakers and their audience, fostering engagement and community building. Additionally, filmmakers can explore diverse revenue streams through advertising and pay-per-view models offered by these platforms, generating income from online distribution.

1.2.2 TV and Radio

The radio and television broadcasting sector comprises three distinct types of businesses. First, there are commercial broadcasters that sustain their operations through advertising revenue. Second, public service broadcasters receive funding from government entities at the central or local level. These broadcasters, on both radio and television, produce and acquire content for broadcasting, encompassing talk shows, news programs, and entertainment shows. Finally, there are specific types of broadcasters that focus on cable and subscription-based content, catering to specialized interests such as sports, education, and children's television.

Television broadcasting includes network-owned stations as well as independently owned stations that are affiliated with networks. Affiliated stations have contractual agreements with networks to broadcast their content, and networks often operate as flagship stations in significant media markets. Leading broadcast networks include ABC, CBS, NBC, and Fox. A typical television station structure comprises various departments such as management (including general manager and vice president); news (including news directors, assignment editors, producers, reporters, anchors, and photographers); production (including directors, technical directors, audio operators, and camera operators); sales (responsible for commercial spot sales); and promotions (involved in creating and editing commercials promoting the station).

In the radio broadcasting industry, companies like Sirius XM Radio and iHeartMedia operate radio broadcast studios that transmit music, talk shows, and other forms of entertainment. Platforms such as Sirius XM's satellite and online radio offer a range of radio programs, including CNBC, the BBC World Service, Bloomberg Radio, and local news channels. Radio networks, syndicates, and stations utilize FM and AM radio channels, as well as digital, satellite, and internet radio channels, to broadcast audio programs.

1.2.3 Print and Publishing

The print industry encompasses a range of businesses involved in publishing periodicals (e.g., newspapers, magazines), books, and journals, as well as their digital counterparts.

Additionally, these businesses may produce directories, mailing lists, and software. Publishers can release works that they have independently created, as well as works for which they have acquired rights from others. Publications are available in various formats, such as traditional print, e-books, and private electronic networks. The "Big Five" publishing conglomerates—Simon & Schuster, Hachette Book Group, HarperCollins, Macmillan, and Penguin Random House—are prominent players in this sector.[37]

Representative players include the following:

- Founded in 1924, Simon & Schuster is a major publishing house known for its diverse range of publications across fiction, non-fiction, children's literature, and more. Atria Books, Gallery Books, and Pocket Books are representative publishers under Simon & Schuster.
- Penguin Random House is one of the largest book publishers in the world, with imprints that include Penguin Books, Knopf Doubleday, Viking Press, and Random House. Penguin Random House publishes over 15,000 titles annually and operates in 20 countries.
- HarperCollins is one of the largest publishing companies in the world. It has an extensive catalog of books and imprints, including Harper, William Morrow, and Avon. HarperCollins publishes books across genres, including literary fiction, romance, mystery, science fiction, and more. News Corp, a global media company, owns HarperCollins. It also operates newspapers such as *The Wall Street Journal* and *The New York Post*.
- Hachette Livre is a French publishing group with imprints such as Little, Brown and Company, Hodder & Stoughton, Grand Central Publishing, and Orbit Books.
- Macmillan is a global publishing company with a rich history dating back to the mid-19th century. It has several imprints, including Farrar, Straus and Giroux, St. Martin's Press, and Tor Books. It is known for publishing award-winning titles and nurturing emerging authors.
- Hearst Magazines is a division of the Hearst Corporation and publishes a wide range of magazines, including *Cosmopolitan*, *Esquire*, and *Harper's Bazaar*. It is one of the largest magazine publishers in the world.
- Conde Nast is another large magazine publisher with titles such as *Vogue*, *Vanity Fair*, and *The New Yorker*.
- Time Inc. is a publishing company with titles such as *Time*, *People*, and *Sports Illustrated*. It is one of the largest magazine publishers in the US.

Within the publishing sector, there are companies that specialize in publishing newspapers, magazines, books, journals, and other periodicals. The organizational structures of publishing companies typically consist of departments such as editorial, creative, contracts and legal, subsidiary rights, sales, marketing, promotion, advertising, publicity, website maintenance, finance, human resources, and information technology. Key roles within the publishing industry include writers, editors, photographers, and photojournalists. Additionally, sales managers, public relations experts, and distributors play crucial roles in the publishing sector.

16 Overview of the Media and Entertainment Industry

1.2.4 Music

The music industry operates through a complex network of collaborations involving various stakeholders.[38] These include businesses and individuals involved in the business side, such as labels, managers, publicists, distributors, booking agents, and performance rights organizations. On the customer side, there are streaming platforms, venues, and public performance platforms like radio. Additionally, there are those involved in creating music, such as singers, songwriters, and producers.

In the 2000s, the recording industry faced significant challenges due to piracy. Over the course of 15 years, the industry experienced three distinct realities: the end of CDs, the rise of digital piracy, and the advent of streaming. These shifts forced labels to adapt their financial models to meet the changing landscape. Even today, the music industry continues to face new challenges, including the rise of independent artists who bypass traditional labels and work directly with artist aggregators. The role of the artist's manager has become increasingly important in promoting new releases.

Publishing is perhaps the most intricate and least understood source of income in the music industry. Music publishers aim to collect royalties related to the rights associated with the musical work itself rather than the recording of it, which falls under the purview of the recording business.

Three major music label companies dominate the market:[39]

- Universal Music Group is the largest record label in the world, with a market share of over 36%. It is home to artists such as Taylor Swift, Drake, and Lady Gaga and has over 50 labels worldwide, including Capitol Records and Interscope Geffen A&M.
- Sony Music Entertainment is the second-largest record label in the world, with a market share of around 26%. It owns labels such as Columbia Records, RCA Records, and Epic Records, and manages artists such as Beyoncé, Adele, and Justin Timberlake.
- Warner Music Group is another major record label with a 20% market share. It manages labels such as Atlantic Records, Warner Bros. Records, and Elektra Records, and is the agency for Ed Sheeran and Bruno Mars.

Digital music distribution, particularly online streaming, has been the most significant transformation in the music business over the past decade. Streaming services continue to strategize ways to expand their user base, enhance their products, increase revenue, and establish a sustainable long-term business plan. The advent of streaming has already reshaped the recording industry and the way people listen to, share, and enjoy music. Streaming platforms have become comprehensive hubs for music consumption, monetization, and discovery. Platforms like Spotify serve as vital channels for music promotion and avenues for artists to monetize their work.

The live and touring industry, represented by companies like Live Nation, remains primarily centered around physical events, making it the least scalable sector in the music industry. Organizing international tours to reach millions of fans requires significant effort and coordination due to the localized and network-based nature of the industry. However, the business landscape may gradually shift toward digitization in the future, as exemplified by the online performances of BTS during the COVID-19 pandemic.[40]

It is crucial for artists to build and maintain a strong relationship with their fan base in order to advance their careers. In the age of social networks, fans actively raise awareness and promote artists within their online communities. The dynamics of artist-fan interactions have transformed from traditional fan clubs to digital platforms, altering how fans engage with artists and each other. Technology has empowered fans, turning them into influential media figures, sometimes surpassing the impact of conventional means of promotion.

1.2.5 Videogames

Big tech companies' newest frontline of competition is gaming. The industry's prosperity has grown over time, with several technical booms fueling its explosive expansion.[41] Console, PC, and mobile gaming are the three primary subsectors of the gaming industry.[42]

The console subsector, which is the oldest and most established, is dominated by major global players such as Nintendo, Sony, and Microsoft. These industry giants have engaged in longstanding competition to secure the largest share of a subsector that generates over 30% of the industry's total revenues.[43] The PC subsector of the gaming industry emerged at a later stage and differs from the console industry by being highly fragmented. Mobile gaming represents the newest and most profitable subsegment of the industry. With its inherent flexibility, mobile gaming has gradually become integrated into users' daily routines, evolving from simple application-based gaming to immersive in-app gaming experiences, as exemplified by mobile platforms like WeChat.

When discussing the growth of the mobile gaming industry, it is essential to mention Activision Blizzard and its highly popular game, *Candy Crush Saga*. *Candy Crush Saga* has played a crucial role in expanding the global community of mobile gamers. Another recent example of a mobile game is *Wordle*, where players are challenged to guess a five-letter word. *Wordle* has gained immense popularity since its release in October 2021, attracting over 45 million players by January 2022. The game's success was further highlighted by its acquisition by the *New York Times*.

From the value chain perspective, the gaming industry can be broadly divided into two businesses—games development and publishing:

- Games development involves the actual creation and design of videogames. Games developers are responsible for designing game mechanics, artwork, storylines, characters, and sound effects. They use various software tools to create and code the game and test it to ensure it functions as intended.
- Publishing manages the marketing, distribution, and monetization of videogames. Games publishers work with game developers to bring the finished product to market. They handle marketing and promotion to create awareness and interest in the game. They also manage the distribution of the game to various platforms and devices, such as consoles, PCs, and mobile devices. Publishers also take care of the monetization aspect of the game, such as in-app purchases, microtransactions, and subscriptions.

In recent years, the e-sports industry has emerged as a thriving sector within the gaming business. This sector revolves around the organization of videogame competitions, where skilled professional gamers compete against each other to win prizes and gain recognition.

E-sports has gained significant popularity, with the establishment of leagues and tournaments featuring popular games like *League of Legends* and *Overwatch*. The global e-sports market was valued at $1.3 billion in 2022, attracting an audience of 532 million people.[44] The Asia-Pacific region stands as the largest market for e-sports, generating over 50% of the total revenue.

Representative companies in the gaming industry include the following:

- Activision Blizzard is a videogame holding company formed in 2008 through the merger of Activision and Vivendi Games. It was acquired by Microsoft in January 2022. It is known for developing and publishing popular franchises such as *Call of Duty*, *World of Warcraft*, and *Candy Crush Saga*.
- Electronic Arts (EA) is an American videogame company founded in 1982. From its early days, EA focused on creating innovative and high-quality games for various platforms, including home computers and consoles. It is known for publishing popular franchises such as *FIFA*, *Madden NFL*, and *The Sims*. It continues to innovate and evolve with advancements in technology, embracing new platforms and exploring emerging trends such as online multiplayer, virtual reality, and live services.
- Nintendo is a Japanese videogame company founded in 1889. It has a rich history in the console gaming industry, with a number of significant milestones and contributions, including the Nintendo Entertainment System (1983), the Nintendo 64 (1996), the GameCube (2001), the Wii (2006), and Nintendo Switch (2017). It is known for developing and publishing popular franchises such as *Super Mario*, *The Legend of Zelda*, and *Pokémon*.
- Tencent Games is a subsidiary of Tencent Holdings Limited, one of the largest technology conglomerates in the world. One of the notable achievements of Tencent Games is the development and release of *PUBG Mobile* in 2018, which has since become one of the most successful mobile games of all time. With its continued focus on mobile gaming, such as *Honor of Kings* and *Call of Duty*, it remains a dominant player in the industry, contributing to the growth and evolution of the global gaming landscape.
- Nexon, a South Korean videogame company founded in 1994, has gained prominence in the gaming industry for its successful implementation of the "freemium" ("free" + "premium") model. It was a trailblazer in offering free-to-play games that generate revenue through in-game purchases and microtransactions. One of Nexon's notable successes is *MapleStory*, an MMORPG that offers players a vast virtual world to explore, engaging in quests and choosing from a wide variety of character classes. While the game is free to play, Nexon monetizes it by offering cosmetic items, convenience features, and additional content through an in-game virtual currency. It has continued to expand its portfolio of freemium games across various genres and platforms, such as *Dungeon Fighter Online* and *KartRider*. Nexon's freemium approach has also made an impact on the global gaming market.
- Riot Games: This is an American videogame company founded in 2006. *League of Legends*, a multiplayer online battle arena game, has become a global phenomenon. Since its release in 2009, *League of Legends* has amassed a massive player base and has established itself as one of the most popular and influential e-sports titles. Its success has led to the development of professional e-sports leagues, such as the *League of*

Legends Championship Series and the *League of Legends* World Championship, which draw millions of viewers and offer substantial prize pools. Riot Games has played a significant role in shaping the e-sports industry.

1.3 Key Facts and Figures of the Media and Entertainment Industry

1.3.1 Overview

According to PwC, the size of the global entertainment and media market decreased to $2 trillion in 2020 as a result of the global recession caused by the COVID-19 pandemic. In the worst year-on-year loss since PwC started monitoring this data 22 years ago, global revenues fell by 3.8% from $2.1 trillion in 2019 to $2 trillion in 2020. The pandemic caused an estimated $53 billion (7.3%) loss in the US market and a $660 billion loss worldwide.[45] The mobile video-on-demand, videogame, and music industries benefited from the rise in streaming services and subscriptions for digital media in 2020; while live performance and touring and movie theaters were forced to change course or shut down as physical media consumption continued to decline.[46]

However, the market increased to $2.2 trillion in 2021, exceeding pre-COVID-19 levels. The coming years will see this figure increase further. This improved growth comes after a dismal pandemic-ravaged 2020 that saw a halt to in-person entertainment, which hit movie theater box office revenues and live performance revenues particularly hard. Entertainment and media business worldwide was projected to expand by 6.5% in 2021 and 6.7% in 2022. The MEI is expected to experience a 5% compound annual growth rate (CAGR),[47] increasing industry revenues to $2.6 trillion by 2025.

The expansion of various industries within the MEI is being driven by high demand for digital content and advertising. According to PwC's projections, the video streaming market is expected to experience a CAGR of 10.6% by 2025, reaching an estimated value of $81.3 billion. Similarly, revenues from videogames and e-sports are anticipated to grow at a CAGR of 5.7%, reaching approximately $200 billion by 2025. The music industry is also poised for growth, with a predicted CAGR of 12.8%, resulting in earnings of $29.3 billion by 2025—primarily driven by digital streaming.

However, certain MEI segments may face challenges in the coming years. PwC's projections indicate that it will likely take until at least 2024 for movie ticket sales to recover to pre-pandemic levels. The traditional television and home video segment, which currently generates $219 billion in sales, is expected to experience a decline, with a CAGR of -1.2% by 2025. Similarly, newspaper and magazine publishing are projected to decline by 1% annually during the same period

Despite the overall positive outlook for the MEI, these projections highlight the potential difficulties some subsectors may face in the near future. The dynamic nature of the MEI suggests that these trends could change as consumer preferences and market dynamics continue to evolve.

1.3.2 By Segment

Film

The global film and video market was expected to grow from $244.43 billion in 2021 to $273.35 billion in 2022 at a CAGR of 11.8%.[48] This growth was mainly due to companies

20 Overview of the Media and Entertainment Industry

restructuring their operations and recovering from the impact of the COVID-19 pandemic, which led to the imposition of restrictive containment measures involving social distancing, remote working, and the temporary cessation of commercial activities, resulting in operational challenges. The market is expected to reach $409.02 billion by 2026 at a CAGR of 10.6%.

Mobile video viewing has increased significantly in recent years and is expected to grow further during the forecast period. This is mainly being driven by the rise in internet penetration and growth in smartphone usage. For example, 57% of global video consumption now takes place on mobile devices.[49] A rapid increase in mobile video consumption is expected to drive the film and video market in the future.

Indeed, within this sector, the most significant growth trajectory is video streaming, with a projected CAGR growth of 10.6% to 2025, propelling the industry to a value of $81.3 billion. On the other hand, the movie theater industry faces challenges, with revenues not anticipated to return to pre-pandemic levels until at least 2024.

TV and Radio

The value of the global TV and radio broadcasting industry increased from $374.55 billion in 2021 to $401.25 billion in 2022, at a CAGR of 7.%.[50] Once again, this growth can be attributed to companies' strategic reorganization efforts and recovery from the adverse effects of the COVID-19 pandemic. The imposition of containment measures such as social distancing, remote work, and the temporary cessation of commercial activities posed significant operational challenges, but companies adapted and are now experiencing positive growth. The market is projected to achieve a CAGR of 5.9%, resulting in a value of $504 billion by 2026.

However, traditional television and home video—while currently the largest consumer segment, with a value of $219 billion—is expected to see a decline in its CAGR by 1.2% by 2026. This suggests that the landscape will be challenging for this particular segment of the MEI.

Print and Publishing

The global print and publishing industry was anticipated to increase from $305.44 billion in 2021 to $320.07 billion in 2022.[51] With a projected CAGR of 3.5%, it is expected to reach a value of $366.73 billion by 2025.

Specifically, the newspaper and magazine market is expanding due to the growing presence of social media and the extensive collection of consumer data. Publishers of newspapers and periodicals can gain a broader and deeper understanding of their readers, distributors, and other stakeholders. Publishers that prioritize a digital business model have made significant investments in their data and analytics teams to capitalize on this trend.

Music

The recorded music market experienced significant growth in 2020, as reported by the International Federation of the Phonographic Industry (IFPI), the global organization promoting the recorded music industry. This marked a sixth consecutive year of expansion, with the market growing by 7.4%. Based on data from the IFPI's *Global Music Report*, total sales for the year amounted to $21.6 billion.[52]

Paid subscription streaming revenue is driving the growth of the music industry, particularly in the streaming sector. In 2020, paid subscription streaming revenues increased by a remarkable 18.5%. By the end of the year, the number of users with paid subscription accounts had reached an impressive 443 million. Overall streaming revenues, encompassing both paid subscriptions and advertising-supported services, also witnessed a significant rise of 19.9%, amounting to $13.4 billion. This accounted for 62.1% of all recorded music sales worldwide. The surge in streaming revenues offset the decline in revenues from other formats, primarily due to the impact of COVID-19. Indeed, the music industry was one of the sectors hit hardest by the pandemic, with live performance revenues plunging by a staggering 74.4% in 2020.

However, despite this setback, the industry is projected to witness substantial growth in the coming years. It is expected that total revenues will experience a CAGR of 12.8%, reaching $29.3 billion by 2025. The primary driver of this growth is the surge in digital streaming, which has become a significant source of revenue for the industry. Additionally, as concert venues reopen and renowned artists resume touring, the return of live performances will contribute to the industry's revenue stream.

Music Industry: Digital Transformation

The music industry has undergone a remarkable transformation and recovery in the face of digitalization. The emergence of digital technologies and the introduction of online platforms have revolutionized the way music is created, distributed, and consumed. Initially, the industry faced significant challenges as piracy and illegal downloads disrupted traditional revenue streams, such as CDs.

However, over time, the industry adapted and found new ways to thrive in the digital era. According to the International Federation of the Phonographic Industry (IFPI) Global Music Report 2023, specifically in the US market, the music industry started turning around in 2016, when growth from streaming services began to outweigh a long-running decline in CD sales.[53] In 2022, revenues from paid subscription services grew by 8%, exceeding $10 billion annually for the first time.[54] The rise of on-demand music services played a pivotal role in this resurgence. These services garnered an average of 92 million paid subscribers per year, showcasing steady growth compared to the average of 84 million subscribers in 2021. This trend highlights the increasing popularity and adoption of streaming platforms among music consumers in the US.

In addition, revenues from advertising-supported services—including popular platforms like YouTube, Spotify, and Facebook—experienced a moderate growth rate, increasing by 6% to reach $1.8 billion in 2022. These ad-supported services, as a new revenue source, contributed approximately 11% to the overall recorded music revenues for the year. By contrast, the IFPI Global Music Report 2023 indicates a decline in revenue from on-demand digital downloads, which saw a substantial drop of 20% to $495 million in 2022.[55] This decrease in revenue was observed for both album downloads and single-track downloads.

These findings highlight the ongoing transition in the music industry toward streaming and ad-supported models, as traditional revenue streams from digital downloads continue to decline.

Videogames

The videogaming industry was expected to reach a value of $178.73 billion in 2021, representing a significant 14.4% increase from the previous year.[56] This growth was a remarkable improvement on earlier projections made in 2016, which had forecast a total value of $90.07 billion. The substantial difference between the two figures indicates the potential for further accelerated growth. The surge can be attributed to the global lockdowns during the COVID-19 pandemic, as individuals compelled to stay at home turned to gaming platforms for entertainment. The pandemic-induced restrictions ushered in a new era for gaming.

Mobile games have emerged as the dominant and fastest-growing segment within the broader videogame industry. In 2021, players spent a staggering $93.2 billion on mobile games, surpassing the combined spending of $87.1 billion on console and PC games.[57]

Another noteworthy development in the videogame industry is the expansion of its demographic reach. While the age distribution of gamers is becoming more diverse, with both older and younger individuals participating, there is also a narrowing gender gap among players. Top-tier gamers who compete in e-sports events have gained enough recognition to qualify for professional athlete visas when traveling to the US.[58]

The videogame industry now surpasses the combined size of the music and film industries. There were over 2.6 billion gamers worldwide as of 2020, representing approximately 30% of the global population.[59] The evolving demographics of gamers are an intriguing aspect of the videogame industry. As more people engage in gaming, there is growing demand for immersive entertainment and easier access to games. This bodes well for the future of the industry, indicating a promising trajectory.

1.4 Emerging Trends in the Media and Entertainment Industry

1.4.1 Production

The past decade has seen some dramatic changes in production (Figure 1.2).

The first trend to be highlighted is the increase in blockbuster productions. A "blockbuster" is a popular and financially successful piece of entertainment—often a

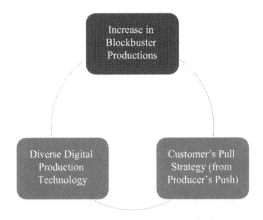

FIGURE 1.2 Emerging Trends in the MEI: Production Aspects.

feature film.[60] However, the phrase has come to apply to any expensive production aimed at broad audiences with accompanying commercialization, often on a scale that might determine the financial success of a film studio or a distributor.

Demand from consumers for media and entertainment products is unpredictable. Entertainment is neither a primary need like food or shelter nor even a secondary need like the need for furnishings or transportation. It is entirely optional to watch a basketball game, a movie, or a song. However, attempting to predict the revenue to be yielded by a hip-hop song or a feature picture is a crapshoot.

The blockbuster approach involves making disproportionately significant investments in a few products designed to appeal to mass audiences. The MEI also follows the "winner takes all" rule, whereby the creators of the most successful content earn much higher revenues than their competitors.[61] In this regard, the most profitable business strategy is blockbusters like *Star Wars*, *Avatar*, and the *Harry Potter* series. There are several explanations of the benefits of betting on blockbusters in recent years:

- Blockbusters attract the best talent. Ambitious projects are often more attractive than cautious projects and a failure in this context will always be forgiven. The most ambitious projects are more efficient in marketing and sales, with big names, higher budgets, and more word of mouth.
- The best predictor of commercial success in the film industry is not the actors or the genre but rather the number of screenings. Distribution plays the same critical role in the music and publishing industries. It is easier to secure access and better conditions with the distribution channels for potential blockbusters.
- Creative products such as films and television shows are generally relatively expensive to produce but very cheap to reproduce with the advancement of digital technologies.[62] For example, making the first copy of a movie can cost hundreds of millions of dollars; but subsequent prints for theatrical release cost only a few thousand dollars apiece and digital distribution is much cheaper. Similar economics apply to hardcover, paperback, and e-books in the publishing industry. The sharp disjunction between costs of production and reproduction means that hit products are disproportionately profitable.

The second trend involves the move from a producer-push strategy to a customer-pull strategy.

The MEI is unique due to its psychological, emotional, and aspirational appeal to customers. Traditionally, content creators decided what to supply; the critical change in this new era is that demand is now wholly consumer-driven. Today's consumer demands the content they prefer in the format they prefer. Additionally, they want to customize that content to their tastes. Quality and acceptance hence become highly subjective to each individual.

In the past, companies in the MEI produced content based on their intuition and creativity without deep consideration of customer needs and expectations. In this way, they created films, TV shows, music albums, books and so on, and pushed potential customers to consume their products. However, with the digital revolution—specifically regarding the availability of granular customer data—players in the MEI have begun to interject more customer-oriented strategies into the production process.[63] Information on

24 Overview of the Media and Entertainment Industry

what people watch, like, and recommend gives producers a far better understanding of the demand side, pulling customers more effectively.

Combined with various analytic techniques, companies have been developing scientific ways to analyze storylines and scripts before they are produced. They can evaluate their casting before actors and actresses get cast, and audience fit before engaging in marketing campaigns. Most of all, they can better forecast sales before a product's release.

Platforms like Netflix and YouTube potentially have an advantage in developing and using these tools, as they collect and control access to much of the relevant data. For example, the platforms rely on algorithm-run recommendation systems to help customers select the next movie or show to watch.

The third trend is the introduction of diverse digital production technology.[64]

The MEI depends on multiple external factors/technology developments like wireless, mobile devices, digitization, internet access speeds, cloud storage, consumer analytics, and social media.[65] It has successfully adapted to these developments in every generation. Since the 1990s, the digitization of content has transformed the creation and delivery of music. The rise of the internet since the 2000s has been a gamechanger for all subsectors of the MEI. Social media has also been instrumental in shaping the present MEI.

For example, virtual production technologies reduce and sometimes eliminate the travel traditionally associated with film and TV productions.[66] Virtual production studios and sound stages, powered by VR and AR, use light-emitting diode walls and green screens to render any given location onto a given set and can replace physical props of all shapes and sizes to help reduce material waste.

Crowdfunding—a digital platform for fundraising—has emerged as a new funding source for production in the MEI. It promotes the launch and scaling of new projects in the MEI by providing networked platforms and handy digital tools.[67]

Excitement is building around NFTs as a vehicle for companies in the MEI to expand engagement with their content and may provide a future production model with the potential for further monetization options.[68] Early NFT initiatives in the MEI include sports, art, collectibles, and more. Businesses and individuals acquire unique digital assets that are easily traded and whose ownership and authenticity are recorded via blockchain technology. By extending the customer relationship into new digital spaces, NFTs enable MEI players to build new communities and create cross-platform consumer involvement grounded in tested IP.

1.4.2 Distribution

Trends in distribution include the expansion of diversified distribution channels, including online and mobile channels (Figure 1.3).

The transition from print to digital platforms has compelled publishing companies to incorporate online content for subscribers while also maintaining print publications or transitioning entirely to e-book publishing and web-based publications. Mobile networks provide round-the-clock access to media and entertainment through smartphones and tablets. Broadcasters and publishers have adjusted their online content to ensure readability on laptops and mobile devices. As digital technology advances, the MEI faces the ongoing challenge of maintaining control over content and retaining audiences. Piracy remains a

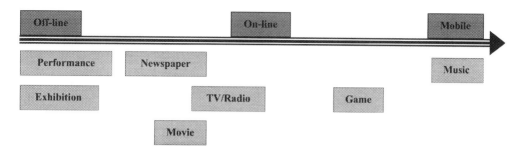

FIGURE 1.3 The Diversification of Distribution Channels in the MEI.

significant issue that broadcasters, film producers, and publishers must collectively battle, requiring continuous efforts to combat IP theft.

The music industry has undergone a profound transformation in distribution channels with the rise of digital music files such as MP3s and illegal music downloads. Traditional physical distribution and the download-to-own business model struggled to compete with online piracy, leading to the decline of the traditional music industry. Although iTunes—initially part of Apple's ecosystem upon its launch in 2001—made significant strides, it could not match the allure of unlimited free music.

The market reached its lowest point between 2010 and 2015. However, a response to digital piracy eventually emerged. Spotify, launched in 2008, expanded its streaming service globally, offering a legal alternative for music consumption. The digital industry has matured, but the physical world still retains its importance. The industry has adapted to the intertwined nature of the digital and physical realms, enabling direct interactions between artists and fans. Artists now stream live shows on social media platforms and announce album releases with a single tweet, exemplifying the fusion of digital platforms with real-world experiences.

In the film industry, major players have repositioned themselves, re-envisioning their business models. After nearly a century of reaching audiences through different intermediaries, such as movie theaters, Disney became the first studio to offer its content directly to consumers through Disney+.[69] Most major Hollywood studios and their parent corporations are now launching their films on online streaming services.

While the COVID-19 pandemic severely affected the film industry, it also presented a chance for the traditional economic models to evolve to better address the challenges of the digital age.[70] In response to profound shifts in audience behavior and content distribution, streaming has become crucial. Traditional approaches to content creation, dissemination, and monetization may face challenges during this transitional period, requiring careful navigation and patience. However, media and entertainment companies that embrace change, recognize its advantages, and adopt innovative thinking can position themselves as influential contributors in shaping the rapidly evolving future.

1.4.3 Marketing

Marketing trends include the growth of online, mobile, and social media marketing, which is more effective in generating word of mouth. There are many advantages to be gained from marketing through these new digital channels.

First, digital marketing channels have global reach. While traditional offline marketing is limited by geography, digital marketing is not. This opens up opportunities for quickly and affordably creating global marketing campaigns. Even a small business can reach an international audience.

Second, digital channels facilitate personalization—something that is difficult in the conventional marketing context. In addition, digital marketing can target specific audiences in an easy and inexpensive way.

Finally, the results of marketing campaigns are measurable. Web analytics and other digital metric tools help businesses track and analyze the effectiveness of online marketing campaigns. They provide detailed information on how customers are responding to advertising and how visitors are interacting with websites.

More importantly, digitalization has created new platforms and tools for marketing purposes. For example, through a crowdfunding campaign, media and entertainment companies can generate PR effects, word of mouth, and initial customer data acquisition—all of which are helpful for marketing purposes.

Crowdfunding platforms like Kickstarter and Indiegogo allow creators to raise money directly from fans and supporters, bypassing traditional funding channels like studios, investors, and grants.[71]

One of the key benefits of crowdfunding is that it allows creators to build a community around their work and engage with fans in a more direct and personal way.[72] By sharing their creative process and offering various rewards based on different levels of support, creators can generate enthusiasm and anticipation for their project while simultaneously raising the necessary funds to bring it to life. Crowdfunding not only provides financial advantages but also aids creators in cultivating a dedicated fan base that can offer ongoing support for future endeavors.

Furthermore, crowdfunding campaigns can serve as a valuable form of market validation, offering creators insight into the level of demand for their work and the specific audience that is expressing interest. A successful crowdfunding campaign can serve as evidence to potential investors, distributors, and other collaborators that a market already exists for the project, enhancing the prospects of securing additional funding and support.

1.4.4 Customers

The MEI has seen the emergence of young customer groups in most major markets, such as music, broadcasting, games, and online services.

These young customers have strikingly different consumption preferences from their older counterparts. For example, they are digital natives, familiar with the internet and mobile. They are also more sensitive to peer culture. Below, we list some exemplary characteristics of these young customer groups:[73]

- From possession to access: This more pragmatic and realistic generation of consumers expects to access and evaluate a broad range of information before purchase.
- At the core of Gen Z is the idea of manifesting individual identity.[74] Consumption thus becomes a means of self-expression—as opposed, for example, to buying or wearing brands to fit in with group norms.

- Radical inclusivity:[75] Gen Z don't distinguish between the friends they meet online and their friends in the physical world. They continually flow between communities that promote their causes by exploiting the high level of mobilization that technology makes possible. Gen Z values online communities because they allow people from different economic backgrounds to connect and mobilize around causes and interests.

Young customer groups have different consumption patterns for media and entertainment products. Music and video streaming and videogames are popular paid services among young customers.[76] This younger demographic also wants more diversity and believes there are gaps in gender diversity, sexual identity, and ethnic representation in media and entertainment content.

Along with good content, they expect ease of discovery. The younger generation, who grew up with social platforms, play a crucial role in discovering new content. They prefer transparent content on social platforms, where the relationship between the creator and the audience is more direct and accessible. Many consumers are willing to pay for content that delivers superior quality, enhanced experiences, and greater convenience.[77]

Given the importance of these young customer groups, seamless and customized experiences will become more critical.[78] They will persist in their quest for distinctive experiences and convenient access to entertainment content. They anticipate seamless interaction at every stage of the customer journey, from sign-up to use and bill management. Bundling options can further enhance the consumer experience by offering a range of integrated services. Leading digital-native streaming platforms cater to video subscribers by providing diverse offerings that include shopping, gaming, devices, and other digital services.

Case Studies

The Walt Disney Company (Disney): Growing Together with the Media and Entertainment Industry

The Walt Disney Company, founded in 1923, has evolved from an animation studio into a global media giant. It introduced iconic characters like Mickey Mouse and pioneered the commercial potential of animation. Over the decades, Disney diversified its ventures into feature films, TV, theme parks, and merchandise. Despite challenges, it acquired Pixar, launched Disney+, and excelled with franchises like *Star Wars* and the Marvel Cinematic Universe. Its success not only established the viability of animation but also revolutionized family entertainment through theme parks. Acquiring ABC, ESPN, Pixar, and Lucasfilm further solidified its industry dominance and adaptation to digital trends. Disney's journey remains a testament to its blend of creativity and commercial success, setting enduring industry standards.

More case details for classroom use are available. Please check the book webpage at www.routledge.com/9781032221212 for more information.

28 Overview of the Media and Entertainment Industry

Vivendi: From a Water Business to a Global Media and Entertainment Giant

Vivendi—initially a 19th-century French water company—has successfully transitioned into a global media and entertainment leader. Faced with regulatory changes, it diversified from water into media in the 1980s, acquiring Canal+ and Seagram in the 1990s. Despite financial challenges, Vivendi strategically sold non-media assets and focused on growth. Its acquisitions of Universal Music Group and Activision Blizzard consolidated its position in the MEI.

More case details for classroom use are available. Please check the book webpage at www.routledge.com/9781032221212 for more information.

ByteDance and TikTok: A Rising Star in the MEI

ByteDance—a Chinese tech company founded in 2012—has swiftly become a major player in the MEI, primarily due to its globally popular app TikTok. By transforming its Chinese app Douyin into TikTok and acquiring Musical.ly, ByteDance expanded its influence. TikTok stands out for its fusion of short videos and social networking, appealing to younger audiences. ByteDance harnessed user-generated content, global accessibility, and data-driven insights to reshape digital content consumption. This success underscores the potency of innovation, data, and user engagement, positioning ByteDance to continue shaping the industry's future through its dynamic content paradigm.

More case details for classroom use are available. Please check the book webpage at www.routledge.com/9781032221212 for more information.

Review

- This opening chapter provides a broad perspective of the MEI's economic worth and multi-dimensional scope, key statistics, and the emerging trends shaping its future. The first section presents an overview of the MEI, underlining its economic significance on a global scale (1.1). With a market value of $2.1 trillion in 2020, the MEI plays a substantial role in the global economy. It is not just an economic powerhouse; it is a source of creativity and enjoyment for billions of individuals across the globe. Furthermore, it provides a platform for storytelling and information exchange that helps shape our cultural landscape.
- The next section delves deeper into the industry's scope, highlighting its comprehensive range (1.2). The MEI includes a broad range of businesses responsible for producing, distributing, and marketing various cultural and entertainment products and services. The MEI is multifaceted and encompasses various subsectors, such as film, TV and radio, print and publishing, music, and videogames. This section outlines a brief history and prospects of each subsector.

- The third section presents key facts and figures that provide more detailed, data-driven insights into the MEI (1.3). It touches on the size and growth projections of each sector. The digital media and entertainment markets are emphasized due to their unprecedented growth. The shift toward digital consumption—especially among younger demographics—is driving the growth in this sector, underscoring the industry's transformation in recent years.
- The final section, on emerging trends in the MEI, offers a forward-looking perspective, dissecting the key forces that are reshaping the industry (1.4). This encompasses various themes, from the disruptive and enabling role of digital technology to the transformation of production, distribution, and consumption practices. Streaming services have revolutionized content consumption, enabling direct and convenient access for audiences and posing new challenges for traditional media, given the changing consumption patterns of younger generations. The future of the MEI hinges on its ability to adapt and innovate amid these transformative changes.

Discussion Questions

Sample answers for classroom discussion are available to instructors. Please check the Instructor Hub on the book webpage (www.routledge.com/9781032221212) for more information.

1 What important roles does the MEI play in the global economy? Which characteristics of the MEI distinguish it from other industries?
2 How can we define the scope of the MEI? What do you think are the most promising subsectors of the industry?
3 How does the shift toward digital media and entertainment influence the MEI's production and distribution practices?
4 How have consumer behaviors and expectations changed through digital technologies in the MEI?
5 How has the rise of streaming services and the direct-to-consumer model impacted traditional media outlets, and how should they adapt?
6 What has been the impact of online marketing channels in the MEI? Which strategies have proven to be most effective for companies in the MEI?

Further Reading

- Mintz, S. (2007) "The Jazz Age: The American 1920s: The formation of modern American mass culture." *Digital History.* www.digitalhistory.uh.edu/disp_textbook. cfm?smtid=3&psid=3397.
- Briggs, A. and Burke, P. (2005) *A social history of the media: From Gutenberg to the internet.* Cambridge, UK: Polity Press.
- McLuhan, M. (1964) *Understanding media: The extensions of man.* New York: McGraw-Hill.
- Ng, S. (2012) "A brief history of entertainment technologies." *Proceedings of the IEEE,* 100, pp. 1386–1390. doi:10.1109/jproc.2012.2189805, https://ieeexplore.ieee.org/stamp/stamp.jsp?arnumber=6182692.

- Albarran, A., Mierzejewska, B., and Jung, J. (2018) *Handbook of media management and economics.* London, UK: Routledge.
- Hennig-Thurau, T., Ravid, S. A. and Sorenson, O. (2021) "The economics of filmed entertainment in the digital era." *Journal of Cultural Economics*, 45(2), pp. 157–170. doi:10.1007/s10824-021-09407-6.
- Ryu, S. (2021) *Beauty of crowdfunding: Blooming creativity and innovation in the Digital Era.* London, UK: Routledge.
- Francis, T. and Hoefel, F. (2018) "'True Gen': Generation Z and its implications for companies." *McKinsey & Company.* www.mckinsey.com/industries/consumer-packaged-goods/our-insights/true-gen-generation-z-and-its-implications-for-companies

References

1. Seth, S. (2022). "The World's Top Media Companies", *Investopedia*, October 30. www.investopedia.com/stock-analysis/021815/worlds-top-ten-media-companies-dis-cmcsa-fox.aspx.
2. The Walt Disney Company. (2022). *Fiscal year 2021 annual financial report.* rep. The Walt Disney Company. https://thewaltdisneycompany.com/app/uploads/2022/01/2021-Annual-Report.pdf, p. 70.
3. The Walt Disney Company. (2022). *Form 10-K: The Walt Disney Company.* rep. U.S. Securities and Exchange Commission. www.sec.gov/Archives/edgar/data/1001039/000100103918000187/fy2018_q4x10k.htm.
4. Yahoo! Finance. (2022). *Apple Inc. (AAPL) stock price, news, Quote & History.* https://finance.yahoo.com/quote/AAPL?p=AAPL&.tsrc=fin-srch.
5. Apple Inc. (2021). *Annual reports on Form 10-K: 2021 10-K.* rep. Apple Inc. https://s2.q4cdn.com/470004039/files/doc_financials/2021/q4/_10-K-2021-%28As-Filed%29.pdf, p. 24.
6. Netflix, Inc. (2022). *Annual reports and proxies: 2021 annual report.* rep. Netflix Investors. https://s22.q4cdn.com/959853165/files/doc_financials/2021/q4/da27d24b-9358-4b5c-a424-6da061d91836.pdf, p. 3.
7. Yahoo! Finance. (2022). *Comcast Corporation (CMCSA) stock price, news, Quote & History.* https://finance.yahoo.com/quote/CMCSA?p=CMCSA&.tsrc=fin-srch.
8. Comcast Corporation. (2022). *2021 Comcast annual review: Annual report on Form 10-K.* rep. Comcast. www.cmcsa.com/static-files/8887f574-dfa9-4480-8c8b-ed7771f7ce44, p. 4.
9. Frater, P. (2022). "Profits Climb at Korea's CJ ENM, but Film Business Retreats Further". *Variety.* https://variety.com/2022/film/asia/cj-enm-korea-profits-film-1235176861/#:~:text=For%20the%20year%20to%20end,a%20regulatory%20filing%20on%20Thursday.
10. The "Korean Wave" is the phenomenon of global interest in South Korean popular culture—including K-pop, K-dramas, and K-movies—which has increased dramatically since the 1990s.
11. Paramount. (2022). *Annual report which provides a comprehensive overview of the company for the past year.* rep. Paramount. https://ir.paramount.com/static-files/357c6440-f534-480a-b0ac-abb13963f070, p. 40.
12. Shim, S. (2022). "Hybe tops 1 tln won in annual sales, first in K-pop industry." *Yonhap News.* https://en.yna.co.kr/view/AEN20220222009851320.
13. Fox Corporation. (2022). *Annual reports: 2021 Annual Report.* rep. Fox. https://investor.foxcorporation.com/static-files/acbeff52-80e1-4945-baba-a58f059f4f32, p. 3.
14. Tencent (2023). *2022 annual report.* https://static.www.tencent.com/uploads/2023/04/06/214dce4c5312264800b20cfab64861ba.pdf.
15. Deng, I. and Qu, T. (2023). "Tencent posts 11 per cent rise in quarterly revenue, buoyed by advertising and game sales as China's economy rebounds." *South China Morning Post.* www.scmp.com/tech/big-tech/article/3220874/tencent-posts-11-cent-rise-quarterly-revenue-buoyed-advertising-and-game-sales-chinas-economy.
16. Sony. (2022). *Quarterly securities report for the three months ended December 31,2021.* rep. Sony Group Corporation. www.sony.com/en/SonyInfo/IR/library/Sony_Quarterly_Securities_Report_2021Q3.pdf, p. 5.
17. [Author removed at request of original publisher.] (2016) "Chapter 1: Media and Culture_1.3 The Evolution of Media," in *Understanding Media and Culture: An Introduction to Mass*

Introduction **31**

Communication. Minneapolis: University of Minnesota Libraries Publishing. https://open.lib. umn.edu/mediaandculture/chapter/1-3-the-evolution-of-media/

18 Vault-Firsthand. (no date). *Media and entertainment: Background.* https://firsthand.co/industries/ media-and-entertainment/background.

19 The Editors of *Encyclopaedia Britannica* (no date). "Benjamin Harris," *Britannica.* www. britannica.com/biography/Benjamin-Harris#ref199198.

20 Vault-Firsthand. (no date). *Media and entertainment: Background.* https://firsthand.co/industries/ media-and-entertainment/background.

21 [Author removed at request of original publisher.] (2016). "Chapter 1: Media and Culture_1.3 The Evolution of Media," in *Understanding Media and Culture: An Introduction to Mass Communication.* Minneapolis: University of Minnesota Libraries Publishing. https://open.lib. umn.edu/mediaandculture/chapter/1-3-the-evolution-of-media/.

22 "News Media and Entertainment" (no date). *Encyclopedia.com.* Great Depression and the New Deal Reference Library. www.encyclopedia.com/economics/encyclopedias-almanacs-transcripts- and-maps/news-media-and-entertainment.

23 "Radio 1929–1941" (no date). *Encyclopedia.com.* Historical Events for Students: The Great Depression. www.encyclopedia.com/education/news-and-education-magazines/radio-1929-1941.

24 [Author removed at request of original publisher.] (2016). "Chapter 1: Media and Culture_1.3 The Evolution of Media," in *Understanding Media and Culture: An Introduction to Mass Communication.* Minneapolis: University of Minnesota Libraries Publishing. https://open.lib. umn.edu/mediaandculture/chapter/1-3-the-evolution-of-media/.

25 Briggs, A. and Burke, P. (2005). *A social history of the media: From Gutenberg to the internet.* Cambridge, UK: Polity Press.

26 Filmsite. (no date). "The History of Film: The Pre-1920s." www.filmsite.org/pre20sintro.html.

27 "Hollywood 1929-1941." (no date). *Encyclopedia.com.* https://www.encyclopedia.com/education/ news-and-education-magazines/hollywood-1929-1941.

28 Stephens, M. (no date). "History of Television." *Grolier Encyclopedia.* https://stephens.hosting. nyu.edu/History%20of%20Television%20page.html.

29 Sewall, S. (2009). "The switch from analog to digital TV." *Nielsen.* www.nielsen.com/insights/ 2009/the-switch-from-analog-to-digital-tv/

30 Bocconi Students Investment Club members (2022). *In depth analysis of the gaming industry: Part 1, Bocconi Students Investment Club (BSIC).* https://bsic.it/in-depth-analysis-of-the- gaming-industry-1/.

31 Kastrenakes, J. (2021). "Beeple sold an NFT for $69 million." *The Verge.* www.theverge.com/ 2021/3/11/22325054/beeple-christies-nft-sale-cost-everydays-69-million.

32 "NBA Top Shot." (no date). https://nbatopshot.com.

33 Goslin, A. (2020). "Fortnite's Travis Scott event drew over 27 million players." *Polygon.* www. polygon.com/fortnite/2020/4/24/21235017/fortnite-travis-scott-event-concert-astronomical-12-3- million-concurrent-players-record#:~:text=Epic%20says%20over%2027.7%20million,players %20attended%20at%20least%20twice.

34 Vault-Firsthand (no date). *Media and entertainment: Structure.* https://firsthand.co/industries/ media-and-entertainment/structure.

35 PwC (no date). *Global Entertainment & Media Outlook 2022–2026.* https://www.pwc.com/gx/en/ industries/tmt/media/outlook.html.

36 The Creative Industries Council (no date). *The Creative Industries Council.* www.thecreative industries.co.uk/.

37 The Best Book Publishers of 2021. (no date). https://jerichowriters.com/best-book-publishers- 2021/.

38 Pastukhov, D. (2019). *How Does the Music Industry Work? Introducing the Mechanics: A 10 Part Series, Soundcharts.* https://soundcharts.com/blog/mechanics-of-the-music-industry.

39 Rys, D. (2022). "Record label market share Q4 2022: Republic's 'Midnights' run outpaces a surging Sony. Billboard. https://www.billboard.com/pro/record-label-market-share-q4-2022- republic-surges-sony-big-year/.

40 Lee, G. (2022). "Are online K-pop concerts and fan interactions here to stay? Experts disagree." *South China Morning Post.* www.scmp.com/lifestyle/entertainment/article/3198701/are-online-k- pop-concerts-and-fan-interactions-here-stay-experts-disagree.

32 Overview of the Media and Entertainment Industry

41 Chikhani, R. (2015). "The history of gaming: An evolving community', *TechCrunch*, 31 October. https://techcrunch.com/2015/10/31/the-history-of-gaming-an-evolving-community.

42 Bocconi Students Investment Club members (2022). *In depth analysis of the gaming industry: Part 1, Bocconi Students Investment Club (BSIC)*. https://bsic.it/in-depth-analysis-of-the-gaming-industry-1/

43 Kirkcaldy, A. (2023). "Video game industry statistics, trends and data in 2023." *WePC*. www.wepc.com/news/video-game-statistics/.

44 Newzoo (no date). "The esports audience will pass half a billion in 2022 as revenues, engagement, & new segments flourish." https://newzoo.com/resources/blog/the-esports-audience-will-pass-half-a-billion-in-2022-as-revenue-engagement-esport-industry-growth.

45 PwC (no date). *2022 outlook segment findings: Markets and industries.* www.pwc.com/gx/en/industries/tmt/media/outlook/segment-findings.html.

46 PwC (no date). *Outlook segment definitions.* www.pwc.com/gx/en/industries/tmt/media/outlook/segment-definitions.html.

47 CAGR is the mean annual growth rate of a market or an investment over a specified period of time longer than one year.

48 ReportLinker (2022). "Film and video global market report 2022." *GlobeNewswire*. www.globenewswire.com/en/news-release/2022/03/08/2398616/0/en/Film-And-Video-Global-Market-Report-2022.html.

49 Low, A. (2017). "We're watching videos on our phones more than ever." *Cnet*. www.cnet.com/tech/mobile/people-are-watching-videos-on-their-phones-more-than-ever/.

50 The Business Research Company (2022). *Global TV and radio broadcasting market report 2022 – market forecast, trends and strategies.* www.thebusinessresearchcompany.com/press-release/tv-and-radio-broadcasting-market-2022.

51 Research and Markets (2022). "$320 billion worldwide print media industry to 2031 – identify growth segments for investment," *GlobeNewswire*. www.globenewswire.com/en/news-release/2022/03/29/2411610/28124/en/320-Billion-Worldwide-Print-Media-Industry-to-2031-Identify-Growth-Segments-for-Investment.html.

52 Hatton, C. (2021). "IFPI issues Global Music Report 2021." *IFPI*. www.ifpi.org/ifpi-issues-annual-global-music-report-2021/.

53 Chambers, D. (2023). "Vinyl records outsell CDs for the first time since 1987." *The Wall Street Journal*. www.wsj.com/articles/vinyl-records-outsell-cds-for-the-first-time-since-1987-49deeef0?fbclid=IwAR3i9qtLKEbNmH8nJDyCB9pevP2zwPfV8cfUy87YplSx1PLj_t4LszeImR8.

54 Chambers, D. (2023). "Vinyl records outsell CDs for the first time since 1987." *The Wall Street Journal*. www.wsj.com/articles/vinyl-records-outsell-cds-for-the-first-time-since-1987-49deeef0?fbclid=IwAR3i9qtLKEbNmH8nJDyCB9pevP2zwPfV8cfUy87YplSx1PLj_t4LszeImR8.

55 Chambers, D. (2023). "Vinyl records outsell CDs for the first time since 1987." *The Wall Street Journal*. www.wsj.com/articles/vinyl-records-outsell-cds-for-the-first-time-since-1987-49deeef0?fbclid=IwAR3i9qtLKEbNmH8nJDyCB9pevP2zwPfV8cfUy87YplSx1PLj_t4LszeImR8.

56 Kirkcaldy, A. (2023). "Video game industry statistics, trends and data in 2023." *WePC*. www.wepc.com/news/video-game-statistics/.

57 Bocconi Students Investment Club members (2022). *In depth analysis of the gaming industry: Part 1, Bocconi Students Investment Club (BSIC)*. https://bsic.it/in-depth-analysis-of-the-gaming-industry-1/.

58 Mordor Intelligence (no date). "Gaming Market Size & Share Analysis – Growth Trends & Forecast (2023–2028)." www.mordorintelligence.com/industry-reports/global-gaming-market.

59 FinanceOnline (no date). "Number of gamers worldwide 2022/2023: Demographics, statistics, and predictions." https://financesonline.com/number-of-gamers-worldwide/.

60 Gray, T. (2015). "'Jaws' 40th anniversary: How Steven Spielberg's movie created the summer blockbuster." *Variety*, 18 June. https://variety.com/2015/film/news/jaws-40th-anniversary-at-40-box-office-summer-blockbuster-1201521198/

61 Braun, W. (2019). "The long tail: When a famous theory got (almost) all wrong." *Medium*, 14 April. https://medium.com/before-the-dot/the-long-tail-when-a-famous-theory-got-almost-all-wrong-12d3c6eb0de9

62 Lambert, C. (2014). "The way of the blockbuster." *Harvard Magazine,* 3 March. www.harvardmagazine.com/2014/01/the-way-of-the-blockbuster

Introduction **33**

63 Hennig-Thurau, T., Ravid, S. A. and Sorenson, O. (2021). "The economics of filmed entertainment in the digital era." *Journal of Cultural Economics*, 45(2), pp. 157–170. doi:10.1 007/s10824-021-09407-6.

64 Hooijdonk, R. van (2021). "The entertainment industry turns to algorithms in search of blockbuster movies." *Richard van Hooijdonk Blog*, 3 June. https://blog.richardvanhooijdonk. com/en/the-entertainment-industry-turns-to-algorithms-in-search-of-blockbuster-movies/

65 Mukherji, P. K. and Sengupta, S. (2022). "Media & Entertainment Industry: An overview." *Avasant.* https://avasant.com/insights/publications/technology-optimization/media-entertainment-industry-an-overveiw/.

66 Whittington, R. (2022). "How film production is becoming more sustainable and profitable." *Forbes*, 2 March. www.forbes.com/sites/sap/2022/02/28/how-film-production-is-becoming-more-sustainable-and-profitable/?sh=a6af95b5bad7.

67 Ryu, S. (2021). *Beauty of crowdfunding: Blooming creativity and innovation in the Digital Era.* London, UK: Routledge.

68 Harrison, J. W. (2022). "Top media and entertainment trends to watch in 2022." *EY.* www.ey. com/en_us/media-entertainment/what-are-the-five-trends-to-watch-in-media-and-entertainment-in-2022.

69 Arkenberg, C. et al. (2020). "Digital media trends: The future of movies." *Deloitte Insights.* www2.deloitte.com/us/en/insights/industry/technology/future-of-the-movie-industry.html.

70 Harrison, J. W. (2022). "Top media and entertainment trends to watch in 2022." *EY.* www.ey. com/en_us/media-entertainment/what-are-the-five-trends-to-watch-in-media-and-entertainment-in-2022.

71 Ryu, S. (2021). *Beauty of crowdfunding: Blooming creativity and innovation in the digital era.* London, UK: Routledge.

72 Ryu, S. and Suh, A., (2021). "Online service or virtual community? Building platform loyalty in reward-based crowdfunding." *Internet Research*, 31(1), pp. 315–340.

73 Francis, T. and Hoefel, F. (2018). "'True Gen': Generation Z and its implications for companies." *McKinsey & Company.* www.mckinsey.com/industries/consumer-packaged-goods/our-insights/true-gen-generation-z-and-its-implications-for-companies.

74 Francis, T. and Hoefel, F. (2018). "'True Gen': Generation Z and its implications for companies." *McKinsey & Company.* www.mckinsey.com/industries/consumer-packaged-goods/our-insights/true-gen-generation-z-and-its-implications-for-companies.

75 Francis, T. and Hoefel, F. (2018). "'True Gen': Generation Z and its implications for companies." *McKinsey & Company.* www.mckinsey.com/industries/consumer-packaged-goods/our-insights/true-gen-generation-z-and-its-implications-for-companies.

76 Price, R. (2020). "Gen Z not only loves content, they pay for it." *Digital Content Next*, 5 February. https://digitalcontentnext.org/blog/2020/02/05/gen-z-not-only-loves-content-they-pay-for-it/.

77 Price, R. (2020). "Gen Z not only loves content, they pay for it." *Digital Content Next*, 5 February. https://digitalcontentnext.org/blog/2020/02/05/gen-z-not-only-loves-content-they-pay-for-it/.

78 Harrison, J. W. (2022). "Top media and entertainment trends to watch in 2022." *EY.* www.ey. com/en_us/media-entertainment/what-are-the-five-trends-to-watch-in-media-and-entertainment-in-2022.

2

THE CHARACTERISTICS OF THE MEDIA AND ENTERTAINMENT INDUSTRY

Outline

Overview	34
2.1 Hedonic Consumption	35
2.2 Window Effect	38
2.3 High Risk and High Return	43
2.4 The Experience Goods Market	46
2.5 The Public Goods Market	48
2.6 Subcultures and Fandom	51
2.7 Cultural Discount and Premium	53
Case Studies	55
Review	56
Discussion Questions	57
Further Reading	57
References	58

Intended Learning Outcomes

- Identify the unique characteristics and corresponding management practices of the media and entertainment industry (MEI).
- Explain cases and examples representing the unique characteristics of the MEI.
- Articulate the challenges and opportunities that the MEI presents for players in relation to those characteristics.

Overview

The MEI has the following unique characteristics (Figure 2.1):

- Hedonic consumption: Customers of the MEI pursue affective and sensory experiences for esthetic pleasure, fantasy, and fun.

DOI: 10.4324/9781003271222-3

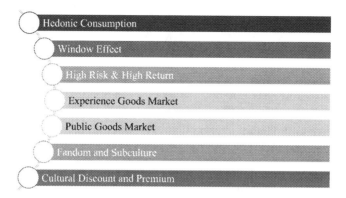

FIGURE 2.1 Seven Unique Characteristics of the MEI.

- Window effect: One popular property with an ensemble of narratives and characters can be developed and exploited across different channels, platforms, and territories.
- High risk and high return: Given uncertain customer demand, the event-based nature of the industry, and diverse risk factors, the MEI involves higher risk by nature. However, significantly lower (or zero) marginal production cost leads to a potentially high return when successful.
- Experience goods market: Unlike search goods, the quality of most MEI goods cannot be evaluated before customers experience them. Because of these characteristics, media, word of mouth, and strong "star systems" (see below) have a significant impact.
- Public goods market: Non-exclusiveness and non-rivalry aspects may lead to a free-rider problem and thus potential market failure in the MEI. To address this issue, players in the MEI have created solutions such as advertising and subscription models.
- Fandom and subcultures: Members of different subcultural groups develop shared tastes and preferences, formulated by socialization and education systems, and their collective experience.
- Cultural discount or premium: The value of cultural goods in one culture is discounted in another due to barriers of language, customs, preferences, and so on. The extent of this discount depends on content genres and characteristics.

In this chapter, we will review the characteristics of the MEI in detail, with some examples from different domains.

2.1 Hedonic Consumption

2.1.1 Definition

In contrast to "utilitarian consumption," which refers to items that are a priority for meeting specific functional purposes, "hedonic consumption" refers to items that elicit emotions, enjoyment, and pleasure through their use or possession. Hedonic consumption focuses on consumer behavior, which seeks sensory pleasures or hedonistic benefits through interaction with goods or services.[1]

A focus on practical needs and functionality characterizes utilitarian consumption. It involves the purchase of products or services needed for day-to-day living, such as

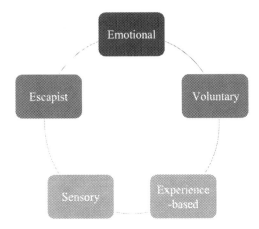

FIGURE 2.2 Hedonic Consumption: Characteristics.

groceries or household items. The primary motivation for utilitarian consumption is to satisfy a need rather than to seek pleasure or enjoyment.

By contrast, hedonic consumption has some unique characteristics (Figure 2.2):

- Emotional: Hedonic consumption is driven by emotions and seeks to provide pleasure and enjoyment to the consumer. It is focused on satisfying emotional needs rather than practical needs.
- Voluntary: Hedonic consumption is typically voluntary and discretionary. Consumers engage in it because they want to, not because they need to.
- Experience-based: Hedonic consumption is experience-based, focusing on the overall experience rather than the specific product or service.
- Sensory: Hedonic consumption is sensory, involving using all five senses to enhance the experience.
- Escapist: Hedonic consumption is used to escape from everyday life or provide temporary relief from stress or negative emotions.

In the hedonic consumption context, customers are emotional; while they are more rational in the utilitarian consumption. Hedonic consumption is underpinned by emotional desire and enjoyment, not utilitarian motives and problem-solving.

2.1.2 Decision-Making Criteria for Hedonic Consumption

Decision-making criteria between the two consumption contexts differ due to the underlying motivations and goals of each type of consumption. In the hedonic consumption context, customers tend to be subjective and follow affective preferences ("want") based on the symbolic attributes of products. Customers tend to be driven by emotional appeal, entertainment value, personal preferences, and brand image. On the other hand, utilitarian consumption is based on instrumental and functional attributes of products and cognitive and reasoned preferences ("should"). Customers are influenced by functionality, quality, convenience, and price (Table 2.1).

Industry Characteristics **37**

TABLE 2.1 Decision Criteria for Hedonic versus Utilitarian Consumption

	Hedonic consumption	*Utilitarian consumption*
Primary decision-making criteria	• Emotional appeal (e.g., the emotional satisfaction and pleasure from the product or experience). • Entertainment value. • Personal preferences: personal tastes and preferences for specific brands are critical factors. • Brand image (e.g., brand reputation of the product or experience). • Price: While price is a consideration, it may not be the primary factor in the decision-making process for hedonic consumption.	• Functionality (e.g., functional benefits of the product or service, such as whether it meets practical needs. • Quality (e.g., durability of the product or service). • Convenience (e.g., accessibility of the product or service). • Price: Consumers may be more price-sensitive for products or services that are necessities rather than luxuries. • Reputation (e.g., the reliability of the brand or provider).

2.1.3 Hedonic Consumption of Media and Entertainment Products

Most products and services in the MEI relate to hedonic consumption.

Media and entertainment products elicit multisensory, fantasy, and emotive responses through the interaction between the consumer, the product, and the consumption.[2] Moreover, the consumption of media and entertainment products (e.g., films, music, and games) has been proven to enhance emotional pleasure and evoke feelings of happiness and satisfaction within consumers.[3]

Media and entertainment products are primarily designed to provide consumers with pleasure, enjoyment, and emotional satisfaction. These products are typically consumed for entertainment value, not practical functionality:

• Emotional appeal: Media and entertainment products such as movies, TV shows, music, and videogames are designed to appeal to consumers' emotions and provide a pleasurable and enjoyable experience.
• Discretionary spending: Consumers often consume media and entertainment products as discretionary spending items, meaning they are not essential for daily living.
• Sensory experience: Many media and entertainment products engage the senses, such as sight, sound, and touch, making the experience more enjoyable and satisfying.
• Escapism: Media and entertainment products can offer consumers an escape from reality and temporary relief from stress and negative emotions.
• Social interaction: Some media and entertainment products, such as movies and videogames, can be consumed with others, providing a social aspect to the consumption experience.

Given the hedonic consumption aspect of the MEI, companies should consider the following points when developing and marketing their products and services:

38 Overview of the Media and Entertainment Industry

- Focus on customer experience: Companies should create a positive and enjoyable customer experience. This can include everything from the quality of content to the overall ambiance and atmosphere of a venue. Companies must also create engaging and interactive experiences that foster customer loyalty.
- Differentiated product offerings: Companies are expected to create differentiated product offerings tailored to specific consumer preferences. These can include different genres of movies or music, different types of videogames, and even different types of theme parks.
- Building brand image and reputation: Brand image and reputation can be essential decision-making criteria for hedonic consumption. Thus, companies should focus on building a strong and positive brand image. This can include creating a unique and recognizable brand identity, investing in advertising and marketing campaigns, and ensuring high-quality customer service.

2.2 Window Effect

Movies and other media and entertainment products are traditionally distributed across distinct sequential channels (e.g., theaters, home video, and video on demand).[4] This practice has been widely employed in the MEI and is referred to by different terms, such as "one source, multi-use" (OSMU), "create once, publish everywhere" (COPE), "media franchises," and "transmedia storytelling."

2.2.1 One Source, Multi-Use

OSMU involves the development of multiple product types from one source.[5] In particular, it is a characteristic of movie products. Although a movie is a work of art, it is not only shown in theaters but also spawns various related products such as videos, TV broadcasting rights, cable TV broadcasting rights, DVDs, novels, games, and character goods. This strategy involves initially creating primary content through meticulous planning, and subsequently transforming it into secondary and tertiary content through reinvestment and licensing.[6]

One example of OSMU is Disney's animation *Mickey Mouse*, which became a massive hit in the 1930s. In response to this success, Disney opened a theme park filled with Mickey Mouse-themed merchandise and characters in 1955. This is a prominent example of OSMU: more than 80 years after its creation, Mickey Mouse continues to be widely recognized due to the diverse range of products produced through OSMU.

Another notable instance of the expansion of this concept is *Star Wars* (Table 2.2). In addition to generating substantial revenue from theaters, the movie series earned multiple times revenues through merchandising sales of character-related goods. This exemplifies how a single source can be utilized across multiple fields and genres, enabling content to extend beyond movies to include games, records, animations, character merchandise, toys, publications, and even the tourism industry.

2.2.2 Create Once, Publish Everywhere

Another term referring to the window effect is "COPE."[7] This is a well-established approach to content creation and distribution. It is commonly understood as the practice

TABLE 2.2 OSMU Case: *Star Wars*

Genre	Description	Cases
Movies	The movie franchise began in 1977 and has since produced over 10 films, with more in development. The films are known for their unique characters, epic storylines, and stunning visual effects.	*Episode IV – A New Hope* (1977), *Episode IX – The Rise of Skywalker* (2019)
Comics and graphic novels	*Star Wars* has been adapted into comic books and graphic novels, which provide fans with additional stories and character development beyond what is seen in the movies and TV shows.	*Star Wars: Darth Vader* series, *Star Wars: Han Solo* series
Television shows	*Star Wars* has been adapted into several television shows. These shows have helped expand the universe and introduce new characters and storylines.	*The Clone Wars* (2008), *The Mandalorian* (2019)
Novels and books	*Star Wars* has been adapted into novels and books, including adaptations of the movies and original stories set within the *Star Wars* universe.	*Heir to the Empire* (1991), *Star Wars: Brotherhood* (2022)
Theme parks	*Star Wars* has been integrated into Disney's theme parks, which allows fans to explore the universe through a fully immersive experience.	Attractions such as Star Wars: Galaxy's Edge.
Soundtracks and music	The music of *Star Wars*, composed by John Williams, is one of the franchise's most iconic and recognizable aspects. The soundtracks have been released as albums, and the music has been used in various other contexts, including commercials, and live orchestral performances.	*Star Wars Live in Concert*
Videogames	*Star* Wars has been adapted into numerous videogames, spanning several different genres, from first-person shooters to roleplaying games.	*Star Wars: Knights of The Old Republic* (2003), *Star Wars Jedi: Survivor* (2023)
Merchandise	A wide range of *Star Wars* merchandise is available, from action figures and clothing to kitchenware and home decor.	*Star Wars* series of Lego and Hasbro
Virtual reality	*Star Wars* has been adapted into virtual reality experiences, allowing players to enter the universe and interact with characters and environments in a fully immersive way.	*Vader Immortal: A Star Wars VR Series* (Oculus, 2019)
Educational programs	*Star Wars* has been used in educational programs, which support charitable causes and encourage young people to unlock their creativity and passion to positively impact the world.	*Star Wars: Force for Change*

40 Overview of the Media and Entertainment Industry

of publishing the same content across all marketing channels. While this approach emphasizes efficiency in content creation and consistency in messaging, it falls short in terms of effectiveness. The crucial aspect that often gets overlooked is the need for content to be tailored and unique to each specific channel.

The concept of COPE gained popularity through its adoption by National Public Radio (NPR) in the US. It is a content management philosophy aimed at enabling content creators to add content in a central location and then repurpose it in various forms across different platforms. In October 2009, David Jacobson—at the time, the director of application development at NPR—authored a guest post titled "COPE: Create Once, Publish Everywhere" on ProgrammableWeb.[8] The article detailed NPR's implementation of a content management architecture that facilitated the publication of each content piece across multiple devices and channels. This encompassed platforms such as NPR.org, diverse mobile apps, station sites, public mashups, NPR widgets, and station modules. NPR's pioneering development of the COPE framework positioned it ahead of the curve and greatly influenced contemporary approaches to content management within organizations.

COPE is a content strategy that revolves around the idea of creating content once and distributing it across multiple channels and platforms. The primary objective of COPE is to optimize the reach and effectiveness of content by ensuring its availability on diverse platforms and devices, catering to audience preferences. The key principle of COPE is to avoid the need to create unique content for each individual channel or platform.

In COPE, content is crafted in a format that can be easily adapted and repurposed for various channels and platforms, such as HTML, XML, or JSON. This allows for seamless distribution of the content to different channels, including social media, email newsletters, mobile apps, websites, and other digital platforms, with minimal or zero customization required.

The main advantages of COPE include the following:

- Time and cost savings: COPE allows organizations to save time and money on content creation and distribution.
- Consistency: COPE helps ensure consistency in messaging, branding, and tone across different channels and platforms, resulting in a strong brand identity and increasing audience engagement.
- Increased reach: COPE enables content to reach a larger and more diverse audience. It aims to increase brand awareness and drive more traffic to websites or other digital properties.
- Data insights: Organizations can gather data and insights on audience engagement and behavior across different channels. This helps inform future content strategies and improve overall performance.

2.2.3 Media Franchise

The term "media franchise" refers to a comprehensive assortment of narratives and characters that can be extensively developed and utilized across various divisions, platforms, territories, and generations. It encompasses a diverse range of media content, including movies, TV shows, books, comics, videogames, and merchandise, all interconnected by a single intellectual property (IP). This IP could represent a fictional universe, a character, or a concept that is employed across different media formats to deliver a unified and immersive experience to the audience. Media franchises typically enjoy a devoted fanbase and can generate substantial revenue for the owning companies.

In addition to *Star Wars*, other representative examples of media franchises include the Marvel Cinematic Universe (MCU), *Harry Potter*, *Pokémon*, and *Hello Kitty*:

- The MCU is an expansive media franchise, showcasing a remarkable series of superhero movies meticulously crafted by Marvel Studios. Its all-encompassing realm extends beyond the silver screen, encompassing TV shows, comics, and merchandise. Within this magnificent tapestry of storytelling, iconic characters such as Iron Man, Captain America, and Spider-Man intertwine, propelling the MCU to awe-inspiring heights of success and unrivaled profitability.
- *Harry Potter* is a prominent media franchise that encompasses a collection of books, movies, videogames, merchandise, and theme parks. Set within a richly imagined world of wizards, the franchise showcases iconic characters and items. With a dedicated fanbase and unwavering popularity, it has proven to be a lucrative venture for owner Warner Bros., generating substantial revenues and leaving an indelible mark on popular culture.
- *Pokémon* is a notable example of a highly successful and enduring multimedia phenomenon. Spanning videogames, animated TV shows, movies, trading cards, and merchandise, the franchise revolves around the concept of trainers capturing, training, and battling creatures known as Pokémon. Enjoying a dedicated fanbase and remarkable longevity, *Pokémon* has established itself as one of the most prosperous and enduring media franchises, resonating with audiences of all ages and continuing to thrive in diverse entertainment sectors.
- *Hello Kitty* is a prominent Japanese media franchise that has garnered significant acclaim and popularity worldwide. Focusing primarily on an extensive range of merchandise, including plush toys, clothing, stationery, and accessories, the franchise revolves around the endearing character of Hello Kitty—a white cat adorned with a distinctive red bow. With a devoted fanbase spanning various age groups, *Hello Kitty* transcends cultural boundaries and serves as a testament to the enduring appeal of character-driven media franchises.

Based on well-established brands with an existing consumer base, media franchises present reduced commercial risks and demand less marketing effort when targeting new and younger audiences. The utilization of franchises allows rights holders to optimize the value of their IP in various ways. By leveraging franchises, synergies can be fostered among different divisions, where a lead medium such as a movie can be accompanied by an array of complementary products, including videogames, TV series, mobile applications, animations, music, books, and theme park attractions. The most successful franchises further augment their revenue streams through licensing and merchandising agreements. For example, fashion retailers may secure the rights to major entertainment brands, allowing them to utilize logos and characters in their clothing and accessories, thereby capitalizing on the popularity and appeal of these franchises.

These are clear benefits of developing a media franchise (Figure 2.3).

First, media franchises enjoy a remarkable level of brand recognition among consumers, providing significant impetus for sales and revenue. The ardent followers of a franchise

42 Overview of the Media and Entertainment Industry

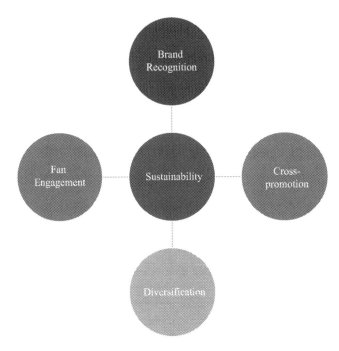

FIGURE 2.3 Benefits of Media Franchises.

exhibit a higher propensity to acquire merchandise and consume content associated with that specific franchise. This consumer loyalty contributes to the establishment of consistent and reliable revenue streams for the franchise owner.

Second, media franchises offer a valuable opportunity for cross-promotion, facilitating the seamless integration of content across diverse media formats. For instance, the release of a movie within the franchise can be effectively promoted through a corresponding TV show, which in turn can be further amplified through a comic book series. Such well-orchestrated cross-promotion builds a cohesive and captivating experience for enthusiasts, immersing them deeply in the world of the franchise.

Third, media franchises enable strategic diversification across a multitude of media formats, effectively mitigating risks and generating revenue from multiple sources. Consider the example of a movie franchise that concurrently embraces TV shows, books, comics, and merchandise—all of which collectively contribute to the overall revenue and success of the franchise. This diversification strategy ensures a robust and well-rounded financial foundation for the franchise owner.

Fourth, they foster an unparalleled level of fan engagement, captivating dedicated fanbases that enthusiastically embrace their content and merchandise. This heightened engagement is manifested in vibrant interactions across social media platforms, dedicated forums, and immersive fan events. The result is the creation of a dedicated, tightly knit community, united by their shared passion for the franchise and their active contribution to its ongoing success.

Taken together, media franchises exhibit remarkable sustainability, not just spanning years but often extending across decades and even generations. This inherent longevity affords consistent revenue streams over extended periods, cementing a lasting legacy for the franchise owner. The enduring appeal of these franchises resonates with successive cohorts of fans, contributing to their sustained success and financial prosperity.

2.2.4 Transmedia Storytelling

Transmedia storytelling is the art of crafting, disseminating, and engaging in a unified narrative experience that transcends various conventional and digital platforms. This approach is employed in domains such as entertainment, advertising, marketing, and even social change initiatives.[9] Utilizing contemporary digital technologies, transmedia story-telling involves the narration of a cohesive story or story experience across diverse platforms and formats.[10]

Telling stories through multiple media simultaneously requires the author and the audience to find new interactive spaces in which they can actively participate in publishing ventures spanning cinema, TV series, advertising campaigns, videogames, mobile apps, cartoons, comics, books, and performative events. It is imperative to respect the distinct characteristics and languages of each medium, even when they are part of a unified system of integrated communication.[11] Transmedia storytelling employs imagery and techniques shared by producers, authors, and audiences within the realms of entertainment, information, and brand communication, which serves to unravel the intricate tapestry of narratives woven within this novel interactive ecosystem.

Drawing on over 50 notable examples of successful projects from across the globe—including *Star Wars*, *The Dark Knight*, *Lost*, *Heroes*, *Dexter*, *Assassin's Creed*, *Lord of the Rings*, and *Avatar*—Max Giovagnoli delves into transmedia storytelling.[12] His comprehensive analysis incorporates valuable insights from prominent producers and international researchers. Readers are offered guidance on crafting compelling products, narratives, and ad campaigns tailored for contemporary audiences. Giovagnoli examines the emerging narrative universes and international franchises of transmedia culture, exploring their distinctive storytelling paradigms, regulations, and opportunities.

2.3 High Risk and High Return

2.3.1 The High-Risk Aspects of the Media and Entertainment Industry

The MEI possesses some unique characteristics that increase the risk involved in managing businesses.

First, it is hard to standardize products given the creativity and imagination involved, which results in uncertain demand. Most products (e.g., film, drama, music, and games) are event-based and initial investment should be considered as a sunk cost without an opportunity to recover from any potential loss. This further increases the risk level.

The diverse risk factors in the MEI, from production to distribution, include the following (Figure 2.4):[13]

- Commercial risks: For the MEI, the most fundamental problem resides in the difficulty of predicting consumer tastes and demand. This risk is inherent to cultural production and is a key focus of economic analysis. The history of the MEI is a long road of unexpected successes and unforeseen failures.

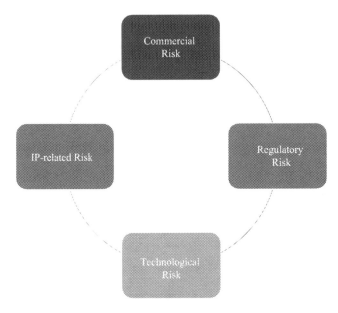

FIGURE 2.4 High-Risk Factors in the MEI.

- Regulatory risks: Media and entertainment companies are subject to various laws—including those related to copyright, data protection, user privacy, consumer protection, and content regulation. Uncertainties for multinationals are increased by the fact that they operate across many jurisdictions. Risks are heightened in countries with opaque and inefficient regulatory regimes. Firms can be affected by sudden changes in laws and regulations that can seriously affect their operations.
- Technological risks: Technological risks are vast in scope. This source of uncertainty stems from the rapid pace of technological change, which continuously opens up new possibilities to disrupt business models (e.g., the proliferation of online platforms) and interrupt income streams (e.g., ad-blocking software and devices).
- IP-related risks: The unauthorized use of IP remains rife and constitutes a formidable challenge for media and entertainment firms. Methods of content theft vary, and digital technologies have exacerbated the problem. Recording devices, including mobile phones, can steal films from movie screens for the copy to be either distributed online or sold on counterfeit DVDs. Peer-to-peer file-sharing websites enable users to exchange pirated content; and streaming websites allow them to watch copyrighted content illegally without downloading it.

2.3.2 The High-Return Potential of the Media and Entertainment Industry

Although there are multiple risk factors, products in the MEI have the potential to yield high returns due to several factors (Figure 2.5).

First, the industry has a diverse range of revenue streams, including movies, television, videogames, music, theme parks, and merchandise. This diversity helps mitigate risks and provides multiple opportunities for revenue growth.

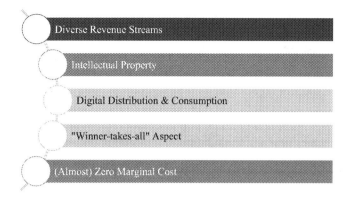

FIGURE 2.5 High-Return Factors in the MEI.

Second, many companies in the industry own valuable IP, such as popular franchises and characters. This IP can be monetized through various channels, such as licensing deals, merchandise sales, and theme park attractions, increasing the chances of success.

Third, the industry is transforming digitally, with more content distributed and consumed through digital formats. This shift has created new revenue opportunities and reduced distribution costs, leading to higher profitability.

Fourth, the MEI is characterized by "winner takes all" aspects, meaning that a small number of companies or individuals tend to dominate the market and capture a disproportionate share of the revenue and attention.

This is partly due to the high fixed costs of producing and distributing media content, which can create barriers to entry for smaller or less established players. Larger companies with more resources are better positioned to invest in content creation, marketing, and distribution, which can lead to competitive advantage and increased market share.

In addition, network effects can reinforce the winner-takes-all dynamic: the value of a product or service increases as more people use it. For example, a social media platform is more valuable to users if more people are on it; this can create a feedback loop, whereby users are incentivized to join the platform with the most users, reinforcing the dominance of a few prominent players.

Finally, products in the MEI also have the potential to yield high returns due to the (almost) zero marginal cost of production and distribution, especially in the digital setting. The turn of the century marked dramatic changes to the business system in the MEI. Digitalization and the convergence of the production system and the development of the internet have influenced the development and implementation of new modes of production and distribution in the MEI.[14]

For example, in the music industry, once a song has been recorded, it can be distributed digitally at minimal cost to an almost unlimited number of listeners. Similarly, in the film industry, once a movie has been produced, it can be distributed digitally or on physical media to an almost unlimited number of viewers. This can create a long-tail revenue model, where many titles generate small revenue, which can add up over time.

Additionally, the low marginal cost of distribution can enable new business models, such as subscription-based streaming services or online marketplaces for digital content, which can generate recurring revenue streams and reduce the risks associated with traditional box-office or sales-driven revenue models.

The emergence of these new business models has profoundly transformed all sectors of the MEI. This is particularly evident in the publishing sector, where the advent of digital technologies quickly gave rise to digital editions of books, newspapers, and magazines. The digitization process has directly impacted the cost paradigm, specifically in terms of total cost distribution. While the cost of producing copy in the magazine industry has remained relatively stable, subsequent units produced have seen significant changes in variable costs. The shift toward digital production of content has directly contributed to decreasing marginal production and distribution costs to almost zero.

2.4 The Experience Goods Market

2.4.1 The Characteristics of Experience Goods

Experience goods can only be evaluated accurately once the product has been purchased and consumed. This contrasts with search goods, which have attributes that can be evaluated prior to purchase or consumption. When it comes to experience goods, consumers are heavily dependent on previous encounters, direct examination of the product, and other information-seeking activities to gather relevant information that aids in the evaluation process. In contrast, most products fall under the search goods category, which includes items like office stationery and home appliances.

Examples of experience goods include movies, concerts, and vacations. Consumers cannot fully evaluate the quality of the product until they have experienced it, making it difficult for them to determine the value of the product before making a purchase decision.

On the other hand, search goods are products that consumers can easily evaluate before purchase. These goods have measurable attributes—such as size, price, and quality—that can be compared across different brands or products. Examples include clothing, electronics, and household appliances. Consumers can easily compare prices, features, and reviews before purchasing them.

Due to the difference in evaluation methods, experience goods are more difficult to market and sell than search goods. For example, marketers of experience goods must rely on branding, reputation, and word of mouth to persuade consumers to purchase their products. They must also create a positive consumer experience to ensure repeat business and positive reviews.

Most media and entertainment products can be classified as experience goods, as consumers of novels, songs, films, paintings, and similar forms of media often face high levels of uncertainty regarding the quality of these products before engaging with them. As a result, consumers frequently encounter feelings of disappointment or other unexpected reactions when experiencing these media forms for the first time.[15]

2.4.2 The Impact of the Media in the Media and Entertainment Industry

Due to the characteristics of the MEI, the media plays a critical role in marketing media and entertainment products because it can significantly influence consumer perceptions of the quality and value of a product. Since experience goods cannot be fully evaluated before purchase, consumers often rely on other factors, such as marketing and reviews, to determine the expected quality of the product. This is where the impact of the media comes into play.

For example, if a movie receives positive reviews from critics and audiences alike, this can significantly increase its perceived value and drive consumer interest and demand. On the other hand, if a movie is heavily criticized or receives negative reviews, this can lower consumer expectations and decrease demand for the movie.

The media can also affect the reputation and brand image of a media or entertainment company. A company that consistently produces high-quality content can build a strong brand reputation and a loyal following, leading to increased demand and revenues over time. In addition, the media can shape consumer preferences and trends. For example, media coverage and marketing campaigns can influence the popularity of specific genres or types of media.

2.4.3 Star Systems in the Media and Entertainment Industry

The concept of "star systems" involves the use of famous actors, musicians, or other celebrities to attract audiences and generate interest in a particular product or production. This may include using a celebrity's name or image in marketing materials, casting them in a lead role in a movie or TV show, or featuring them in a promotional event. From a risk reduction perspective, star systems are critical because they can help mitigate some of the uncertainties associated with producing and marketing media and entertainment products.

The effect of star power on box office revenue has been studied extensively. For example, casting a well-known actor in a lead role can help increase the perceived value of a movie or TV show, since consumers are more likely to trust and be interested in a production featuring a familiar face. This can help reduce the risk of low box office revenues or poor ratings.

2.4.4 The Importance of Word of Mouth in the Media and Entertainment Industry

Word of mouth—the sharing of information about products or services among customers—has garnered attention from marketers and researchers as a potential alternative to traditional advertising, which has become less effective due to increased competition.[16] Studies have shown that word of mouth is particularly influential when customers are considering purchasing new or unfamiliar products or services.

Where customers have limited knowledge of a product or service, WOM can play a powerful role in shaping their buying decisions. It serves as a valuable source of information and guidance, allowing customers to gain insights from the experiences and recommendations of others.

As commercial advertising faces challenges in capturing consumer attention, word of mouth emerges as a compelling and trusted way in which customers can seek information and make informed choices. Its effectiveness lies in its ability to bridge the gap between unfamiliar products/services and the customer's need for reliable guidance.

The evaluation of media and entertainment products by consumers is often limited, prompting them to rely on the opinions and experiences of others to make informed decisions.

This is where word of mouth comes into play. It can have a significant impact on consumer interest, demand, and revenue for such products.[17] Recommendations from

48 Overview of the Media and Entertainment Industry

friends, family, trusted sources, online reviews, and social media discussions all contribute to positive word of mouth, which can amplify consumer interest in a media or entertainment product.

For example, if a friend personally recommends a movie or TV show, the recipient is more likely to trust the suggestion and develop an interest in the product. Similarly, positive online reviews and social media buzz can greatly enhance consumer interest and drive demand.

Conversely, negative word of mouth can severely hinder the success of a media or entertainment product. Negative reviews, criticism, or backlash can significantly lower consumer expectations and dampen demand.

Therefore, word of mouth plays a critical role in shaping consumer perceptions, preferences, and purchasing decisions—particularly for experience goods in the MEI. As a result, media companies should recognize the significance of word of mouth and implement strategies to generate positive buzz and recommendations from consumers and trusted sources.

Online consumer reviews have emerged as a major competing form of word of mouth, and arguably are now more widely consulted than the quality signals presented by certified experts.[18] Word of mouth volume has significantly impacted box office revenue, whereas audience scores have not. If the expectations of a movie are higher before release, the valence of word of mouth is higher before release than after release.[19] The valence of word of mouth may not significantly impact box-office revenue, according to relevant studies.

2.5 The Public Goods Market

2.5.1 Definition

Media and entertainment products are partially public goods, in light of the characteristics that define whether a specific product is a "public good."[20] The two main criteria are that a public good must be non-rivalrous and non-excludable. "Non-rivalrous" means that the good does not dwindle in supply as more people consume it; "non-excludable" means that the good is available to all citizens:

- Non-rivalrous: The good or resource can be used or enjoyed by multiple individuals simultaneously without diminishing its availability for others. In other words, consumption of the good by one person does not diminish its availability or utility for others.
- Non-excludable: The good or resource cannot be restricted or denied to individuals. It is not possible to prevent anyone from accessing or using the good, regardless of their willingness or ability to pay for it.

According to this definition, a good that exhibits the traits of non-rivalry and non-exclusiveness is referred to as a pure "public good," as opposed to a "private good." "Partially public goods" are goods that satisfy the two public good conditions only to a certain extent or only some of the time.

The free-rider problem is a significant concern associated with public goods. Public goods are accessible to all individuals, irrespective of whether they contribute financially toward them. This creates the potential for certain members of society to benefit from the goods without bearing the associated costs. For instance, individuals who do not pay taxes essentially enjoy a "free ride" by benefiting from the revenues funded by those who do pay taxes. Similarly, turnstile jumpers in a subway system are engaging in a form of free riding by utilizing the service without paying for it.

2.5.2 Media and Entertainment Products as Public Goods

Media and entertainment products—for example, video content on an online platform—can be treated as a public good.[21] Because public goods are non-rivalrous and non-excludable, they do not operate as other commodities do. Media and entertainment products are not only public goods in an economic sense (especially in their digital form); they also constitute public goods in a socially beneficial sense.

First, access and inclusion stand as fundamental values. Media and entertainment services are available to all individuals, regardless of background or circumstances. By embracing inclusivity, media and entertainment content can foster a sense of fairness and create an environment in which everyone can partake in the experiences they offer.

Second, quality of life is another societal value that is deeply intertwined with the MEI. The industry has the potential to greatly enhance quality of life by offering products and services that support work-life balance and overall wellbeing. Through the provision of content and experiences that contribute to personal growth, relaxation, and entertainment, the MEI can significantly impact individuals' lives and contribute to their happiness and fulfillment.

Third, belonging to a community is another societal value associated with the MEI. It creates spaces in which people with shared interests can connect and communicate, fostering a sense of belonging and promoting social cohesion. For example, by participating in virtual communities centered on specific interests, individuals can find likeminded people, build relationships, and contribute to the development and growth of their communities.

Fourth, the MEI can greatly influence educational empowerment. Specifically, educational content tailored to children's needs can shape the minds of individuals and contribute to their intellectual development. By providing informative and educational materials, the MEI helps nurture knowledge, critical thinking skills, and creativity.

Fifth, the MEI helps foster cultural understanding. Content that reflects and strengthens cultural identities plays an important role in building inclusive and harmonious societies. By producing content that celebrates cultural diversity and encourages empathy, the industry can help create a more interconnected world, in which cultural differences are respected and appreciated.

2.5.3 The Potential Market Failure of the Media and Entertainment Industry—and Solutions

The MEI has many unique characteristics. There are several reasons why this completely unregulated market could fail, given the potential free rider problem.[22] Market failure occurs when market prices cannot sustain the market structure. The failure of an entire market segment has far-reaching, fundamental effects. Content and other information products are characterized by high fixed costs, cheap distribution, economies of scale with incentives to oversupply, and commoditization. The prices of content and network

50 Overview of the Media and Entertainment Industry

TABLE 2.3 Societal Values Created by the MEI

Societal Values	Effects
Access and inclusion	• Enabling universal access and fostering inclusivity.
	• Facilitating equal opportunities.
Quality of life	• Enhancing wellbeing
	• Contributing to a balanced and fulfilling life.
	• Elevating the standard of living.
Community engagement	• Cultivating a sense of belonging and connection.
	• Empowering individuals to actively engage with their communities.
Empowering education	• Promoting the educational value derived from content.
	• Enhancing learning, knowledge acquisition, and creativity.
Cultural enrichment	• Strengthening cultural identities.
	• Nurturing cultural diversity and cultural expression.

distribution are collapsing across a broad front. It has become difficult to charge anything for information products and services. This is a symptom of a chronic price deflation that shows no sign of abating. While this may be good news for consumers, it is bad news for providers. The price is approaching marginal cost, which can be near zero.[23]

The MEI has employed the advertising model to address the potential free rider and market failure problem.[24] The fundamental business model of many MEI players revolves around advertisers' desire to reach potential customers. This model has significant implications for market performance, as viewer preferences indirectly influence the dynamics. Viewers are drawn to programming, despite their general aversion to the ads contained within it; while advertisers seek viewers as potential consumers. The coordination between these two sides is facilitated by broadcasters and platforms, which determine the levels of advertising to allow and the types of programs to carry, with advertising revenues funding the programming. Competition for viewers within specific demographic segments implies that programming choices will be influenced by the preferences of those specific demographics.

Introducing subscription pricing as an alternative approach can potentially enhance performance by catering to the preferences of underrepresented individuals.[25] However, higher overall prices tend to benefit broadcasters at the expense of viewers and advertisers. Where there is a weakening in advertising demand, program selection may become excessively imbalanced as broadcasters strive to avoid engaging in ruinous competition based on subscription prices. Conversely, where advertising demand remains strong, there may be intense competition among broadcasters for viewers, leading to minimal differentiation. Certain markets, such as newspapers, may only be served by a monopoly because advertisers prefer to place ads in publications with the highest readership, while readers prefer to purchase publications with the greatest volume of content, including ads.

Economists have studied the economic benefits of both advertising and direct subscription payments in supporting radio and television programming.[26] The results of this research suggest that a mix of the two mechanisms is likely to be the optimal approach. Advertisers are likely to be motivated by the desire to maximize their reach among a target population at the lowest possible cost, consistent with persuading consumers of the attractiveness of their products. For this reason, they are likely to eschew the support of programming (or other software) that appeals to a narrow set of potential consumers. Thus, in most circumstances, advertiser-supported services are likely to be less finely differentiated than subscriber-supported services. If some consumers are unwilling to pay much for highly differentiated services, their economic welfare will be greater with advertiser-supported services. For this reason, presumably, more than one-third of all households now served by cable television do not currently subscribe, even though cable offers a much greater choice than the available array of broadcast stations in even the largest markets.

On the other hand, some consumers may desire more choice than can be supported by advertising alone. Subscriber-supported services can reflect the intensity of consumer preferences, not simply their willingness to use a service—the critical criterion for advertisers. This is why pay-cable and pay-per-view services have proliferated in the current multichannel video environment. Only a few hundred thousand subscribers, each paying a substantial one-time user fee, may be required to support two or three hours of a nationally distributed service or event. Foreign soccer games, obscure older feature films, and live concerts may be offered for a one-time charge; while more popular events may be advertiser-supported.

A third possibility for supporting services in the current or future information infrastructure is a mix of user charges and advertiser support for the same service. Pay-per-view services could still carry advertising billboards or even interspersed advertising messages. For example, video cassettes and motion picture theaters are now supported by both subscriber charges and advertising. In addition, the same programming could be offered simultaneously without advertising but with a subscriber fee, or with advertising but without a subscriber fee. This combination of support mechanisms could lead to greater diversity and a more extensive array of available services.

2.6 Subcultures and Fandom

2.6.1 Understanding Subcultural Groups in the Media and Entertainment Industry

The existence of different subcultures is another essential characteristic of the MEI. In the field of sociological and cultural anthropology, the concept of a "subculture" is defined by the *Oxford English Dictionary* as "an identifiable subgroup within a society or group of people, esp. one characterized by beliefs or interests at variance with those of the larger group; the distinctive ideas, practices, or way of life of such a subgroup."[27] The differences in fantasy and emotion among various subcultural groups arise from the distinct socialization and educational systems in which members participate, leading to the acquisition of "learned" emotions and collective experiences.

Subcultural groups can be categorized based on various attributes, including age, gender, social class, ethnic background, and specific preferences toward particular genres or content.

Age and gender are two of the most common subcultural bases for segmentation in consumer research.[28] One stream of studies has investigated the influence of these two factors on individual preferences for consuming different forms of media and entertainment products. For instance, one recent study revealed that nearly one-third of older men and women continue to subscribe to cable and satellite TV; whereas only approximately one-quarter of younger women choose to pay for conventional TV services.[29] Furthermore, in terms of subscription services for media and entertainment products, younger women tend to have a higher average number of subscriptions compared to men of the same age and older individuals of any gender. Another study reveals that there are notable distinctions between men and women in their use of subscription services.[30] For

52 Overview of the Media and Entertainment Industry

example, men exhibit a greater tendency to cancel services than women. As an illustration, during the pandemic, 20% of men canceled their streaming video subscriptions, whereas only 13% of women did so. Men are also twice as likely as women (22% compared to 11%) to discontinue a streaming video service in order to subscribe to a new one.

With regard to age, new media is a potent force for young consumers.[31] Among individuals aged 15–29, the top three entertainment brands are YouTube, Netflix, and TikTok. In contrast, for individuals aged 30–44, the top brands are Netflix, YouTube, and Facebook. It is noteworthy that traditional TV and cable networks are positioned toward the lower end of the rankings for both age groups. Furthermore, individuals aged 60 or older are twice as inclined as those under the age of 30 to choose television as their preferred means of entertainment.

The notion of subcultures based on fandom for a specific genre or content was introduced by Dick Hebdige in his 1979 book *Subculture: The Meaning of Style*.[32] Hebdige argued that communities centered around punk, hipster, and other musical genres formed unique cultural entities. Rather than engaging in explicit political protests or violent confrontations with authority, these groups challenged established mainstream culture through their distinct cultural style. This style encompassed elements such as unconventional clothing, pierced ears and noses, and other visible signs that unsettled and disrupted the prevailing societal norms.

2.6.2 Fandom as a Key Component of the Media and Entertainment Industry

"Fandom" refers to a subculture of passionate and dedicated fans who are deeply engaged with a particular media property, such as a film, TV show, book series, or videogame.[33] Communities of fans are formed around common interests, and actively contribute to the fandom by creating fan art, fan fiction, and other forms of fan-generated content. Fandom plays a significant role in the MEI as it fosters engagement, loyalty, and financial success.

One notable advantage of fandom is its ability to cultivate a devoted and dedicated audience for a specific media property. Fans exhibit high levels of engagement, closely following news and updates while enthusiastically sharing their passion. This organic word-of-mouth promotion generates buzz around the property, increasing awareness and attracting new audiences.

Moreover, fandom serves as a valuable revenue source for media and entertainment companies. Fans are willing to invest in a wide range of products and experiences associated with their beloved properties, including merchandise, events, and digital content. Capitalizing on fandom, media companies can develop new revenue streams by offering exclusive content, establishing fan clubs or subscription services, and organizing fan events and conventions.

Beyond its revenue-generating potential, fandom plays a crucial role in building brand equity and fostering a strong emotional bond between fans and media properties. Fans who are highly engaged with a particular property tend to exhibit greater loyalty, actively sharing positive opinions and recommendations. They also develop a sense of personal ownership and investment in the success of the property.

Fandom can form around various types of content and genres, creating passionate communities. Examples of content and genres known for their dedicated fandoms include the following:

- *Harry Potter*: The *Harry Potter* books and movies have spawned a massive fandom, with fans deeply invested in Hogwarts and its characters. The fandom encompasses many activities, from fan fiction and art to cosplay and wizard rock music.
- *Stranger Things*: This popular Netflix series has a large and active fandom, including fans of the show's 1980s nostalgia, supernatural themes, and memorable characters. The fandom has created its own fan art, fan fiction, and merchandise, and has even inspired its own *Stranger Things*-themed bar and restaurant.
- *Anime*: Japanese *anime* has a dedicated fandom worldwide, with fans passionate about the art form and its unique storytelling style. The *anime* fandom includes many subgenres and properties, from classic series like *Sailor Moon* and *Dragon Ball* to newer properties like *Attack on Titan* and *My Hero Academia*.
- K-pop: Korean pop music has a massive and dedicated fandom worldwide. K-pop fans are known for their intense loyalty to their favorite groups and artists, and their extensive use of social media to support and promote their idols.

2.7 Cultural Discount and Premium

2.7.1 Cultural Discount: Theory and Practice

"Cultural discount" refers to the phenomenon whereby the value of cultural goods in one culture is discounted in another because of barriers in terms of language, customs, preferences, and so on. The reduced value of media and entertainment products in the international market is due to their different cultural backgrounds, which may not be recognized or understood by audiences in other regions.[34]

The term "cultural discount" captures the notion that a particular program or feature film rooted in one culture and thus attractive in that environment will have diminished appeal elsewhere, as viewers will find it difficult to identify with the styles, values, beliefs, institutions, and behavior patterns that are portrayed.[35] The notion explains why fictional drama—which potentially minimizes the cultural discount—is widely traded, while there is very limited trade in informational programming.

The cultural discount theory originated in the field of media economics and initially sought to explain why some domestically successful media products perform poorly in foreign markets. One stream of research proposes that culture can play an essential role in the international dissemination of new products, particularly entertainment products.[36] Research ascribes a significant role to the construct of national culture, primarily because cultural values are potent forces that shape perceptions and behaviors. Cultural boundaries may also act as barriers and impede the flow of ideas, communication, and products from one culture to another. Importantly, in an increasingly global economy, one central issue is how consumers of various cultures accept objects and ideas from other cultures. In particular, how residents accept imported products with cultural implications has been crucial in understanding cross-culture predictability—that is, the extent to which the performance of products in one culture can be predicted by the performance of the same products in another culture [37]

Media and cultural economists have commonly used movies as a representative cultural product category to examine the theory of cultural discount and local reception. For example, Lee (2006) examines two quantitative aspects of the cultural discount phenomenon.[38] First, a media product may be valued to a lesser extent by foreign audiences that

54 Overview of the Media and Entertainment Industry

lack the cultural background needed for full appreciation. Second, differences in esthetic tastes, social and cultural values, language, and other factors may lead to different judgments of whether certain products are better. Therefore, the values of cultural products in a foreign market are not completely predictable from their performance in their original market. This challenge invokes the concept of cross-culture predictability. For example, suppose the value of a movie can be discounted due to cultural differences. In that case, we can expect a country's audience will be more receptive to movies from a closer culture.

Suppose the distance between cultures is not considerable as they share the same language, race, or religion; or have similar customs, emotions, and cultural inclinations. In that case, you can easily understand and enjoy content from the other cultures without significantly discounting your own cultural experience. For example, when a Korean drama is aired, it is relatively easily accepted in Japan and China, where cultural and emotional tendencies are similar. However, acceptance is lower in Europe and Africa, where the cultural soil is utterly different from Korea. The term for this is the "cultural discount rate."

A high cultural discount rate means that acceptance of the cultural products of one country is low in another country; while a low cultural discount rate means that acceptance is higher. The cultural discount rate is used as an index to evaluate the potential for the exchange of popular culture between countries.[39]

Due to the characteristics of cultural products, the cultural discount rate is low for sports, nature documentaries, animation, and games; while the cultural discount rate is high for movies, dramas, entertainment programs, and plays. In addition, cultural products that focus on visual effects have a lower cultural discount rate.

One of the reasons why K-pop culture (e.g., dramas, movies, popular music) has permeated East Asia (e.g., Japan, China, Taiwan, and Hong Kong) and Southeast Asia (e.g., Thailand and Vietnam), creating the Korean Wave, is cultural familiarity. In other words, the cultural discount rate was low. When the MEI produces cultural products with the global market in mind, one strategy to consider is lowering the cultural discount rate.

Conversely, we can expect movies with more culturally specific content to perform relatively worse in foreign markets. Lee (2006) empirically tests this hypothesis by using genres as indicators of movie content.[40] His studies find that US comedies, which tend to be more culturally specific, perform relatively worse than non-comedies in many East Asian countries. By contrast, US adventure movies are less culturally specific and perform better than non-adventure movies. This research maintains that cultural content can vary significantly even within the same genre.

The Dark Knight (2008) and Avatar (2009) can be classified as action movies. However, The Dark Knight—which contained many cultural elements about American crimes—reaped only 47% of its worldwide revenues outside the North American market. By contrast, Avatar—which relied on universal 3D technologies and environmentalism—collected 73% of its revenues outside the North American market (Box Office Mojo).[41]

2.7.2 Cultural Premium

"Cultural premium" refers to the added value or appeal that a particular culture or subculture can bring to a creative work, such as a movie, TV show, or music album.[42] The concept of cultural premium proposes that certain cultural elements can increase a product's perceived quality or desirability, leading to greater consumer interest and financial success.

The hit Marvel movie *Black Panther* is a prime example of how cultural premium can play a role in the success of a film. The movie featured an almost all-black cast, with a storyline celebrating African culture and traditions. This cultural premium helped to generate widespread interest and excitement among audiences, leading to the movie grossing over $1.3 billion worldwide.[43]

The relationship between cultural discount and cultural premium often depends on the cultural context in which a creative work is produced and consumed. For example, a movie featuring predominantly white male actors and directors may be seen as culturally discounted in specific markets with strong demand for diverse representation. Conversely, a movie that celebrates a particular culture or subculture may have a cultural premium in markets where that culture or subculture is highly valued. A movie that features diverse representation may be seen as having a cultural premium in some markets, but may face a cultural discount in others where audiences are less receptive to such representation.

For example, the movie *Crazy Rich Asians* was celebrated for representing Asian culture and diversity in Hollywood, leading to a cultural premium in markets where Asian representation is highly valued. However, in some Asian markets, the movie was criticized for perpetuating stereotypes and not accurately representing the diversity of Asian cultures, leading to a cultural discount.

In conclusion, cultural discounts and premiums are not mutually exclusive and can coexist in different contexts. From a managerial perspective, international distributors that understand the delicate implications of the match/mismatch of their general national culture and the imported product's specific cultural content can better predict the international success of imported media and entertainment products.

Case Studies

Star Wars: How to Build an Intergenerational Media Franchise Kingdom

Star Wars stands as a prime example of effective media franchise management. With Disney's 2012 acquisition of Lucasfilm, the franchise underwent a strategic transformation to engage a new generation of fans. Through transmedia storytelling, animated series like *The Clone Wars* captivated younger audiences, while theme park integration and digital strategies expanded its reach. Successes such as *The Force Awakens* and *Rogue One* bridged generational gaps by introducing new characters while honoring the original trilogy. *Star Wars'* adaptability, innovative storytelling, and diversified approaches—like the launch of the original Disney+ series—make it a vital case study in appealing to both existing and emerging audiences in the MEI.

More case details for classroom use are available. Please check the book webpage at www.routledge.com/9781032221212 for more information.

56 Overview of the Media and Entertainment Industry

Riot Games: Unlocking the Potential of *League of Legends*

Riot Games, founded in 2006, gained recognition with *League of Legends* (*LOL*), a representative multiplayer online battle arena game driving the explosion of e-sports. Diversifying its IP, Riot expanded *LOL's* reach via music, virtual idols, and comics. Collaborating with Fortiche, it crafted *Arcane: League of Legends*—an animated series globally released on the Netflix and Tencent Video platforms. Strategically aligned with the *LOL* World Championship, the series delves into two game characters, bolstering storytelling and engagement. Riot Games aims to harness its strong IP to attract new players while retaining fans. This project showcases its strategy to redefine the scope of game-adapted content.

More case details for classroom use are available. Please check the book webpage at www.routledge.com/9781032221212 for more information.

Review

- This chapter presents many concepts and factors that shape and influence the MEI. It begins by exploring hedonic consumption (2.1), explaining how consumers derive intrinsic pleasure and satisfaction from media and entertainment products. This emotional and psychological fulfillment elucidates unique consumer behaviors within the industry, setting it apart from other industries.
- Next, the window effect is discussed (2.2). This strategy is employed to maximize a product's revenue potential by sequentially releasing it across different channels and platforms. This approach creates a series of revenue "windows," ensuring a longer life for the product and encouraging consumers to build a long-term relationship with the product.
- The MEI's high-risk, high-return nature is then discussed (2.3). The industry is fraught with significant uncertainties and unpredictability, often resulting in substantial financial losses. Despite these risks, the potential for high returns attracts players, driving continued growth and dynamism in the industry.
- The MEI is an experience goods market, as the quality and value of media and entertainment products mostly cannot be known before consumption (2.4). This characteristic presents unique challenges and opportunities for marketing practices in the MEI. The industry addresses this through promoting word of mouth and leveraging star systems.
- The chapter also considers the characteristic of the public goods market within the MEI (2.5). It emphasizes how this characteristic presents significant challenges for the industry. It also forces the industry to innovate and seek new ways to generate revenue and protect IP rights, such as advertising and subscription models.
- The importance of fans in the MEI is then underscored (2.6). This section explains how the deep engagement of fans drives loyalty, engagement, and revenue. It further provides insights into how these loyal groups challenge mainstream culture and influence the acceptance and popularity of new media and entertainment content and formats.

- The chapter concludes by discussing cultural discount and cultural premium (2.7). The impact of cultural factors on the acceptance and successful use of media and entertainment products plays different roles in foreign markets. Cultural dynamics significantly affect the international success of media and entertainment products, providing insights for global players to make informed decisions.

Discussion Questions

1 How does *hedonic consumption* influence consumers' behavior in the MEI? Can you think of examples from your own experience?
2 Discuss the significance of the *window effect* in the MEI. How has the emergence of digital platforms affected this strategy?
3 Considering the MEI's *high-risk, high-return* nature, what factors should potential players consider when launching a media and entertainment project?
4 Why are media and entertainment products considered *experience goods*? How does this influence marketing strategies within the industry?
5 How does the MEI's *public goods market* nature pose revenue generation challenges? Can you suggest strategies to combat potential market failure in the digital era (e.g., piracy, illegal downloading)?
6 How does fandom contribute to the success of a media and entertainment product? Provide examples of successful leveraging of fandom in the marketing strategies of the MEI.
7 How can the concepts of *cultural discount and cultural premium* impact the international success of a media and entertainment product? Provide examples of a media and entertainment product that experienced a cultural discount or premium in a foreign market.

Further Reading

- Hirschman, E. C. and Holbrook, M. B. (1982). "Hedonic consumption: Emerging concepts, methods and propositions." *Journal of Marketing*, 46(3), pp. 92–101.
- Johnson, D. (2013). *Media franchising: Creative license and collaboration in the culture industries.* New York: NYU Press.
- Mudambi, S. M. and Schuff, D. (2010). "What makes a helpful review? A study of customer reviews on Amazon.com." *MIS Quarterly*, 34(1), pp.185–200.
- Vogel, H.L. (2020). *Entertainment industry economics: A guide for financial analysis.* Cambridge: Cambridge University Press.
- Gray, J., Sandvoss, C. and Harrington, C. L. (eds.) (2017). *Fandom: Identities and communities in a mediated world.* New York: NYU Press.
- Moon, S. and Song, R. (2015). "The roles of cultural elements in international retailing of cultural products: An application to the motion picture industry." *Journal of Retailing*, 91(1), pp. 154–170.
- Ryu, S. (2023). "Unlocking the intellectual property (IP) potential of Riot Games' League of Legends." *SAGE Business Cases.*" SAGE Publication, London, UK.

58 Overview of the Media and Entertainment Industry

References

1 "Hedonistic consumption" (2020) *The Universal Marketing Dictionary*. https://marketing-dictionary.org/h/hedonistic-consumption/#cite_ref-1.
2 Hirschman, E. C. and Holbrook, M. B. (1982) "Hedonic consumption: Emerging concepts, methods and propositions." *Journal of Marketing*, 46(3), pp. 92–101.
3 Alba, J. W. and Williams, E. F. (2013) "Pleasure principles: A review of research on hedonic consumption." *Journal of Consumer Psychology*, 23(1), pp. 2–18.
4 Hennig-Thurau, T. et al. (2007) "The last picture show? Timing and order of movie distribution channels." *Journal of Marketing*, 71(4), pp. 63–83.
5 Jang, H., Hong, S., Kim, K., Kim, J. J. (2011). "Applied method for one source multi use (OSMU) in the broadcasting communication convergence environment." In: J. J. Park, L. T. Yang, C. Lee (eds.) *Future Information Technology. Communications in Computer and Information Science*, vol 185. Berlin, Heidelberg, Germany: Springer. https://doi.org/10.1007/978-3-642-22309-9_27.
6 Korean Creative Content Agency (2010). "Trend of smartphone technology and industry." *In-depth Report of Culture Technology, No. 3*.
7 "Create once, publish everywhere: (no date) *Hannon Hill*. http://dwmofqygvzj39.cloudfront.net/files/1/2853-hannon-hill-cascade-createoncepubikheveryywhere.pdf.
8 Jacobson, D. (2009) "Clean content = portable content." *NPR*, 4 February. www.npr.org/sections/inside/2009/02/clean_content_portable_content.html.
9 Jenkins, H. (2003) "Transmedia storytelling." *MIT Technology Review*, 15 January. www.technologyreview.com/2003/01/15/234540/transmedia-storytelling/.
10 Jenkins, H. (2007) "Transmedia Storytelling 101." *Henry Jenkins Blog*, 21 March. http://henryjenkins.org/blog/2007/03/transmedia_storytelling_101.html.
11 Giovagnoli, M. (2011) *Transmedia storytelling imagery, shapes and techniques*. Pittsburgh, PA: ETC Press. https://kilthub.cmu.edu/articles/journal_contribution/Transmedia_Storytelling_Imagery_Shapes_and_Techniques/6687011.
12 Giovagnoli, M. (2011) *Transmedia storytelling imagery, shapes and techniques*. Pittsburgh, PA: ETC Press. https://kilthub.cmu.edu/articles/journal_contribution/Transmedia_Storytelling_Imagery_Shapes_and_Techniques/6687011.
13 Chalaby, J. K. (2018) "Hedging against disaster: Risk and mitigation in the media and entertainment industries." *International Journal of Digital Television*, 9(2), pp. 167–184.
14 Lozic, J. (2019) "Zero marginal cost in magazine industry: Changing of cost paradigm in 'new' magazine industry." *44th International Scientific Conference on Economic and Social Development*. www.researchgate.net/publication/342004623_Zero_marginal_cost_in_magazine_industry_Changing_of_cost_paradigm_in_new_magazine_industry.
15 English, J. F. (2014) "The economics of cultural awards." In V. A. Ginsburgh and D. Throsby (eds.) *Handbook of the economics of art and culture, Volume 2*. Oxford, UK: North-Holland Elsevier, pp. 119–143.
16 Buttle, F. A. (1998) "Word of mouth: understanding and managing referral marketing." *Journal of Strategic Marketing*, 6(3), pp. 241–254.
17 Liu, Y. (2006) "Word of mouth for movies: Its dynamics and impact on box office revenue." *Journal of Marketing*, 70(3), pp. 74–89.
18 Duan, W., Gu, B. and Whinston, A. B. (2008) "Do online reviews matter? An empirical investigation of panel data." *Decision Support Systems*, 45(4), pp. 1007–1016.
19 Liu, Y. (2006) "Word of mouth for movies: Its dynamics and impact on box office revenue." *Journal of Marketing*, 70(3), pp. 74–89.
20 Fernando, J. (2022) "What are public goods? Definition, how they work, and example." *Investopedia*, 20 March. www.investopedia.com/terms/p/public-good.asp.
21 Pennings, A. J. (2011) "Media content as a 'public good.'" *Anthony J. Pennings, PhD*, 23 February. http://apennings.com/media-strategies/media-content-as-a-public-good/.
22 "Annex 11: Market failure in broadcasting" (no date). *Ofcom*. www.ofcom.org.uk/__data/assets/pdf_file/0022/32665/annex11.pdf.
23 Row, H. (2004) "Market failure in the media sector." *Fast Company*. www.fastcompany.com/664862/market-failure-media-sector.

24 Anderson, S. P. and Gabszewicz, J. J. (2006) "The media and advertising: A tale of two-sided markets." In V. A. Ginsburgh and D. Throsby (eds.) *Handbook of the economics of art and culture, Volume 1*. Oxford, UK: North-Holland Elsevier, pp. 567–614.

25 Anderson, S. P. and Gabszewicz, J. J. (2006) "The media and advertising: A tale of two-sided markets." In V. A. Ginsburgh and D. Throsby (eds.) *Handbook of the economics of art and culture, Volume 1*. Oxford, UK: North-Holland Elsevier, pp. 567–614.

26 Crandall, R. W. (no date) *Funding the national information infrastructure: Advertising, subscription, and usage charges, White Papers*. https://nap.nationalacademies.org/resource/wpni3/ch-18.html.

27 "Subcultures and scenes" (no date). *New York University Libraries*. https://guides.nyu.edu/subcultures.

28 Hirschman, E. C. and Solomon, M. R. (1983) "The relationship of age and gender subcultures to the consumption of rational and irrational experiences." In R. P. Bagozzi, A. M. Tybout and A. Abor (eds.) *Advances in Consumer Research*, 10, pp. 334–338.

29 "Media consumption across gender" (2021) *Collage Group*. www.collagegroup.com/2021/10/18/media-consumption-across-gender/.

30 Loucks, J. and Locker, M. (2020) "Should media and entertainment companies focus on female consumers to boost subscriptions?" *Deloitte Insights*. www2.deloitte.com/us/en/insights/industry/technology/media-subscriptions-gender-gap.html/#endnote-1.

31 Bridge, G. (2022) "Demographic divide: How age differences continue to drive consumer trends in media and tech." *Variety*. https://s3.amazonaws.com/media.mediapost.com/uploads/Variety_VIP_Study.pdf.

32 Sullivan, J. L. (2020) "Chapter 8: Media fandom and audience subcultures." In *Media audiences: Effects, users, institutions, and power*. Thousand Oaks, CA: SAGE Publications, Inc., pp. 189–212. www.sagepub.com/sites/default/files/upm-binaries/50993_ch_8.pdf.

33 Pearson, R. (2010) "Fandom in the digital era." *Popular Communication*, 8(1), pp. 84–95.

34 Lee, F. (2006) "Cultural discount and cross-culture predictability: Examining the box office performance of American movies in Hong Kong." *Journal of Media Economics*, 19(4), pp. 259–278.

35 Hoskins, C. and Mirus, R. (1988) "Reasons for the US dominance of the international trade in television programmes." *Media, Culture & Society*, 10(4), pp. 499–515.

36 Moon, S. and Song, R. (2015) "The roles of cultural elements in international retailing of cultural products: An application to the motion picture industry." *Journal of Retailing*, 91(1), pp. 154–170.

37 Lee, F. (2006) "Cultural discount and cross-culture predictability: Examining the box office performance of American movies in Hong Kong." *Journal of Media Economics*, 19(4), pp. 259–278.

38 Lee, F. (2006) "Cultural discount and cross-culture predictability: Examining the box office performance of American movies in Hong Kong." *Journal of Media Economics*, 19(4), pp. 259–278.

39 Shin, S. and McKenzie, J. (2019) "Asymmetric cultural discounting and pattern of trade in cultural products: Empirical evidence in motion pictures." *The World Economy*, 42(11), pp. 3350–3367.

40 Lee, F. (2006) "Cultural discount and cross-culture predictability: Examining the box office performance of American movies in Hong Kong." *Journal of Media Economics*, 19(4), pp. 259–278.

41 Moon, S. and Song, R. (2015) "The roles of cultural elements in international retailing of cultural products: An application to the motion picture industry." *Journal of Retailing*, 91(1), pp. 154–170.

42 Moon, S. and Song, R. (2015) "The roles of cultural elements in international retailing of cultural products: An application to the motion picture industry." *Journal of Retailing*, 91(1), pp. 154–170.

43 Johnson, T. (2018) "Black Panther is a gorgeous, groundbreaking celebration of black culture." *Vox*. www.vox.com/culture/2018/2/23/17028826/black-panther-wakanda-culture-marvel#.

MODULE II

The Fundamentals of Management

3

WHAT IS MANAGEMENT? A MEDIA AND ENTERTAINMENT INDUSTRY PERSPECTIVE

Outline

Overview	63
3.1 The Concept of Management	64
3.2 A Brief History of Management	66
3.3 The Roles of Managers	69
3.4 Management and Managers in the Media and Entertainment Industry	77
3.5 Challenges for Management in the New Digital Era	80
Case Studies	84
Review	85
Discussion Questions	86
Further Reading	86
References	86

Intended Learning Outcomes

- Understand the development of management concepts and theories.
- Explain the roles of a manager in general and in the media and entertainment industry (MEI) specifically.
- Describe emerging challenges for managers and management.

Overview

- Management is the process of planning, organizing, leading, and controlling resources to achieve organizational goals. It facilitates effective resource utilization, the achievement of goals, enhanced productivity, reduced uncertainty, and innovation.

DOI: 10.4324/9781003271222-5

64 The Fundamentals of Management

- This chapter traces the evolution of management theories in line with business and societal changes.
- The key functions of managers include planning, organizing, leading, and controlling. The chapter emphasizes the varying importance of and balance between these functions depending on the managerial level and the nature of the job.
- The unique management roles in the MEI involve balancing creativity and business objectives, managing talent, fostering innovation, and adapting to changing consumer preferences and technologies.
- The complexities of globalization and digital technologies, and the growing importance of environmental, social and governance (ESG) factors in business, are new challenges for management in the digital era.

3.1 The Concept of Management

Management involves the coordination and administration of tasks with the aim of achieving a goal. It encompasses activities such as strategizing and organizing, as well as coordinating the efforts of employees to effectively utilize available resources in order to accomplish the desired objectives.

Definitions and concepts of management include the following:

- "[A] vulnerable force, under pressure to achieve results and endowed with the triple power of constraint, imitation and imagination, operating on subjective, interpersonal, institutional and environmental levels"—Ghislain Deslandes.[1]
- "[T]he art of getting things done through people" —Mary Parker Follett.[2]
- "[T]o manage is to forecast and to plan, to organize, to command, to coordinate and to control"—Henri Fayol.[3]
- "Management is the coordination of all resources through the process of planning, organizing, directing and controlling in order to attain stated objectives"—Louis Allen.[4]
- "Management is the planning, organizing, leading, and controlling of human and other resources to achieve organizational goals efficiently and effectively"—Henry Mintzberg.[5]

Management encompasses various aspects, including determining the purpose, goals, protocols, and regulations of an organization; optimizing the human resources within an organization to drive its success; and establishing a hierarchy among staff members based on seniority level.

To excel as a manager, one must cultivate a range of skills, such as planning, communication, organization, and leadership. A comprehensive understanding of the company's objectives and the ability to guide employees, sales activities, and other operational aspects are also crucial in order to achieve those goals.

According to French management theorist Henri Fayol, management activities may consist of five functions: planning, organizing, commanding, coordinating, and controlling (Figure 3.1):[6]

- Planning—the first function of management—is a crucial and complex task that encompasses all departments and functions within a business, particularly management. Fayol outlines four key components of planning: the desired outcome or goal; the

What is Management? 65

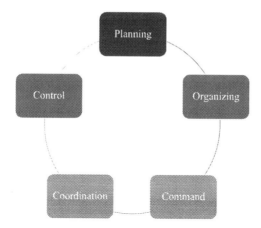

FIGURE 3.1 Fayol's Five Functions of Management.

actions required; the stages involved; and the methods to be employed. When creating a plan, a manager must carefully consider the tangible and intangible resources of the organization, ongoing work, emerging trends, and future events. A well-designed plan exhibits characteristics such as unity, continuity, flexibility, and specificity.

- Organizing—the second function—entails providing all necessary resources, both physical and human, to execute the plan of action effectively. Staffing, often overlooked but vital, is a critical aspect of management. Managers must ensure that they have the right individuals in the appropriate positions and attend to matters like workplace policies and organization. Retaining top talent necessitates offering incentives such as benefits, paid time off, and comprehensive training programs.
- Command—the third function—revolves around obtaining optimal performance from all employees within a manager's unit for the benefit of the entire organization. This entails having competent personnel; understanding employees thoroughly; fulfilling the organization's obligations to its staff; collaborating with other managers to ensure unity of direction and effort; leading by example; conducting regular performance audits; and refraining from excessive involvement in trivial details.
- Coordination—the fourth function—involves ensuring that all personnel comprehend their responsibilities, and that resources and activities across the organization are harmonized to achieve the desired goals. Effective managers recognize that coordination is pivotal for implementing strategies and sustaining ongoing operations. Management must be capable of addressing questions regarding who is responsible, which tasks need to be completed, and when and where activities are taking place—all in alignment with the organization's mission.
- Control—the final function—focuses on verifying whether operations conform to the adopted plan, issued instructions, and established principles. Employees within an organization need a clear understanding of the goals they are striving to achieve and the metrics that will be employed to evaluate their success. Different staff members have distinct roles and corresponding levels of responsibility. A manager must exercise control over their actions, methods, and progress measurement. Maintaining control over these factors enables managers to navigate the path toward success.

66 The Fundamentals of Management

Fayol's Five Functions of Management represent a significant milestone in the field of management theory. These functions—planning, organizing, leading, controlling, and coordinating—are attributed to Fayol as he originally conceptualized them. They have since become widely recognized and adopted as a fundamental framework in the field of management worldwide. In order to effectively guide a team toward achieving business objectives, it is imperative for managers to grasp these five foundational operations.

One perspective often associates management exclusively with "business administration," thereby excluding its application in non-commercial domains such as charities and the public sector. However, management transcends these narrow boundaries and extends to encompass all types of organizations. Regardless of the nature of the entity, effective management is required to optimize the performance of its work, personnel, processes, technology, and other vital components. As a result, management exhibits a pervasive presence and a broader scope of application.

Communication and the cultivation of a positive working environment are two essential aspects of management. Whether pursued within an enterprise or through individual endeavors, effective communication plays a crucial role in facilitating coordination and achieving desired outcomes. Additionally, fostering a positive work culture enhances employee engagement and productivity.

The need to employ specific tools and techniques—such as plans, measurements, motivational psychology, goals, and economic measures—may vary depending on the context and the specific requirements of management. While these elements are often utilized to support and enhance management practices, their application is contingent upon the unique circumstances and objectives of each situation.

3.2 A Brief History of Management

3.2.1 Before the Industrial Revolution

The origins of management can be traced back to the earliest forms of human organization and the need to direct and coordinate the efforts of individuals.[7] As a formal field of study and practice, management emerged during the Industrial Revolution in the 18th and 19th centuries. However, the principles and practices of management have deep historical roots that can be observed throughout various ancient civilizations and societal systems.

Ancient civilizations such as Egypt, Mesopotamia, and China demonstrated early applications of management principles in their endeavors. Notably, these civilizations employed management techniques to organize and oversee large-scale projects, including the construction of monumental structures like pyramids, canals, and other infrastructure. The successful completion of these projects required the efficient management of diverse resources such as labor, materials, and finances.

In ancient Greece, management principles found expression in the realm of civic administration. Elected officials were entrusted with the responsibility of managing the affairs of the city-state; and prominent philosophers like Plato emphasized the significance of wise and just leadership in achieving societal harmony and progress.

The Roman Empire provides another example of the application of management principles on a vast scale. The Roman military—renowned for its organizational prowess—employed clear lines of command and control, ensuring efficient coordination and effective governance of the territories under Roman rule.

During the medieval period in Europe, management principles were evident in the feudal system. In this hierarchical system, lords assumed responsibility for managing their lands and the people residing on them. Feudalism relied on a structured framework of power and authority, with well-defined lines of responsibility and accountability.

These historical examples demonstrate that even before the formal emergence of management as a distinct field, principles of coordination, organization, and leadership were integral to human endeavors. The evolution of management as a discipline builds upon this rich historical foundation, incorporating contemporary theories and practices to address the complexities of modern organizational environments.

3.2.2 The Industrial Revolution Era

The development of management as a formal discipline took shape during the era of industrialization, which unfolded during the 19th century. This period was characterized by significant societal and economic changes, driven by technological advancements and the rise of large-scale corporate organizations.[8]

The Industrial Revolution, spanning from the late 1700s to the 1800s, transformed the way people lived and worked.[9] Prior to this period, agricultural activities and small-scale craftsmanship were the primary means of livelihood, and rural communities predominated. However, the invention of the steam engine sparked a series of innovations that revolutionized industries. These advancements included the mechanized extraction of coal from underground mines, the establishment of factories capable of mass-producing goods, and the development of efficient railroad transportation networks. The expansion and increased productivity of these factories necessitated effective management and coordination. For instance, Henry Ford's implementation of the moving assembly line for automobile production in the early 1900s exemplified the need for efficient management in large-scale manufacturing. By standardizing parts and streamlining the production process, Ford significantly reduced the time required to build a Model T car.[10] Skilled artisans were no longer the primary workforce, and the use of lower-cost labor and the implementation of assembly lines called for effective guidance and management of these complex operations.[11] A shift in organizational structure and management practices was necessary to harness the benefits of these new technologies and drive efficiency and productivity.

The changes brought about by industrialization highlighted the need for systematic approaches to managing resources, coordinating tasks, and directing the efforts of individuals within organizations. This demand led to the development of management theories and principles aimed at optimizing productivity, improving organizational efficiency, and effectively utilizing human and material resources. Over time, management evolved as a distinct field of study and practice, drawing insights from various disciplines such as engineering, psychology, economics, and sociology to address the complexities of modern organizations.

The Industrial Revolution served as a catalyst for the formalization and advancement of management, setting the stage for subsequent developments in management theory and practice that continue to shape the field today.

68 The Fundamentals of Management

3.2.3 The Scientific Era

The rapid advancements in technology during the industrial era brought forth a pressing need for enhanced productivity and efficiency in business operations. Managers sought to understand and analyze work processes, with the aim of optimizing and improving their execution. One notable figure in this context was Frederick Taylor, who pioneered the measurement of human output. Taylor emphasized that increasing efficiency and reducing costs were crucial objectives of management. His theories revolved around calculating the number of units produced within a specific timeframe.[12] Taylor conducted time studies to determine the quantity of units that could be produced by a worker within a specified timeframe. Other management theorists such as Frank Gilbreth, Lilian Gilbreth and Harrington Emerson expanded on the concept of management reasoning, focusing on efficiency and consistency to optimize output. This objective remained consistent across industries, from automobile manufacturing to coal mining and steel production. The primary goal was to maximize productivity by efficiently utilizing labor.

Concurrently, the need to manage worker output and align the entire organization toward a shared objective became increasingly apparent. As industries grew in complexity, management faced the challenge of organizing multifaceted processes within larger enterprises. Fayol is credited with developing key management concepts such as the five functions of management: planning, organizing, coordination, command, and control. These concepts laid the foundation for the modern-day principles of management: planning, organizing, leading, and controlling.[13]

The management principles developed during this period responded to the demands of industrialization, with the aim of optimizing work processes, increasing productivity, and ensuring coordination across various organizational functions. These foundational ideas continue to shape management practices today, providing a framework for effective decision-making, resource allocation, leadership, and performance evaluation.

3.2.4 The Modern Era

Peter Drucker, often regarded as the father of modern management, revolutionized the field with his concept of "managing by objective" (MBO).[14] Drucker—an influential author, educator, and management consultant—believed in aligning individual objectives with organizational goals to drive success.[15] MBO involves a systematic process of defining specific and measurable objectives that are necessary to achieve the overall objectives of the organization.

The beauty of Drucker's MBO concept lies in its ability to provide employees with a clear understanding of their organization's objectives and their individual responsibilities in contributing to those objectives. For instance, consider a sales department within a company. The organizational goal may be to achieve a 5% increase in sales revenue in the upcoming fiscal year.

In practice, the first step in the MBO process involves consulting with the relevant individuals in the sales department to assess the feasibility of the 5% sales growth objective. Once it has been determined that this is achievable, the objective is communicated throughout the sales department and each individual is assigned specific targets that will collectively contribute to the 5% increase. For instance, in a regional firm with seven sales representatives, each representative would have a designated goal that, when combined with the efforts of their colleagues, would lead to the overall sales growth target.

In the MBO cycle, management plays a critical role in supporting, monitoring, and evaluating performance. Should any issues arise, it becomes management's responsibility to take corrective actions to address them. Furthermore, if the 5% sales objective is met or surpassed, rewards can be shared among the sales team. Importantly, the MBO approach applies to every department within an organization, regardless of its size, and is an ongoing and iterative process.

Drucker's contributions to modern management extend beyond the MBO concept. Throughout his extensive career, he emphasized the fundamental role of businesses in creating and satisfying customers. He regarded marketing and innovation as two essential functions that drive organizational success. Drucker believed that businesses often fail when they neglect to ask the critical question: "What business are we in?"[16] Many companies encounter challenges or even face demise when they fail to adapt to changing industry dynamics or venture into markets beyond their core competencies. Notable examples include Blockbuster, Kodak, BlackBerry, and Yahoo.

As the field of management continued to evolve, other influential thinkers made lasting contributions. One such figure is Henry Mintzberg, who challenged the traditional notion of managers as detached strategists. Mintzberg observed that management is hard work, requiring managers to be actively engaged in attending meetings, managing crises, and interacting with internal and external stakeholders. Depending on their specific roles, managers fulfill multiple duties, acting as spokespersons, leaders, resource allocators, and negotiators.[17]

Another prominent figure in modern management thinking is Michael Porter, a renowned professor at Harvard Business School. Porter's significant contribution lies in his exploration of strategic reasoning and the pursuit of long-term competitive advantages. He proposed three fundamental ways in which firms can gain such advantages: cost leadership (i.e., being the lowest-cost producer); differentiation (i.e., offering unique products or services at premium prices); and focus (i.e., competing in a specialized niche market).[18]

These thinkers have enriched the field of management with their profound insights and concepts, shaping the way organizations approach goal setting, strategic thinking, and achieving sustainable competitive advantages.

3.3 The Roles of Managers

3.3.1 Definition

A "manager" is a professional who takes a leadership role in an organization and manages a team of employees.[19] In many organizations, managers are assigned to oversee specific departments, each with their own unique responsibilities. While the exact roles and titles may vary, managers typically have duties such as conducting performance evaluations, making decisions, and ensuring efficient operations within their respective departments. They serve as the vital link between employees and executives, facilitating effective communication and coordination between different levels of the company hierarchy.

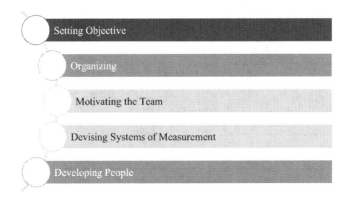

FIGURE 3.2 The Five Primary Functions of a Manager.

In general, there are five primary functions of a manager: setting objectives, organizing, motivating the team, devising systems of measurement, and developing people (Figure 3.2).[20]

Setting Objectives

Setting and achieving objectives is how a manager accomplishes and maintains success. Managers must also be able to convey these objectives to their staff or employees in a compelling manner. For instance, a restaurant manager could state they want to improve service times and remind employees that faster service will increase revenue and tips.

Organizing

Managers evaluate the type of work to be conducted, divide it into achievable tasks, and effectively delegate those tasks to staff. The organization consists of relationships among individual staff and departments or entities inside the organization. It is the manager's responsibility to ensure that these individuals and entities work together in harmony, which includes motivating staff members and departments to stay on task. A good manager is skilled at building interpersonal relationships among team members and can troubleshoot if members are confused or encounter challenges.

The organization also requires a manager to establish relationships of authority among their team members. Maximizing organizational arrangements can help businesses enhance the company's efficiency in the market, reduce business costs, and improve productivity.

Motivating the Team

In addition to the tasks of organization and delegation, motivation includes having the skills to handle different types of personalities in a team. An effective manager must know how to form and lead successful teams and galvanize team members around a cause.

Devising Systems of Measurement

As for the other management functions, measurement is critical to improving business performance. Managers need to set targets or key performance indicators for the team, and then develop ways to measure whether the team is on track to meet those goals. Because developing measurable ways of assessing performance can be challenging, managers must often be creative and thoughtful.

Developing People

In addition to leading their team toward a goal and measuring their progress along the way, good managers invest in their staff's development. Managers can, for example, work with their team to help them set goals to advance in their careers.

Managers must have leadership skills to use these five operations successfully. They are responsible for coaching team members by helping them recognize their strengths and weaknesses and improve their performance. Different managers may have different styles of leadership. Managers should develop their leadership skills to be effective supervisors regardless of style.

3.3.2 What Managers Do

There have been many studies on what managers do. The most famous of these was articulated by Henry Mintzberg in the early 1970s.[21] Mintzberg's enduring influence can be attributed to the relatively stable nature of managerial work over time, despite a few notable changes such as the shift toward empowered relationships between top managers and other stakeholders, advancements in technology, and the exponential increase in data and information.

Through his extensive observations of managers in action, Mintzberg discovered that managers adopt multiple roles to effectively handle the diverse demands they face in their roles. A "role" can be defined as a structured set of behaviors, and Mintzberg identified 10 distinct roles that are commonly performed by managers. These roles can be further categorized into three groups: interpersonal, informational, and decisional. The performance of these roles can vary in terms of their prominence and the extent to which they are fulfilled, depending on the managerial level and specific organizational functions. While each role is described individually, they collectively form an interconnected whole.

These 10 roles provide a comprehensive framework for understanding the complex nature of managerial work (Figure 3.3). Managers must adeptly navigate their interpersonal relationships, actively seek and disseminate information, and make crucial decisions to effectively fulfill their responsibilities. The dynamic interplay between these roles ensures that managers can effectively address the multifaceted challenges they encounter in their managerial roles.

The interpersonal roles link all managerial work together. There are three primary interpersonal roles that managers undertake.

- Figurehead: In this role, the manager acts as a representative of the organization, especially in formal settings. For example, top-level managers may attend conferences or events to represent the company and establish its presence in the industry. Similarly, supervisors act as representatives of the workgroup, conveying information and decisions from higher management to the employees.

72 The Fundamentals of Management

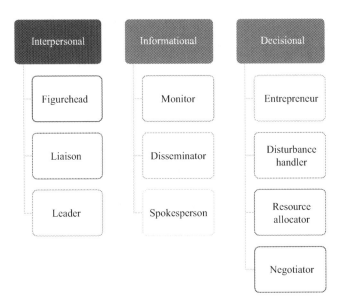

FIGURE 3.3 Ten Roles of Managers.

- Liaison: Managers—particularly top-level managers—interact with individuals and groups both inside and outside the organization. Through this role, they establish networks, build relationships, and gather valuable information. Top-level managers utilize the liaison role to cultivate strategic alliances, seek support, and gain insights into industry trends. On the other hand, supervisors rely on the liaison role to ensure smooth coordination and communication within their workgroups.
- Leader: Managers are responsible for defining and managing relationships between themselves and their employees. They provide guidance, motivation, and support to their team members, fostering a positive work environment. Effective leaders empower their employees, encourage collaboration, and inspire high performance. Supervisors, in particular, play a crucial role in day-to-day leadership, overseeing the work of team members and ensuring their needs are met.

The information roles ensure that information is acquired and shared. The manager's direct interactions with individuals in their interpersonal roles provide them with a distinct advantage in obtaining valuable information. As a result, the three informational roles primarily focus on the information-related aspects of managerial responsibilities. These roles are specifically designed to ensure the effective gathering, dissemination, and utilization of information within the managerial context:

- Monitor: This role involves actively seeking and receiving information from various sources. Managers continuously scan their internal and external environments to stay informed about market trends, competitor activities, and industry developments. By monitoring information, managers gain valuable insights that enable them to make informed decisions and take appropriate actions.

What is Management? **73**

- Disseminator: Managers act as conduits of information within the organization. They share relevant information with their team members, departments, or other stakeholders. For example, a manager may communicate new policies, procedures, or strategic goals to ensure everyone is aligned and well-informed.
- Spokesperson: At the top level, managers represent the organization to external parties. They serve as ambassadors, conveying the organization's vision, mission, and achievements to the public, industry experts, and other stakeholders. By effectively disseminating the organization's information into the external environment, top-level managers establish the company's reputation and build relationships with key stakeholders.
- At the lower levels of management, supervisors play a crucial role as spokespersons within their specific unit or department. They communicate important updates, developments, and challenges to team members and act as subject-matter experts within their domain.

Managers make significant use of this information in their decisional roles. Managers' unique access to information places them at the center of organizational decision making. There are four decisional roles managers play:

- Entrepreneur: Managers are responsible for identifying opportunities and initiating innovative ideas that can drive organizational growth and competitiveness. They take calculated risks, explore new markets, develop new products and services, and seek ways to adapt to changing environments. For instance, a manager in a technology company may spearhead the development of a new cutting-edge product line to capture a niche market segment.
- Disturbance handler: Managers are equipped to tackle and resolve crises or conflicts that may arise within the organization. They navigate challenging situations—such as internal disputes, sudden market shifts, or unexpected disruptions—to minimize negative impacts and maintain organizational stability. For example, a manager in a manufacturing company may swiftly address supply chain disruptions caused by natural disasters by identifying alternative suppliers and implementing contingency plans.
- Resource allocator: This role involves making decisions on the allocation of organizational resources such as budget, personnel, and equipment to different projects, departments, or initiatives. Managers analyze priorities, evaluate resource needs, and make strategic choices to optimize resource utilization and achieve organizational goals. For example, a manager in a retail company may allocate a larger portion of the marketing budget to launch a new advertising campaign targeting a specific customer segment.
- Negotiator: Managers engage in discussions, bargaining, and conflict resolution to protect the organization's interests and secure advantageous outcomes. They negotiate contracts, resolve disputes with external stakeholders, and collaborate with partners or suppliers to establish mutually beneficial agreements. A manager in a global company may negotiate pricing and terms with suppliers to ensure favorable supply agreements that support cost savings and product quality.

3.3.3 Managers: Different Levels

Within the organizational framework of large businesses and corporations, a hierarchical structure commonly comprises three main tiers of management: lower-level management, middle-level management, and senior-level management (Figure 3.4):

- Low-level managers (e.g., team manager, line manager): Examples of low-level management positions include frontline team leaders, section leads, and supervisors. Operating at the lowest tier in the management hierarchy, these individuals are responsible for supervising the daily tasks of individual employees and providing them with guidance. Their duties typically involve ensuring the quality of work, directing staff in their day-to-day activities, addressing employee concerns through proper channels, overseeing team supervision and career development, and offering performance feedback to subordinates.

  For example, line managers are responsible for achieving specific outputs. Typically, their responsibilities relate to their company's products or services. Line managers often communicate with a company's upper management and report results to them. Team managers, referred to as "supervisors," oversee specific groups or functions of an organization. They may be tasked with supervising projects or keeping teams on track. Like line managers, team managers report results to the company's upper management.
- Middle-level managers (e.g., general managers): Middle-level managers occupy the layer above low-level managers and are supervised by senior management. Middle management comprises individuals serving as department, regional, or branch managers. Their role primarily involves cascading the strategic objectives formulated by senior management to frontline managers. In contrast to senior management, middle managers allocate a significant portion of their time to directional and organizational functions. This involves establishing and communicating essential policies for lower-level management, offering guidance to enhance their performance, and executing organizational plans under the guidance of senior management.

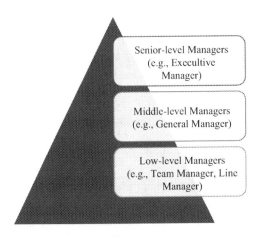

FIGURE 3.4 Different Levels of Managers.

For example, general managers are responsible for various management tasks, including overseeing product production. They typically set goals for employees and create product plans. A general manager's usual goal is to increase the company's revenue.

- Senior-level managers (e.g., executive managers): At the pinnacle of the management hierarchy is senior management, comprising individuals such as the chief executive officer, president, vice president, and board members. It is the responsibility of senior management to establish the overarching goals and direction of the organization. They develop strategic plans, formulate company-wide policies, and make high-level decisions that shape the organization's trajectory. Additionally, senior-level managers often play a crucial role in securing external resources and are held accountable to shareholders and the public for the organization's performance.

Executive managers are typically involved in shaping the overall strategy of the company and may oversee multiple departments. They are tasked with ensuring that various tasks and projects align with the overarching mission of the company.

3.3.4 Different Management Styles

There are different types of effective leadership styles. There is no best management style, and some people will feel more personally suited to one type. You can also select elements of different management styles to create the optimal archetype for you and your company. Here, we briefly review three positive management styles that can help make any manager a more effective leader:

- Persuasive: A compelling leader spends much of their time with team members. Influential managers are aware of team members' daily work and are involved in their work lives. Being engaged with employees allows persuasive managers to lead by example and secure buy-in and compliance from the team by persuading rather than instructing or demanding.
- Democratic: A democratic manager invites the team to be directly involved in decision-making. Open lines of communication between democratic managers and employees allow these managers to understand the skills and advantages each employee brings. Open participation and exchange of ideas among different levels of employees allow everyone to contribute to the outcome of a decision or project. This management style is more successful when managers develop organized and streamlined decision-making processes. Otherwise, accepting input from everyone can make the process sluggish and disorganized.
- *Laissez-faire*: The *laissez-faire* manager functions almost more like a mentor than a manager. They empower employees to step up and make decisions. This allows the team to feel like they own part of each project. The manager takes a backseat role, offering advice or getting things back on track if something goes wrong. Otherwise, they stand aside, allowing employees to flourish creatively and exercise leadership.

3.3.5 Management Skills for Managers

To be a successful manager, students may consider developing the following skills (Figure 3.5):

76 The Fundamentals of Management

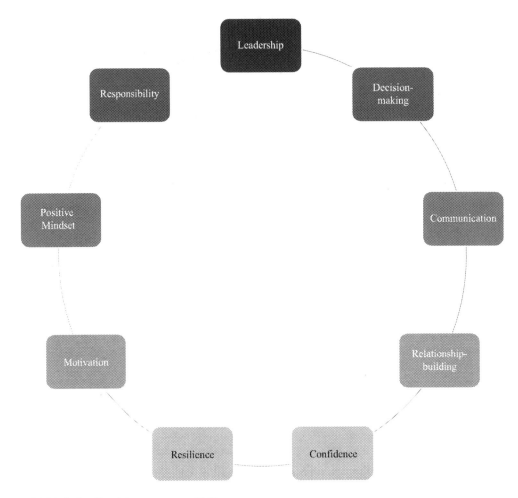

FIGURE 3.5 Key Management Skills.

- Leadership: This is a core skill for managers, as one of their primary responsibilities is leading their team. Managers often lead by example, encouraging employees to mirror their actions and work ethic.
- Decision-making: Managers must often make tough decisions for their teams, so strong decision-making skills are essential. Often, managers develop their decision-making processes to help them handle decisions and other issues in the workplace. Great managers are also willing to ask other company employees for feedback as they make decisions.
- Communication: Managers also need communication skills to succeed, as they frequently communicate with their employees and other company members. Usually, managers also need good written communication skills, as they may be responsible for writing reports and emails. Active listening is also categorized as a communication skill, and managers need this skill to communicate effectively. Active listening includes eye contact, body language, and smiling.

- Relationship-building: Great managers also build relationships with their employees. They may do this through frequent communication and relationship-building exercises. When managers form strong relationships with their employees, it can help increase mutual trust and boost employee morale.

Other characteristics of great managers include confidence, resilience, motivation, a positive mindset, and responsibility, among others. For example, confidence can equip managers to handle difficult situations and lead their employees effectively. It can help them make solid decisions and lead by example. Great managers also know how to motivate their employees. They may use incentives to motivate their employees, such as employee of the month programs or other rewards. They can lead effectively even under challenging circumstances, maintain a positive attitude, and encourage their employees to do the same. They think optimistically and show positivity in their interactions with others.

In addition, customer service skills can be helpful for managers. Sometimes, managers communicate directly with customers, acting as a communication line between customers and senior management. This makes customer service skills helpful, including empathy, patience, and persuasion.

3.4 Management and Managers in the Media and Entertainment Industry

The role of managers in the MEI is different from the role of ordinary managers. This is because the MEI is unique in its nature, characteristics, and challenges, and specialized skills and knowledge are thus required to manage successfully.

Media and entertainment companies operate in a highly dynamic and constantly evolving environment, which demands an agile and flexible approach to management. The industry is also highly competitive, with new entrants constantly disrupting traditional business models. Therefore, managers in media and entertainment companies must be innovative and adaptive, able to identify and respond quickly to changing market conditions.

In addition, the MEI has unique legal and regulatory requirements that managers must be familiar with. For example, intellectual property (IP) laws, copyright laws, and licensing agreements can be complex, and managers must understand them to effectively manage the company's assets and protect its interests.

Moreover, the MEI is highly creative, so managers must balance business objectives with creative goals. This requires a deep understanding of the creative process and the ability to work effectively with creative professionals such as writers, producers, and artists.

While working closely with the creative side of the industry, management in the MEI is focused on managing and delivering creative content.[22] Roles include administrative management positions (e.g., strategic planning, sales, human resources, finance and accounting, marketing, and public relations) and "creative management" positions (e.g., producer, executive, and agent). Starting in the mailroom at a talent agency or management company is often a pathway to other business-side opportunities in entertainment, especially TV or film.

The roles and responsibilities of management and managers can differ across domains. For example, the music business is a unique industry with multiple moving parts. There are various areas with opportunities to develop a career on the business, creative, or tech side. Key functions in music management include artist and repertoire, artist relations

78 The Fundamentals of Management

and talent management, business strategy and operation, marketing and digital media, sync, licensing, music publishing, sales and distribution, and technology.

The responsibilities of a manager in the MEI can vary significantly based on their specific role.[23] For example, in artist management, managers collaborate with various artists—such as actors, musicians, and writers—to assist them in effectively organizing and sustaining their careers. They primarily collaborate with artists, particularly those involved in performing arts or writing. Managers are typically hired by creative individuals to assist them in planning and executing various aspects of their careers.

These managers may either discover aspiring artists seeking representation or be sought out by prospective clients themselves. Once hired, the manager's primary role is to oversee the practical business aspects of the client's career, allowing the client to concentrate on their artistic pursuits. Duties may include assisting the client in finding an agent, establishing connections with producers or studios, and aiding in financial planning.

Also, opportunities exist for event managers who aspire to work in event coordination for prominent clubs, hotels, and celebrities within the industry. They focus on organizing and executing events, social functions, and parties. These managers often assume a multifaceted role, acting as a hybrid of an agent, financial advisor, and public relations manager, while also providing additional services that may not fall strictly within the scope of these other positions.

In the MEI, managers should possess a foundational understanding of various aspects of business administration, contracts, IP matters, event management, artist management, marketing, promotion, and branding. Additionally, expertise in areas such as artist management, concert promotion, music publishing, recording, publicity, and marketing/promotion firms is necessary to effectively navigate the industry.

Key differences between managers in the MEI and in traditional industries include the following:

- Creative versus operational: In the MEI, managers must possess a deep understanding of the creative process and effectively collaborate with creative professionals. Unlike traditional industry managers, who mainly focus on operational or managerial aspects, managers in the MEI must embrace the artistic vision and support its realization. For example, a film producer in the MEI will work closely with directors, writers, and actors to bring their creative vision to the screen, emphasizing storytelling and artistic expression.
- Fast-paced versus predictable: Managers in the MEI thrive in a fast-paced and ever-evolving environment. They must adapt quickly to changes in technology, consumer trends, and market demands. In contrast, traditional industry managers often follow more predictable workflows and operate within established systems. For instance, a social media manager in the MEI must stay up to date with the latest social media platforms and engagement strategies to effectively promote clients' content and engage with their audience.
- IP versus physical property: Managers in the MEI must navigate the complexities of IP laws, copyright regulations, and licensing agreements. They must protect and monetize creative works, such as films, music, and designs. In contrast, traditional industry managers primarily deal with physical assets, such as manufacturing goods or managing inventory. An example of IP management in the MEI is a music manager

who ensures that artists' songs are properly registered, licensed, and protected against unauthorized use.

- Risk-taking versus risk avoidance: Managers in the MEI embrace diverse risks and innovation to remain competitive in a dynamic industry. They explore new ideas, experiment with emerging technologies, and venture into uncharted territories. Traditional industry managers often prioritize stability and risk avoidance to ensure consistent operations. For example, a gaming studio manager may invest in the development of an innovative and untested game concept, pushing the boundaries of interactive entertainment.
- Emotional intelligence versus technical expertise: Managers in the MEI must possess high emotional intelligence to navigate the unique dynamics of working with creative professionals. They must understand the importance of collaboration, motivation, and addressing the emotional needs of their team. On the contrary, managers in traditional industries rely heavily on technical expertise and proficiency in their field.

Given the differences between the roles of managers in the MEI and those in other industries, managers in the MEI must develop a unique set of attitudes and skills.

First, they must understand and appreciate the creative process and effectively collaborate with creative professionals. Fostering an environment that promotes creativity and innovation of individuals or teams is crucial.

Second, they should be able to adapt to new technologies, emerging trends, and evolving consumer preferences. This requires the capability to quickly adjust strategies, make timely decisions, and seize opportunities in a dynamic industry landscape.

Third, managers in the MEI must have a strong grasp of the legal and policy information around IP, copyright, and licensing. This is essential as they need to protect and leverage the intellectual assets of artists, content creators, and organizations to maximize their value and prevent unauthorized use.

TABLE 3.1 Differences between Managers in the MEI and Traditional Industries

	Managers in the MEI	*Managers in traditional industries*
Skills and characteristics	• Creativity and a deep understanding of the creative process. • Emotional intelligence and the ability to work effectively with creative professionals. • Knowledge of IP laws, copyright laws, and licensing agreements. • Willingness to take risks and experiment with new ideas. • The ability to work in a fast-paced, constantly evolving environment. • Strategic thinking and the ability to balance business objectives with creative goals. • Excellent communication and networking skills. • Openness to feedback and collaboration.	• Technical expertise in their field. • Strong organizational skills and attention to detail. • The ability to manage and motivate employees. • Familiarity with industry-specific regulations and compliance requirements. • Knowledge of supply chain management and logistics. • Analytical skills and the ability to interpret data and make informed decisions. • Strategic thinking and the ability to adapt to changing market conditions. • Strong financial management skills.

80 The Fundamentals of Management

Fourth, they are expected to take calculated risks and embrace innovation to remain competitive in a rapidly changing industry. This involves experimenting with new ideas, exploring unconventional approaches, and being willing to challenge the status quo.

Lastly, they need high emotional intelligence to navigate the unique challenges of working with creative professionals.[24] Building strong relationships, fostering collaboration, and effectively managing conflicts are vital for maintaining productive and harmonious working environments while spearheading creativity and innovation.

3.5 Challenges for Management in the New Digital Era

Managers in the 21st century must confront challenges their counterparts of even a few years ago could hardly imagine. Ongoing technological advances such as artificial intelligence (AI), and the evolving nature of globalization are chief among the demands today's managers will face.

3.5.1 Technology

The exponential growth of technology has been widely discussed. Reports suggest that the computing power of today's iPhone surpasses that of the computer that facilitated the moon landing by more than 100,000 times.[25] In this rapidly evolving technological landscape, management faces the challenge of harnessing the vast amounts of data available for informed decision-making. Data analytics—the examination of datasets—provides valuable insights into customer behavior, preferences, personalized marketing, and online engagement. However, managers must navigate the complexities of data analytics without becoming overwhelmed, making the collection, organization, and utilization of data in a logical, timely, and cost-effective manner a new standard of managerial competence.

Moreover, emerging technologies such as AI, blockchain, the metaverse, and drones present exciting opportunities that require a fresh set of managerial skills. Each of these advancements necessitates a new level of expertise to effectively integrate it into business practices. AI in particular is a gamechanger, leading to concerns about job displacement. While some industries have already experienced the replacement of workers by AI to some extent, it also offers the potential to automate mundane tasks, allowing managers to focus on core responsibilities. This shift emphasizes the importance of human skills such as empathy, employee development, coaching, and creative thinking as essential qualities for today's managers.

3.5.2 Globalization

Globalization continues to progress steadily. As markets mature, more countries are transitioning from emerging status and witnessing the rise of a burgeoning middle class with increased purchasing power. This new class of consumers has created demand for previously inaccessible goods and services, prompting companies worldwide to expand beyond their national boundaries to cater to these needs. However, management in the era of globalization presents a unique set of challenges.[26]

Global managers must navigate various complexities, including adapting to diverse cultures and understanding different legal frameworks, tariffs, import/export regulations, human resources considerations, logistics, marketing strategies, supply chain management, currency fluctuations, foreign investments, and government policies. Despite these formidable demands, global trade has experienced unprecedented growth.

Expanding beyond one's home country gives rise not only to traditional obstacles, but also to new challenges such as unexpected trade barriers, blocked acquisitions, and heightened regulatory scrutiny. These factors underscore the need for a new generation of managers equipped with the skills to thrive in this complex business environment. The conventional command and control management model that may have sufficed in previous decades is insufficient in today's world, where technology, globalization, nationalism, and other hurdles require a flatter, more agile organizational structure led by managers who possess the appropriate new competencies.

Management in the global environment entails two interrelated aspects. First, it involves the challenges associated with globalization—particularly the openness required in a global context. Globalization brings about increased interconnectedness and interdependence among economies, creating a highly competitive and dynamic business landscape. Managers must understand and adapt to the complexities of operating in multiple markets, each with its own unique cultural, economic, and regulatory nuances. Second, it revolves around effectively managing a global workforce. With globalization, organizations have expanded their operations across borders, resulting in a diverse and multicultural workforce. Managing such a workforce requires special skills and approaches to harness the collective talent and potential of employees from different backgrounds.

To meet these challenges, managers must cultivate cultural intelligence.[27] Cultural intelligence is a conceptual understanding of culture, including its variations and influence on behavior. It requires mindfulness: the ability to pay attention to signals and reactions in diverse cross-cultural situations. Also, behavioral skills should be developed by utilizing knowledge and mindfulness to exhibit appropriate behaviors in those situations.

Management in today's global environment is complex and demanding. Global managers must possess the knowledge and skills to navigate the challenges of globalization, while also demonstrating cultural intelligence to effectively manage a diverse global workforce.

3.5.3 Sustainability

"Sustainability," in the business and management setting, refers to the conduct of business operations in a way that considers the environmental, social, and economic impacts of those operations in both the short and long term.[28] Sustainability involves harmonizing economic growth with environmental preservation and social accountability to safeguard the capacity of future generations to fulfill their own requirements.

Sustainability in business and management encompasses a range of practices, such as environmental, social, and economic sustainability (Figure 3.6):[29]

- Environmental sustainability involves reducing waste and pollution, conserving natural resources such as water and energy, and mitigating the impact of business operations on the environment.
- Social sustainability involves promoting social equity and justice, respecting human rights, and providing safe and healthy working conditions for employees and other stakeholders.

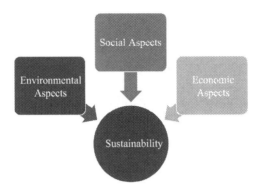

FIGURE 3.6 Sustainability in Business and Management.

- Economic sustainability includes ensuring that business operations are financially viable and sustainable over the long term while contributing to the economic development of the communities in which they operate.

Sustainability is not only a moral and ethical obligation but also a strategic imperative for businesses. By prioritizing sustainability, companies can improve their reputation, lower costs, mitigate risks, adhere to regulations, and attract and retain talented employees.

In the realm of business and management, two key concepts have emerged to aid companies in incorporating sustainability into their practices and strategies: the United Nations Sustainable Development Goals (SDG) and ESG criteria. The SDGs provide a framework for addressing global challenges and promoting sustainable development across various sectors. ESG criteria, on the other hand, assess a company's performance in areas such as environmental impact, social responsibility, and corporate governance.

The SDGs were adopted by the United Nations in 2015 as a global call to action to end poverty, protect the planet, and ensure that all people can enjoy peace and prosperity.[30] The 17 SDGs cover various issues such as climate change, social inequality, and sustainable economic growth. The SDGs offer a valuable framework for companies to harmonize their strategies and operations with global sustainability objectives. Companies can identify pertinent sustainability concerns that are applicable to their business and establish specific targets to tackle them. Engaging in efforts to achieve the SDGs not only bolsters a company's reputation, but also attracts and retains customers and employees while mitigating the risks associated with sustainability-related challenges.

The 17 SDGs are as follows:

- No poverty: End poverty in all its forms everywhere.
- Zero hunger: End hunger, achieve food security and improved nutrition, and promote sustainable agriculture.
- Good health and wellbeing: Ensure healthy lives and promote wellbeing for all people of all ages.
- Quality education: Ensure inclusive and equitable quality education and promote lifelong learning opportunities for all.
- Gender equality: Achieve gender equality and empower all women and girls.

- Clean water and sanitation: Ensure the availability and sustainable management of water and sanitation for all.
- Affordable and clean energy: Ensure access to affordable, reliable, sustainable, and modern energy for all.
- Decent work and economic growth: Promote sustained, inclusive, and sustainable economic growth, full and productive employment, and decent work for all.
- Industry, innovation, and infrastructure: Build resilient infrastructure, promote inclusive and sustainable industrialization, and foster innovation.
- Reduced inequalities: Reduce inequalities within and among countries.
- Sustainable cities and communities: Make cities and human settlements inclusive, safe, resilient, and sustainable.
- Responsible consumption and production: Ensure sustainable consumption and production patterns.
- Climate action: Take urgent action to combat climate change and its impacts.
- Life below water: Conserve and sustainably use the oceans, seas, and marine resources for sustainable development.
- Life on land: Protect, restore, and promote the sustainable use of terrestrial ecosystems, sustainably manage forests, combat desertification, halt and reverse land degradation, and halt biodiversity loss.
- Peace, justice and strong institutions: Promote peaceful and inclusive societies for sustainable development, provide access to justice for all, and build effective, accountable, and inclusive institutions at all levels.
- Partnerships for the SDGS: Strengthen the means of implementation and revitalize the global partnership for sustainable development.

Relatedly, ESG criteria are crucial to consider when assessing a company's sustainability performance.[31] These are employed by investors to assess a company's sustainability performance and guide investment choices. Similar to the SDGs, ESG criteria offer a framework for companies to evaluate and address sustainability-related risks and opportunities. Environmental factors cover aspects like climate change, resource efficiency, and pollution. Social factors encompass labor practices, human rights, and community engagement. Governance factors deal with board composition, executive compensation, and transparency. Numerous studies have shown a positive correlation between strong ESG practices and financial outperformance.[32]

Sustainability is a critical issue for managers and management in the MEI.[33]

Consumers increasingly seek to support businesses that demonstrate a commitment to sustainability as they become more aware of the issues. With sustainable practices and the promotion of environmental and social responsibility, media and entertainment companies can enhance their reputation and appeal to socially conscious consumers. Furthermore, the MEI significantly influences public opinion and can help raise awareness of sustainability issues. Different players in the industry can encourage positive change by promoting sustainable lifestyles and behaviors through their content. The adoption of sustainable practices can drive innovation and create new business opportunities. For example, the shift toward digital content and distribution has led to new sustainable business models and revenue streams.

84 The Fundamentals of Management

For this reason, many media and entertainment companies are implementing sustainability practices such as the following:

- Environmental practices: Companies are adopting sustainable practices to reduce environmental impact. These include measures such as reducing energy consumption and carbon emissions, using renewable energy sources, and implementing waste reduction and recycling programs. For example, Disney has set a goal to achieve net-zero greenhouse gas emissions for its direct operations by 2030 and is working toward using 100% renewable energy sources.[34] Disney has also implemented waste reduction and recycling programs and sustainable sourcing practices for its products and materials.
- Diversity and inclusion: Many media and entertainment companies focus on improving diversity and inclusion within their organizations. This includes promoting diversity in hiring, creating a more inclusive workplace culture, and increasing representation in content production and distribution. For example, Netflix aims to increase the representation of underrepresented groups in its content production and distribution.[35] It has implemented various measures to achieve this, such as investing in employee diversity and inclusion training programs, and partnering with diverse talent organizations.
- Community engagement: Media and entertainment companies engage with their communities to address social issues and promote positive change. This includes partnering with nonprofit organizations, promoting social causes through their content, and supporting local initiatives. ViacomCBS has implemented several community engagement initiatives to promote sustainability, such as the Viacommunity program, which provides funding and resources for community-driven sustainability projects.[36] ViacomCBS collaborates with local organizations and governments to support environmental conservation and education efforts.

Case Studies

LEGO: Promoting Creativity and Imagination in Everyday Management

LEGO's management style is about nurturing creativity and imagination through experimentation, play, collaboration, learning, and leadership. Encouraging risk-taking, the company values learning from failures. Playfulness is integrated into its culture, allowing employees to explore ideas with enjoyment. Collaborative settings and cross-functional teams encourage diverse viewpoints. The emphasis on learning is visible in extensive training, while Lego's unique "Leadership Playground" model promotes inclusive leadership. This approach not only sparks creativity but also influences the future of play and innovation in the MEI.

More case details for classroom use are available. Please check the book webpage at www.routledge.com/9781032221212 for more information.

Netflix's ESG Management: Driving Sustainable Growth of the Online Streaming Platform

Global streaming giant Netflix exemplifies strong ESG management for sustainable growth. In addition to achieving net-zero emissions in 2022 through eco-friendly practices, it emphasizes diversity, equity, and inclusion in its workforce and content. Initiatives like the Netflix Fund for Creative Equity support underrepresented voices. With robust governance structures, including an independent board and a Code of Ethics, Netflix ensures transparency and ethical conduct. This ESG model enhances its reputation, broadens its audience, and establishes a benchmark for sustainable success in the MEI.

More case details for classroom use are available. Please check the book webpage at www.routledge.com/9781032221212 for more information.

Review

- This chapter begins by discussing the notion of management (3.1). Management is the process of planning, organizing, leading, and controlling resources to achieve organizational goals. Effective management is critical for any organization, as it helps efficiently utilize resources, achieve organizational goals, enhance productivity, reduce uncertainty, and foster innovation.
- Tracing the history of management (3.2), the chapter explores the evolution of management theories and practices over time. This reveals how our understanding of management has evolved in response to changing business environments and societal contexts.
- The next section identifies the roles of managers, specifically in relation to the key functions they perform, including planning, organizing, leading, and controlling (3.3). These roles demand various skills, and the significance of each function and the balance between them may vary depending on the manager's level in the organization and the nature of their job.
- In the MEI context, the following section examines how the roles and responsibilities of management and managers take a unique shape (3.4). Due to the MEI's creative and rapidly changing nature, managers are tasked with balancing creativity and business objectives, managing talent, fostering innovation, and responding to rapidly changing consumer preferences and technological advancements.
- Management faces new challenges and opportunities as the world moves into a new era (3.5). The digital transformation has led to the rise of new business models, technologies, and consumer behaviors in the MEI. It has also brought about unique challenges related to data privacy and security, the digital divide, and the need for digital literacy. Globalization and the rise of digital technologies have introduced another layer of complexity to management. This shift requires managers to develop new skills and capabilities. The importance of ESG in the MEI is also highlighted, emphasizing the growing importance of sustainability for businesses.

86 The Fundamentals of Management

Discussion Questions

1 How has the evolution of management theories influenced current management practices? Can you identify aspects of different theories in contemporary management styles?
2 What are the key management activities of a manager? What do you think is the most important activity and why?
3 How do the roles and responsibilities of managers in the MEI differ from those in other industries? Can you provide specific examples?
4 How are the challenges of the new digital era reshaping the role and skills of managers? Discuss the implications of digital transformation for management practices in the MEI.
5 Discuss the importance of ESG factors in the MEI. How are companies implementing sustainable practices and what role does management play?
6 Looking toward the future, what impact may technologies like AI and machine learning have on management in the MEI? What opportunities and challenges may they present?

Further Reading

- Witzel, M. (2016) *A history of management thought* (2nd ed.). London: Routledge.
- Buckingham, M. (2005) "What great managers do." *Harvard Business Review,* 83(3), pp. 70–79. https://hbr.org/2005/03/what-great-managers-do.
- McCord, P. (2014) "How Netflix reinvented HR." *Harvard Business Review,* 92(1) pp. 71–76. https://hbr.org/2014/01/how-netflix-reinvented-hr.
- Steers, R. M. and Nardon, L. (2015) *Managing in the global economy* (1st ed.). London: Routledge.
- PwC (2022) *Tackling 'ESG' in the media and entertainment industry.* https://www.pwc.com.au/industry/entertainment-and-media-trends-analysis/esg-trends.html.

References

1 Deslandes, G. (2014) "Management in Xenophon's Philosophy: A retrospective analysis." *38th Annual Research Conference.* Chicago, IL: Philosophy of Management.
2 Jones, N. L. (2013) 'Chapter 2: Of poetry and politics: The managerial culture of sixteenth-century England." In P. I. Kaufman (ed.) *Leadership and Elizabethan culture.* New York: Palgrave Macmillan (Jepson Studies in Leadership), pp. 17–36.
3 Ward, P. (2021) "Management theory of Henri Fayol: Summary, examples." *NanoGlobals.* https://nanoglobals.com/glossary/henri-fayol-management-theory/.
4 Allen, L. A. (1971) *Management and organization.* New York: McGraw-Hill.
5 Mintzberg, H. (1973) *The nature of managerial work.* New York: Harper & Row.
6 Ward, P. (2021) "Management theory of Henri Fayol: Summary, examples." *NanoGlobals.* https://nanoglobals.com/glossary/henri-fayol-management-theory/.
7 Lloyd, R. and Aho, W. (2020) *The history of management: The four functions of management.* Montreal, QC: FHSU Digital Press. https://fhsu.pressbooks.pub/management/chapter/the-history-of-management/.
8 Zamaros, P. (no date) "A brief history of management." *The Drz Network.* www.zamaros.net/mgt%20reading%202%20-%20history%20of%20mgt.pdf

9 Lloyd, R. and Aho, W. (2020) *The history of management: The four functions of management.* Montreal, QC: FHSU Digital Press. https://fhsu.pressbooks.pub/management/chapter/the-history-of-management/.

10 Klaess, J. (2021) "The history and future of the assembly line." *Tulip.* https://tulip.co/blog/the-history-and-future-of-the-assembly-line/.

11 Wilson, J. M. (2015) "Ford's development and use of the assembly line, 1908–1927." In B. Bowden and D. Lamond (eds.) *Management history: Its global past and present.* Charlotte, NC: Information Age Publishing Inc., pp. 71–92.

12 DiFrancesco, J. M. and Berman, S. J. (2000) "Human productivity: The New America Frontier." *National Productivity Review*, 19(3), pp. 29–36.

13 Fayol, H. (1949) *General and industrial management.* Translated by Constance Storrs. London, UK: Sir Isaac Pitman & Sons.

14 Wren, D. A. and Bedeian, A. G. (2009) *The evolution of management thought.* Hoboken, NJ: John Wiley & Sons, Inc.

15 Edersheim, E. H. (2007) *The definitive Drucker: Challenges for tomorrow's executives -- Final advice from the father of modern management.* New York: McGraw-Hill.

16 Drucker, P. F. (2008) *Management: Revised edition.* New York: Collins Business.

17 Mintzberg, H. (1973) "The nature of managerial work." In S. Crainer (ed.) *The ultimate business library.* Chichester, UK: Capstone Publishing, pp. 174.

18 Dess, G. G. and Davis, P. S. (1984) "Porter's (1980) generic strategies as determinants of strategic group membership and organizational performance." *Academy of Management Journal*, 27(3), pp. 467–488.

19 Buckingham, M. (2005) "What great managers do." *Harvard Business Review*, March. https://hbr.org/2005/03/what-great-managers-do.

20 Dessler, G., Cole, N. D. and Chhinzer, N. (2015) *Management of human resources: The essentials.* London, UK: Pearson.

21 Mintzberg, H. (1973) *The nature of managerial work.* New York: Harper & Row.

22 Harvard FAS Mignone Center for Career Success (no date). "Entertainment, media, music, sports." https://careerservices.fas.harvard.edu/channels/entertainment-media-music-sports/.

23 Wiesen, G. (2023) "What does an entertainment manager do?" *PracticalAdultInsights.* www.practicaladultinsights.com/what-does-an-entertainment-manager-do.htm (Accessed: 16 June 2023).

24 Landry, L. (2019) "Why emotional intelligence is important in leadership." *Harvard Business School Online.* https://online.hbs.edu/blog/post/emotional-intelligence-in-leadership.

25 Kendal, G. (2019) "The first moon landing was achieved with less computing power than a cell phone or a calculator." *Pacific Standard.* https://psmag.com/social-justice/ground-control-to-major-tim-cook.

26 Amin, S. (2014) *Capitalism in the age of globalization: The management of contemporary society.* London: Bloomsbury Publishing.

27 Earley, P. C. and Mosakowski, E. (2004) "Cultural intelligence" *Harvard Business Review*, 82(10), pp. 139–146.

28 Spiliakos, A. (2018) "What is sustainability in business?," *HBS Online: Business Insights Blog.* https://online.hbs.edu/blog/post/what-is-sustainability-in-business.

29 "Economic, social, and environmental sustainability areas" (2021) *The Social Ripples.* www.thesocialripples.com/blog/sustainability/economic-social-amp-environmental-sustainability-areas.

30 "The 17 goals | sustainable development" (no date) *United Nations.* https://sdgs.un.org/goals.

31 Bucaille, A. (no date) "ESG in technology, media & telecommunications: Driving value through sustainability." *Deloitte.* www.deloitte.com/global/en/Industries/tmt/perspectives/esg-in-tmt-driving-value-through-sustainability.html.

32 Khan, M., Serafeim, G. and Yoon, A., (2016) "Corporate sustainability: First evidence on materiality." *The Accounting Review*, 91(6), pp. 1697–1724.

33 "Tackling 'ESG' in the media and entertainment industry" (2022) *PwC.* www.pwc.com.au/industry/entertainment-and-media-trends-analysis/esg-trends.html.

34 Mitchell, B. (2021) "Disney's new CSR report highlights environmental goals for 2030." *Blooloop.* https://blooloop.com/theme-park/news/disney-csr-social-responsibility-report-environmental-goals/.

88 The Fundamentals of Management

35 Netflix (2023) "Making progress: Our latest film & series diversity study and Netflix Fund for Creative Equity Updates." https://about.netflix.com/en/news/making-progress-our-latest-film-and-series-diversity-study-and-netflix-fund.
36 Barnes, C. (2020) "How employees around the world have found new ways to give back for the company's annual day of service." *Paramount*. www.paramount.com/news/life-at-viacomcbs/viacomcbs-gives-back-with-virtual-community-day.

4

ORGANIZATIONAL BEHAVIOR IN MEDIA AND ENTERTAINMENT ORGANIZATIONS

Outline

Overview		89
4.1	Decision-Making	90
4.2	Planning	92
4.3	Organizational Structure	96
4.4	Leadership	100
4.5	Controlling and Coordinating	103
4.6	Organizational Communication	105
4.7	New Themes of Organizational Behavior	110
Case Studies		115
Review		116
Discussion Questions		117
Further Reading		118
References		118

Intended Learning Outcomes

- Understand the fundamentals of individual behavior in organizations.
- Analyze group dynamics and team functioning.
- Examine organizational structures and dynamics.
- Apply organizational behavior theories to the media and entertainment context.

Overview

- Organizational behavior (OB) is a business discipline that studies individual behavior, group behavior, and organizational aspects within the workplace. It aims to explain, predict, and influence behavior to improve individual and organizational effectiveness.

DOI: 10.4324/9781003271222-6

90 The Fundamentals of Management

- OB examines attitudes, values, personalities, motivations, perceptions, and emotions to understand individual behavior. It also analyzes group behavior and focuses on team dynamics, communication, leadership, decision-making, and conflict resolution. Furthermore, OB explores organizational structures, communication channels, power dynamics, change management, and culture to study organizational aspects.
- The goals of OB include explaining behavior by identifying influencing factors, predicting behavior through pattern analysis, and influencing behavior through applying theories and interventions. Organizations can enhance employee motivation, teamwork, leadership effectiveness, and overall organizational performance by understanding and leveraging these aspects.

4.1 Decision-Making

4.1.1 Decision-Making in Organizations

Decision-making is an inherent aspect of daily life, as we are constantly faced with choices that shape our lives. Decision-making permeates every aspect of our existence—whether that be selecting our attire, choosing our meals, determining our place of residence and employment, or even selecting our life partner.

Top management team members regularly make decisions that have far-reaching implications for the organization and its stakeholders. These decisions can determine the long-term success or failure of the organization. Well-informed and strategic decisions can position the organization for growth and sustainability; while poor decisions can have detrimental consequences, potentially leading to bankruptcy. Although managers at lower levels may not have the same impact on the overall survival of the organization, their decisions can still significantly influence their respective departments and the wellbeing of their employees.

In the organizational context, it is important to recognize that effective decision-making requires two key elements: access to relevant and comprehensive information, and the capacity to analyze and interpret it. While the availability of appropriate information depends on external sources, the capability to make informed decisions is a characteristic that resides within an individual.[1] Therefore, proficient managers can consider various viewpoints and differing perspectives to reach a well-informed decision.

Decision-making involves the act or process of carefully considering potential choices and ultimately choosing one option.[2] Managers play a crucial role in decision-making, as their choices have a direct and substantial impact on the effectiveness of the organization and its stakeholders, including all individuals or groups who are influenced by the actions and outcomes of the organization. It is important to acknowledge the significance of managerial decision-making and its implications for the wellbeing and satisfaction of the various stakeholders involved.

In the current business environment, numerous companies provide examples of strategic errors resulting from poor decision-making by managers. Another crucial aspect of decision-making in an organizational context is the need for comprehensive and accurate information. In economics, the concept of "information asymmetry" highlights how incomplete or inadequate information can lead to erroneous decisions and unfavorable choices.[3] This concept underscores that insufficient or flawed information often results in "analysis paralysis," hampering effective decision-making. Furthermore, even with reliable and precise information, decision-makers must possess strong problem-solving skills and discerning decision-making abilities to make sound judgments regarding everyday problems and challenges.

A fundamental principle in decision-making is that the decision-maker must possess both legitimacy and authority over the individuals or groups affected by the decision. The success of decision-makers relies on their decisions being respected and implemented by those impacted. It is important to highlight this aspect because the fragmented structure of organizations, with various factions representing different interests, can hinder the decision-making abilities of decision-makers. It is crucial to empower decision-makers with the necessary authority to effectively make decisions.

4.1.2 Decision-Making Process

The five steps involved in the managerial decision-making process are explained below:[4]

- Establishing the objective: The first step in the decision-making process is to establish the objective of the business enterprise. The critical objective of a private business enterprise is to maximize profits. However, a business firm may have other objectives, such as maximization of sales or growth. The objective of a public enterprise is normally not to maximize profits but to follow benefit-cost criteria. To achieve this objective, a public enterprise should evaluate all social costs and benefits when deciding whether to build an airport, a power plant, a steel plant, and so on.
- Defining the problem: The second step in the decision-making process is to define or identify the problem. Defining the nature of the problem is essential because decision-making is, after all, meant to solve the problem. For instance, a company may find that its profits are declining. It must investigate what is causing the problem of decreasing profits—for example, the wrong pricing policy or the use of outdated technology. Once the source or reason has been identified, the problem can be defined.
- Identifying possible alternative solutions (i.e., alternative courses of action): Once the problem has been identified, the next step is to find alternative solutions. This will require consideration of the variables that have an impact on the problem. In this way, a relationship between the variables and the problems is established. Various hypotheses can be developed in this regard, which will become alternative courses for solving the problem.

    The choice between these alternative courses of action depends on which will bring about the largest profit increase.
- Evaluating alternative courses of action: The next step in business decision-making is to evaluate the alternative courses of action. This requires the collection and analysis of relevant data. Some data will be available within the various departments of the firm itself. Other data may be obtained from the industry and from government.

    The data and information obtained can be used to evaluate the outcome or results expected from each possible course of action. Methods such as regression analysis, differential calculus, linear programming, and cost-benefit analysis are used to arrive at the optimal course of action. The optimum course of action is that which best helps to achieve the established objective of the firm.

92 The Fundamentals of Management

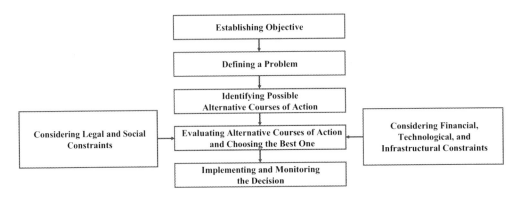

FIGURE 4.1 The Decision-Making Process in Business and Management.

Managers must work under certain constraints in choosing an optimal solution to the problem. Those constraints may be legal, such as laws on pollution and disposal of harmful wastes; they may be financial (e.g., limited financial resources); they may relate to the availability of physical infrastructure and raw materials; or they may be technological, imposing limits on the possible output to be produced per unit of time. The crucial role of a business manager is to determine the optimal course of action within the scope of these constraints.

- Implementing the decision: Once the alternative courses of action have been evaluated and the optimal course of action has been selected, the final step is to implement the decision. Implementing the decision requires constant monitoring to obtain the expected results from the optimal course of action. If it is found that the expected results are not forthcoming due to the incorrect implementation of the decision, remedial measures should be taken.

However, once a course of action has been implemented to achieve the established objective, changes may become necessary from time to time in response to changes in conditions or the firm's operating environment.

The five steps of the decision-making process are shown in Figure 4.1.

4.2 Planning

4.2.1 Definition

Planning is crucial to achieve desired goals and organize necessary actions. It involves creating and maintaining plans, utilizing conceptual skills, and evaluating planning capabilities through tests. Planning is an integral aspect of intelligent behavior and is important in various occupations, particularly management and business. Different plans are employed in each field to enhance efficiency and effectiveness.

Forecasting is closely linked to planning: it involves predicting future outcomes, while planning focuses on shaping and preparing for desired future scenarios. By combining forecasting with scenario development and response strategies, planning enables individuals and organizations to proactively navigate potential challenges. Planning plays a vital role in project and time management, as it facilitates the identification of the steps needed to achieve specific goals. Effectively following a plan allows for progress toward the desired outcome to be assessed, similar to using a map to monitor progress toward a destination.

In dynamic environments, planning faces contemporary challenges. It requires the development of specific yet flexible plans to adapt to changing circumstances. Even in highly uncertain environments, continuous planning is crucial to maintain preparedness and responsiveness. Additionally, empowering lower organizational levels to set and develop plans is essential in dynamic contexts where top-down goal dissemination may be time-constrained. Environmental scanning, including competitive intelligence, is another contemporary planning issue that aids in analyzing the external environment and gaining insights into competitors' actions.

4.2.2 Foundation of Planning

Strategies, and creating action plans to guide work activities. The objectives of planning are to provide clear direction, reduce uncertainty, eliminate inefficiencies, and establish performance standards for control. Research on the correlation between planning and performance indicates that formal planning is associated with desired financial outcomes.[5] However, the quality and execution of planning hold greater importance than the extent of planning activities. External environmental factors often impact the ability of companies to achieve high performance despite their planning efforts. Additionally, the planning-performance relationship is influenced by the timeframe within which planning occurs.

Goals and Plans

Goals and plans play a key role in achieving desired outcomes. Goals represent desired outcomes, while plans outline the specific actions and strategies to achieve those goals. Goals can be strategic, focusing on the organization's overall direction or financial targets. They can be stated goals that are explicitly defined or actual goals that emerge from the organization's actions.

Strategic plans encompass the entire organization, guiding its overall direction; while operational plans are specific to a particular functional area, such as marketing or finance. Plans can also be classified based on their timeframe, with long-term plans extending beyond three years and short-term plans covering a year or less.

When it comes to specificity, plans can be either specific or directional. Specific plans leave no room for interpretation, providing clear guidelines on what needs to be done. Directional plans are flexible, offering general guidelines that allow for adaptation and adjustment based on circumstances.

Additionally, plans can be categorized as single-use or standing plans. Single-use plans are designed to address unique situations or events that are not expected to recur, while standing plans are ongoing and guide activities that are performed repeatedly.

Management by Objectives

Management by objectives is a process that involves setting goals that are mutually agreed upon between managers and members.[6] These goals serve as a basis for evaluating organizational performance.[7] In the traditional goal-setting approach, top-level goals are

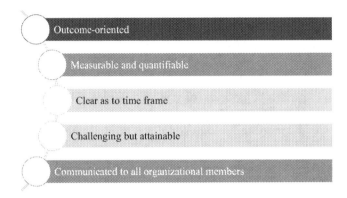

FIGURE 4.2 Characteristics of Good Goals.

cascaded down to lower organizational levels, becoming subgoals for each area. Well-written goals possess some key characteristics: they are written in terms of outcomes; measurable and quantifiable; clear in terms of the timeframe; challenging yet attainable; and communicated to relevant members of the organization (Figure 4.2).

The goal-setting process typically involves several steps: reviewing the organization's mission; evaluating available resources; determining goals individually or collaboratively; documenting them; and communicating them to all relevant organizational members. Regular review and adjustment of goals based on results are also integral to the planning process.

Diverse factors—such as the manager's position, environmental uncertainty, and future commitments—can influence the planning process. These factors will determine the complexity and extent of planning required in an organization.

Two main approaches to planning exist. The traditional approach involves top managers developing plans that flow down through the organizational hierarchy, often with the support of a formal planning department. The more modern approach aims at greater engagement of organizational members in the planning process, encouraging collaboration and diverse perspectives.

By understanding and applying effective goal-setting and planning practices, aspiring media and entertainment management professionals can enhance their ability to navigate complex challenges and achieve organizational success.

4.2.3 Planning Techniques and Skills

Several skills and techniques help managers assess the organization's environment and plan its next steps: environmental scanning, forecasting, benchmarking, budgeting, and scheduling.[8]

Environmental Scanning

How can managers become aware of significant environmental changes? Managers in both small and large organizations use environmental scanning to screen large volumes of information to anticipate and interpret environmental changes.[9] Extensive environmental scanning will likely reveal issues and concerns affecting an organization's current or planned activities. Research has shown that companies that use environmental scanning have better performance.[10]

Competitor intelligence has emerged as a significant component of environmental scanning, whereby organizations collect information about their competitors to gain insights into their activities and assess potential impacts on their operations.[11] Gathering information about competitors involves answering critical questions such as identifying who they are, understanding their actions, and evaluating the implications of their strategies on the organization. A substantial portion of the necessary competitor information can be obtained from internal sources such as employees, suppliers, and customers. Engaging in competitor intelligence does not necessarily involve unethical or secretive practices, but rather relies on readily accessible sources such as ads, promotional materials, press releases, government reports, annual reports, job ads, news articles, and industry studies.

Global scanning has gained immense importance in environmental scanning efforts in today's globalized markets.[12] Given the complexity and dynamism of world markets, managers recognize the need to expand their scanning activities to gather crucial information on global forces that may impact their organizations. The value of global scanning for managers depends on the extent of the organization's global activities. Companies with significant global interests can greatly benefit from comprehensive global scanning, as it provides insights into global trends, geopolitical factors, economic conditions, and cultural influences that shape markets and industries worldwide. By incorporating global scanning into their planning and decision-making processes, media and entertainment management professionals can effectively navigate the complexities of global markets and gain a competitive edge.

Forecasting

The second technique managers can use to assess the environment is forecasting. Forecasting is an essential part of planning, and managers need forecasts that will allow them to predict future events effectively and in a timely manner. Environmental scanning establishes the basis for forecasts, which are predictions of outcomes.

Forecasting techniques fall into two categories: quantitative and qualitative. Quantitative forecasting applies mathematical rules to a series of data to predict outcomes. Qualitative techniques are typically used when precise data is limited or hard to obtain. Quantitative techniques are preferred when managers have sufficient hard data that can be used. In contrast, qualitative forecasting uses knowledgeable individuals' judgment and opinions to predict outcomes.

Quantitative forecasting involves applying mathematical rules to historical data to predict outcomes, while qualitative techniques rely on expert judgments and opinions when precise data is limited. Using both quantitative and qualitative forecasting methods can help managers make more accurate predictions and adjust their plans accordingly.

Benchmarking

Benchmarking is another valuable technique that managers can utilize to improve performance. It involves analyzing and adopting best practices from leading organizations in various fields. For example, a streaming platform may benchmark against a competitor to improve its user interface and enhance the overall user experience. Benchmarking allows

96 The Fundamentals of Management

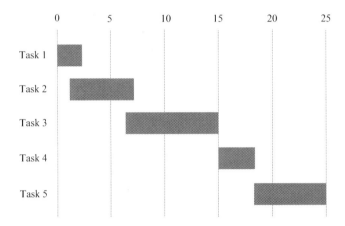

FIGURE 4.3 Gantt Charts: Example.

managers to identify areas of improvement and implement strategies that have proven successful in other organizations, leading to increased efficiency and effectiveness.

Budgeting

Allocation of resources is a critical aspect of planning. Two techniques commonly employed by managers are budgeting and scheduling. Budgeting involves creating a numerical plan to allocate resources for specific activities, including revenues, expenses, capital expenditures, and resource utilization.

Key practices to improve budgeting processes and outcomes include aligning goals with budgets; being flexible; and collaborating, communicating, and coordinating budgeting throughout the organization.

Scheduling

Scheduling allocates resources by determining the sequence, responsible individuals, and completion deadlines. Managers use scheduling techniques such as Gantt charts to effectively plan and organize tasks.[13]

Gantt charts provide a graphical representation of project timelines, showing each task's start and end dates, as well as the duration and dependencies (Figure 4.3). Gantt charts enable project managers to visualize progress, identify critical paths, allocate resources efficiently, and manage project schedules effectively. Using bars or blocks to represent tasks and their durations, Gantt charts provide a clear overview of the project timeline, allowing for better planning, coordination, and decision-making.

4.3 Organizational Structure

4.3.1 Organization and Organizing: Concepts and Components

Organizing is a systematic process of structuring, integrating, and coordinating task goals and activities to resources to achieve objectives.[14] Organizational design encompasses several key elements that shape the structure and functioning of an organization. These

Organizational Behavior **97**

TABLE 4.1 Key Elements of Organizational Design

Key elements	Description
Work specialization	Dividing work activities into separate tasks.
Chain of command	Hierarchical structure with lines of authority and communication.
Span of control	Number of employees a manager can effectively supervise.
Departmentalization	Grouping jobs based on criteria such as functions, products, geography, processes, or customers.
Authority	Rights inherent in a managerial position to give instructions and expect compliance.
Responsibility	Obligation or expectation to perform assigned duties.
Unity of command	Each employee reporting to only one manager to avoid conflicting directives.
Centralization vs. Decentralization	Deciding whether decision-making authority resides with upper-level managers versus lower-level employees.
Formalization	Reliance on standardization and strict rules for consistency and control in an organization.

include work specialization, chain of command, span of control, departmentalization, centralization-decentralization, and formalization (Table 4.1).

Work specialization involves dividing work activities into separate tasks. While traditionally seen as an effective organizing mechanism, it is now recognized that excessive specialization can lead to challenges such as limited employee engagement and narrow skills development.

The chain of command and concepts like authority, responsibility, and unity of command were traditionally crucial to maintain control within organizations. In contemporary organizations, these concepts have become less relevant as organizations have become flatter and more flexible.

The span of control refers to the number of employees a manager can effectively supervise. While the traditional view emphasizes a limited span of control, the contemporary perspective recognizes that the optimal span of control depends on various factors, including the manager's and employees' skills and abilities, and the specific situation.

Departmentalization is the grouping of jobs based on various criteria. For example, functional departmentalization groups jobs by the functions performed, while product departmentalization groups jobs based on product lines. Geographical departmentalization groups jobs by geographical regions, and process departmentalization groups jobs based on the flow of products or customers. Customer departmentalization groups jobs based on specific customer groups.

The authority to give instructions and expect compliance is inherent to a managerial position. The acceptance view of authority recognizes that authority is derived from the willingness of subordinates to accept it. Line authority grants a manager the power to direct an employee's work; while staff authority provides support, assistance, and advice, and relieves some informational burdens on managers.

Responsibility is the obligation or expectation to perform assigned duties. Unity of command emphasizes that employees should have only one manager to report to, ensuring clarity and avoiding conflicting directives.

98 The Fundamentals of Management

Centralization-decentralization are structural approaches determining who has decision-making authority within the organization. Centralization involves decision-making authority residing with upper-level managers, while decentralization involves delegating decision-making to lower-level employees.

"Formalization" refers to the extent to which an organization relies on standardization and strict rules to ensure consistency and control. Formalization provides clear guidelines for employees but can also limit flexibility and creativity.

With these key elements of organizational design, managers can structure their organizations to enhance efficiency, effectiveness, and adaptability to the changing business environment.

4.3.2 Organizational Design

Traditional Organizational Design

Traditional organizational design includes various structures that are commonly used in organizations. One such structure is the simple structure, which features low departmentalization, wide spans of control, centralized authority in a single person, and minimal formalization. This is found in small businesses or startups where decision-making is centralized.

Another traditional design is the functional structure, which groups employees with similar or related occupational specialties. This structure allows for efficient coordination within departments but can create challenges in communication and coordination across different functional areas.

A divisional structure organizes the firm into separate business units or divisions based on products, services, customers, or geographical locations. Each division operates independently, providing a higher level of autonomy but potentially duplicating functions and increasing costs.

Adaptive Organizational Design

Adaptive organizational design encompasses more flexible structures and is responsive to the dynamic business environment.[15] The team structure is an example: the entire organization comprises work teams, which promotes collaboration, employee empowerment, and faster decision-making.

The matrix structure combines functional and project-based structures. It assigns specialists from different departments to work on projects led by project managers. This structure enables resource sharing and the utilization of expertise across functional areas but can lead to complex reporting relationships and power struggles.

The project structure is employed when employees consistently work on projects rather than in traditional functional roles. This structure is common in the media and entertainment industry (MEI), given the nature of event-based products such as films and live performances.

Virtual organizations consist of a small core of full-time employees who collaborate with outside specialists temporarily as needed for specific projects. This structure allows for flexibility and access to specialized skills. Relatedly, network organization relies on a network of outside suppliers to provide specific product components or work processes. The organization focuses on its core competencies while leveraging external resources.

The increasing use of adaptive organizational design has also led to a rise in flexible work arrangements. For example, telecommuting allows employees to work from home while staying connected to the workplace through computer technology.[16] Flextime allows employees to vary their work hours within certain limits while still meeting weekly requirements.[17]

These flexible work arrangements enable organizations to adapt to changing employee preferences, enhance work-life balance, and improve employee satisfaction and productivity. They all have their own advantages and considerations, and organizations must evaluate their feasibility and compatibility with their specific operations and work culture.

4.3.3 Managing Human Resources

Human resource management (HRM)—the strategic approach of managing people as an organization's most valuable assets—plays a crucial role. First, it can be a significant source of competitive advantage.[18] By effectively managing and developing their workforce, organizations can enhance productivity, innovation, and customer satisfaction, giving them an edge over competitors. For example, companies like Alphabet, Meta, and Amazon are renowned for HRM practices that attract and retain top talent, fostering a culture of creativity and innovation.

Second, HRM is an integral part of organizational strategies.[19] The alignment of HRM practices with overall business strategy ensures that the workforce has the necessary skills and competencies to achieve organizational goals. Companies like Zappos have strategically focused on building a strong corporate culture and delivering exceptional customer service, which requires them to hire and train employees who are aligned with their values and goals.

More importantly, the treatment of employees significantly impacts organizational performance.[20] Research has shown that satisfied and engaged employees are more productive, committed, and likely to stay with the organization.[21] Organizations that prioritize employee wellbeing and development tend to experience lower turnover rates and higher levels of employee satisfaction. For example, companies like Patagonia have gained recognition for their employee-friendly policies, such as flexible work arrangements, generous benefits, and supportive work environments.

4.3.4 Formation and Management of Teams

A group is formed when two or more individuals unite and engage in mutual interactions to accomplish particular objectives. Within an organization, the structure defines formal groups, which are assigned specific tasks to achieve organizational goals; and informal groups, which emerge organically through social affiliations.

The group development process involves several stages: forming, storming, norming, performing, and adjourning.[22] Each stage has its own dynamics and activities, such as joining the group, resolving conflicts, establishing norms, and working together on tasks.

In assessing group performance and satisfaction, several significant components come into play: external conditions, group member resources, group structure, group processes, and group tasks.[23] These elements collectively shape the dynamics and outcomes within a group setting.

100 The Fundamentals of Management

External conditions are the contextual factors that influence work groups. These include the availability of resources, organizational goals, and other environmental factors. Alignment with organizational goals can provide clarity and direction, but a group with limited resources may face challenges in achieving its objectives.

Group member resources—encompassing knowledge, skills, abilities, and personality traits—directly impact individual contributions and overall group effectiveness. The diverse capabilities and attributes of group members influence what tasks they can perform and how proficiently they can execute them.

Group structure is crucial in defining roles and relationships within a group. Roles can be task-oriented, focused on achieving work objectives; or socio-emotional, aimed at maintaining group cohesion and member satisfaction. The optimal size of a group depends on the specific task it is aiming to accomplish. Different tasks require varying degrees of coordination, communication, and decision-making, which can be affected by group size.

Group norms—shared expectations and standards of behavior—have a profound influence on individual performance and group dynamics. They govern key factors such as work output levels and adherence to established practices. However, the pressure to conform to norms can strongly influence individual judgment and attitudes, potentially leading to biased groupthink. Relatedly, cohesiveness—the degree of unity and solidarity among group members—is closely related to group productivity. Higher levels of cohesiveness tend to foster better cooperation, communication, and overall performance.

The status system within a group can serve as a significant motivator, as it impacts individual behaviors and interactions. Incongruence or discrepancies in status levels may affect individual engagement and collaboration.

Group decision-making and conflict management are critical processes that significantly influence performance and satisfaction. Depending on the objectives and circumstances, different approaches may be appropriate. Group decisions are advantageous when accuracy, creativity, and acceptance are crucial. Effective communication and managing conflicts are particularly relevant for group performance when tasks are complex and interdependent.

4.4 Leadership

4.4.1 Leaders and Leadership

A leader possesses the ability to influence and guide others toward the achievement of organizational goals.[24] Leadership is a fundamental aspect of management, and managers are expected to exhibit effective leadership skills as part of their overall responsibilities.

Early attempts to define leadership traits proved unsuccessful at identifying specific characteristics that can universally predict leadership effectiveness. However, subsequent research and observations have identified several traits associated with leadership. These include self-confidence, determination, integrity, effective communication, adaptability, and the ability to inspire and motivate others.[25] Leaders who possess these traits can inspire and guide their team members toward success.

For example, consider Steve Jobs, the co-founder of Apple Inc. His visionary leadership, creativity, and ability to think outside the box enabled him to revolutionize the technology industry and propel Apple to great success. Jobs' charismatic and innovative leadership style inspired his teams to think differently and strive for excellence.

Leadership styles can also vary depending on the situation and the team or organization's needs. For instance, a leader may adopt a democratic leadership style, involving team members in decision-making and valuing their input. This approach promotes employee engagement and fosters a sense of ownership and commitment to the team's goals.

On the other hand, in a crisis where immediate action is required, a leader may adopt a more autocratic leadership style, making quick decisions and providing clear direction to ensure the team's safety and success.

Effective leadership is not limited to specific traits or styles. Different situations and contexts may call for different leadership approaches. Successful leaders adapt their style and behavior based on the needs of their team and the challenges they face.

4.4.2 Characteristics of Good Leaders

Leadership is a complex and multifaceted concept critical in achieving goals and inspiring organizational members to reach their full potential.[26] Effective leaders can positively impact their teams and organizations, driving innovation, collaboration, and success. Good leaders in business and management possess various characteristics that enable them to guide their organizations to success.

Key characteristics of good leaders in business and management (Figure 4.4) include the following:[27]

- Vision: Good leaders have a clear vision of where they want their organization to go and how they plan to get there. They can communicate this vision to their team and inspire them to work toward achieving it.
- Strategic thinking: Good leaders can think strategically and make decisions that align with their organization's goals and values. They can anticipate challenges and opportunities and adjust their strategies accordingly.
- Communication skills: Good leaders are skilled communicators who can clearly and concisely convey their ideas and vision to their team. They are also good listeners who are open to feedback and can communicate effectively with stakeholders inside and outside the organization.

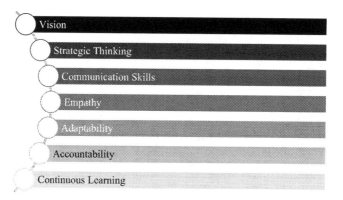

FIGURE 4.4 Characteristics of Good Leaders.

- Empathy: Good leaders can understand and empathize with team members and stakeholders. They can see situations from multiple perspectives and build strong relationships with their team.
- Adaptability: Good leaders can adjust their strategies and tactics in response to changing circumstances. They remain calm and focused during times of uncertainty and can guide their team through difficult situations.
- Accountability: Good leaders take responsibility for their decisions and actions, and hold themselves accountable for their organization's success or failure. They are transparent and open about their decisions and actions, and can admit when they have made mistakes.
- Continuous learning: Leaders should be lifelong learners committed to self-improvement and growth. They seek out new opportunities to learn and develop their skills, and can apply what they learn to their leadership roles.

4.4.3 Leadership Style

A leader's behavior generally has a dual focus: the task and the people. Fiedler's model measured two leadership styles—relationship-oriented or task-oriented—using the least preferred coworker questionnaire and defined the best style to use in particular situations.[28] He examined three contingency dimensions: leader-member relations, task structure, and position power. The model suggests that task-oriented leaders perform best in favorable and unfavorable situations, while relationship-oriented leaders perform best in moderately favorable situations.

Hersey and Blanchard's situational leadership theory focused on followers' readiness.[29] They identified four leadership styles: telling (high task-low relationship); selling (high task-high relationship); participating (low task-high relationship); and delegating (low task-low relationship). They also identified four stages of readiness: unable and unwilling (use telling style); unable but willing (use selling style); able but unwilling (use participative style); and able and willing (use delegating style).

The path-goal model developed by Robert House identified four leadership behaviors: directive, supportive, participative, and achievement-oriented (Figure 4.5).[30] House

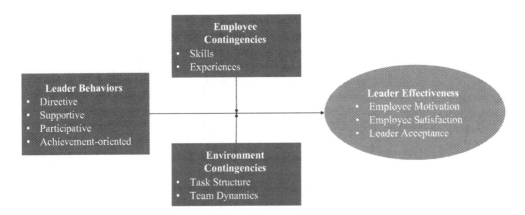

FIGURE 4.5 Path-Goal Leadership Theory.

assumed that a leader can and should be able to use any of these styles. In his model, the two situational contingency variables were the environment and the follower. The path-goal model says that a leader should provide direction and support as needed—that is, structure the path so the followers can achieve the goals.

4.5 Controlling and Coordinating

4.5.1 Definition

Organizational control is a critical aspect of the management process that involves assessing whether the organization is on track to achieve its desired objectives and taking corrective actions when necessary. It is closely linked to planning, as it evaluates whether the planned activities are being executed effectively. The specific coordination methods employed within an organization depend on its preferred management style.

Controlling involves monitoring, comparing, and correcting work performance. As the final step in the management process, it serves as a feedback mechanism to ensure that goals and targets are being met. Without control, managers will lack the necessary information to determine whether the organization is progressing as intended.[31]

The importance of control can be understood from three perspectives:

- Control gives managers the means to ascertain whether organizational goals are being achieved and, if not, to identify the reasons behind the deviations. This knowledge allows them to take timely corrective actions to bring performance back on track.
- Control is crucial in providing information and feedback that empowers managers to delegate authority and responsibility to employees. When managers have confidence in the control systems, they can trust employees to perform their tasks effectively, fostering a sense of empowerment and autonomy within the organization.
- Control is a protective mechanism for the organization and its assets. By monitoring and evaluating activities, control systems can detect and prevent potential risks, fraud, or misuse of resources. This safeguards the organization's interests and helps maintain its long-term sustainability.

Coordination, on the other hand, focuses on integrating and aligning organizational activities to achieve common goals. It involves bringing together different parts of the organization, ensuring effective collaboration, resolving conflicts, and managing dependencies. Coordination is essential to achieve synergy, teamwork, and innovation in organizational operations.

While control ensures consistency and alignment of activities with established goals, coordination ensures the integration and synchronization of these activities. Effective control relies on effective coordination, as well-coordinated activities are more likely to meet established standards and benchmarks. Similarly, effective coordination depends on effective control, as it is challenging to achieve synergy and innovation if organizational activities are not aligned with established goals and objectives.

Control and coordination are interrelated concepts fundamental to an organization's effective functioning. Control provides the framework for assessing and correcting work performance, while coordination ensures the integration and alignment of activities. Together, they enable organizations to achieve their objectives efficiently and effectively.

104 The Fundamentals of Management

4.5.2 The Control Process

The three steps in the control process are measuring, comparing, and taking action.[32] In the process, the standards are goals that were developed during the planning process. These goals provide the basis for the control process, which involves measuring actual performance and comparing it against the standard. Depending on the results, a manager may decide to do nothing, correct the performance, or revise the standard:

- Measuring is about deciding how to measure actual performance and what to measure.
- Comparing involves looking at the variation between actual performance and the standard. Deviations outside an acceptable range of variation need attention.
- Taking action can include doing nothing, correcting the performance, or revising the standards. Correcting the actual performance can involve different corrective actions, either immediate or essential. Standards can be revised by either raising or lowering them.

4.5.3 Controlling for Organizational Performance

Organizational performance is the accumulated results of all the organization's work activities. Two frequently used organizational performance measures are:

- productivity—the output of goods or services produced divided by the inputs needed to generate that output; and
- effectiveness—the measure of how appropriate organizational goals are and how well those goals are being met.[33]

There are diverse tools used for measuring organizational performance. For example, balanced scorecards provide a way to evaluate an organization's performance in four different areas rather than just from a financial perspective.

The balanced scorecard is a strategic management tool that helps organizations translate their mission and strategy into measurable goals and objectives. Robert Kaplan and David Norton developed it in the early 1990s, and it has since become widely used in private and public organizations.[34]

The balanced scorecard consists of four critical perspectives, each representing a different aspect of organizational performance (Figure 4.6):

- Financial perspective: This focuses on financial goals and objectives, such as revenue growth, cost reduction, and profitability. It helps organizations ensure that their financial goals are aligned with their overall strategy and mission.
- Customer perspective: This focuses on customer goals and objectives, such as customer satisfaction, loyalty, and retention. It helps organizations ensure that they are meeting the needs and expectations of their customers.
- Internal business processes perspective: This focuses on internal processes and operations that drive organizational performance, such as quality, efficiency, and innovation. It helps organizations ensure that their internal processes are aligned with their overall strategy and mission.

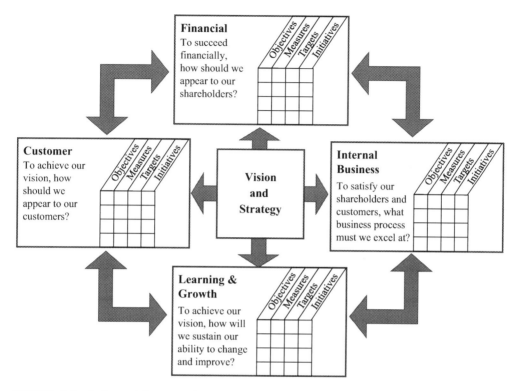

FIGURE 4.6 Balanced Scorecard.

- Learning and growth perspective: This focuses on developing organizational capabilities and resources, such as employee skills and knowledge, information technology, and organizational culture. It helps organizations invest in the right areas to support their strategy and mission.

The balanced scorecard provides a comprehensive and integrated view of organizational performance, helping ensure that all aspects of the organization are aligned with its overall mission and strategy. Each perspective is represented by objectives and measures that track and monitor performance over time. It is a valuable tool for strategic planning, performance management, and organizational communication.

4.6 Organizational Communication

4.6.1 Communication Process

Communication involves the transmission and comprehension of meaning. Its functions encompass the regulation of employee behavior, the motivation of employees, the expression of emotions, the fulfillment of social needs, and the provision of information. "Interpersonal communication" refers to interactions between two or more individuals; while "organizational communication" encompasses the various patterns, networks, and communication systems within an organization.

For communication to take place, there must be a purpose expressed as a message that needs to be conveyed. This message originates from a source (sender) and is transmitted to a receiver. The message is encoded into a symbolic form and transmitted through a chosen medium or channel to the receiver. The receiver then decodes the message, translating it to its original meaning. As a result, meaning is transferred from one person to another.

The communication process involves the following elements:[35]

- Sender: The individual or entity initiating the communication to convey information or a message to the receiver
- Encoding: The transformation of the message into a form that the receiver can comprehend and transmit. This can take the form of verbal or nonverbal elements, such as gestures or facial expressions
- Message: The specific information or content being conveyed by the sender.
- Channel: The medium utilized to transmit the message, such as face-to-face conversation, email, text message, or social media.
- Decoding: The process undertaken by the receiver to interpret the message, involving understanding the message within the context of the sender's intended meaning and considering the receiver's own experiences and background.
- Receiver: The individual or entity that receives the message from the sender.
- Feedback: The response or reaction of the receiver to the message, which can be expressed verbally or nonverbally. It provides insight into how well the message was understood and whether further clarification or information is required.

Figure 4.7 illustrates the elements of the communication process. The entire process is susceptible to noise—disturbances that interfere with a message's transmission, receipt, or feedback. Anything that interferes with understanding can be noise, distorting any point in the communication process.

4.6.2 Definition

Communication is an essential aspect of every organization.[36] On the one hand, effective organizational communication can increase the general efficiency of the organization. On

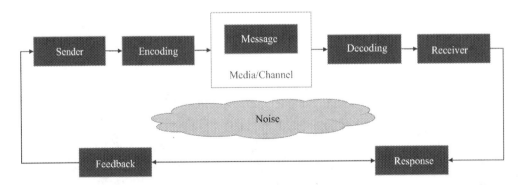

FIGURE 4.7 Communication Process.

the other hand, ineffective communication can decrease people's motivation and performance. Organizational communication theory suggests that there are five main functions of communication:[37]

- Management: Managing employee behavior regarding roles, compliance, etc.
- Feedback: Initiating feedback for employees in terms of performance.
- Information: Creating information exchange within the organization.
- Persuasion: Convincing others—for example, leaders encourage employees to commit to the organization's mission.
- Emotional sharing: Allowing members to express their satisfaction or dissatisfaction.

The importance of communication in an organization can be emphasized in different respects.[38]

First, communication promotes motivation by informing employees of the task, how they are performing it, and how to improve their performance if it is not up to the mark.

Second, communication plays a crucial role in altering an individual's attitude. A well-informed person tends to have a more favorable attitude than someone with limited information. Organizational magazines, meetings, and other forms of oral and written communication help form and strengthen employee attitudes.

Third, communication is a source of information to organizational members for decision-making, as it helps identify and assess alternative courses of action.

Fourth, communication assists in controlling the process. It helps shape organizational members' behavior in various ways. Organizational members are expected to adhere to hierarchical structures, follow established principles and guidelines, conform to organizational policies, and effectively communicate work-related issues to their managers.

Lastly, communication helps in socializing. It is an indispensable aspect of human existence, as effective communication is essential to thrive in social settings.

Organizational communication can vary, with different styles and directions.

Formal versus Informal Communication

Communication within an organization can be formal or informal (Table 4.2).[39]

"Formal communication" refers to communication that takes place within prescribed organizational work arrangements. The organization's structural hierarchy does not define informal communication. Communication in an organization can flow downward, upward, laterally, and diagonally. For example, when a manager asks an employee to

TABLE 4.2 Formal versus Informal Organizational Communication

Items	Formal	Informal
Place	Working places, e.g., office	Non-working places, e.g., rest area
Time	Working time	After work, break time
Direction	Hierarchical, top-down	Horizontal
Message Characteristics	Task-oriented, official, preparation	Non-task-oriented Private, emotional, flexible, immediate

108 The Fundamentals of Management

complete a task, or when an employee communicates a problem to their manager, that is formal communication.

"Informal communication" is organizational communication not defined by the organization's structural hierarchy. When employees talk with each other in the lunchroom, as they pass in hallways or work out at the company wellness facility, they communicate through informal communication. Employees may form friendships and communicate with each other.

Informal communication fulfills two purposes in organizations: it permits employees to satisfy their need for social interaction; and it can improve an organization's performance by creating alternative and frequently faster and more efficient communication channels.

Workplace design also influences organizational communication.[40] That design should support four types of employee interaction: focused work, collaboration, learning, and socialization. In each of these circumstances, communication must be considered.

Directional Communication

Basic forms of organizational business communication are also directional. Information can flow downward, upward, or horizontally.[41]

"Downward communication" refers to the transmission of messages from managers and supervisors to frontline employees. This type of communication typically includes instructions, tasks, organizational policies, and performance evaluations that employees must fulfill. While written forms like emails, memos, and policy guidelines are commonly used for downward communication, verbal channels such as meetings and phone calls also serve this purpose.

In contrast, "upward communication" refers to messages sent from lower-level employees to their managers. This form of communication allows employees to share projects, materials, and other relevant information with their managers. It also enables employees to provide feedback and suggestions regarding their job roles, performance, or overall company operations. Such communication channels offer upper management valuable insights and data for important decision-making processes.

Organizational communication also occurs horizontally, involving interactions among employees with the same hierarchical positions. These individuals may belong to the same department or different organizational areas. Similar to informal communication, horizontal communication is typically quick and spontaneous. It predominantly takes the form of verbal exchanges rather than written communication.

Internal Communication versus External Communication

Another classification of organizational communication is internal or external.

Internal communication is the exchange of information among members within an organization. It can occur at various levels, encompassing company-wide communication and interactions within smaller groups such as departments or project teams. Formal internal communication is predominantly conveyed in written form, comprising materials such as company updates and sales performance reports. These communications are typically intended for employees.

External communication entails messages specifically aimed at individuals or entities outside the organization, such as customers, prospects, partners, the media, or regulatory bodies like the government. Businesses devote careful attention to crafting messages targeted at external audiences to ensure a favorable perception of the organization. External communication is primarily formal, structured, and transmitted through specific channels to effectively reach the intended audience.

External communication often serves the purpose of persuasion, while internal communication primarily focuses on the dissemination of information. Businesses frequently employ promotional methods as part of their external communication efforts, ensuring that their messages effectively reach and resonate with the intended audience. To select the most appropriate promotional channels, businesses engage in research to gain a better understanding of their target audience.

Oral Communication versus Written Communication

Organizational communication can be either oral or written.

Oral communication can occur in various settings, including one-on-one conversations, small group discussions, or company-wide gatherings like an annual meeting. Despite its perceived informality, oral communication can often be structured and well prepared. For instance, a business owner engaging with potential investors at a charity dinner may conduct extensive research on the investors beforehand, allowing them to lead the conversation and address their specific interests.

Written communication is vital to business operations. Entrepreneurs frequently need to develop detailed and intricate business plans before launching a business. Additionally, they may be involved in drafting contracts and financial documents. These forms of business communication tend to be formal and often require the involvement of subject-matter experts such as lawyers and accountants.

However, not all written communication within a business is strictly formal. Day-to-day interactions between employees, known as horizontal communication, often adopt a more informal tone. Colleagues may exchange quick emails to ask each other questions or seek clarification on certain matters.

Businesses commonly utilize instant messaging programs or collaboration tools like Microsoft Teams, Slack, and Notion to facilitate written communication. These tools enable colleagues to receive and respond to messages promptly, ensuring that time-sensitive business activities can proceed according to plan.

Promoting Effective Organizational Communication

Promoting effective organizational communication is essential for the success of any business or organization.[42]

First, organizations should develop a comprehensive communication plan. This includes defining methods for sharing information, assigning communication responsibilities, and establishing mechanisms for evaluating and enhancing communication effectiveness over time.

Second, organizations must deliver timely and relevant information to ensure that communication is timely and tailored to the needs of employees and the organization.

110 The Fundamentals of Management

This involves providing regular updates on significant projects, sharing important news or changes, and establishing channels for receiving input and feedback.

For this purpose, employing diverse communication channels—such as email, social media, newsletters, meetings, and face-to-face interactions—is key. By employing multiple channels, different audiences can access the necessary information in a way that suits their preferences and needs. Relatedly, organizations should use technology tools such as project management software, messaging applications, and video conferencing platforms to facilitate communication and collaboration within teams and across the organization.

Third, organizations should foster two-way communication and encourage a culture of open feedback between managers and employees, and among different departments and teams. Actively promote an environment in which all individuals feel comfortable sharing their thoughts and opinions. This includes nurturing a transparent culture where information is readily shared, and employees feel empowered to ask questions and provide feedback.

Offering training programs that equip employees with practical communication skills can be helpful. This may include training in active listening, effective message delivery, and the appropriate use of communication channels for different purposes.

4.7 New Themes of Organizational Behavior

4.7.1 Managing Creativity and Innovation

Creativity is the capacity to combine ideas in unique ways or establish uncommon connections between different concepts. Creativity serves as a driving force that enables products, advertising, and marketing campaigns to transcend the competition. The success of numerous renowned companies can be attributed to creativity.[43] However, the creative capacity within most organizations is limited, requiring managers to comprehensively understand how to harness and leverage creativity effectively.

Creativity consists of two distinct elements: originality and usefulness.[44] For example, a captivating ad can employ a highly original creative idea to capture attention. A new product may incorporate a creative idea that builds on existing features, resulting in lower originality. Still, this idea can be exceptionally valuable in effectively meeting consumers' unmet needs.

A study by Berend Wierenga and his colleagues points out that creative ideas come mainly through three processes: fluency, persistence, and flexibility.[45] Fluency involves generating many ideas in the hope that some will be brilliant. Persistence involves digging deeper to make incremental changes. Flexibility involves switching between idea perspectives and out-of-the-box thinking to find radical innovations. They highlight eight action points for managers to effectively manage organizational creativity:

- Choosing between originality and usefulness: Consider the specific requirements, constraints, and objectives of your marketing domain before deciding on the level of originality or usefulness needed.
- Selecting the proper process for the desired outcome: Select the appropriate idea generation process based on the type of innovation sought, such as fluency for a wide range of ideas, persistence for incremental innovations, or flexibility for radical innovations.

Organizational Behavior **111**

- Allocating individual resources to the task: Recruit creative and motivated individuals, enhance the creative performance of existing employees through training or exposure to creative influences, and seek creative input from external sources.
- Tackling creative tasks with teams: Assemble teams with domain expertise for in-depth exploration or diverse backgrounds to generate a large number or diverse ideas.
- Choosing creativity-enhancing practices and tools: Offer creativity training, provide domain-specific training where necessary, use extrinsic motivation, and employ input constraints to stimulate deeper exploration.
- Adopting the best management style: Foster a supportive and empowering style that encourages risk-taking, tolerates failure, and provides developmental feedback.
- Selecting the right IT-enabled tools: Utilize creativity support systems with knowledge activation and idea production support.
- Assessing the outcome(s) of the creative task: Evaluate generated ideas with domain experts or target consumers, pilot test the best ideas, assess the effectiveness of creativity-enhancing techniques, and document the results of implemented ideas.

4.7.2 Managing Change and Innovation

Organizational changes are significant modifications or transformations implemented within an organization.[46] These can cover various aspects of the organization, such as its structure, processes, culture, strategies, systems, or technologies. Organizational changes are driven by internal or external factors that necessitate adaptation and improvement. Organizational changes are complex and require effective change management strategies to minimize resistance and maximize the benefits of the change.

Organizational changes often need someone to act as a catalyst and take responsibility for managing the change process—a change agent.[47]

Change agents can come from various organizational positions and need not necessarily be managers. Implementing change may include modifying structural components such as reporting relationships, coordination mechanisms, employee empowerment, and job redesigns.

Changes in technology pertain to alterations in work processes or the tools and techniques utilized. Importantly, changing individuals and groups requires transformations in attitudes, expectations, perceptions, and behaviors.

Organizational culture—which consists of shared values—tends to be relatively stable and resistant to change. To successfully drive change, the organization should focus on building change capability, ensuring managers understand their role, and involving individual employees. Managers can contribute to this by serving as positive role models; creating new narratives, symbols, and rituals; selecting, promoting, and supporting employees who embrace the new values; redesigning socialization processes; modifying the reward system; setting clear expectations; challenging existing subcultures; and encouraging employee participation.

Stress arises when individuals face excessive pressure from demanding situations, constraints, or opportunities.[48] To help employees cope with stress, managers can address job-related factors by ensuring employees' abilities align with job requirements, improving organizational communication, implementing performance planning programs, and redesigning jobs. Addressing personal stress factors may be more challenging,

112 The Fundamentals of Management

but managers can offer employee counseling, promote time management practices, and provide wellness programs.

4.7.3 Managing Global Teams

When it comes to managing global teams, unique challenges arise due to the diverse resources group members possess—in particular as a result of their cultural backgrounds.[49] Global teams often comprise individuals from different countries or regions, with different perspectives, values, and communication styles. Effectively leveraging this diversity while maintaining cohesion can be complex for managers.

Group structure in a global team context also presents specific challenges. Conformity to norms and expectations can vary across cultures, requiring sensitivity and adaptability to ensure everyone feels included and valued. Cultural hierarchies and power systems may influence team status dynamics.

Effective communication becomes even more critical. Cultural differences in communication styles, language barriers, and varying time zones can hinder information sharing, understanding, and coordination. Managers must facilitate open and inclusive communication channels, encourage active listening, and foster an environment in which diverse perspectives are valued and respected.

Conflict management is another essential process in global teams, especially in the case of virtual global teams.[50] Cultural differences can lead to misunderstandings, disagreements, and conflicts. Managers must possess intercultural competence and employ conflict resolution strategies that promote constructive dialog, mutual understanding, and finding common ground.

Understanding the informal connections and relationships within global teams is also vital. Informal networks and social relationships can significantly influence team dynamics, communication patterns, and the flow of information. Managers should recognize and leverage these informal connections to foster collaboration, knowledge sharing, and effective teamwork.

Managing global teams involves paying attention to the diverse resources of group members, addressing cultural differences, navigating group structure challenges, promoting effective communication, managing conflicts constructively, and adopting a coaching role as a manager.

4.7.4 Managing Diversity

Diversity has become one of the most widely discussed subjects in the business world in recent decades,[51] alongside other key business topics like quality, leadership, and ethics. Despite its prevalence, diversity remains a contentious and often misunderstood issue. Diversity has significant importance in modern workplaces.

Figure 4.8 illustrates various types of workplace diversity.

Despite the benefits of workforce diversity for organizations, managers still face challenges in creating accommodating and safe work environments for diverse employees.

For example, "bias" is a term that describes a tendency or preference toward a particular perspective. Our personal biases result in preconceived notions about individuals or things. Prejudice—a product of our biases—involves preconceived beliefs, opinions, or judgments

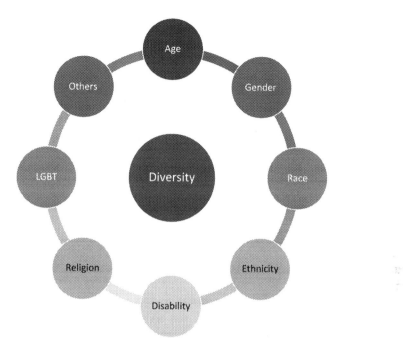

FIGURE 4.8 Diversity in Organization.

toward individuals or groups. Prejudice can stem from various forms of diversity, including race, gender, ethnicity, age, disability, religion, and other personal characteristics.

Stereotyping plays a significant role in fostering prejudice, as it involves judging individuals based on perceived group characteristics. Both prejudice and stereotyping can lead to unequal treatment of individuals belonging to specific groups, known as "discrimination."

Discrimination, regardless of intention, can result in detrimental consequences for employers. The ramifications extend beyond potential financial implications, including reduced employee productivity, disruptive conflicts, increased turnover, and a negative work environment. Therefore, it is crucial for managers to proactively address and eliminate unfair discrimination, even if the organization has never faced an employment discrimination lawsuit.

One form of discrimination in organizations is the gender gap.[52] The term "glass ceiling," first used in a *Wall Street Journal* article in 1986, refers to the invisible barrier that separates women (and other minorities) from top management positions.[53] Studies investigating the glass ceiling phenomenon have revealed the organizational practices and biases that hinder women's progress in advancing their careers. These studies have identified various factors, such as the absence of mentorship opportunities, pervasive gender stereotypes, the perception that leadership effectiveness aligns with masculine traits, and supervisors' perceptions of conflicts between family and work responsibilities.

To address these challenges, organizations have implemented initiatives to manage workplace diversity effectively. These encompass several key elements, including the commitment of top management to promoting diversity; the establishment of mentoring

114 The Fundamentals of Management

programs in which experienced members guide less-experienced individuals; diversity skills training to enhance understanding and inclusion; and the creation of employee resource groups that bring together employees who share common dimensions of diversity, fostering support and collaboration within the organization.

Managing diversity is particularly vital for media and entertainment companies. Media and entertainment companies must create content that resonates with a diverse audience. Having a diverse workforce will help them create content that reflects the diversity of their audience and avoid unintentionally perpetuating stereotypes or excluding certain groups. Moreover, diverse teams can bring various perspectives and experiences, leading to more significant innovation and creativity. This can help companies stay ahead of the curve and produce content that is engaging and impactful.

4.7.5 Managing Social Responsibility

"Social obligation" refers to actions taken by a company based on its responsibility to meet specific economic and legal requirements. Under this approach, the organization fulfills its obligations but does not go beyond that. This concept is considered the classical perspective of social responsibility.[54]

Social responsibility is the intention of a business to go beyond its legal and economic duties and act in ways that are morally right and beneficial for society.[55] A socially responsible business complies with the law. It considers the interests of shareholders but also recognizes an ethical imperative to contribute to the betterment of society and refrain from actions that may harm it.

As managers engage in planning, organizing, leading, and controlling, they must consider ethical dimensions. Ethics are the principles, values, and beliefs guiding decisions and behaviors in determining right and wrong. Many managerial decisions require an evaluation of the decision-making process and the potential impact on those that will be affected by the decision. Managers play a critical role in creating an environment that fosters the adoption of the organization's culture and desired values by employees in their job performance. Research indicates that managers help influence an individual's decision to act ethically or unethically.[56] A strong organizational culture impacts employees' ethical behaviors more than a weak culture. A robust culture that upholds high ethical standards exerts a powerful and positive influence on ethical behavior.

The behavior exhibited by managers has a significant impact on whether employees behave ethically. Ethical leaders are characterized by honesty, transparent communication of values, an emphasis on essential shared values, and fair utilization of the reward system. Managers can effectively address ethical lapses and social irresponsibility by demonstrating strong ethical leadership and protecting employees who raise ethical concerns. Managers can encourage them to come forward and foster a culture in which employees feel comfortable expressing complaints without fearing negative consequences.

Media and entertainment companies have a significant social responsibility to their audiences, employees, and communities:[57]

- Accuracy and truthfulness: Media and entertainment companies are responsible for providing accurate and truthful information to their audiences. This includes verifying sources, fact-checking information, and correcting errors promptly.

- Responsible content: Media and entertainment companies are responsible for creating content that does not promote hate speech, violence, or other harmful messages. They should also consider the potential impact of their content on vulnerable audiences, such as children.
- Diversity and representation: As mentioned, media and entertainment companies are responsible for reflecting the diversity of their audiences and communities. This includes promoting diversity and inclusion in their content and workforce, and avoiding perpetuating stereotypes or discriminatory messaging.
- Data privacy and security: With the increasing reliance on digital media, media and entertainment companies are responsible for protecting the privacy and security of their audiences' data.
- Environmental sustainability: Companies in the MEI are responsible for minimizing their environmental impact by reducing waste, conserving resources, and promoting sustainable practices.[58]

Case Studies

Best Decision-Making in the Media and Entertainment Industry

The Acquisition of Pixar by Disney

In 2006, Disney acquired Pixar Animation Studios for $7.4 billion. This decision has been credited with revitalizing Disney's animation division and helping to create some of the most successful animated films of all time, such as *Toy Story*, *Finding Nemo*, and *The Incredibles*. The acquisition of Pixar also brought key creative talent, such as John Lasseter, to Disney. It helped to consolidate the studio's position as a major player in the MEI.

Apple's Introduction of the iPod

In 2001, Apple introduced the iPod, a portable media player that allowed users to store and play music files. The iPod was a major success and helped to transform the way people consume music. The introduction of the iPod also laid the groundwork for developing the iTunes store, which allowed users to purchase and download music online.

Worst Decision-Making in the Media and Entertainment Industry

AOL's Acquisition of Time Warner

In 2000, AOL acquired Time Warner for $164 billion in the largest merger in history. The merger was intended to create a new media powerhouse that would combine AOL's dominance in the digital space with Time Warner's vast media assets. However, the merger was a disaster, as the two companies could not integrate effectively and struggled to adapt to the changing media landscape. The merger is often cited as one of the worst in history, leading to significant losses for both companies.

116 The Fundamentals of Management

Blockbuster's Failure to Adapt to the Digital Age

In the early 2000s, Blockbuster was the dominant video rental chain in the United States. However, the company failed to adapt to the rise of digital streaming and the decline of physical media. Blockbuster declined to purchase Netflix for $50 million in 2000 and instead attempted to launch its digital rental service, which ultimately failed. Blockbuster filed for bankruptcy in 2010 and was eventually liquidated.

Representative Leaders in the Media and Entertainment Industry

Oprah Winfrey

Oprah Winfrey is a media personality, producer, and philanthropist who has significantly impacted the MEI. She previously hosted *The Oprah Winfrey Show*, the highest-rated talk show in the United States. She is now the chairperson and chief executive officer (CEO) of Harpo Production and the chairperson, CEO, and chief operating officer of the Oprah Winfrey Network. Winfrey has supported charitable causes, including education and empowerment initiatives for women and girls. She is an inspirational leader with high emotional intelligence. Her traits as a great leader also include being resilient, focused, and confident. [59]

Bob Iger

Bob Iger is the former CEO of The Walt Disney Company, one of the world's largest and most successful media and entertainment companies. Under Iger's leadership, Disney acquired several major media properties, including Pixar, Marvel, and Lucasfilm, and launched the successful Disney+ streaming service. Iger is also known for his leadership style, emphasizing collaboration, innovation, and risk-taking.

In his 2019 book *The Ride of a Lifetime: Lessons Learned from 15 Years as CEO of the Walt Disney Company*, Iger broke down 10 core principles of outstanding leadership: optimism, courage, focus, decisiveness, curiosity, fairness, thoughtfulness, authenticity, the relentless pursuit of perfection, and integrity. [60] These 10 principles defined his leadership style, which helped him implement Disney's strategy to improve the company.

Review

- In exploring organizational behavior, we discuss the decision-making process (4.1). It tackles the crucial role that problem identification, alternative evaluation, choice, and implementation play in an organization's survival and success. This process forms the basis of strategic planning and is paramount in today's fast-paced and ever-changing business environment.
- Planning is an essential activity that involves creating and maintaining plans (4.2), utilizing conceptual skills, and evaluating planning capabilities. Dynamic environments require specific yet flexible plans that can be adapted to changing circumstances. The foundation of planning involves defining goals, establishing strategies, and

developing plans for organizational activities. Planning techniques and skills include environmental scanning, forecasting, benchmarking, budgeting, and scheduling.

- The organizational structure encompasses various key elements that shape an organization's operations (4.3). Traditional organizational designs include simple, functional, and divisional structures; while adaptive designs include team, matrix, and project structures. Effective human resource management is essential for competitive advantage, strategic alignment, and employee satisfaction. The formation and management of teams involve stages of development, external conditions, member resources, group structure, processes, and tasks.
- Leaders influence and guide others toward achieving group or organizational goals (4.4). Traits associated with effective leadership include self-confidence, determination, integrity, effective communication, adaptability, and the ability to inspire and motivate others. Good leaders possess vision, strategic thinking, communication skills, empathy, adaptability, accountability, and a commitment to continuous learning.
- Control involves assessing whether organizational objectives are being met and taking corrective actions; while coordination integrates organizational activities to achieve common goals, fostering teamwork and innovation (4.5). Control and coordination are interrelated, with effective control relying on effective coordination.
- Organizational communication is the transfer and understanding of meaning within an organization (4.6). Effective communication is crucial for managing employee behavior, providing information, motivating employees, and fulfilling social needs. Businesses should promote effective communication by creating a communication plan, using multiple channels, encouraging two-way communication, providing training, fostering transparency, sharing timely and relevant information, and utilizing technology.
- New themes of organizational behavior include the management of creativity, change and innovation, global teams, diversity, and social responsibility (4.7). The management of creativity involves fostering original and useful ideas. Change and innovation can be managed by addressing people, structure, and technology changes. The management of global teams involves leveraging diverse perspectives and addressing communication challenges and conflicts. Overcoming personal biases, promoting inclusivity, and improving ethical considerations are the main components of managing diversity and social responsibility.

Discussion Questions

1 Discuss the role of the organizational decision-making process in the survival and success of media and entertainment companies. How can these companies ensure effective decision-making in a fast-paced and ever-changing industry?

2 How does an organization's structure influence its culture, decision-making process, and overall functioning? How can managers effectively navigate these dynamics?

3 Discuss the respected business leaders in the MEI. What makes them distinguishable from others?

4 Discuss the relationship between control and coordination in business and management. What practices can companies in the MEI implement to balance them?

118 The Fundamentals of Management

5 What unique challenges are faced in managing global teams, particularly within the MEI? How can these challenges be addressed to promote effective teamwork and collaboration?

6 Discuss the importance of diversity, ethics, and social responsibility within organizations, particularly in the MEI. How can these aspects influence a company's business?

Further Reading

- Greenwood, R. C. (1981) "Management by objectives: As developed by Peter Drucker, assisted by Harold Smiddy." *Academy of Management Review*, 6(2), pp. 225–230.
- Iger, R. (2019) *The ride of a lifetime: Lessons learned from 15 years as CEO of the Walt Disney Company*. New York: Random House.
- Kirton, G. and Greene, A. M. (2021) *The dynamics of managing diversity and inclusion: A critical approach.* London: Routledge.
- Luecke, R., (2003) "Harvard Business Essentials: managing creativity and innovation." Cambridge, MA: Harvard Business Press.
- Miller, K. and Barbour, J. (2014) *Organizational communication: Approaches and processes.* Singapore: Cengage Learning.
- Simons, R. (1995) "Control in an age of empowerment." *Harvard Business Review*, 73(2), pp. 80–88.
- Vogel, D. J. (2005) "Is there a market for virtue? The business case for corporate social responsibility." *California Management Review*, 47(4), pp.19–45.

References

1 Juneja, P. (no date) "Decision making in an organizational context." *MSG Management Study Guide*. www.managementstudyguide.com/decision-making-in-organizational-context.htm.

2 Bright, D. S. et al. (2019) *Principles of management.* Houston, TX: OpenStax, Rice University. https://openstax.org/books/principles-management/pages/2-1-overview-of-managerial-decision-making.

3 "Information asymmetry" refers to a situation where one party in a business transaction possesses a greater amount of information than the other. This disparity in access to relevant and current information can lead to imbalances in business negotiations.

4 Dutta, N. (2015) "Managerial decision making process (5 steps)." *Economics Discussion*. www.economicsdiscussion.net/decision-making/managerial-decision-making-process-5-steps/6099.

5 Armstrong, J. S. (1982) "The value of formal planning for strategic decisions: Review of empirical research." *Strategic Management Journal*, 3(3), pp.197–211.

6 Greenwood, R. C. (1981) "Management by objectives: As developed by Peter Drucker, assisted by Harold Smiddy." *Academy of Management Review*, 6(2), pp. 225–230.

7 Rodgers, R. and Hunter, J. E. (1991) "Impact of management by objectives on organizational productivity." *Journal of Applied Psychology*, 76(2), pp. 322–336.

8 "Planning techniques" (no date) *Université Larbi Ben M'hidi Oum El Bouaghi*. http://tele-ens.univ-oeb.dz/moodle/pluginfile.php/298850/mod_resource/content/2/Planning%20Techniques.pdf.

9 "Basics of environmental scanning" (no date) *SHRM*. www.shrm.org/resourcesandtools/tools-and-samples/hr-qa/pages/basics-of-environmental-scanning.aspx.

10 Yasai-Ardekani, M. and Nystrom, P. C. (1996) "Designs for environmental scanning systems: Tests of a contingency theory." *Management Science*, 42(2), pp. 187–204.

11 Walton, A. (2022) "8 reasons why competitive intelligence is important." *Competitive Intelligence Alliance.* www.competitiveintelligencealliance.io/why-is-competitive-intelligence-important/ (Accessed: 29 January 2023).

12 Kobrin, S. J. (1991) "An empirical analysis of the determinants of global integration." *Strategic Management Journal*, 12(S1), pp. 17–31.

13 Hennigan, L. and Bottoeff, C. (2022) "PERT Chart Vs. Gantt Chart: Which System is Best for Project Management?" *Forbes*, 4 July. www.forbes.com/advisor/business/pert-chart-vs-gantt-chart/.

14 "Global Innovative Leadership Module: Business Management and Organization" (2015) *Erasmus+*. https://ec.europa.eu/programmes/erasmus-plus/project-result-content/9a1c8bee-11f3-48f0-8e25-c86b14cf445a/Business%20Management%20And%20Organization%20Booklet.pdf.

15 Mackenzie, K. D. (1988) "Designing the adaptive organization." In R. J. Niehaus and K. F. Price (eds.) *Creating the competitive edge through human resource applications.* Boston, MA: Springer, pp. 63–64. https://link.springer.com/chapter/10.1007/978-1-4613-0969-7_6.

16 Tung, L. L. and Turban, E. (1996) "Information technology as an enabler of telecommuting." *International Journal of Information Management*, 16(2), pp. 103–117.

17 Gonsalves, L. (2020) "From face time to flex time: The role of physical space in worker temporal flexibility." *Administrative Science Quarterly*, 65(4), pp. 1058–1091.

18 Barney, J. B. and Wright, P. M. (1998) "On becoming a strategic partner: The role of human resources in gaining competitive advantage." *Human Resource Management*, 37(1), pp. 31–46.

19 Wright, P. M. and McMahan, G. C. (1992) "Theoretical perspectives for strategic human resource management." *Journal of Management*, 18(2), pp. 295–320.

20 Delery, J. E. and Doty, D. H. (1996) "Modes of theorizing in strategic human resource management: Tests of universalistic, contingency, and configurations. Performance predictions." *Academy of Management Journal*, 39(4), pp. 802–835.

21 Harter, J. K., Schmidt, F. L. and Hayes, T. L. (2002) "Business-unit-level relationship between employee satisfaction, employee engagement, and business outcomes: A meta-analysis." *Journal of Applied Psychology*, 87(2), pp. 268–279.

22 Tuckman, B. W. and Jensen, M. A. (1977) "Stages of small-group development revisited'." *Group & Organization Studies*, 2(4), pp. 419–427.

23 Robbins, S. P., Judge, T. A. and Vohra, N. (2019) *Organizational behavior.* 18th edn. Harlow, UK: Pearson.

24 Yukl, G. (2008) "How leaders influence organizational effectiveness." *The Leadership Quarterly*, 19(6), pp. 708–722.

25 Northouse, P. G. (2021) *Leadership: Theory and practice.* 9th edn. Los Angeles, CA: SAGE Publishing.

26 Yukl, G. (2008) "How leaders influence organizational effectiveness." *The Leadership Quarterly*, 19(6), pp. 708–722.

27 "The 10 characteristics of a good leader" (2023) *Center for Creative Leadership.* www.ccl.org/articles/leading-effectively-articles/characteristics-good-leader/.

28 Uță, I.-C. (2021) "Fiedler's contingency model of leadership explained." *BRAND MINDS.* https://brandminds.com/fiedlers-contingency-model-of-leadership-explained/.

29 Cairns, T. D. et al. (1998) "Technical note: A study of Hersey and Blanchard's situational leadership theory." *Leadership & Organization Development Journal*, 19(2), pp. 113–116.

30 "House's path goal theory" (no date) *MSG Management Study Guide.* www.managementstudyguide.com/houses-path-goal-theory.htm.

31 Simons, R. (1995) "Control in an age of empowerment." *Harvard Business Review*, 73(2), pp. 80–88.

32 Simons, R. (1995) 'Control in an age of empowerment." *Harvard Business Review*, 73(2), pp. 80–88.

33 Kanter, R. M. and Brinkerhoff, D. (1981) "Organizational performance: Recent developments in measurement." *Annual Review of Sociology*, 7(1), pp. 321–349.

34 Kaplan, R. S. and Norton, D. P. (1992) "The balanced scorecard: Measures that drive performance." *Harvard Business Review*, 70(1), pp. 71-79. https://hbr.org/1992/01/the-balanced-scorecard-measures-that-drive-performance-2.

35 Hawes, L. C. (1973) "Elements of a model for communication processes." *Quarterly Journal of Speech*, 59(1), pp. 11–21.

36 Eisenberg, E. M. and Witten, M. G. (1987) "Reconsidering openness in organizational communication." *Academy of Management Review*, 12(3), pp. 418–426.

37 Weick, K. E. and Browning, L. D. (1986) "Argument and narration in organizational communication." *Journal of Management*, 12(2), pp. 243–259.

120 The Fundamentals of Management

38 Goldhaber, G. M., Porter, D. T., Yates, M. P. and Lesniak, R. (1978) "Organizational communication." *Human Communication Research*, 5(1), pp. 76–96.

39 Johnson, J. D., Donohue, W. A., Atkin, C. K. and Johnson, S. (1994) "Differences between formal and informal communication channels." *Journal of Business Communication*, 31(2), pp. 111–122.

40 Smollan, R. K. and Morrison, R. L. (2019) "Office design and organizational change: The influence of communication and organizational culture." *Journal of Organizational Change Management*, 32(4), pp. 426–440.

41 Amed, A. (2019) "Types of organizational communication." *Bizfluent*. https://bizfluent.com/list-7613677-types-organizational-communication.html.

42 Eliadis, A. (2020) "The five elements of effective organizational communication." *Forbes*, 14 April. www.forbes.com/sites/forbescoachescouncil/2020/04/14/the-five-elements-of-effective-organizational-communication/.

43 IEDP Editorial (2017) "Managing creativity in organizations." *IEDP*. www.iedp.com/articles/managing-creativity-in-organizations/.

44 Wierenga, B. and Althuizen, N. (2017) "Managing the supply and demand of creativity." *RSM Discovery Magazine*, 27 November. https://discovery.rsm.nl/articles/319-managing-the-supply-and-demand-of-creativity/.

45 Wierenga, B. and Althuizen, N. (2017) "Managing the supply and demand of creativity." *RSM Discovery Magazine*, 27 November. https://discovery.rsm.nl/articles/319-managing-the-supply-and-demand-of-creativity/.

46 Nadler, D. A. and Tushman, M. L. (1990) "Beyond the charismatic leader: Leadership and organizational change." *California Management Review*, 32(2), pp. 77–97.

47 Ottaway, R. N. (1983) "The change agent: A taxonomy in relation to the change process." *Human Relations*, 36(4), pp. 361–392.

48 Dahl, M. S. (2011) "Organizational change and employee stress." *Management Science*, 57(2), pp. 240–256.

49 Bouncken, R., Brem, A. and Kraus, S. (2016) "Multi-cultural teams as sources for creativity and innovation: The role of cultural diversity on team performance." *International Journal of Innovation Management*, 20(1), p. 1650012.

50 Montoya-Weiss, M. M., Massey, A. P. and Song, M. (2001) "Getting it together: Temporal coordination and conflict management in global virtual teams." *Academy of Management Journal*, 44(6), pp. 1251–1262.

51 Gilbert, J. A., Stead, B. A. and Ivancevich, J. M., (1999) "Diversity management: A new organizational paradigm." *Journal of Business Ethics*, 21(1), pp. 61–76.

52 Wright, E. O., Baxter, J. and Birkelund, G. E. (1995). "The gender gap in workplace authority." *American Sociological Review*, 60(3), pp. 407–435.

53 Zimmer, B. (2015) "The phrase 'glass ceiling' stretches back decades." *Wall Street Journal*. www.wsj.com/articles/the-phrase-glass-ceiling-stretches-back-decades-1428089010.

54 Davis, K. (1973). "The case for and against business assumption of social responsibilities." *Academy of Management Journal*, 16(2), pp. 312–322.

55 Vogel, D. J. (2005). "Is there a market for virtue? The business case for corporate social responsibility." *California Management Review*, 47(4), pp. 19–45.

56 Reiss, M. C. and Mitra, K. (1998). "The effects of individual difference factors on the acceptability of ethical and unethical workplace behaviors." *Journal of Business Ethics*, 17(14), pp. 1581–1593.

57 "Media and entertainment: Achieving a more sustainable, inclusive media and entertainment industry" (no date) *BSR*. www.bsr.org/en/topics/media-and-entertainment.

58 "Tackling 'ESG' in the media and entertainment industry" (2022) *PwC*. www.pwc.com.au/industry/entertainment-and-media-trends-analysis/esg-trends.html.

59 Sattar, S. B. (2021) "Leadership qualities: Styles, traits and skills of Oprah Winfrey." *The Strategy Watch*. www.thestrategywatch.com/leadership-oprah-winfrey/.

60 Denning, S. (2019) "Ten leadership lessons from Disney's Bob Iger." *Forbes*, 28 December. www.forbes.com/sites/stephaniedenning/2019/12/28/ten-leadership-lessons-from-disneys-bob-iger/?sh=1e10cdea26fc.

5

STRATEGIC MANAGEMENT IN THE MEDIA AND ENTERTAINMENT INDUSTRY

Outline

Overview	121
5.1 The Concept of Strategic Management	122
5.2 Vision and Goals	126
5.3 External/Internal Analysis	129
5.4 Business vs. Corporate Strategy: Overview	137
5.5 Business Strategy	139
5.6 Corporate Strategy	146
5.7 New Strategic Management Components	150
Case Studies	153
Review	154
Discussion Questions	155
Further Reading	155
References	156

Intended Learning Outcomes

- Identify the concepts and frameworks of strategic management and the core strategic management activities of an organization.
- Explain the concept and framework of business and corporate strategy.
- Compare different approaches to business and corporate strategy.
- Apply the knowledge to analyze an organization's strategy formulation and implementation.

Lost Boy: "Let's go get 'em!"
John Darling: "Hold on a minute. First we must have a strategy."
Lost Boy: "Uhh? What's a strategy?"
John Darling: "It's er … It's a plan of attack."

—Walt Disney's Peter Pan

DOI: 10.4324/9781003271222-7

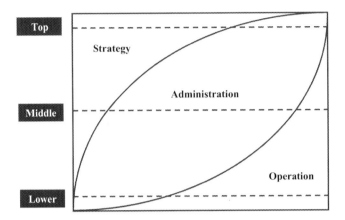

FIGURE 5.1 Management Activities by Different Levels.

Overview

The main components of strategic management are discussed in this chapter, as follows (Figure 5.1):

- Corporate vision and goals: Defining the organization's overall purpose, mission, and long-term goals.
- External analysis: Assessing the external environment (e.g., market trends, competition, and regulatory factors that may impact the organization).
- Internal analysis: Evaluating the organization's strengths and weaknesses (e.g., resources and capabilities).
- Business strategy: Developing specific strategies for each business unit or product line based on three generic strategic approaches: cost leadership, differentiation, and focus strategy.
- Corporate strategy: Determining the overall direction and scope of the organization, including its portfolio of businesses and its approach to growth (e.g., related diversification or unrelated diversification).
- Corporate governance: Establishing the organizational structure and processes to ensure effective decision-making and oversight (e.g., the role of the board of directors and other governance mechanisms).
- Non-market strategy: Developing strategies to manage the organization's relationships with stakeholders outside the market.
- Strategy implementation: Executing the strategy and translating it into action (e.g., setting objectives, allocating resources, and monitoring progress).

5.1 The Concept of Strategic Management

Why do individuals or organizations fail? Failures are often caused by insufficient effort or unexpected negative events. But working hard may produce the very same outcome

FIGURE 5.2 Strategic Management Process.

when it comes to strategic thinking. Examples of the lack of strategic thinking include the following:

- No thought on interrelationships among works: No integrative approach.
- No thought on the sequence of works: No systematic perspective.
- No thought on what is important: No prioritization.
- No thought on the future: No long-term plan.

Without strategic thinking, an organization cannot expect to win the competition. Recognizing the significance of strategic thinking within an organizational context, managers engage in strategic management to formulate the organization's strategies. These strategies constitute the approach through which the organization can fulfill its business objectives, compete successfully, and attract and satisfy customers.

In a nutshell, strategy involves the determination of an enterprise's long-term goals, the adoption of courses of action, and the allocation of the necessary resources to achieve those goals.[1] Strategic management calls for an integrated perspective and is undertaken by the organization's top management. The starting point is an acknowledgement that competition is ubiquitous and that businesses must be strategic in order to survive.

A company's competitive advantage—in other words, what sets it apart from the pack—is crucial to strategic management. It serves as the basis for choosing an appropriate competitive strategy.

Key management activities include strategy, administration, and operation. Management activities are conducted through different hierarchies. The top management team primarily undertakes strategic management, while administration and operation management are covered by middle- and lower-level management teams (Figure 5.2).

Strategic management is vital for three reasons:

- It makes a difference in how thriving organizations perform. Through the systematic and deliberate implementation of strategic management practices, organizations are better positioned to achieve their objectives, outperform their competitors, and secure sustainable growth.
- It is crucial to help managers cope with continually changing situations. Through the strategic management process, managers gain the necessary insights, tools, and frameworks to analyze and interpret these changing situations, enabling them to identify opportunities, anticipate threats, and adapt their strategies accordingly.
- Finally, it helps coordinate and focus employee efforts on what is important. This coordination ensures that individual efforts are aligned with broader organizational goals and promotes a sense of shared purpose, enhancing employee engagement and motivation.

124 The Fundamentals of Management

5.1.1 Development of Strategic Management Theory

There are four phases in the evolution of formal strategic planning:[2]

- Basic financial planning (meet budget): In the early stages of formal strategic planning, organizations focus primarily on budgeting and financial planning. This approach to planning is largely reactive, with organizations responding to changes in the external environment as they occur. The goal is to meet budget targets and ensure the organization remains financially stable.
- Forecast-based planning (predict the future): In the next phase, organizations begin to use forecasting techniques to predict future trends and developments. This allows them to be more proactive in planning and anticipate external environment changes. Forecast-based planning involves analyzing historical data, identifying trends, and using that information to make predictions.
- Externally oriented planning (think strategically): In this phase, organizations think more strategically about their future. They recognize the need to look beyond their internal operations and consider the broader external environment. This involves analyzing the competitive landscape, identifying emerging trends, and assessing the organization's strengths and weaknesses relative to its competitors. Externally oriented planning involves engaging with stakeholders and considering the broader community's interests.
- Strategic management (create the future): In the final phase, formal strategic planning becomes a core part of strategic management. Organizations develop a clear and comprehensive strategic plan that guides all aspects of their operations. This involves aligning the organization's activities with its strategic goals and objectives, and continuously monitoring progress to ensure the organization remains on track. Strategic management also involves being flexible and adaptable, able to adjust the plan as circumstances change and new opportunities emerge.

In the third phase (i.e., externally oriented planning), the concept of strategic business units (SBUs) is introduced. An SBU is a self-contained division or unit within an organization that operates as a distinct business entity with its own unique mission, goals, and strategies.[3] An SBU is typically managed as a separate business with its own resources, processes, and operations, and is often responsible for a particular product or service line.

An SBU typically has its own set of objectives and targets and is responsible for its budget and financial performance. It operates independently of other SBUs within the same organization, although there may be some degree of coordination and sharing of resources between units.

To be considered an SBU, a business unit should meet specific criteria, such as having a clearly defined product or service offering, a distinct customer base, and a unique competitive position in the market. SBUs are typically evaluated on their ability to generate revenue, profitability, and return on investment; and are expected to contribute to the overall performance of the organization.

While business-unit decisions affect only the individual SBU, corporate decisions affect the shape and direction of the whole enterprise.

The key point is to link strategic planning to operational decision-making. A "planning framework" refers to the practice of cutting across organizational boundaries and facilitating strategic decision-making for the whole organization. Throughout the planning process, top managers are expected to stimulate entrepreneurial thinking to create a future in which the organization can outperform its competitors. Finally, a corporate value system will reinforce the commitment to the strategy.

5.1.2 The Strategic Management Process

Strategic management is a multi-step approach encompassing strategy planning, implementation, and evaluation.

There are six steps in the strategic management process (Figure 5.3):

- Decide the corporate vision and primary goals: This initial step involves establishing a clear and compelling corporate vision that defines the desired future and purpose of the organization. Alongside this vision, primary goals are formulated, outlining the specific objectives that the organization is aiming to achieve. This step sets the direction and provides a framework for subsequent strategic decisions.

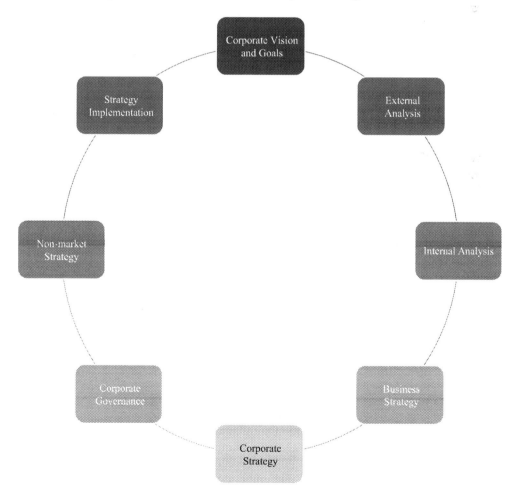

FIGURE 5.3 Components of Strategic Management.

126 The Fundamentals of Management

- Analyze the external competitive environment to identify opportunities and threats: In this phase, organizations conduct a comprehensive analysis of the external factors that impact their operations. This entails identifying opportunities, which are favorable external conditions that can be capitalized upon; and threats, which are external factors that pose challenges or risks to the organization.
- Analyze the organization's internal condition to identify its strengths and weaknesses: This step involves a thorough assessment of the organization's internal strengths and weaknesses. By evaluating its resources, capabilities, and core competencies, managers can identify areas of competitive advantage and areas that require improvement.
- Generate strategic alternatives: Building on the understanding of the external and internal environment, this phase focuses on generating a range of strategic alternatives. These alternatives represent different courses of action that the organization can pursue to achieve its goals and capitalize on the identified opportunities.
- Select strategies (strategy formulation): In this stage, the organization evaluates the strategic alternatives and selects the most promising ones to pursue. The company assesses each option's feasibility, its potential impact on competitiveness, its alignment with the corporate vision and goals, and the resources and capabilities needed to pursue it. The selected strategies serve as a blueprint for the company's future direction and guide subsequent decision-making.
- Implement the strategy: This is the critical phase in which the chosen strategies are translated into action. The main activities in this step include allocating resources, setting specific objectives, establishing timelines, and designing the necessary organizational structures and processes to execute the strategy.

5.2 Vision and Goals

5.2.1 Corporate Vision

The corporate vision is a clear, compelling statement of the company's aspirations and its unique purpose.[4a] It sets boundaries for the scope of the company's activities.

Companies need vision to:

- provide direction and purpose to the organization;
- guide the development of strategies and the whole organization and teams; and
- energize and inspire people to action.

First, a clear vision serves as a guiding star that sets the course for the organization. It provides a sense of direction, offering a long-term perspective on where the company aims to go and what it aspires to achieve. A well-crafted vision helps leaders and employees make informed decisions, prioritize initiatives, and stay focused on activities that contribute to the realization of the vision.

Second, a strong vision influences the development of strategies and shapes the organization's growth trajectory. It serves as a strategic anchor, informing the formulation of goals, objectives, and action plans. A well-aligned vision ensures that strategic choices are harmonized with the organization's purpose, enhancing the chances of success and sustainable growth.

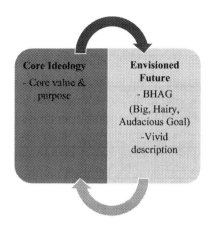

FIGURE 5.4 Articulating a Vision.

Finally, a compelling vision can ignite enthusiasm, passion, and commitment among employees. It creates a sense of purpose and meaning, fostering a shared identity and a collective sense of belonging. A vision that resonates with employees' values and aspirations fosters a positive and engaging work culture, helping to attract and retain top talent.

To articulate a vision, a core ideology and an envisioned future are key components (Figure 5.4)[4b]. The core values and purpose of a company formulate the core ideology.

The core values represent the fundamental principles and beliefs that guide the organization's behavior and decision-making. These values embody the organization's identity and serve as a compass for its actions. For example, Disney's core values of creativity, dreams, and imagination reflect its commitment to fostering a culture of innovation, storytelling, and magical experiences.

The core purpose defines the reason for the organization's existence beyond financial considerations. It captures the essence of the organization's mission and outlines the impact it aims to have on society. For example, 3 M's core purpose is to solve unsolved problems innovatively, emphasizing its commitment to addressing challenges through inventive solutions.

5.2.2 Goals

An organization's envisioned future can be presented in the form of "big, hairy, audacious goals" (BHAGs). This concept—coined by Jim Collins and Jerry Porras in their book *Built to Last: Successful Habits of Visionary Companies*[5]—encapsulates a vivid description of the desired outcome that a company is seeking to realize.

Examples of BHAGs include the following:

- Ford (1900s): Democratize the automobile.
- Stanford University (1940s): Become the Harvard of the West.
- Nike (1960s): Crush Adidas.

In strategic management, goals provide a clear sense of direction and purpose for an organization. They also provide a basis for measuring and evaluating progress and the success of the strategy. Goals inspire and motivate employees within the company and assist in prioritizing activities and allocating resources. Finally, goals help facilitate effective communication and alignment across different levels and functions in the company.

Given these purposes of setting goals, good goals should have the following characteristics:

- Be precise and measurable: A good goal should be specific and well defined so that progress can be tracked and measured over time. It should help ensure accountability and allow for adjustments to be made if necessary.
- Address important issues: A good goal should be aligned with the organization's overall mission and strategic objectives and address essential issues or opportunities relevant to the organization's stakeholders.
- Be challenging but realistic: A good goal should be challenging enough to motivate individuals or teams to work toward achieving it but not so difficult that it is unattainable. Goals that are too easy may not be motivating, while goals that are too difficult may be demotivating.
- Be time specified: A good goal should have a clear timeline or deadline. This helps ensure that progress is being made toward the goal and that resources are allocated appropriately. It is also important to balance short-term and long-term goals, as both are necessary for sustainable success.

Alternatively, SMART goals have the following characteristics that help companies focus and evaluate goals as needed (Figure 5.5):[6]

- Specific: Specific goals are those that have a well-defined desired outcome, ensuring a clear understanding of what is to be achieved. Whether a goal pertains to a sales target or a product launch objective, it should be articulated in a manner that aligns with everyone's understanding and objectives.
- Measurable: Measurable goals are characterized by their quantifiable nature. It is important to establish a means of tracking progress by defining the specific metrics or data that will be used to measure the goal.
- Achievable: Goals should be realistic to maintain motivation and enthusiasm toward their attainment. While it is beneficial to set ambitious goals, breaking them down into smaller, more manageable targets can help ensure their achievability.

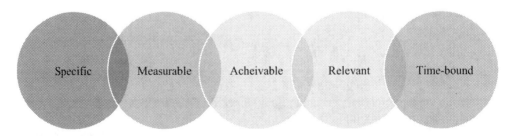

FIGURE 5.5 SMART Goals.

- Relevant: Goals should be directly aligned with the mission and objectives of the company. It is essential to establish the relevance of a goal, ensuring that it contributes meaningfully to the overall purpose and strategy of the organization.
- Time-bound: Setting a deadline for goals is crucial to establish a sense of urgency and enable effective evaluation of success or failure. A goal without a specified timeframe lacks a clear benchmark for measuring progress. Although the deadline marks an evaluation point, it does not imply that all work will be completed; rather, it serves as a milestone to assess progress and set new goals accordingly.

5.3 External/Internal Analysis

5.3.1 Role of Analysis

Analysis is helpful in various respects:

- It facilitates evidence-based decision-making by providing relevant data, information, and insights to decision-makers, enabling them to make informed choices.
- It enables the identification of patterns, trends, and correlations within data, allowing for predictive modeling and forecasting. This can aid in proactive decision-making and help mitigate potential risks.
- Through analysis, decision-makers can gain a comprehensive understanding of the strengths, weaknesses, opportunities, and threats (SWOT) associated with a particular situation or problem. This knowledge can inform strategic planning and resource allocation.
- It promotes effective resource utilization by identifying inefficiencies, redundancies, and areas for improvement. By optimizing processes and operations, organizations can increase productivity and reduce costs.
- It supports effective risk management by assessing and evaluating potential risks and their potential impact. By analyzing risk factors, decision-makers can implement risk mitigation strategies and contingency plans to safeguard the organization's interests.
- It fosters innovation by uncovering insights and trends that can lead to the development of new products, services, or business models. By analyzing emerging market trends and customer preferences, organizations can stay ahead of the competition and adapt their strategies accordingly.
- It improves transparency and accountability by providing a factual basis for decision-making. It allows decision-makers to justify their choices based on objective data and analysis, enhancing trust and credibility among stakeholders.
- It facilitates effective communication and collaboration among team members and stakeholders by providing a common language and framework for discussing complex issues. Through analysis, diverse perspectives can be integrated, leading to more inclusive and well-rounded decision-making processes.

There is a Chinese saying: "If you know your enemies and know yourself, you will not be imperiled in a hundred battles."

Business guru Gary Hamel once said: "Developing a sound and healthy organization requires understanding the environment as much as understanding the organization."

Charles Darwin argued: "It is not the strongest of the species that survives, nor the most intelligent, but the most responsive to change."

The common thread in the three quotes above is the importance of understanding external (e.g., enemies, environment, change) and internal (e.g., yourself, organization, responsive) aspects. When conducting analysis, both external and internal analysis should be considered.

5.3.2 External Analysis

On the one hand, external analysis aims to analyze the dynamics of the industry in which an organization competes. An organization can understand opportunities and threats around its businesses through external analysis:

- Opportunities: Conditions in the environment that a company can take advantage of to become more profitable.
- Threats: Conditions in the environment that endanger the integrity and profitability of the company's business.

Porter's Five Forces Model

Porter's Five Forces Model (Figure 5.6) is a suitable analysis framework for this purpose.[7] The Five Forces model, developed by Michael E. Porter, serves as a framework for assessing the competitive dynamics within industries. The model is widely used to analyze the competitive intensity, attractiveness and profitability of an industry or market. It examines five key forces that influence an industry, offering valuable insights to enhance a company's long-term profitability. This versatile model can be effectively applied to any industry, enabling a comprehensive understanding of the competitive landscape and aiding in strategic decision-making.

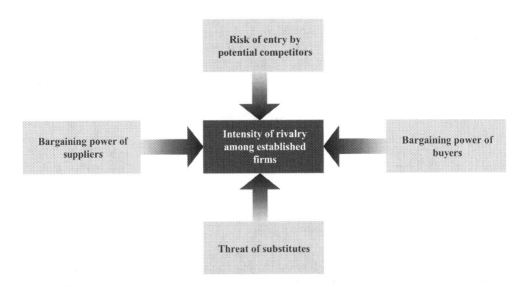

FIGURE 5.6 Porter's Five Forces Model.

The five forces are:

- industry rivalry (competition in the industry);
- threat of entry (potential for new entrants to break into the industry);
- bargaining power of suppliers;
- bargaining power of buyers (or customers); and
- threat of substitutes.

Industry Rivalry

The first force examined in the model pertains to the level of competition within the industry. This factor considers the number of competitors and their ability to offer similar products or services at competitive prices. If there are numerous rivals and a wide range of comparable offerings, this diminishes a company's leverage. Suppliers and buyers are more likely to seek alternative options, resulting in reduced pricing power for the company. Conversely, when competitive rivalry is low, a company gains greater power to set higher prices and dictate favorable terms, leading to increased profits.

Threat of Entry

The potential for new competitors to enter an industry impacts a company's position. The ease with which new entrants can establish themselves as effective competitors, and the associated time and cost factors, influence the strength of established companies. Industries with significant barriers to entry favor existing companies, as they can command higher prices and negotiate more favorable terms due to limited competition.

Bargaining Power of Suppliers

The third element of the model evaluates the influence suppliers hold over a company. It considers the number of suppliers providing essential inputs, the uniqueness of those inputs, and the cost involved in switching to alternative suppliers. When few suppliers are available, a company becomes more dependent on them, granting them more power to increase input costs and gain other advantageous terms. Conversely, a company benefits from a larger pool of suppliers or low switching costs between rival suppliers, allowing for lower input costs and improved profitability.

Bargaining Power of Buyers

The bargaining power of buyers to impact business is another force examined in the model. It is influenced by the number of buyers, the significance of each buyer, and the cost associated with acquiring new buyers or entering new markets. A smaller, more influential buyer base empowers companies to negotiate for lower prices and better deals. In contrast, a supplier dealing with numerous smaller, independent buyers can charge higher prices, leading to increased profitability.

132 The Fundamentals of Management

Threat of Substitutes

The final force focuses on the presence of substitute goods or services that can fulfill the same purpose as a company's offerings. Substitutes pose a threat by potentially diverting customers away from a company's products or services. Companies offering goods or services without close substitutes have greater power to increase prices and secure favorable terms. However, when close substitutes are readily available, customers have the option to forgo a company's offerings, potentially weakening its position.

Porter's Five Forces Model Exercise: The Media and Entertainment Industry

- Industry rivalry: The media and entertainment industry (MEI) is highly competitive, with many players vying for audience attention and spend. The level of competitive rivalry can be affected by factors such as brand recognition, pricing, and the quality and popularity of content.
- Threat of entry: The MEI can be difficult to enter due to the high costs associated with creating and distributing content. However, the rise of digital platforms and the increasing ease of self-publishing have lowered barriers to entry in some sectors of the industry.
- Bargaining power of suppliers: In the MEI, suppliers can include artists, performers, writers, and other content creators. The bargaining power of these suppliers can be high if they are in hot demand, have a unique skill set, or have other bargaining advantages.
- Bargaining power of buyers: The bargaining power of buyers in the MEI can vary depending on the type of content and the distribution channel. For example, buyers of movie tickets may have limited bargaining power due to the high demand for popular films. In contrast, streaming service buyers may have more bargaining power due to the many choices available.
- Threat of substitutes: In the entertainment industry, substitutes can include other forms of media, such as books, music, or videogames. The availability of substitutes can impact demand for specific types of entertainment and may also affect pricing.

Key Success Factors

An expected outcome from the analysis of the Five Forces is identifying key success factors (KSFs) (Figure 5.7). KSFs state the essential elements a company needs to compete in its target markets. In effect, they articulate what the company must do and do well to achieve the goals outlined in its strategic plan. Examples include agility, reliability, diversity, and emotional connection with clients. An analysis of the competition in an industry should answer the questions such as the following:

- What (forces) drive competition?
- What are the main dimensions of competition?
- How intense is the competition?
- How can we secure a superior competitive position?

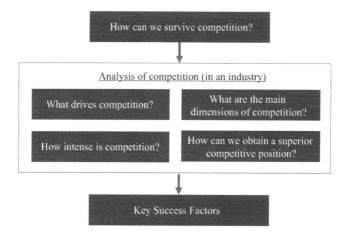

FIGURE 5.7 Identifying Key Success Factors.

Exercise: Key Success Factors in the Media and Entertainment Industry

- Production and sourcing of quality content (e.g., film, drama, music).
- Diverse distribution channels.
- Strong brand power.
- Stable customer base.
- Creative and talented human resources.
- Technological capability.

5.3.3 Internal Analysis

Internal analysis involves identifying the strengths and weaknesses of the company. Managers must understand the following:

- the role of resources, capabilities, and distinctive competencies in the process through which companies create value and profit;
- the importance of superior efficiency, innovation, quality, and responsiveness to customers; and
- the sources of the company's competitive advantage (strengths and weaknesses).

Resources, Capabilities, and Core Competence

On the one hand, resources are capital or financial, physical, social or human, technological, and organizational factor endowments (tangible and intangible). Firm-specific or difficult-to-imitate resources and valuable resources that drive strong demand can be sources of core competence.

134 The Fundamentals of Management

On the other hand, capabilities are a company's skills in coordinating and using its resources, including organizational structure, processes, and control systems. Firm-specific capabilities to manage resources can be a source of core competence.

Core competence is the collective learning in the organization—especially the capacity to coordinate diverse production skills and integrate streams of technologies. To elaborate, "core competence" refers to the unique combination of knowledge, skills, and technologies that an organization has developed over time, which sets it apart from its competitors. Core competence can be complex for competitors to replicate or imitate and can provide a sustainable competitive advantage for the organization.

If a company has specific and valuable resources, it must also be able to use them effectively to create core competence. However, a company can also create core competence without such resources if it has unique capabilities.[8] The following conditions are key to core competence:

- The ability to contribute to value creation: Core competence must be relevant to the organization's business and be able to contribute to the creation of value for customers. This means that core competence should be aligned with the organization's overall strategy and goals.
- Relative superiority to competitors: Core competence should give the organization a competitive advantage. This means that the competence must be better than what competitors possess to create value for customers and outperform competitors.
- Causal ambiguity and uncertain imitability: Core competence should be rare and difficult for competitors to replicate. This can be due to several factors, such as the knowledge being tacit, hard to communicate, or challenging to acquire. In addition, the processes and techniques used to develop the competence may be difficult to imitate. These factors create causal ambiguity and uncertain imitability, making it difficult for competitors to replicate the core competence.
- Applicable to other businesses: Core competence should be applied to other businesses within the organization or in other industries. This allows the organization to leverage its unique strengths and resources across multiple domains and create value in new areas.

Examples of core competence in the MEI include a studio's expertise in producing high-quality blockbuster films or a streaming service's ability to personalize content recommendations using advanced algorithms and user data.

Organizations must identify and leverage their unique strengths and resources to develop core competence. This requires a deep understanding of the organization's internal capabilities and the external environment in which it operates. Additionally, organizations must be able to continuously adapt and evolve their core competence to remain competitive in a rapidly changing market.

Competitive Advantage

By leveraging its core competence an organization can develop a competitive advantage to achieve superior profitability. This is why core competence is considered a critical factor in strategic management, as it can help organizations create sustainable competitive advantages and generate long-term value for shareholders.

Strategic Management **135**

A competitive advantage can take many forms, such as cost advantage, differentiation, or focus. "Cost advantage" means an organization can produce goods or services at a lower cost than its competitors. In contrast, "differentiation" means an organization offers a unique product or service perceived as superior to its competitors. "Focus" means that an organization specializes in serving a particular niche or segment of the market.

When an organization has a competitive advantage, it can generate superior profitability compared to its competitors. This is because a competitive advantage allows an organization either to charge a higher price for its products or services (in the case of differentiation) or to operate at a lower cost (in the case of cost advantage). Both of these outcomes can result in higher profits (Figure 5.8).

Profitability is influenced by three key factors—value, price, and cost (Figure 5.9):

- Value is the perceived worth or benefit that customers associate with a company's products or services. It represents the value customers place on what the company offers. The higher the value customers perceive, the greater the potential for generating revenue and achieving profitability.

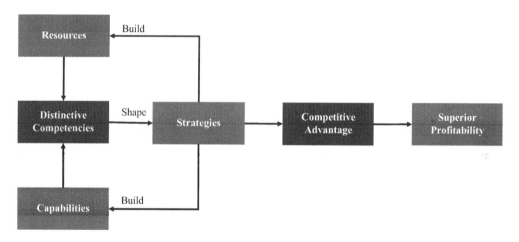

FIGURE 5.8 Distinctive Competencies to Superior Profitability.

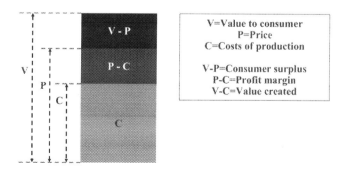

FIGURE 5.9 Value-Price-Cost Framework.

136 The Fundamentals of Management

- Price is the amount of money charged by a company for its products or services. It is a critical element that directly impacts revenue and profitability. The gap between value and price is customer benefit (or consumer surplus). The price should be set strategically, taking into consideration factors such as production costs, market demand, competition, and customer perceptions of value. Finding the right balance between price and value is essential to maximize profitability.[9]
- Cost represents the expenses incurred by a company in creating the value offered to customers. It includes various components, including raw materials, labor, marketing expenses, and operational costs. The gap between price and cost is the profit that the company can obtain, so effective cost management is vital to maintaining profitability. By optimizing costs without compromising on value or quality, a company can improve its profit margins and overall financial performance.

To achieve profitability, companies must align these factors. They need to deliver products or services that are perceived as valuable by customers, set appropriate prices that reflect the value provided, and effectively manage costs to ensure profitability is improved.

5.3.4 SWOT Analysis

SWOT analysis is a framework used to evaluate a company's competitive position and to develop strategic planning.[10]

SWOT analysis combines internal and external factors to evaluate an organization's current state and future potential. By leveraging both internal and external data, this technique assists businesses in identifying strategies that are more likely to yield success while avoiding those that have led to or are likely to lead to failure:

- Strengths are the areas in which an organization excels and sets itself apart from competitors. These may include a strong brand, a loyal customer base, a solid financial position, unique technological advancements, and other advantages.
- Weaknesses represent areas in which an organization falls short of optimal performance. These are aspects that need improvement for the company to remain competitive. Examples include a weak brand presence, high employee turnover, inadequate supply chain management, or insufficient capital resources.
- Opportunities are favorable external factors that can provide a competitive advantage to an organization. For instance, if a country reduces tariffs, a car manufacturer can seize the opportunity to expand into a new market, thereby increasing sales and market share.
- Threats are external factors that have the potential to harm an organization's operations or success. These may include droughts impacting crop yields for a wheat-producing company, escalating costs of raw materials, intensifying competition, a limited labor supply, and other factors that pose risks to the business.

Internal factors play a significant role in identifying the strengths and weaknesses of a company within the SWOT analysis. External factors are equally important in determining the success of a company. These external influences provide valuable insights for identifying both

TABLE 5.1 SWOT Analysis and Potential Question List

		Favorable	Unfavorable
Internal		Strengths	Weaknesses
		• In which areas are we demonstrating excellence?	• What are the factors that hinder our progress?
		• What is our most valuable resource or advantage?	• Which product lines are underperforming?
External		Opportunities	Threats
		• What emerging trends are shaping the marketplace?	• How many competitors are present and what is their market share?
		• Which demographic segments are we currently not reaching?	• Are there any new regulations that pose risks to our operations or products?

opportunities and threats. By considering both internal and external aspects, a comprehensive list of strengths, weaknesses, opportunities, and threats can be generated (Table 5.1).

5.4 Business vs. Corporate Strategy: Overview

Every company requires strategies to achieve its objectives and stay competitive in its respective market. Two common approaches are business strategies and corporate strategies. While these strategies differ from each other, they work in conjunction to enhance performance and drive profitability for companies.

Business strategies are formulated by organizations to achieve specific goals. A business strategy entails a plan to attract customers, secure their business, and generate profits by offering products or services in a targeted market. A business strategy includes approaches for acquiring customers, choosing which product or service to offer, increasing customer satisfaction, and increasing profits.

A business strategy aims to enable a company to gain a competitive advantage in its market:[11]

- Competitive strategy: A business strategy pertains to the methods and approaches employed by a company to establish a competitive advantage in the market. This includes various strategies—such as cost leadership, differentiation, or focus—aimed at outperforming competitors.
- Market oriented: A business strategy should be market oriented, indicating it should be tailored to meet the needs of the target market. This necessitates a thorough understanding of customer preferences, market trends, and the competitive landscape within the industry.
- Market strategies: A business strategy is a company's specific tactics to compete in the market. These tactics may include pricing strategies, product development initiatives, distribution plans, and promotional activities.
- Focus on a specific business: A business strategy should maintain a clear focus on a particular business domain—be it a specific product line, a business unit, or the entire organization. This enables the company to allocate resources effectively and concentrate its efforts on achieving strategic objectives.

138 The Fundamentals of Management

Businesses leverage corporate strategies when they are trying to diversify or enter a new market.[12] A corporate strategy is a strategic plan that assists an organization in determining which markets it intends to enter and how to do so effectively. This strategy serves as a roadmap for the company's growth and expansion.

Corporate strategies are utilized by business stakeholders and top-level management to make informed decisions regarding the industries in which the company should operate. It also guides them in identifying and acquiring business units that can contribute to the overall success of the organization. A corporate strategy includes targeting markets where the organization aims to establish its competitive presence, strategic considerations regarding the timing and pace of the company's growth, and deciding how to enter a new market.

The corporate strategy is aimed at identifying the industries in which the firm should engage:

- Portfolio strategy: Portfolio strategy involves evaluating a company's business portfolio and deciding which businesses to retain and which to divest. This assessment considers factors such as growth potential, profitability, and strategic alignment for each business unit.
- Organization-oriented: A corporate strategy should be oriented toward optimizing the overall performance of the organization. This entails understanding the firm's capabilities, resources, and corporate culture, and leveraging them to achieve strategic goals.
- Market and non-market strategies: A corporate strategy should consider both market strategies, focusing on competition in the marketplace; and non-market strategies, addressing regulatory, political, and social factors that impact the business.
- Focus on business portfolio: A corporate strategy should prioritize the management of the business portfolio, strategically allocating resources across different businesses to achieve desired objectives. These might include investing in high-growth ventures, divesting underperforming units, or acquiring new businesses to expand the organization.

In conclusion, business and corporate-level strategies diverge primarily in their objectives (Table 5.2). While a business strategy concentrates on competition within the marketplace, a corporate strategy prioritizes organizational growth and profitability. A business strategy centers on delivering value to consumers, attaining competitiveness in the market through unique products or services compared to competitors, or achieving cost leadership within the industry. A corporate strategy aims to enhance overall company value, pursue growth through diversification or expansion, and implement necessary downsizing.

TABLE 5.2 Key Differences between Business and Corporate Strategy

Type	Business strategy	Corporate strategy
Characteristics	• Competitive strategy. • Market oriented. • Market strategies. • Focused on a specific business.	• Portfolio strategy. • Organization oriented. • Market + non-market strategies. • Focused on the business portfolio.

5.5 Business Strategy

5.5.1 The Three Generic Business Strategies

A business strategy determines how a firm competes within a particular business to establish a competitive advantage over its rivals. Managers can employ a business strategy to:

- establish a concise and actionable business plan for employees and department leaders;
- evaluate their products, target audience, and competition to identify their competitive advantage;
- enhance their understanding of the existing business model, including its strengths, opportunities, and areas for improvement;
- determine the necessary resources and steps to enhance competitiveness within the market;
- inspire and motivate employees by setting achievable goals; and
- demonstrate success and credibility through measurable results.

Managers develop business strategies to address ongoing operational challenges and achieve quantifiable objectives, such as acquiring a specific number of customers or generating targeted revenue. These strategies are instrumental in enabling teams to meet short-term and dynamically evolving goals, enabling them to effectively compete within a specific market segment.

The three generic business strategies can be explained through the lens of the value-price-cost framework (Figure 5.10):

- Cost leadership: The aim is to achieve the lowest cost of production and distribution in the industry while maintaining acceptable levels of quality. The goal is to offer products or services at a lower price than competitors while maintaining profitability. The company can achieve this by optimizing its processes, reducing waste, and leveraging economies of scale.
- Differentiation: The objective is to create unique products or services that are perceived as better than those of competitors and for which customers are willing to pay a premium. A company can achieve this by investing in research and development (R&D), creating a solid brand identity, and delivering exceptional customer service.

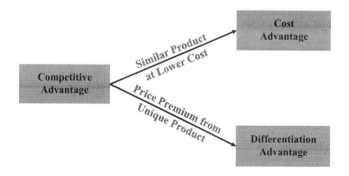

FIGURE 5.10 Sources of Competitive Advantage.

FIGURE 5.11 Type of Generic Business Strategy.

- Focus: The company targets a specific segment or niche within the industry and tailors its products or services to satisfy the needs of that segment. It can achieve this by understanding the needs and preferences of the target segment, and developing a specialized offering that meets those needs better than competitors.

These strategies are designed to create customer value while capturing value for the company. By optimizing costs, creating differentiation, or focusing on a specific segment, companies can build a sustainable competitive advantage that enables them to thrive in their industry (Figure 5.11).

5.5.2 Cost Leadership Strategy

A cost leadership strategy is a company's plan to become a cost leader in its category or market. Cost leadership occurs when a company is the category leader for low pricing.[13] To achieve this without drastically cutting revenue, a business must reduce costs in all other business areas, such as marketing, distribution, and packaging.

There are many benefits to being a cost leader. Cost leaders can charge the lowest amount for a product while remaining profitable. Other companies may have to sell their products at a loss to compete with the cost leader's prices.

Cost leaders can also withstand recessions better than competitors because they are experienced at appealing to consumers with budgets in mind. A company with meager operational costs can go longer without achieving sales goals than a company with high costs.

Also, cost leaders can be more flexible. Since their costs are low, they can discount prices more often or potentially try out other product offerings that other companies might be unable to. Companies with flexibility are likely to attract a more extensive customer base.

While there are numerous advantages associated with being a cost leader, it is important to recognize that opting for a cost leadership strategy entails certain risks. Unlike companies that offer superior products or possess strong brand appeal, the primary value proposition of a cost leader often revolves around low pricing. Consequently, if a competitor manages to achieve even greater cost reductions, it can pose a significant threat to the cost leader's customer base.

Most cost leaders employ a combination of various methods to maintain their status by consistently minimizing operational costs. Drivers of cost advantages encompass factors such as economies of scale, economies of learning, and other cost-related considerations like production techniques, product design, capacity utilization, and residual efficiency (e.g., education and corporate culture).

Strategic Management   **141**

Economies of Scale

The term "economies of scale" refers to the cost benefits that companies can gain as their production processes become more efficient.[14] Companies can take advantage of economies of scale by increasing production and lowering costs. This is possible because the costs are spread across a larger quantity of goods. These costs can be both fixed and variable. The concept of economies of scale is applicable to businesses across various industries, as it represents the cost savings and competitive advantages that larger companies have over smaller ones.

Economies of scale occur when increasing business size affords certain advantages. For example, a business may experience an economy of scale when it engages in bulk purchasing. By buying a larger quantity of products at once, it can negotiate a lower price per unit compared to its competitors.

There are several drivers enabling economies of scale to give rise to lower per-unit costs. First, there is the benefit of labor specialization and more integrated technology that allows for increased production volumes. When tasks are specialized and technology is optimized, efficiency improves, resulting in lower costs per unit. Second, economies of scale can be achieved through bulk orders from suppliers, larger advertising purchases, or reduced costs of capital. Third, spreading internal function costs across a larger number of units produced and sold contributes to cost reduction. Fixed costs—such as administrative expenses, R&D costs, and overhead costs—can be distributed over a larger production volume, reducing the per-unit burden on these expenses.

Economies of scale can be achieved through two primary methods. First, a company can achieve internal economies of scale by restructuring the allocation and utilization of its resources, including equipment and personnel. By optimizing these internal factors, the company can enhance efficiency and reduce costs.

Second, external economies of scale can be achieved by expanding the company's size relative to its competitors. This increased scale enables the company to leverage its market presence and engage in competitive practices, such as negotiating advantageous discounts for bulk purchases.

The significance of economies of scale lies in their ability to confer a competitive edge on businesses within their industry. Consequently, companies strive to capitalize on economies of scale whenever feasible.

Exercise: Economies of Scale

Suppose the fixed cost is $10,000 for any number of production units and the variable cost is $1 per unit.

- **Calculate the total cost of production**
  (Tip: Total cost of production = Fixed cost + Variable cost X number of production units)

  - For 1,000 units
  - For 10,000 units

- **Calculate the cost of production per unit.**
  (Tip: Cost of production per unit = Total cost of production/number of production units)

  - For 1,000 units
  - For 10,000 units

  Which case has a lower cost of production per unit? Why?

In the media and entertainment industry (MEI), economies of scale can be observed in various aspects, such as content production, distribution, and marketing expenses. One notable example of economies of scale in the industry is the production of blockbuster films.[15]

When a production studio invests in producing a big-budget film, the costs associated with production, marketing, and distribution can be quite substantial. However, if the film becomes a success, the studio can reap significant benefits from economies of scale. As the film gains in popularity and attracts a larger audience, the revenues generated from ticket sales, merchandise, licensing, and international distribution increase exponentially.

With a successful blockbuster film, the studio can leverage its established brand and reputation to negotiate better deals with distribution partners, theaters, and promotional channels.[16] It can secure more favorable terms, such as lower distribution fees, wider release, and increased marketing support. The success of a blockbuster film can also lead to higher demand for ancillary products and licensing opportunities, further increasing revenue streams.

Economies of scale come into play when a studio can spread the fixed costs of production, marketing, and distribution across a larger audience base. As the film reaches more theaters and generates more ticket sales, the average cost per viewer decreases, resulting in higher profit margins. The studio can also benefit from increased bargaining power when negotiating deals with suppliers, talent, and production crews, leading to potential cost savings.

Economies of Learning (Experience Curve)

Economies of learning are derived from the knowledge and expertise gained through experience.[17] Unlike economies of scale, which have a threshold, economies of learning continue to improve efficiency over time. The key distinction between economies of scale and economies of scope is that economies of learning are not directly tied to production levels. It is not about producing more quantity or a broader range of products, but rather about becoming a specialist in a specific field by accumulating a greater volume of production for the same product.

The concept of the experience curve was first introduced by Bruce D. Henderson, the founder of the Boston Consulting Group, in the 1960s.[18] It visualizes the phenomenon of learning by doing, illustrating that as cumulative production volume increases, the direct cost per unit produced decreases. As a result, the experience curve has a convex shape with a downward slope, reflecting the decreasing cost per unit with increased cumulative production volume.

The experience curve is a broader phenomenon that encompasses the total output of various functions within a firm, such as manufacturing, marketing, and distribution.

The implications of the experience curve are significant. As direct costs decrease with the increase in cumulative output, firms that have been producing more and for a longer period enjoy lower direct costs per unit. This competitive advantage can lead to their dominance in the market.

An example of economies of learning in the MEI can be observed in the production of television shows. As a production team creates more episodes of a particular show, they become more experienced and efficient in various aspects of the production process.

Initially, the team may face challenges in coordinating the actors, setting up the equipment, and managing the overall production workflow. However, as they gain experience and learn from their mistakes, they can streamline their processes, optimize resource allocation, and improve overall production efficiency. The team may become faster at setting up scenes, require fewer retakes, and better anticipate potential production issues. As a result, the time and resources required to produce each subsequent episode decrease, leading to lower average production costs per episode.

Additionally, the accumulated knowledge and experience gained by the production team can enhance the creative quality of the show. The team has become more adept at storytelling, character development, and delivering engaging content, which can contribute to the show's success and audience appeal.

The concept of economies of learning is evolving into that of a "learning economy," where efficiency and growth are propelled by training and specialization. This leads to the production of profitable goods and services with high added value.

5.5.3 Differentiation Strategy

Product differentiation is a marketing strategy that distinguishes a company's products or services from the competition.[19] Successful product differentiation involves the identification and effective communication of the unique qualities that set a product or company apart from its competitors. It entails highlighting the distinct differences and value propositions that make that product or company appealing to a specific target market or audience.

A differentiation strategy is a deliberate approach that businesses adopt to provide customers with something unique and distinguishable from what their competitors offer. The primary goal is to gain a competitive advantage by leveraging the strengths, weaknesses, and value proposition of the business while meeting the needs of customers.

In the MEI, there are various strategies companies employ to differentiate themselves and signal quality to their customers.

One approach to differentiation is through the use of a strong brand name. Building a reputable and recognizable brand can instill trust and confidence in customers. For example, Disney has established itself as a renowned brand in the MEI, known for its

144 The Fundamentals of Management

high-quality content and family-friendly image. The Disney brand serves as a signal of quality and helps differentiate its offerings from competitors.

Another way to signal quality is by providing extended warranties or guarantees. Companies may offer extended warranties on electronic devices, such as gaming consoles or televisions, to assure customers of their durability and reliability. This differentiation strategy not only signals quality but also provides customers with peace of mind and confidence in their purchase.

Luxurious packaging is another way to differentiate products. Packaging plays a significant role in shaping customers' perceptions of quality. Companies may invest in visually appealing and premium packaging to create a sense of luxury and value. For example, high-end audio equipment manufacturers often package their products in sleek and sophisticated boxes, emphasizing the premium nature of their offerings.

Utilizing celebrities for marketing purposes is a prevalent differentiation strategy in the MEI. By associating their brand or products with well-known personalities, companies aim to leverage the credibility and appeal of those celebrities to attract customers. This can be seen in endorsements or collaborations between fashion brands and popular actors, musicians, or athletes.

Sponsorship of sports and cultural events is a common strategy. By associating their brand with prestigious events, companies can enhance their reputation and reach a broader audience. Sports apparel brands often sponsor major sporting events (e.g., the Olympics) or teams to align themselves with the excitement and passion of sports, differentiating themselves from competitors in the market.

Differentiation strategies provide several advantages that can help businesses carve out a unique niche within their industry:

- Reduced price competition: By differentiating products or services, companies can compete in the market based on factors other than just lower prices. This reduces direct price-based competition and attracts customers seeking specific qualities or preferences.
- Unique products: A differentiation strategy leverages the unique qualities and features of products or services. By identifying and highlighting the characteristics that competitors lack, companies can differentiate their offerings in the market. Effective marketing and advertising efforts can effectively communicate these unique attributes to the target audience, creating a distinct identity and positioning for the brand.
- Improved profit margins: When products are differentiated and positioned as higher-quality or higher-value offerings, this opens up opportunities for larger profit margins. Customers who value and are willing to pay a premium for superior quality or unique features provide the potential for increased revenue with fewer sales. This can contribute to enhanced profitability and financial performance.
- Consumer brand loyalty: Successful differentiation can foster brand loyalty among customers. When a business consistently delivers on its perceived quality and unique value proposition, it builds trust and loyalty.

Differentiation strategies also come with certain disadvantages and challenges that businesses should consider.

First, differentiation requires businesses to invest in R&D, product design, quality control, and marketing efforts to create and maintain unique features or attributes. These additional costs can impact profit margins, especially if customers are not willing to pay a premium price for the differentiated product or service.

Moreover, when a business successfully differentiates itself and gains market recognition, it may attract the attention of competitors, which may attempt to replicate or imitate the differentiated features. This can erode the competitive advantage and uniqueness initially achieved, leading to increased competition and potential loss of market share.

Relatedly, maintaining a differentiation strategy requires ongoing innovation and adaptation to stay ahead of competitors and meet evolving customer needs. This demands substantial resources, time, and effort, as well as a proactive approach to market research and product development.

Finally, introducing new or unique features can create uncertainty and perceived risk among customers, who may be hesitant to adopt unfamiliar products or services. The challenge lies in effectively communicating and convincing customers about the value and benefits of the differentiated offering to overcome this perceived risk.

5.5.4 Focus Strategy

A focus strategy involves developing, marketing, and selling products to a niche market—which could be a type of consumer, product line, or geographical area. A focus strategy aims to build a strong connection with target customers and establish the company as a key player within that niche.

The advantages of adopting a focus strategy lie in offering customers either the same value at a lower price or a superior value at a higher price. This approach allows the company to differentiate itself within the niche market and capture the attention and loyalty of its target customers.

This can be done by adopting either of the following types of focus strategies:

- Low-cost focused strategy: In this strategy, an organization identifies a micro or geographically concentrated market. Within this market, all customers with a particular need can be provided with a product designed and delivered at a lower cost than mass marketers. The competition, in this case, is with cost leaders. By controlling these aspects internally, the organization can save on costs for distribution, transportation, and channel partner margins. At the same time, raw materials can be locally sourced, and the production process can be optimized to reduce product costs.
- Focused differentiation strategy: An organization does not try to reduce prices in this strategy. Instead, the focus is on customizing a product and adding specifically sought-out value propositions. The targeted customers can then be encouraged to pay more than they would for standard solutions. With this type of focused strategy, niche market segments that are geographically distributed can also be captured. At the same time, the organization can continue to innovate and improve its offerings to match market demands. The competition, in this case, is with differentiated brands.

Table 5.3 presents the differences between three generic business strategies in terms of their strategic choices, advantages, and disadvantages.

146 The Fundamentals of Management

TABLE 5.3 Three Generic Business Strategy Directions

Business strategy	Strategic choices	Advantages	Disadvantages
Cost leadership	• Aimed at the average customer. • Increase efficiency and lower costs.	• Protected from competitors and new entrants by cost advantage. • Less vulnerable to powerful suppliers/buyers.	• Tied to maintaining low labor costs. • Risk of imitation by competitors. • Risk of not responding to changes in customer tastes.
Differentiation	• Pursue a high level of product differentiation. • Engage in the maximum amount of market segmentation. • Develop skills relevant to the source of differentiation.	• Protected from competitors and new entrants by brand loyalty. • Less vulnerable to moderate increases in the cost of inputs.	• Pressure to maintain perceived uniqueness. • The importance of differentiation may diminish over time.
Focus	• Choose a specific niche market or several niche markets. • Develop relevant skills according to the adoption of cost leadership or differentiation.	• Protected from competitors and new entrants by the uniqueness of product or service and customer loyalty. • An increase in the cost of inputs can be passed on to targeted customers, who are willing to pay a higher price. • Forms a strong relationship with customers.	• Production costs can be high, reducing profitability. • The niche market may not be stable.

5.6 Corporate Strategy

Top executives design corporate strategies to achieve long-term goals, such as sustainable growth, and solve comprehensive issues affecting the entire organization, like diversification.[20] A corporate strategy is usually long-lasting and based on the company's vision.[21] The company might measure this strategy's success over many years.

Executive leaders can utilize corporate strategies to:

- determine the trajectory, pace, timing, and scope of the company's growth;
- explore new business prospects and evaluate their viability;
- enhance efficiency by consolidating departments, sharing resources, or engaging in the acquisition or divestiture of business units;
- make informed decisions regarding competition, market entry strategies, and market dominance;
- delineate the position the company aims to occupy within its industry; and
- provide managers with guidance for achieving long-term goals.

Firms using diversification strategies enter entirely new industries, expanding their operations beyond their existing value chain. Diversification involves venturing into new value chains. This expansion into new industries can be achieved through mergers, acquisitions, or independent entry.

To assess the viability of a proposed diversification move, companies typically subject it to three critical tests:

- Attractiveness test: This evaluates the attractiveness of the industry that the firm intends to enter. It assesses the industry's profit potential and market dynamics. If the industry does not offer strong profit potential or if the market conditions are unfavorable, entering it may be risky and not conducive to diversification.
- Cost of entry test: This examines the costs associated with entering the target industry. Executives should carefully evaluate the financial implications and determine if the firm can recover the expenses incurred during the diversification process. This will ensure that the potential benefits outweigh the costs and justify the investment.
- Better-off test: This focuses on assessing whether both the new unit and the firm as a whole will benefit from diversification. It examines whether the diversification move will lead to a competitive advantage for either the new unit or the existing firm. Diversification should be pursued only if it will enhance the overall competitive position and create value for the organization.

A proposed diversification move should pass these tests or be rejected.[22]

5.6.1 Related Diversification

Because it leverages strategic fit, companies that engage in related diversification are more likely to achieve gains in shareholder value.[23] Related diversification occurs when a firm enters a new industry that shares significant similarities with its existing industry or industries. This strategic approach allows companies to leverage their existing capabilities and resources to gain a competitive advantage in the new industry.[24]

Disney's acquisition of ABC and ESPN is an example of related diversification, as both films and television are part of the MEI. By expanding into a related industry, companies can unlock synergies and benefit from shared knowledge, distribution channels, and customer base.

Some firms pursue related diversification with the goal of developing and exploiting a core competency, which is a unique skill set that is challenging for competitors to replicate. This core competency can be leveraged across different businesses and contributes to the value experienced by customers in each business.

For example, News Corp. ventured into new business areas, such as the broadcasting and film industries, by identifying shared commonalities in the components of the value chains. By capitalizing on these synergies, companies can enhance their competitive position and create value for stakeholders.

Value creation through related diversification can be achieved through various mechanisms, including economies of scope and transferring competencies.

148 The Fundamentals of Management

Economies of Scope

Economies of scope, often referred to as "portfolio effects," occur when different business units within a diversified company can share resources and functions.[25] By leveraging shared resources, such as production facilities, distribution networks, or marketing expertise, these business units can achieve higher asset utilization and lower operating costs. This sharing of resources leads to efficiency gains and cost savings, ultimately creating value for the company. However, it is important to carefully consider coordination costs to ensure that the benefits of resource sharing outweigh any potential drawbacks.

Transferring Competencies

Transferring competencies is another avenue for value creation in related diversification. When a company enters a new industry that aligns with its existing competencies, it can leverage its expertise and knowledge to lower the cost of value-creation activities. For example, a technology company with expertise in software development may enter a related industry, such as telecommunications, using its technological capabilities to develop innovative products or services at a lower cost compared to competitors. This competency transfer can also create opportunities for differentiation, allowing the company to offer unique features or superior quality that justifies premium pricing. By leveraging existing competencies across different businesses, the company can generate additional value and establish a competitive advantage.

5.6.2 Unrelated Diversification

The decision of a soft-drink company like Coca-Cola to acquire a movie studio might seem perplexing at first glance. This unconventional move represents an example of unrelated diversification, whereby a company ventures into an industry that lacks any significant similarities to its existing industry or industries. Coca-Cola's purchase of Columbia Pictures in 1982 for $750 million exemplifies this type of diversification.[26] Surprisingly, this seemingly odd acquisition turned out to be a successful investment for Coca-Cola, as Columbia Pictures was later sold to Sony for a substantial $3.4 billion just seven years later in 1989.[27]

Virgin Group provides another notable example of unrelated diversification.[28] The company has successfully entered into various business areas that seemingly have no apparent relationship with each other or with Virgin's initial industry. Virgin Group, originally known for its music label, expanded its operations into sectors such as airlines (Virgin Atlantic), telecommunications (Virgin Mobile), healthcare (Virgin Care), and even space tourism (Virgin Galactic).

Despite lacking a direct connection to its initial music industry, Virgin Group's diversification strategy has proven to be largely successful. The company's founder, Richard Branson, has emphasized the importance of leveraging Virgin's brand reputation and customer-centric approach in entering new markets.[29] This approach has allowed Virgin to carve out unique positions in each industry it enters and to differentiate itself from competitors.

However, most unrelated diversification attempts do not yield favorable outcomes. Some companies, despite their iconic brands and resources, have experienced disappointing results when branching out into unrelated businesses. For example, Starbucks, renowned for its coffee, began offering an online retailing platform for furniture, Living.com.[30] In 2014, Amazon attempted to diversify into the smartphone market with the release of the Fire Phone.[31] The phone incorporated Amazon's ecosystem and features, such as Firefly, allowing users to easily purchase products from Amazon. Unfortunately, both endeavors ended in failure. Despite their strong brand recognition, the strategic resources and expertise of Starbucks and Amazon did not effectively transfer to the online furniture retailing and mobile phone businesses, respectively.

These examples highlight the inherent risks associated with unrelated diversification. While some companies may achieve success through such ventures, many others find that their core competencies and brand value do not translate effectively into unrelated industries. Therefore, careful consideration and strategic evaluation are crucial when pursuing unrelated diversification, as it presents unique challenges and uncertainties that may not align with a company's existing strengths and capabilities.

Assessment of Business Attractiveness in Diversification

When assessing the business attractiveness of potential diversification opportunities, there are three key criteria to consider (Figure 5.12):

- Industry and business scale/growth: Factors to assess include market size, growth potential, competitive landscape, regulatory environment, and technological advancements. A larger and rapidly growing industry with favorable market conditions presents more attractive opportunities for diversification. Businesses should analyze their own scale and growth potential within the new industry, considering factors such as economies of scale, market share potential, and customer demand.
- Expected return and risk: The potential return on investment and associated risks are important considerations when assessing the attractiveness of diversification. The expected return should account for revenue growth, cost efficiencies, and profitability potential. It is essential to conduct thorough financial analysis, including revenue projections, cost estimates, and cash flow forecasts. Simultaneously, businesses must evaluate the risks inherent in entering a new market, such as competitive pressures, market volatility, technological disruptions, regulatory challenges, and operational complexities. The balance between expected return and risk will influence the overall attractiveness of the diversification opportunity.

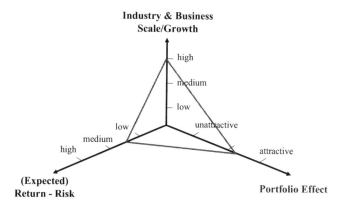

FIGURE 5.12 Assessment of Business Attractiveness in Diversification.

150 The Fundamentals of Management

- Portfolio effect: Diversification should be evaluated in the context of the existing business portfolio. The portfolio effect considers the potential synergies, complementarities, and risk diversification benefits that the new venture can bring to the overall business. By adding a new business unit or entering a different industry, companies seek to reduce their overall risk exposure, optimize resource allocation, and enhance the stability of their revenue streams. Assessing the fit between the proposed diversification and the existing portfolio is the most important factor in determining the overall attractiveness and strategic fit of the opportunity.

5.6.3 Vertical Integration versus Horizontal Integration

Vertical integration and horizontal integration are two common strategies used by businesses to diversify their operations and enter new markets.

Vertical integration involves expanding a company's operations by acquiring or controlling businesses at different stages of the same supply chain. For example, a company that produces raw materials may vertically integrate by acquiring a company that manufactures finished products using those raw materials. By integrating vertically, the company gains greater control over its supply chain, leading to greater efficiencies, cost savings, and increased profitability.

In the MEI, vertical integration can include owning or controlling various stages of the production and distribution process. For example, a media and entertainment company may vertically integrate by acquiring a production studio or partnering with independent producers to create original content. This allows them to have greater control over the development and production of TV shows, films, or other forms of entertainment. Vertical integration can also involve acquiring and operating distribution channels such as cable networks, streaming platforms, or movie theaters. By vertically integrating into distribution, a company can ensure a direct pipeline to reach audiences with its content.

Horizontal integration involves growing a company's businesses by acquiring or merging with businesses that operate in the same stage of the supply chain or offer similar products or services. For example, a company that produces soft drinks may horizontally integrate by acquiring a competitor that produces similar soft drinks. By integrating horizontally, the company gains greater market share, economies of scale, and increased bargaining power.

Examples of horizontal integration in the MEI include media conglomerates that acquire or merge with other companies in the same industry to expand their reach, diversify their content offerings, and gain a larger market share. For example, the merger of CBS Corporation and Viacom in 2019 aimed to create a more robust media company with a broader content portfolio and enhanced distribution capabilities. Also, with the rise of streaming platforms, there has been significant horizontal integration through mergers and acquisitions. The acquisition of Hulu by Disney and the merger of WarnerMedia and Discovery to form Warner Bros. Discovery are examples of horizontal integration in the streaming space.[32]

5.7 New Strategic Management Components

Managers face three current strategic management issues: corporate governance, non-market strategy, and strategy implementation.

5.7.1 Corporate Governance

"Corporate governance" refers to the mechanisms and structures that govern how a company operates and is managed, as well as the relationships between various stakeholders.[33] At its core, corporate governance aims to establish a framework that guides the actions and responsibilities of the board of directors, management, and other key individuals within the organization. By implementing effective corporate governance practices, companies can ensure that they operate in the best interests of their stakeholders, including shareholders, employees, customers, suppliers, and the wider community.

First, corporate governance establishes mechanisms for setting and pursuing the company's objectives, ensuring that strategic decisions are made in alignment with the organization's mission and values.[34] This includes defining roles, responsibilities, and processes for decision-making, risk management, and compliance.

Second, corporate governance ensures that the interests of all stakeholders are taken into account, and that their rights are protected.[35] This is about fostering open communication channels and engaging stakeholders in decision-making processes to build trust and maintain positive relationships. Corporate governance essentially involves balancing the interests of a company's many stakeholders, such as shareholders, customers, suppliers, financiers, the government, and the community.

Third, corporate governance promotes accountability by monitoring and assessing the performance of the board, management, and the company as a whole.[36] It also emphasizes transparency in financial reporting, disclosure of information, and adherence to ethical standards, enabling stakeholders to make informed decisions. Relatedly, corporate governance ensures that companies comply with applicable laws, regulations, and industry standards.

Companies that prioritize good corporate governance not only fulfill their legal and ethical obligations but also gain a competitive edge. Sound corporate governance practices can enhance a company's reputation, attract investment, and foster long-term sustainability. Aligning the interests of stakeholders and promoting responsible decision-making, corporate governance contributes to the overall success and resilience of a company.

5.7.2 Nonmarket Strategy

The nonmarket strategy recognizes businesses as social and political beings, not just economic agents.[37] As companies play a crucial role in creating and delivering value, they are often influenced by various stakeholders, through both formal channels, such as laws and regulations, and informal channels, such as social pressure and activism. To navigate this landscape effectively, savvy executives recognize the importance of engaging with the social and political environment. By actively participating in shaping rules and norms, they reduce the risk of being constrained by external factors. However, developing a successful nonmarket strategy requires significant effort and long-term commitment, which many companies are hesitant to undertake. Furthermore, only a few truly grasp the integration of market and nonmarket strategies to maintain a sustainable competitive advantage.[38]

152 The Fundamentals of Management

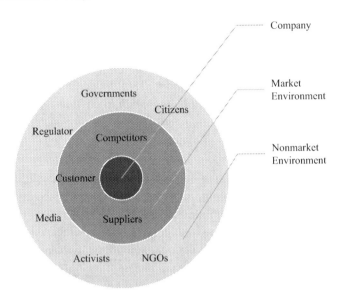

FIGURE 5.13 Nonmarket Environment.

The nonmarket environment surrounding markets plays a significant role in shaping market dynamics. Social, political, and cultural factors inevitably influence and impact the functioning of markets (Figure 5.13).[39] Recognizing this interplay, the next frontier in strategic management is the deliberate shaping of the nonmarket environment.[40] However, embracing this approach requires a mindset shift within the top executive team. It necessitates acknowledging that corporations are not solely economic entities but also social and political actors. Neglecting the company's role in the nonmarket environment and focusing solely on economic aspects leaves the shaping of that environment to external stakeholders such as politicians, regulators, and activists. If companies do not actively participate in shaping the nonmarket environment, they risk being subjected to new rules and regulations imposed by others.

Leading corporations recognize the importance of stretching the competitive playing field beyond the market realm. They embrace social and political issues not as mere nuisances but as strategic opportunities. These companies can proactively shape the rules of the game, seize strategic advantages, and establish themselves as influential actors in both market and nonmarket arenas.

Market-based strategies are good in the short term but are not enough to gain and sustain a competitive advantage for the long term in this age of volatility, uncertainty, complexity, and ambiguity. Market-based strategies have a severe weakness in dealing with these issues.[41] Given that they are not just shareholder issues but stakeholder issues, most are not just a matter of profitability but also involve moral and reputational issues that require a different lens.

5.7.3 Strategy Implementation

Strategy implementation involves translating plans into actionable steps to achieve the desired outcomes.[42] It is essentially the practice of bringing ideas and intentions to

Strategic Management **153**

fruition. The ultimate success of any organization hinges on its ability to effectively execute decisions and carry out essential processes in a consistent and efficient manner. How can one ensure the successful implementation of a strategy?

Successfully implementing and executing strategy depends on "delivering what's planned or promised on time, on budget, at quality, and with minimum variability—even in the face of unexpected events and contingencies."[43]

While formulating a strategy is an initial step toward implementing organizational change, the actual implementation is crucial to the success of a company. Even the most well-crafted plans may not materialize without an efficient implementation process.

For managers seeking to implement strategic change within their organization, the following practices can lead to the successful introduction and rollout of a new strategy:[44]

- Ensure the alignment of plans with the organization's mission, vision, and values. This ensures that everyone is working toward the same objectives and fosters a shared sense of purpose.
- Establish an organizational structure capable of effectively executing the strategy. Identify and address any obstacles or bottlenecks within the structure that may impede progress.
- Allocate sufficient resources to activities essential for the success of the strategy.
- Develop policies that promote and support the strategy.
- Implement programs and initiatives that foster continuous improvement. Create an implementation plan outlining specific steps, timelines, budgets, and required resources to achieve the strategic objectives.
- Align the reward system to incentivize the attainment of desired outcomes.
- Demonstrate strategic leadership throughout the implementation process. Identify and develop leaders with the necessary skills, experience, and vision to guide the organization toward its goals.
- Regularly review and report on progress: Monitor implementation progress to identify any issues or obstacles, allowing for necessary adjustments to be made.
- Make strategic adjustments as needed. Remain flexible and willing to adapt the strategy to ensure its relevance and achievability.
- Foster an organizational culture that supports strategy implementation. Cultivate a culture of innovation, collaboration, and continuous improvement, ensuring that all employees are aligned in working toward the goals and objectives of the strategy.

Case Studies

News Corp. versus Virgin Group—How to Diversify Businesses

News Corp. and Virgin Group represent different diversification strategies in the MEI. News Corp., founded by Rupert Murdoch, pursued related diversification, expanding its newspaper origins into TV, film, digital media, and publishing. This strategy leverages expertise, resources, and distribution for synergy, market access, and risk reduction. In

154 The Fundamentals of Management

contrast, Richard Branson's Virgin Group excelled at unrelated diversification, entering various sectors using its brand, entrepreneurship, and core strengths. Ventures like airlines, music, and telecommunications capitalize on Virgin's brand reputation and cross-industry competencies. Both strategies highlight diversification's role in shaping success in the MEI.

More case details for classroom use are available. Please check the book webpage at www.routledge.com/9781032221212 for more information.

CJ E&M: Corporate Strategy with Vertical Integration

CJ E&M, a leading South Korean entertainment company, has executed a successful vertical integration strategy across diverse business sectors. Starting as a content producer, it now controls content distribution through TV channels, digital platforms, and live event venues. Its vertical integration extends to merchandising through an e-commerce platform and intellectual property development via CJ ENM IP. This holistic approach has enabled efficiencies, cost savings, and revenue growth, while fostering a strong brand presence and global reach. By managing content creation, distribution, and monetization together, CJ E&M has cultivated a devoted fan base and emerged as a significant global player in the MEI.

More case details for classroom use are available. Please check the book webpage at www.routledge.com/9781032221212 for more information.

Review

- This chapter provides an in-depth look into strategic management by examining its key components: the concept of strategic management (5.1); vision and goals (5.2); external and internal analysis (5.3); business strategy and corporate strategy (5.4, 5.5, 5.6); and new strategic management components (5.7).
- Section 5.1 discusses the development of strategic management theories and strategic management processes.
- Section 5.2 underlines the importance of a clear vision and goal as the cornerstone of any successful strategy. It emphasizes how a clear and compelling vision, bolstered by well-defined and achievable goals, engenders a sense of commitment and drives improved performance, fostering organizational success.
- Section 5.3 delivers valuable insights into a business's internal and external context. Employing analysis frameworks like Porter's Five Forces Model and SWOT analysis, it showcases how businesses can identify opportunities and threats in their external environment while understanding their inherent strengths and weaknesses. This understanding facilitates timely strategic adjustments to navigate the ever-changing business landscape.
- The chapter then distinguishes business strategy and corporate strategy (5.4). The business strategy focuses on a company's competitive positioning within a specific market or industry (5.5). Generic business strategy includes cost leadership, differentiation, and focus strategies. Corporate strategy deals with the holistic view of how various business

units and markets integrate and interact (5.6). Corporations can grow their businesses with either related diversification or unrelated diversification. These parts underscore the need for these strategies to work in harmony, aligned with the overarching company vision and goals for sustainable growth and competitive advantage.

- Next, the chapter introduces the three new strategic management components (5.7), including corporate governance, non-market strategy, and strategy implementation. Good corporate governance seeks to balance the interests of all stakeholders, such as shareholders, senior management, customers, and the community. Companies should also proactively shape their nonmarket environment, transforming social and political issues from mere disturbances into strategic opportunities. Finally, the chapter offers guidelines on implementing strategy, from creating a strategy-equipped organization to reviewing and making necessary strategic adjustments.

Discussion Questions

1 How can the establishment of a clear vision and set of goals positively impact the strategic direction of a company? Can you give examples of companies significantly affected by their vision and goals?
2 Discuss the importance of external/internal analysis in strategic management. How do frameworks like Porter's Five Forces Model and SWOT enhance our understanding of a company's strategic position?
3 Compare and contrast business strategy and corporate strategy. How do they complement each other, and why must these strategies align?
4 How does corporate governance impact a company's reputation and relationship with stakeholders? Discuss the implications of poor corporate governance practices, providing real-world examples.
5 The nonmarket strategy recognizes businesses as social and political beings. Discuss how a company can proactively engage with its nonmarket environment and turn social and political issues into strategic opportunities.
6 Strategy implementation is seen as the most challenging part of strategic management. Discuss why this is so and suggest how the process can be improved.

Further Reading

- Aaker, D. A. (1984) "How to select a business strategy." *California Management Review*, 26(3), pp. 167–175.
- Elberse, A. (2013) *Blockbusters: Why big hits–and big risks–are the future of the entertainment business.* London: Faber & Faber.
- Feldman, E. R. (2020) "Corporate strategy: Past, present, and future." *Strategic Management Review*, 1(1), pp. 179–206.
- Prahalad, C. K. and Hamel, G. (1990) "The core competencies of the corporation." *Harvard Business Review*, 86(1), pp. 79–91.
- Porter, M. E. (1987) "From competitive advantage to corporate strategy", *Harvard Business Review*, 65(3), pp. 102–121.

156 The Fundamentals of Management

References

1 Chandler, A. (1962) *Strategy and structure: Chapters in the history of industrial enterprise.* New York: Doubleday.
2 Gluck, F. W., Kaufman, S. P. and Walleck, A. S. (1980) "Strategie management for competitive advantage." *Harvard Business Review*, 58(4), pp. 154–161.
3 Govindarajan, V. (1986) "Decentralization, strategy, and effectiveness of strategic business units in multibusiness organizations." *Academy of Management Review*, 11(4), pp. 844–856.
4a Lyons, S. (2022) "How to develop your corporate vision', *Forbes*, 14 December. www.forbes.com/sites/forbescoachescouncil/2020/12/15/how-to-develop-your-corporate-vision/.
4b Collins, J. C., and Porras, J. I. (1996). "Building your company's vision." Harvard Business Review, 74 (5), 65–78.
5 Collins, J. and Porras, J. (2005) *Built to Last: Successful Habits of Visionary Companies.* New York: Random House.
6 Leonard, K. and Watts, R. (2022) "The ultimate guide to S.M.A.R.T. goals." *Forbes.* www.forbes.com/advisor/business/smart-goals/.
7 Porter, M. E. (1980) *Competitive strategy: Techniques for analyzing industries and competitors.* New York: Free Press.
8 Prahalad, C. H. and Hamel, G. (1990) "The core competence of the corporation'. *Harvard Business Review*, 68(3), pp. 295–336.
9 Marn, M. V. and Rosiello, R. L. (1992) "Managing price, gaining profit." *Harvard Business Review.* https://hbr.org/1992/09/managing-price-gaining-profit.
10 Kenton, W. (2023) "SWOT analysis: How to with table and example." *Investopedia.* www.investopedia.com/terms/s/swot.asp.
11 Aaker, D. A. (1984) "How to select a business strategy." *California Management Review*, 26(3), pp. 167–175.
12 Feldman, E. R. (2020) "Corporate strategy: Past, present, and future." *Strategic Management Review*, 1(1), pp. 179–206.
13 Indeed Editorial Team (2023) "What is cost leadership strategy?" *Indeed.* www.indeed.com/career-advice/career-development/create-cost-leadership-strategy.
14 Silberston, A. (1972) "Economies of scale in theory and practice." *The Economic Journal*, 82(325), pp. 369–391.
15 Elberse, A. (2008) "Should you invest in the long tail?" *Harvard Business Review*, 86(7/8), pp. 88–97.
16 Elberse, A. (2013) *Blockbusters: Why big hits – and big risks – are the future of the entertainment business.* Faber & Faber.
17 "Economies of learning" (2022) *Policonomics.* https://policonomics.com/economies-of-learning/.
18 "Experience Curve" (2022) *Policonomics.* https://policonomics.com/video-c9-experience-curve/.
19 MacMillan, I. and McGrat, R. (1997) "Discovering new points of differentiation." *Harvard Business Review*, July-August. https://hbr.org/1997/07/discovering-new-points-of-differentiation.
20 Prahalad, C. K. and Hamel, G. (1990) "The core competencies of the corporation." *Harvard Business Review*, 86(1), pp. 79–91.
21 Porter, M. E. (1987) "From competitive advantage to corporate strategy." *Harvard Business Review*, 65(3), pp. 102–121.
22 Porter, M. E. (1987) "From competitive advantage to corporate strategy." *Harvard Business Review*, 65(3), pp. 102–121.
23 Markides, C. C. and Williamson, P. J. (2007) "Related diversification, core competences and corporate performance." *Strategic Management Journal*, 15(S2), pp. 149–165.
24 Markides, C. C. (2014) "To Diversify or Not to Diversify." *Harvard Business Review.* https://hbr.org/1997/11/to-diversify-or-not-to-diversify
25 Nayyar, P. R. (1993) "Stock market reactions to related diversification moves by service firms seeking benefits from information asymmetry and economies of scope." *Strategic Management Journal*, 14(8), pp 569–591.
26 Berry, J. F. (1982) "Coca-Cola to acquire Columbia Pictures." *The Washington Post*, January 20. www.washingtonpost.com/archive/business/1982/01/20/coca-cola-to-acquire-columbia-pictures/871c846f-01c4-4674-8038-989c4fc40791/.

27 Fabrikant, G. (1989) "Sale to Sony approved by Columbia Pictures." *The New York Times*, September 28. www.nytimes.com/1989/09/28/business/sale-to-sony-approved-by-columbia-pictures.html.

28 Pisano, G. P. and Corsi, E. (2012) "Virgin Group: finding new avenues for growth." *Harvard Business School Case* (Case No: 612070).

29 Clarkson, N. (2015) "Richard Branson: My four tips for growing a business." *Virgin Group.* www.virgin.com/about-virgin/latest/richard-branson-my-four-tips-growing-business.

30 Martinson, J. (2000) "Setback for Starbucks as online venture fails." *The Guardian*, August 17. www.theguardian.com/technology/2000/aug/17/internetnews.business2.

31 Schneider, J. (2014) "The Amazon Fire launch: What's new and what they stole from Apple. *Harvard Business Review*, June 19. https://hbr.org/2014/06/the-amazon-fire-launch-whats-new-and-what-they-stole-from-apple.

32 Baysinger, T. (2022) "Discovery and WarnerMedia close $43 billion merger." Axios, April 9. www.axios.com/2022/04/08/discovery-warnermedia-close-merger.

33 The Chartered Governance Institute UK & Ireland (no date) "What is corporate governance?" *The Chartered Governance Institute.* www.cgi.org.uk/about-us/policy/what-is-corporate-governance.

34 Nicholson, G. J. and Kiel, G. C. (2007) "Can directors impact performance? A case-based test of three theories of corporate governance." *Corporate Governance: An International Review*, 15(4), pp. 585–608.

35 Heath, J. and Norman, W. (2004) "Stakeholder theory, corporate governance and public management: What can the history of state-run enterprises teach us in the post-Enron era?: *Journal of Business Ethics*, 53(3), pp. 247–265.

36 Nicholson, G. J. and Kiel, G. C. (2007) "Can directors impact performance? A case-based test of three theories of corporate governance." *Corporate Governance: An International Review*, 15(4), pp. 585–608.

37 Minor, D. B. (2015) "The organization of non-market strategy." In J. de Figueiredo et al. (eds) *Strategy beyond markets Vol. 34: Advances in strategic management.* Emerald Group Publishing, forthcoming. https://dash.harvard.edu/bitstream/handle/1/26964421/minor_the-org-of-nonmarket-strategy.pdf;jsessionid=1CD355468EC0EB08FCE1E366E5433967?sequence=1.

38 Mellahi, K. et al. (2015) "A review of the nonmarket strategy literature: Toward a multi-theoretical integration." *Journal of Management,* 42(1), pp. 143–173.

39 Bach, D. and Allen, D. B. (2010) "What every CEO needs to know about nonmarket strategy." *MIT Sloan Management Review*, April 1. https://sloanreview.mit.edu/article/what-every-ceo-needs-to-know-about-nonmarket-strategy/.

40 Figueras, T. Y. (2017) "Non Market Strategy." (CK85092). *Esade.* http://prodesade.esade.edu/gea/generate/9A_EN/report.html?sby=16CK85092

41 Aggarwal, V. K. (2003) "Analyzing American firms' market and nonmarket strategies in Asia." In V.K. Aggarwal (ed.) *Winning in Asia, U.S. style: Market and nonmarket strategies for success.* New York: Palgrave Macmillan, pp. 3–25. https://basc.berkeley.edu/pdf/articles/Analyzing%20American%20Market%20and%20Nonmarket%20Strategies.pdf.

42 Miller, K. (2020) "A manager's guide to successful strategy implementation." *Harvard Business School Insights Blog.* https://online.hbs.edu/blog/post/strategy-implementation-for-managers.

43 Miller, K. (2020) "A manager's guide to successful strategy implementation." *Harvard Business School Insights Blog.* https://online.hbs.edu/blog/post/strategy-implementation-for-managers.

44 "Implementing strategy" (2020) *CMI.* www.managers.org.uk/knowledge-and-insights/research/implementing-strategy/.

MODULE III
Marketing Management

6

MARKETING MANAGEMENT IN THE MEDIA AND ENTERTAINMENT INDUSTRY

Outline

Overview	161
6.1 Marketing Paradigm	162
6.2 Marketing Analysis	167
6.3 Segmentation-Targeting-Positioning Strategy	171
6.4 Marketing Mix	173
6.5 Brand Management	188
Case Studies	197
Review	197
Discussion Questions	198
Further Reading	199
References	199

Intended Learning Outcomes

- Identify the concepts of the marketing paradigm.
- Articulate the marketing analysis frameworks and tools.
- Explain the process and components of marketing strategy and marketing mix.
- Describe the key concepts and frameworks of brand management.

Overview

- The concept of customer-centric marketing focuses on maximizing profits through customer satisfaction and encompasses the multifaceted interactions of customers with the company.

DOI: 10.4324/9781003271222-9

- It is important to analyze both macroenvironments and microenvironments to grasp market dynamics. Macro factors include demographics, economics, technology, politics, and social elements; while micro factors cover competitors and customers.
- The segmentation-targeting-positioning (STP) strategic framework explains the process of segmenting the market based on various characteristics, targeting specific market segments, and positioning offerings to align with target segment preferences.
- This chapter breaks down each component of the "4 P" marketing mix—product, price, place, and promotion—and discusses the strategies and considerations involved in aligning products and services with customer expectations, differentiating from competitors, and fostering effective customer interactions.
- Finally, the chapter outlines approaches to brand management, including building brand equity, enhancing brand loyalty, and managing brand communities. In discussing strategies like brand leveraging and extensions with real-life examples, the chapter emphasizes the significance of strong branding and the risks of poor brand management.

6.1 Marketing Paradigm

6.1.1 What is Marketing?

"Marketing" is "the activity, set of institutions, and processes for creating, communicating, delivering, and exchanging offerings that have value for customers, clients, partners, and society."[1] At its most basic level, marketing, as a market-oriented approach, aims to maximize profits through customer satisfaction (Figure 6.1).

According to this definition, there are four components of marketing:

- Creating: The collaborative process of involving suppliers and engaging customers in developing valuable offerings to satisfy customer needs.
- Communicating: Effectively conveying information about these offerings and gaining insights from customers.
- Delivering: Efficient and effective distribution of offerings to consumers in a way that optimizes value.
- Exchanging: Engaging in transactions where value is traded for these offerings

FIGURE 6.1 The Objectives of Marketing.

An important goal of marketing is facilitating a company's growth. This can be achieved by attracting and retaining new customers. Marketing covers all actions a company undertakes to draw in customers and maintain relationships with them. For this purpose, marketing aims to match a company's products and services to customers who want access to those products. Matching products to customers ultimately ensures the profitability and growth of the company. In summary, marketing seeks to identify target customers, address their unmet needs through a product or service, and draw their attention to that product or service.

Value in the Marketing Paradigm

Value is at the center of marketing. "Value" describes the advantages that customers receive in satisfying their needs—what they gain from purchasing and consuming a company's offering. Therefore, while the company is responsible for creating the offering, it is ultimately customers who determine its value.

Furthermore, marketing aims to create a profitable exchange for customers. "Profitable" means the customer's personal value equation is positive. The personal value equation is:

Value = Benefits Received − [Price + Hassle]

"Hassle" refers to the amount of time and effort invested by customers during the shopping process. This equation is subjective, as each customer evaluates the benefits of a product differently, and their shopping efforts also vary.

Value is subjective and varies among customers based on their individual needs. The marketing concept, which serves as the underlying philosophy for marketers, emphasizes the importance of satisfying customer desires and requirements. Companies that embrace this philosophy are considered market oriented. However, market-oriented companies also understand the significance of conducting profitable exchanges in order to achieve success. Being market oriented does not justify a failure to generate profits.

The Marketing Concept and Market Orientation

Companies have not always embraced the marketing concept and market orientation.[2] Beginning with the Industrial Revolution, companies were production oriented, which subsequently evolved to product oriented, selling oriented, and marketing oriented.[3]

- Production oriented: The oldest concept in business, the production concept asserts that consumers will prefer products that are widely available and affordable. Managers adhering to this concept focus on achieving high production efficiency, reducing costs, and implementing mass distribution strategies. It assumes that consumers are mainly interested in product availability and low prices. This orientation is particularly applicable in developing countries where consumers prioritize obtaining the product rather than its specific features.
- Product oriented: This concept holds that consumers will favor products that offer superior quality, performance, or innovative features. Managers following this concept concentrate on developing and continuously improving high-quality products. They

164 Marketing Management

assume that consumers appreciate well-crafted products and possess the ability to evaluate quality and performance. However, these managers may sometimes become overly enamored with their own products and fail to understand the market's needs.
- Selling oriented: This posits that consumers and businesses will not naturally purchase sufficient quantities of the selling company's products. Therefore, companies must engage in aggressive selling and promotional efforts. This concept assumes that consumers typically exhibit buying inertia or resistance and must be persuaded to make a purchase. It also presupposes that the company possesses effective selling and promotional tools to stimulate greater buying. Many firms adopt the selling concept when they have excess production capacity and aim to sell what they make rather than aligning their offerings with market demand.
- Market oriented: A business philosophy that challenges the aforementioned orientations, the market-oriented concept emerged in the 1950s. It asserts that the key to achieving organizational goals lies in being more effective than competitors in creating, communicating, delivering, and exchanging customer value to target customers. The market-oriented concept (or marketing concept) is based on target market identification, an understanding of customer needs, and integrated marketing efforts.

Differences between Sales and Marketing

Sales and marketing both focus on generating revenue and maximizing profit for a company. However, marketing mainly focuses on long-term goals, whereas sales have a relatively short-term perspective (Table 6.1).[4]

On the one hand, sales departments tend to operate under tight periodic targets. Their main focus is on generating immediate revenue through direct product sales and promotional activities. On the other hand, marketing goals are often more intangible and may not have an immediate impact on revenue. Marketing campaigns aim to create awareness, build brand recognition, and cultivate a larger customer base. While marketing efforts may not directly translate into immediate sales, they contribute to the overall growth of the company by expanding its customer reach and enhancing brand perception.

The sales concept traditionally focuses on the needs of the seller. It focuses on converting products into sales and maximizing sales growth. The primary objective is to

TABLE 6.1 Examples of Sales and Marketing Goals

Examples of marketing goals	Examples of sales goals
• Research customer needs and interests.	• Increase monthly sales.
• Build a brand.	• Expand to new customer groups.
• Improve product awareness.	• Close sales.
• Increase customer satisfaction.	• Lower customer acquisition cost.
• Maintain customer relationships.	• Retain existing customers.
• Launch a new product.	
• Reposition a brand or product.	

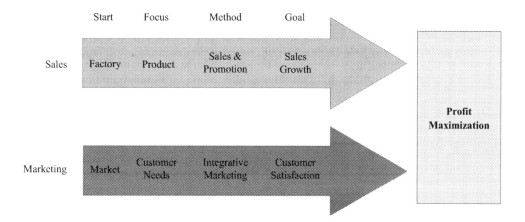

FIGURE 6.2 Marketing versus Sales.

sell what the company produces. In contrast, the marketing concept shifts the focus to the needs of the market (or customers). It emphasizes understanding and satisfying the needs of customers by providing products or services that offer solutions to their problems or fulfill their desires. This concept recognizes that successful marketing creates value for customers beyond the transaction itself and thus satisfies them in a long-term relationship (Figure 6.2).

In the end, the marketing paradigm seeks to answer the following questions:

- "Who are our customers?"
- "What do our customers value?"
- "How can we create value for our customers?"

6.1.2 The Concept of the Customer

Two terms—"customers" and "consumers"—are used interchangeably in the marketing context, but there is a contextual difference between them. In general, "customers" are individuals or businesses that purchase products or services from a company by directly engaging with it.[5] "Consumers" are defined as those who consume or use products and services. By definition, "consumers" can be "customers."

In the marketing paradigm, the "ideal" customer is someone who interacts with the company by custom; believes in the company; praises the company; and preaches about the company:

- Interacts with the company by custom: A customer regularly engages with the company by making repeated purchases or utilizing its services. They establish a relationship with the company through their continued interactions, including repeat purchases, subscriptions, or ongoing service engagements.
- Believes in the company: A customer not only chooses to do business with the company, but also has a sense of belief or confidence in its products, services, or brand.

166 Marketing Management

They have trust in the company's ability to deliver on its promises and meet their needs or expectations.

- Praises the company: A customer who is satisfied with their experience may express positive feedback and praise for the company. They may openly commend the company's offerings, customer service, or overall performance, which can contribute to building a positive reputation for the company.
- Preaches about the company: A highly engaged customer may go beyond mere praise and actively advocate for the company. They may recommend the company's products or services to others; share positive experiences through word of mouth, social media, or online reviews; and act as brand ambassadors for the company.

Customers are essential because they drive revenues; businesses cannot exist without them. All businesses compete with other players to attract customers by aggressively advertising their products, lowering prices, or developing unique products and experiences. To understand how to better meet the needs of customers, some businesses closely monitor their customer relationships to identify ways to improve products and services. The way businesses treat their customers can give them a competitive edge.

6.1.3 Marketing Planning Process

The marketing planning process begins by aligning with the corporate and business strategies of the company. The overall vision and goals of the organization, along with the existing business or product portfolio, guide the formulation of the marketing strategy. This ensures that marketing efforts are in sync with the broader objectives of the company.

The marketing strategy is established through a three-step approach: segmenting the market; targeting specific and desired segments; and positioning the product or service within those target segments. Market segmentation involves dividing the market into distinct groups of customers based on shared characteristics, needs, or behaviors. Targeting seeks to select the most attractive segments that align with the company's objectives and allocate resources to reach and serve those segments effectively. Positioning involves creating a distinctive image and positive perceptions of the product or service in the minds of target customers, emphasizing its unique value proposition and competitive advantage.

To support the positioning and implementation of the marketing strategy, companies develop and manage a set of marketing components collectively known as the "marketing mix." These components include the "4Ps" of product offering, pricing, place (or distribution), and promotion (or marketing communication). The marketing mix allows companies to strategically blend these elements to create a compelling and competitive offering that satisfies the needs and desires of target customers.

Finally, throughout the process, companies should analyze the environment around them to construct and implement a strategic marketing plan.

Figure 6.3 summarizes the marketing planning process. The following sections cover each component of the marketing planning process.

FIGURE 6.3 Marketing Planning Process.

6.2 Marketing Analysis

There are two elements involved in analyzing the environment around marketing strategy: micro and macro.[6] Some of these environmental factors are beyond the control of managers, but they still influence the decisions in a strategic marketing plan.

6.2.1 Macroenvironment Factors

To analyze the microenvironmental context, companies should take a look at the different external forces shaping economic development and consumption trends. These forces include economic factors, social/cultural factors, technological factors, and political/legal factors. For example, the economic environment can impact the organization's production and the consumer's decision-making process. Social and cultural forces include demographic trends, social values and norms, lifestyle and psychographic factors, and cultural influences on consumer behavior. Technological forces include the influence of advancements and innovations in the technological landscape on the marketing environment and consumer behavior. Technological developments may impact communication, information access, product development, distribution channels, and consumer expectations. The political and legal environment—including government policies, regulations, and the legal framework—influences businesses and consumer behavior in a significant way, so it is important for companies to examine these forces (e.g., laws, regulations, trade policies, taxation, government stability, political ideologies) before developing marketing strategies.

6.2.2 PEST Analysis: A Framework for Macroenvironment Analysis

PEST analysis is a framework used in macroenvironment analysis to examine the external factors that influence a business or industry,[7] which focuses on political, economic, social, and technological factors:

- Political factors: These relate to the influence of political systems, government policies, and regulations on the industry. For example, the media and entertainment industry (MEI) can be influenced by political factors, including censorship laws, content

168 Marketing Management

regulations, intellectual property rights, and media ownership regulations. In certain countries, strict censorship laws may restrict the type of content that can be produced or distributed, impacting the creative freedom and potential growth of media and entertainment companies.

- Economic factors: Economic factors encompass the overall economic conditions, trends, and influences that impact the industry and businesses. These include economic growth, inflation, exchange rates, and consumption patterns. For example, during an economic downturn, consumers may cut back on discretionary entertainment expenses, impacting sales for entertainment businesses such as movies, concerts, or live events.
- Social factors: These are the cultural, societal, and demographic aspects that shape consumer behavior and preferences. In the MEI, social factors may include shifts in consumer tastes and lifestyle trends. For example, changing consumer preferences toward streaming services have disrupted traditional television and movie distribution models, leading to the rise of streaming platforms like YouTube and Netflix and the decline of cable television viewership.
- Technological factors: Technological factors are advancements and innovations in technology that impact the industry. In relation to the MEI, they include the emergence of new technologies such as digital platforms, mobile devices, artificial intelligence, and the metaverse. These have revolutionized content production and distribution, consumption habits, and the overall customer experience. For example, the proliferation of mobile devices and high-speed internet has fueled the growth of mobile entertainment apps and platforms, transforming how consumers access and engage with media and entertainment content.

More recently, this framework has been extended to PESTLE analysis through the addition of legal factors and environmental factors (Table 6.2).[8] Legal factors encompass laws, regulations, and legal frameworks that impact the industry. Environmental factors examine the influence of environmental issues and sustainability considerations on the industry.

These frameworks help companies adapt their strategies to align with the political, economic, social, and technological landscape, and thus enable them to stay competitive and satisfy the fast-changing needs and preferences of the market.

6.2.3 Microenvironment Factors

The microenvironment encompasses the immediate factors around stakeholders that directly influence a company's marketing planning and implementation. Compared to the macroenvironment, these factors are within the control or influence of the company.

Customers are at the core of any microenvironment analysis. Understanding their needs, preferences, behaviors, and purchasing patterns is crucial to developing effective marketing strategies.

Competitors play a significant role in shaping a company's marketing strategy. Analyzing competitors' strategies, strengths, weaknesses, and market positioning helps businesses differentiate themselves and identify areas of opportunity or threats. Monitoring competitors' pricing, product features, marketing campaigns, and customer satisfaction levels is essential to maintain a competitive edge.

TABLE 6.2 PESTLE Analysis Examples

Political	Economic	Social	Technological	Legal	Environmental
• Government policy. • Political stability. • Tax policy. • Trade policy.	• Economic growth. • Inflation rates. • Interest rates. • Disposable income. • Exchange rates. • Unemployment rates.	• Demographic factors. • Population growth. • Lifestyle. • Cultural trends.	• Innovation level. • Technological awareness. • Digital infrastructure. • Cybersecurity.	• Health and safety laws. • Consumer safety. • Copyright protection. • Employment law.	• Environmental policy. • Climate/weather change. • Pollution. • Recycling. • Sustainability.

170 Marketing Management

Internal stakeholders such as employees, management, and shareholders influence a company's marketing efforts. Employee engagement, training, and motivation are critical for delivering consistent and high-quality customer experiences. Strong leadership and alignment with the company's vision and objectives are essential for developing effective marketing strategies and implementing them successfully.

Other stakeholders, such as suppliers and distributors, can influence a business's success when they hold power. Also, the general public may prevent a company from achieving its goals. The company's actions must be considered from the perspective of the general public and how they are affected.

6.2.4 3C Analysis: A Framework for Microenvironment Analysis

3C analysis is a framework used to analyze the microenvironment around a business. Management guru Kenichi Ohmae coined the "3Cs" of customers, competitors, and corporation.[9] By analyzing these three components, companies can find the key success factor and create a viable marketing strategy.

Customer Analysis

Conducting comprehensive customer analysis is critical for businesses to effectively appeal to their target market. For example, demographic data plays a significant role in this analysis, as it helps identify the business's target market and its desires. More specifically, businesses gain valuable insights into customers' motivations, pain points, and expectations. Understanding customer segments, consumption behaviors and decision-making processes helps businesses tailor their products, services, and marketing efforts.

In-depth interviews, questionnaires, and user tests provide valuable answers that can be used to facilitate the successful introduction of their product or service into the market.

Competitor Analysis

Once the main competitors have been identified, it is essential to conduct a thorough analysis. This includes understanding their overall marketing strategies and the level of effort they put into their marketing activities. Competitors should be examined from multiple angles to gain a comprehensive understanding of their marketing practices.

This analysis allows a business to learn from its successful and unsuccessful marketing decisions, leveraging that knowledge to drive success. This knowledge is invaluable in guiding effective marketing strategies and staying competitive in the market.

Corporation Analysis

Building on the customer and competitor analyses conducted, the company should identify the strong points and resources that contribute to its performance. This includes assessing the company's strengths, weaknesses, core competencies, and unique value proposition. With this analysis, businesses can identify areas for improvement, capitalize on existing strengths, and align their resources with market opportunities.

Some companies may encounter difficulties in identifying these aspects. Thus, seeking the opinions of customers and other stakeholders can be valuable. Companies can gather points of comparison with competitors and gain insights into how customers might respond to current and future marketing activities.

6.3 Segmentation-Targeting-Positioning Strategy

The STP marketing strategy shifts the focus of marketing away from the product and onto the customer.[10] Through this strategy, a company divides its customer base into specific groups (or segments) based on different criteria, such as interests, needs, and demographics. The company then can determine which customer segments to focus on for its marketing efforts. This process allows the company to develop effective marketing strategies and approaches that appeal to its target segments. Companies can also leverage the STP strategy to understand the characteristics of their target customers and the best way to communicate with them.

6.3.1 Segmentation

The first element of the STP strategy is segmentation. This includes creating different categories for a customer base. Each group can have specific criteria based on certain issues and features (Figure 6.4):

- Geographic segmentation: Companies can categorize their audience based on their location, including region, state, or country.
- Demographic segmentation: Companies should consider arranging their customers by traits such as age, gender, education level, occupation, and income.
- Behavioral segmentation: This approach groups customers based on how they interact with the company. For example, companies can review which products customers buy, how frequently they make purchases, and which items they view when shopping.
- Psychographic segmentation: Companies can classify their consumers based on characteristics such as interests, opinions, and activities. Relatedly, companies can divide their audience based on religious, cultural, and political beliefs.

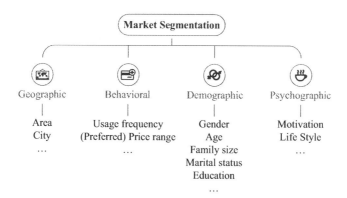

FIGURE 6.4 Market Segmentation Criteria.

6.3.2 Targeting

Targeting is the second step in the STP strategy. The company analyzes the customer segments and focuses on a specific group for a targeted marketing campaign. This selection can be based on factors such as demographics, whereby customers who frequently engage with a product or service or exhibit higher purchasing rates are chosen as the target segment.

Many aspects might inform targeting decisions, depending on the specific needs of the business and the preferences of consumers. Considerations often include the size of each segment, its growth potential, profitability, and accessibility. The targeting phase allows companies to focus their efforts on specific customer segments, tailoring their marketing strategies to effectively reach and engage with the chosen target audience.

Exercise: Segmenting and Targeting Movie Theater Customers

Suppose you manage a movie theater business near a university town and want to segment the whole customer group (i.e., university students in their 20s) and target a specific customer segment. After extensive analysis, you identify gender and relationship status are two relevant segmentation criteria.

Questions

- Given these two criteria, choose the most appropriate target segment and discuss why.
- Which other segmentation criteria can be employed? With these criteria, which customer segments should be targeted?

6.3.3 Positioning

Positioning occurs when you use customer data to develop a unique, personalized marketing strategy. This can allow you to fulfill consumer needs and offer your goods or services to solve customers' problems. This advertising approach might also give you

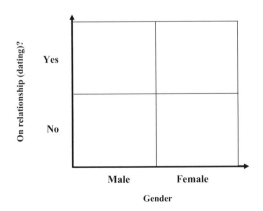

FIGURE 6.5 Market Segmentation: Exercise.

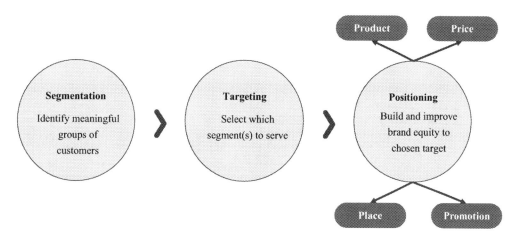

FIGURE 6.6 STP Strategy.

some advantage over competitors, as consumers may find targeted ads more persuasive than commercials intended for a general audience. As a result, a company might experience more overall sales through this customization process.

How should you position your product/service in target customers' minds?

- Only one specific position.
- Unique and consistent.
- Differentiation from competitors.
- Development and optimization of the marketing mix.

Create a Marketing Mix

A marketing mix is a type of plan that allows you to oversee multiple marketing elements and achieve a cohesive marketing strategy. You can use this technique to support your product positioning and better reach your target audience. By relying on a marketing mix to help prepare an STP marketing strategy, you can focus more effectively on customer requirements (Figure 6.6). The next section presents the concepts and components of the marketing mix.

6.4 Marketing Mix

The marketing mix plays a fundamental role in marketing a product or service. Harvard Business School Professor Neil Borden popularized the idea of the marketing mix—commonly known as the "4Ps" (product, price, place, and promotion)—and demonstrated how companies can use these tactics to engage consumers.[11]

They are influenced by internal and external factors within the overall business environment and have significant interdependencies. With the marketing mix, companies can address crucial aspects of their marketing strategy, including understanding customer needs, assessing how their product or service aligns with those needs, evaluating perceptions of their offering in the market, differentiating themselves from competitors, and effectively engaging with customers:

- Product: This is defined as a bundle of attributes (e.g., features, functions, benefits) capable of exchange or use—usually a mix of tangible and intangible forms.[12] A product can be an idea, a physical good, advice, or any combination of these. It exists for exchange in the satisfaction of individual and organizational objectives. The term "products and services" is occasionally used.

    To meet customer demand and capitalize on market opportunities, it is essential for the product to address an unfulfilled need in the market. Managers must acquire a thorough understanding of the product itself. This includes the distinctive features that set it apart from competitors, the potential for product bundling or diversification into related product lines, and the existence of substitute products within the market.
- Price: This is how much the company will sell the product for.[13] When determining a price, businesses need to take into account factors such as the cost per unit, marketing expenses, and distribution costs. Additionally, they should assess the prices of similar products in the market to ensure that their proposed price offers a viable choice for consumers. Price represents the monetary value customers must pay to obtain a product.
- Place (or distribution): This refers to marketing and distributing products to consumers. It also describes the extent of market coverage for a given product. Key considerations include whether the company will sell the product through a physical store, online, or through wholesale channels.
- Promotion: As defined by the Association of National Advertisers, this includes strategies aimed at increasing sales and engaging customers.[14] It can be quantified in terms of volume, market share, and profitability. Illustrative examples of promotional tactics include coupons, sweepstakes, rebates, premiums, unique packaging, cause-related marketing, and licensing.

More recently, the 4Cs marketing mix—a variation of the 4Ps with a more customer-oriented approach—has gained more attention. The 4C marketing mix consists of consumer wants and needs, cost, convenience, and communication (Figure 6.7).[15]

- Customer wants (or needs): The initial element in this marketing mix is about understanding and fulfilling the wants or needs of customers. Instead of solely focusing on the product, businesses should strive to address a customer's specific

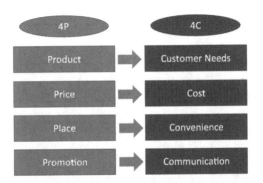

FIGURE 6.7 4P versus 4C Marketing Mix.

needs or requirements. By understanding the target customer, the process of creating a product that provides genuine benefits becomes more valuable.
- Cost: The second component is cost. It is essential to differentiate between the price of the product and its overall cost to the customer. Cost may include factors beyond the product's price, such as the time and effort expended by the customer to access the product or the associated expenses, like transportation. Cost also encompasses the perceived value or benefit that the product provides to the customer.
- Convenience: Convenience represents the third component, similar to the "place" aspect of the traditional marketing mix. Convenience takes a more customer-centric approach by focusing on optimizing the accessibility and ease of obtaining the product, ensuring a seamless and hassle-free experience for the customer.
- Communication: The final C is communication. Communication is a fundamental aspect of successful marketing, as it enables the effective implementation of the other three marketing mix components. Unlike traditional promotion, which can often be manipulative and ineffective, communication is more customer oriented. It emphasizes meaningful interaction between the company and customers, fostering a genuine connection and understanding.

6.4.1 Product

Product Types

Products can be categorized into three distinct types: functional products, experiential products, and symbolic products (Figure 6.8).[16] Each type serves a specific purpose and provides different value to consumers.

Functional products are designed to fulfill practical needs and solve problems for consumers. These products primarily focus on their utilitarian functionality. Examples of functional products include smartphones, streaming devices, and software applications. These products are primarily chosen for their ability to perform specific tasks efficiently, such as facilitating communication, accessing digital content, or editing videos.

Experiential products provide consumers with immersive experiences, emotional stimulation, and sensory enjoyment.[17] These products focus on creating memorable and pleasurable experiences for consumers. Examples include theme parks, live concerts, and interactive videogames. The goal of experiential products is to engage consumers on a deeper level and evoke positive emotions, excitement, and entertainment.

Symbolic products are associated with social identity and self-expression. These products allow consumers to communicate their values, beliefs, and aspirations through

FIGURE 6.8 Three Types of Products.

the brands they choose to associate with. Examples include fashion items endorsed by celebrities and luxury goods. Consumers purchase these products not only for their functional or experiential qualities but also to align themselves with a particular brand or image, projecting their desired self-identity to others.[18]

Understanding the distinctions between functional, experiential, and symbolic products helps marketers tailor their strategies to meet specific consumer needs and desires.

Product Lifecycle

The product lifecycle is the time from the introduction of a product to consumers on the market until its removal from the market.[19] Product lifecycles follow a similar trajectory to human lifecycles.

The product lifecycle comprises four distinct stages—introduction, growth, maturity, and decline—which help guide product lifecycle management strategies to sustain and nurture a product throughout its lifespan. This concept is utilized by management and marketing professionals to make informed decisions regarding advertising efforts, pricing adjustments, and market expansion at different stages of the product lifecycle (Figure 6.9):

- Introduction: During this stage, a significant allocation of resources is dedicated to advertising and implementing a targeted marketing campaign aimed at creating consumer awareness regarding the product and its associated advantages.
- Growth: If the product succeeds, it moves to the growth stage. This is characterized by growing demand, a surge in production levels, and expanded market reach.
- Maturity: This is the most profitable stage, as the production and marketing costs decline.
- Decline: As the product gains traction and achieves success, it inevitably attracts competition from other companies seeking to replicate its achievements, often by introducing enhancements or offering lower prices. Consequently, the product may experience a decline in market share as competitors enter the scene.

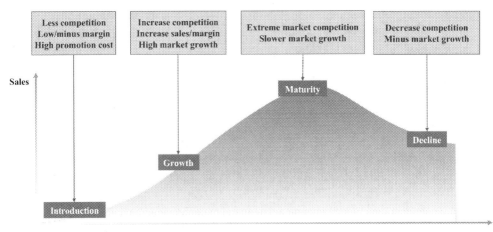

FIGURE 6.9 Product Lifecycle.

Marketing Management **177**

TABLE 6.3 Branding versus Hit Paradigms

Branding paradigm	Hit paradigm
• Long term.	• Short term.
• Strategy and implementation.	• High uncertainty and risk.
• Market analysis.	• Intuition-based.
• Minimize uncertainty.	• Adjust to uncertainty.
• Consistency.	• Responsive to trends.

Branding versus Hit Paradigm

The branding and hit marketing paradigms represent different marketing approaches. The choice between these two paradigms depends on the marketing goals and objectives of the company (Table 6.3).

The branding paradigm focuses on building a solid and consistent brand over time, which requires a long-term commitment. A branding strategy tends to have a clear plan that guides all marketing activities to ensure consistency and alignment with the brand's values and vision. For this reason, understanding the market and consumer needs is crucial in the branding paradigm to develop a marketing strategy that resonates with the target audience. It aims to minimize uncertainty by relying on research and data-driven insights to develop a marketing strategy. Consistency is key in all marketing activities to build a strong brand identity that resonates with the target audience.

In contrast, the hit marketing paradigm focuses on short-term results that can be achieved quickly to respond to trends and changes in the market. By nature, it involves taking risks due to uncertain and unpredictable market trends. This approach relies more on intuition and creativity than data-driven insights to develop marketing campaigns. Because of this, this paradigm requires marketers to adjust their strategies quickly based on changes in the market and consumer trends.

Given the different characteristics between the hit and branding paradigms, most media and entertainment products are driven by the hit marketing paradigm because of the nature of the industry. Most media and entertainment products have a short shelf life, with new products quickly replacing old ones. A hit marketing approach can quickly generate interest in a product and maximize its impact while it is still relevant and in demand.

The MEI is highly competitive, with numerous products vying for consumer attention. Moreover, those products are highly dependent on consumer tastes and preferences, which can be unpredictable and subject to change. In this highly competitive environment, hit marketing tactics are often used to create a buzz around a product and generate interest from consumers quickly.

Therefore, the success of media and entertainment products depends on their ability to capture the public's attention and generate significant traction. Some marketing tactics, such as creating viral campaigns and leveraging popular trends, can effectively achieve this goal.

In some cases, it is also possible to use a hit marketing approach to enhance the effectiveness of a branding strategy (Figure 6.10). For example, *Harry Potter* and *Star Wars* are both highly successful and recognizable brands in the MEI. They have consistent themes and values across the franchise, creating a cohesive brand identity that is easily recognizable to fans. Also, there is a wide range of merchandise available,

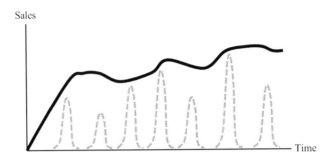

FIGURE 6.10 Branding Through Hit Marketing.

including books, movies, videogames, clothing, and toys. This merchandising helps to reinforce the brand identity and creates a sense of community among fans.

6.4.2 Pricing

Price is the cost of a product for consumers. Customers primarily assess the value they will receive from a product before evaluating the price they are willing to pay. Managers should link the price to the product's value, but they also must consider cost and competitors' prices (Figure 6.11).[20] Pricing strategy follows the golden rule, where the value delivered by a product or service takes precedence over its price, and the price must be higher than the cost. Furthermore, competitors' pricing should be considered.

Customers' perceptions of price are influenced by several factors that shape their understanding and evaluation of the cost associated with a product or service.

First, customer expectations play a significant role in their perceptions of price. For example, customers may have different price expectations when comparing the cost of purchasing a product from a convenience store versus a hotel bar. These expectations are influenced by factors such as perceived value, brand image, and the overall experience associated with the purchase.

Second, customers may evaluate the fairness of a transaction by comparing the perceived price with their expectations and the perceived value of the product. If the price aligns with the expected cost and customers perceive that they are receiving fair value for their money, they are more likely to accept the price as reasonable.

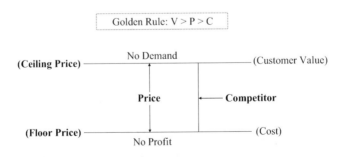

FIGURE 6.11 Golden Rule of Pricing: Value > Price > Cost.

Third, the category to which a product belongs can impact customers' perceptions of its price. Necessity goods, such as basic food items or household essentials, are often evaluated based on their affordability and essentiality, while luxury goods are associated with higher price points due to their exclusivity and premium features.

Finally, customers tend to compare the price of a product to reference prices, the prices of similar products in the market. If the price of a product is significantly higher or lower than the reference price, it can influence customers' perceptions of the product's value and affordability.

Different Pricing Approaches

Cost-Based Pricing

Cost-based pricing is the simplest method of determining price and embodies the basic idea behind doing business.[21] Many companies calculate their production costs, determine their desired profit margin, and apply this figure to a large number of products. This method often overlooks crucial factors such as comprehensive market research, consumer preferences, and competitive strategies. Consequently, it fails to adequately align pricing strategies with market dynamics and customer expectations.

Competition-Based Pricing

Competition-based pricing involves setting prices in relation to competitors' prices.[22] Based on information about competitors' prices, prices are set in consideration of the differences between the company's products or services and those of competitors. In contrast to alternative pricing strategies, such as value-based pricing or cost-plus pricing, where prices are determined based on factors such as consumer demand or production costs, this pricing approach takes a different perspective.

Value-Based Pricing

Value-based pricing is setting prices based on a consumer's perceived value of a product or service.[23] Value-based pricing is the most customer-focused pricing approach. Companies base their pricing on how valuable the customer believes a product to be. This pricing mainly applies to markets where possessing an item enhances a customer's self-image.

Some Repeated Mistakes in Pricing

Pricing is not an easy task for most companies, given the dynamics around the market. If a company can avoid some repeated mistakes in pricing, it can generate more significant marketing outcomes:

- Mistake #1—Only considering the cost of the product: When companies only consider the cost of producing a product, they may set prices too low to cover all of their expenses or too high to attract customers. Pricing should also take account of the value that customers place on the product, competitors' pricing, and the company's overall marketing strategy.

180 Marketing Management

- Mistake #2—No response to changes in the market: Pricing should be flexible and responsive to changes in the market. If the market becomes more competitive, prices should be adjusted accordingly to maintain market share. Similarly, if demand for a product increases, companies can increase prices to capture additional revenue and profit.
- Mistake #3—No consideration of other marketing mix components: Pricing should be considered in the context of other marketing mix components, such as product, promotion, and place. The price should align with the overall marketing strategy and objectives.
- Mistake #4—No price discrimination: Price discrimination is the practice of charging different prices to different groups of customers for the same product or service. Companies can maximize revenue and profit by using price discrimination strategies, such as segmenting customers based on willingness to pay, demographics, or geographical location.
- Mistake #5—Too much price discount for short-term performance: While discounts can be effective in generating short-term sales, they can also undermine the perceived value of a product and erode profit margins. Companies should carefully consider the long-term impact of price discounts before implementing them.
- Mistake #6—Ignoring customers' expectations/perceptions: Customers' perceptions of a product's value can influence their willingness to pay. Companies should consider customer perception when setting prices. If a product is perceived as low quality, customers may be unwilling to pay a high price. Similarly, customers may be willing to pay a premium price if a product is perceived as high quality.

New Product Pricing: Penetration Pricing versus Skimming Pricing

When introducing a new product to the market, companies may consider two competing pricing strategies: penetration pricing and skimming pricing (Table 6.4).

Penetration pricing involves attracting customers to a new product or service by charging a lower price during its initial offering.[24] This lower price serves as a means of penetrating the market and attracting customers away from competitors. Penetration pricing utilizes the strategy of setting low prices initially to generate awareness of a new product among a wide range of customers. The objective of penetration pricing is to attract customers to experience a new product and establish a strong market presence.

Companies like Netflix and Disney+ employ penetration pricing by offering discounted or free trial periods to attract new subscribers. These promotional offers aim to penetrate the market, gain a significant customer base, and establish a strong presence in the market.

TABLE 6.4 Penetration Pricing versus Skimming Pricing

Penetration pricing Sell as fast/much as possible!	*Skimming pricing* You can buy it if you want!
• Price-sensitive customers.	• High demand from customer.
• Economies of scale.	• No benefit from large-scale production.
• Higher entry barriers.	• No potential competitors.
• Network externalities.	• Quality signaling.

Skimming pricing is a pricing strategy through which a company charges the highest initial price that customers will pay and then lowers it over time.[25] Skimming pricing is commonly employed when introducing a new product category to the market. The primary objective is to maximize revenue during a period when consumer demand is high and competition remains limited.

Once these objectives have been achieved, the original product creator may adjust prices to attract cost-conscious buyers while maintaining competitiveness in the face of lower-priced alternatives that emerge in the market. This phase typically arises when sales volume declines at the highest price level, necessitating a price reduction to meet market demand.

When virtual reality (VR) headsets were first introduced to the market, they were priced at a premium. Companies like Oculus positioned their VR headsets as cutting-edge technology with a higher price tag, targeting early adopters and technology enthusiasts who were willing to pay a premium for the immersive VR experience.

Price Discrimination

Price discrimination is a pricing strategy that charges different customer segments different prices for the same product or service based on the seller's assessment of what each customer is willing to pay (Figure 6.12).[26] Price discrimination relies on the seller's belief that customers in certain groups can be persuaded to pay higher or lower prices based on how they value the product or service.[27]

In "absolute" price discrimination, the seller charges each customer the maximum price they are willing to pay. In more general situations, customers are grouped based on specific characteristics or attributes, and each group is charged a different price.

The effectiveness of price discrimination depends on whether the profit gained from separating the markets outweighs the profit from keeping the markets combined. The success of price discrimination depends on the relative elasticities of demand in the different segments. Customers in less price-sensitive segments pay higher prices, while those in more price-sensitive segments pay lower prices.

One example of price discrimination can be observed in the airline industry. Customers who purchase tickets several months in advance usually pay lower prices compared to those who buy last-minute tickets. When demand for a particular flight is high, airlines adjust ticket prices accordingly.

There are several conditions that must be met for successful price discrimination:

- Segmentation of customer groups should be possible: Price discrimination requires the identification of customers with different willingness to pay for the same product or service.
- Responses to price should differ by segment: Different customer groups must respond differently to price changes. For example, some customers may be willing to pay a

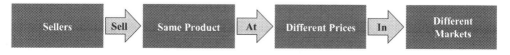

FIGURE 6.12 Concept of Price Discrimination.

182 Marketing Management

higher price for a premium product, while others may only be willing to pay a lower price for the same product.

- There should be no chance of "arbitrage": The prices charged to different customer groups should not be easily transferable between groups. This means that customers should not be able to buy the product or service at a lower price and resell it at a higher price to another group.
- The costs of implementation should be lower than the benefits to be gained: The cost of implementing the price discrimination strategy should be less than the benefit to be obtained from charging different prices to different customer groups.
- Customers should not feel negatively about paying a higher price; Customers who pay a higher price should not feel cheated or bothered by the fact that others are paying a lower price for the same product or service. This may involve subtly differentiating the products or services to avoid direct comparisons.
- There should be no legal issues: Price discrimination should not violate any laws or regulations related to discrimination or unfair competition.

If these conditions are satisfied, companies can successfully implement price discrimination strategies to capture additional revenue from different customer groups. However, companies should also take care to ensure that their pricing strategies are fair, have no negative impact on customers and do not violate any legal or ethical standards.

Price Discrimination in Movie Ticket Pricing

Movie ticket prices often differ at different times of the day due to a form of price discrimination known as "temporal price discrimination." This pricing strategy aims to optimize revenue by charging different prices at different times of the day based on demand.

Movie theaters typically charge higher prices for tickets during peak hours, such as evenings and weekends, when more people can attend movies. Lower prices are charged during non-peak hours, such as weekday afternoons, when fewer people are likely to attend movies.

This pricing strategy helps movie theaters maximize their revenue by charging premium prices for tickets during peak hours when demand is higher and offering discounted prices during off-peak hours to attract more customers. It also helps manage the theater's seating capacity by encouraging customers to attend movies during non-peak hours when the theater may have more available seating.

Price discrimination helps balance supply and demand by varying prices according to the time of day, optimizing revenue for movie theaters and providing different options for customers based on their preferences and budgets.

6.4.3 Place

In the marketing mix, "place," or marketing channel, refers to where products or services are sold. In other words, it is about how a company distributes its products or services to

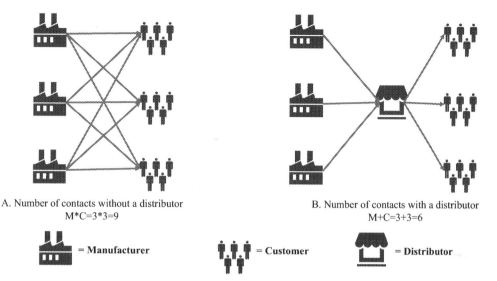

FIGURE 6.13 Key Roles of Marketing Channels.

customers. For tangible products, this will include physical locations such as brick-and-mortar stores. It can also include other methods to purchase, like online or mobile channels.

Distributors play a key role in reducing the number of contacts between companies and customers, which can help improve the efficiency of the distribution process (Figure 6.13). They consolidate demand for a product or service from multiple customers and place a larger order with companies. Furthermore, they handle logistics such as warehousing, transportation, and inventory management. They can also provide customer services such as order tracking, returns and refunds, and technical support to customers, such as installation, maintenance, or repair services. This allows the company to focus on producing and marketing the product or service.

Direct and Indirect Marketing Channels

There are two main types of distribution channels: direct and indirect. In a direct channel, a company (or manufacturer) directly provides the product to consumers. In this instance, the business may own all elements of its distribution channel or sell through a specific retail location.

In an indirect channel, a company uses an intermediary to sell its product to consumers. The company may sell to a wholesaler which further distributes to retail outlets. This may raise product costs, since each intermediary will get a percentage of the profits. This channel may become necessary for large companies that sell their products through many retailers.

Direct and indirect marketing channels both have their advantages and disadvantages (Table 6.5).

Direct marketing channels give the seller greater control over the marketing mix, including product, price, promotion, and place (distribution). They also allow the company

TABLE 6.5 Advantages and Disadvantages of Direct versus Indirect Marketing Channels

	Direct marketing channels	Indirect marketing channels
Advantages	• Control. • Relationship building. • Feedback.	• Broader reach. • Economies of scale. • Reduced risk.
Disadvantages	• Limited reach. • Resource-intensive. • Time-consuming.	• Limited control. • Reduced customer feedback. • Channel conflict.

to build a direct relationship with customers, which can lead to greater customer loyalty. Relatedly, direct marketing channels provide the company with direct customer feedback, which can help improve the product and marketing practices. However, direct marketing channels are typically limited, as the company must bear the costs of reaching each customer directly. It can be resource intensive and time consuming.

In contrast, indirect marketing channels can provide the company with a broader reach, as intermediaries such as wholesalers, retailers, and distributors can reach many customers at once. It can potentially benefit from economies of scale, as intermediaries can purchase products in bulk and reduce costs. However, indirect marketing channels give the seller less control over the marketing mix, as intermediaries may decide on some components, such as pricing and promotion. It can also lead to channel conflict where the company operates its own direct channels at the same time.

Each marketing channel has its value-add of sales and cost per transaction (Figure 6.14). Companies should choose the most appropriate channel or combination of channels based on their target customer segments, product or service characteristics, and budget:

- Salesforces: These are teams of sales representatives who promote and sell a company's products or services directly to customers. The value-add of sales for this channel is

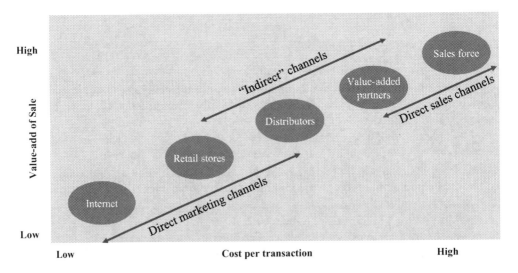

FIGURE 6.14 Type of Marketing Channels.

high, as they can provide personalized attention to customers and answer any questions about the product or service. However, the cost per transaction for this channel is also high, as teams require salaries, training, and other expenses.

- Value-added partners: These are companies or individuals that add value to a product or service before it reaches the end customers. For example, a company may provide installation or maintenance services for a product. The value-add of sales for this channel is high, as these partners can provide specialized services that enhance a product's value. The cost per transaction for this channel can vary, but it is often lower than a salesforce channel, as partners may be paid based on performance or commission.
- Distributors: These buy products or services from a manufacturer or supplier and sell them to retailers or end customers. The value-add of sales for this channel is moderate, as distributors can help reach a broader customer base and handle logistics and inventory management. The cost per transaction for this channel is mostly lower than salesforces or value-added partners, as distributors may purchase products in bulk and sell them to retailers or end customers.
- Retail stores: These are physical locations where customers can buy a company's products or services directly. The value-add of sales for this channel is moderate, as customers can see, touch, and try products before buying. The cost per transaction for this channel is relatively low, as stores may handle a few components of marketing distribution, such as logistics and inventory management.
- Internet channel: This involves selling products or services through an online platform. The value-add of sales for this channel is limited, as customers should browse and buy products or services by themselves. The cost per transaction is also cheaper than most other marketing channels, as it does not require physical infrastructure; and companies can use information systems for operating transactions.

New Marketing Channel Strategy: Digital (Online) Channel

Digital marketing leverages digital channels to market products and services in order to reach consumers.[28] This type of marketing includes the utilization of websites, mobile devices, social media platforms, and search engines. Its rise in popularity coincided with the emergence of the internet in the 1990s.

In essence, digital marketing shares fundamental principles with traditional marketing but offers companies a fresh approach to connecting with consumers and gaining insights into their behavior. Many companies integrate both traditional and digital marketing strategies to maximize their reach and effectiveness.

Digital marketing offers numerous advantages:

- Digital marketing channels are generally much more cost effective than traditional marketing methods. Online marketing also can reach a wider audience since the internet is accessible globally.
- Digital marketing channels allow customers to shop from anywhere at any time. Additionally, online stores can offer a wider variety of products and services than brick-and-mortar stores due to not being limited by physical space.

186 Marketing Management

- Digital marketing enables a high level of customization, from targeted ads to personalized content marketing. This customization can result in a better customer experience.
- Digital marketing channels provide quick and direct customer feedback through reviews, comments, and social media interactions. This feedback can help businesses improve their products and services and adjust their marketing strategies accordingly.

On the other hand, digital marketing channels are not without their disadvantages:

- One major disadvantage of digital marketing is that it can lead to price competition. With the ease of comparison shopping and the abundance of options available online, businesses may be forced to lower their prices to stay competitive.
- Another disadvantage is the potential for security breaches. Online transactions and data storage are vulnerable to hacking and cyberattacks, which can result in the loss of sensitive information and damage a company's reputation.
- Digital marketing channels lack the personal touch that traditional marketing methods provide. Customers may feel disconnected from the brand, leading to a lack of loyalty and engagement.

Table 6.6 summarizes the advantages and disadvantages of digital marketing channels.

The MEI can benefit significantly from digital marketing channels to reach and engage its target audience. For example, the emergence of online streaming channels has transformed the MEI in recent years. These channels allow users to access a vast library of content on-demand without subscribing to traditional cable or satellite TV services.

Online streaming platforms are major players in creating original content, producing movies, TV shows, documentaries, and more. Online streaming channels allow media and entertainment companies to distribute their content directly to viewers without going through traditional distribution channels. This gives them more control over their content and allows them to reach a wider audience.

Another benefit of online streaming channels is the collection of data on user behavior and preferences, which can be used to improve recommendations and personalize the user experience. Creators can also use this data to better understand their audience and create content that resonates with them.

6.4.4 Promotion

Marketing promotion is planned, persuasive, targeted, and goal-driven communication with (potential) customers. It is used to make the offer known to potential customers and

TABLE 6.6 Advantages and Disadvantages of Digital Marketing Channels

Advantages	Disadvantages
• Low cost/wider area.	• Price competition.
• Convenient access.	• Security issues.
• Diverse assortment.	• Lack of personal touch.
• Customization.	• Information overload.
• Quick feedback from customers.	

persuade them to investigate it further.[29] In other words, it is the medium used to directly communicate and engage with customers.

With the advancement of modern technology, companies have more channels than ever through which to communicate. This allows a business to tailor its message to a specific customer and communicate how the product will satisfy their needs.

Different organizations have different expectations for their promotional activities. These expectations are developed into objectives, shaping the selection and execution of these activities:[30]

- Building awareness: A product or brand must often create an identity within the market. For the most part, this applies to a new company, a new brand, or a new product; but it may also be often needed when rebranding or building up a failing product. The aim is to select promotional activities that help inform the customer about the company and the product.
- Creating interest: If the customer is already aware of the product or has been made aware of it through certain activities, it becomes necessary to move them along to actual purchasing behavior. The aim here is to identify a need that the product fulfills and ensure that the customer recognizes this need as something unfulfilled.
- Providing information: Sometimes a company may need to provide necessary information regarding the product, its benefits, features, or usage to the consumer. This may be the case if a new product is introduced.
- Stimulate demand: A company may seek to enhance its sales through promotion. If sales have been lower than usual, the aim may be to get them back up to the target level by re-engaging old customers and encouraging new ones to try a product. In other instances, the aim may be to increase sales at certain times of the year, such as near a major holiday. Free demonstrations or special deals may be used to achieve these ends.
- Reinforcing the brand: One primary aim of promotional activity may be to further strengthen the brand and its place in the market. This helps turn first-time purchasers into lifetime purchasers. This can also help create advocates for the product from within the customer base.

Five methods make up a promotional mix, as follows:[31]

- Advertising: This promotional method involves paid communication through various mass media channels such as television, radio, newspapers, magazines, billboards, websites, brochures, and direct mail. While advertising was traditionally one-sided, the advent of new media platforms like the internet allows for quicker feedback and interaction with consumers.
- Public relations (PR) and sponsorship: PR activities aim to generate positive mentions and coverage of a product or brand in influential media outlets such as newspapers, magazines, talk shows, social networks, and blogs. This can involve both paid and unpaid efforts. Sponsorship of major events or collaborations with influencers and super users can also increase brand visibility and generate positive word of mouth.
- Personal selling: Personal selling is based on direct interaction between company representatives and consumers. This approach focuses on building personal relationships

188 Marketing Management

and creating a connection between the client and the brand or product. Personal selling can take place in person, over the phone, via email, or through chat platforms.

- Direct marketing: Direct marketing targets specific influential potential customers through methods like telemarketing, personalized letters, emails, and text messages. This approach allows for targeted communication and customized offers tailored to the preferences and needs of individual customers.
- Sales promotions: Sales promotions are short-term tactical activities designed to stimulate immediate sales. Examples include bundle discounts (e.g., "buy one, get one"), seasonal discounts, and time-limited coupons. These activities aim to create a sense of urgency and incentivize customers to make a purchase within a specific timeframe.

A company may use one or more of the above methods in harmony to ensure a clear, compelling, and direct message reaches the customer. The selection of the portfolio of activities may depend on the company's marketing strategies.

The MEI is known for innovative and creative marketing promotion activities aimed at attracting and retaining audiences. Movie trailers are a classic example of marketing promotion in the movie industry. They are typically released months before a movie's release date and provide a sneak peek of its plot, cast, and production values. The trailer for *The Blair Witch Project* (1999) used a viral marketing campaign to create a buzz around the movie.[32] The filmmakers created a fake documentary-style website and online forums, suggesting that the events in the movie were real. This generated intense curiosity among viewers and the movie was massively success. The trailer for *Deadpool* (2016) was widely praised for its irreverent and humorous tone, which perfectly captured the spirit of the movie. The trailer also featured innovative uses of pop culture references, which helped it stand out from other superhero movies.[33]

6.5 Brand Management

6.5.1 Brand Concept

A brand is what people say about you when you are not in the room.

—Jeff Bezos

Products are made in the factory, but the brands are created in mind.

—Walter Landor

The Concept of Brand

According to branding guru Seth Godin, a "brand" is "the set of expectations, memories, stories and relationships that, taken together, account for a consumer's decision to choose one product or service over another."[34]

The American Marketing Association defines a "brand" as "a name, term, design, symbol, or any other feature that identifies one seller's good or service as distinct from those of other sellers."[35]

A brand encompasses the perception or image that individuals associate with specific products, services, or activities offered by a company. This includes both practical aspects, such as the product's features; and emotional elements, such as the feelings evoked when engaging with the brand. It is not limited to physical attributes but also covers the emotional connection consumers develop toward the company or its offerings, which is triggered by elements like the name, logo, visual identity, and messaging.[36]

Branding has a rich history, with its origins dating back centuries. For example, Italians used watermarks on paper as a form of branding, while cattle ranchers in rural America marked their livestock for identification purposes. The concept of branding gained traction in the 19th century when companies started packaging their goods to differentiate themselves from competitors.

A brand serves as an intangible asset that helps consumers identify a particular company and its products, especially in a competitive marketplace where differentiation is crucial.[37] This is especially true when companies must set themselves apart from others who provide similar products.

It is important to distinguish between a brand and marketing tools like logos or slogans (although these terms are often used interchangeably). Logos and slogans are promotional tools utilized by companies to market their offerings; while together, they contribute to create a brand identity. Effective marketing helps keep a company's brand at the forefront of consumers' minds, influencing their preference for one brand over another.

A brand is recognized as one of a company's most valuable and significant assets. Some companies are synonymous with their brands, becoming inseparable from them.

Ultimately, a brand encapsulates the intuitive feeling individuals have about a specific product or company. Each person develops their own perception of a brand, and the popularity of brands can fluctuate based on consumer sentiment and experiences.

Why Brands are Good for Both Customers and Companies

Brands are beneficial for customers in several ways:

- Reduced search costs: Brands help customers easily identify products or services that match their needs and preferences. This reduces the time and effort required to search for and compare different options, making the decision-making process easier and more efficient.
- Quality assurance: A well-established brand is typically associated with high-quality products or services. Customers can have confidence in the product or service quality based on their past experiences or the experiences of others who have used the brand.
- Improved buying experience: Brands can enhance the overall buying experience for customers. By providing consistent quality and service, customers can feel confident and comfortable in their purchase decisions. They are also more likely to be loyal to a brand that consistently meets or exceeds their expectations.
- Emotional connection: Strong brands can also create an emotional connection with customers by evoking positive feelings and associations. Customers may feel a sense of pride or identity in using a particular brand, which can lead to increased loyalty and repeat purchases.

190 Marketing Management

TABLE 6.7 Benefits of Brands for Customers and Companies

Benefits for customers	*Benefits for company*
• Helps the decision-making process, (e.g., by reducing search cost, providing quality information). • Improves the buying experience, (e.g., can predict the quality of product, comfort, and confidence).	• Sustainable competitive advantages: differentiation, price premium. • Helps customer retention. • Easier to launch new products. • Advantages in hiring and retaining talent.

Brands are also beneficial for companies in different ways:

- Sustainable competitive advantages: A well-established brand can create a sustainable competitive advantage for a company. A strong brand can differentiate a company's products or services from competitors, allowing it to charge a premium price for its offerings.
- Customer retention: Brands help companies to build a loyal customer base. Customers are more likely to continue purchasing from a brand they know and trust, which can help increase customer retention rates.
- Easier product launches: A strong brand can make it easier for a company to launch new products or services. If a company has an established brand, customers are more likely to be willing to try new offerings from that brand, making introducing new products or services easier.
- Advantages in hiring and retaining talent: A strong brand can also help companies attract and retain top talent. Companies with strong brands are often seen as more desirable places to work, which can help attract high-quality candidates. Additionally, employees who feel a sense of pride in their brand are more likely to be loyal to the company and stay with the organization for extended periods.

Table 6.7 sets out the benefits of brands for customers and companies.

Branding

Branding is the process of endorsing products and services with the power of a brand, shaping the perceptions of organizations, companies, products, or services in the minds of consumers.[38] It is a strategic process that aims to enable consumers to quickly identify and connect with a company, giving them a reason to choose the company's offerings over those of competitors. By clarifying the unique attributes and value proposition of the brand, companies seek to attract and retain loyal customers and stakeholders that align with the brand's promises.

The impact of branding extends to various parties, from consumers to employees, investors, shareholders, suppliers, and distributors. A strong brand not only helps consumers differentiate similar products but also contributes to a company's reputation. For example, individuals who feel disconnected from a brand are less likely to seek employment with that company; whereas those who resonate with a brand and find its products inspiring are more likely to seek opportunities to be part of its world.

When a company establishes its brand as its public image, it must define its brand identity, which encompasses how it wants to be perceived. This often involves incorporating the company's message, slogan, or product into elements such as a logo or symbol. The goal is to create a memorable and appealing brand that accurately conveys the desired message or feeling to consumers. When a brand generates positive sentiment among its target audience, it builds brand equity, which signifies the value and strength of the brand in the marketplace.

Well-executed branding not only boosts sales of the specific product being sold but also has a positive impact on the sales of other products offered by the same company. A trusted brand fosters consumer trust, and a positive experience with one product increases the likelihood of trying other products associated with the same brand. This phenomenon is commonly known as "brand loyalty."

6.5.2 Brand Equity

Brand equity is the value of a brand.[39] It is the simple difference between the value of a branded product and that product without that brand name attached to it. Brand equity is based on consumer attitudes about positive brand attributes and favorable consequences of brand use.[40] Brand equity is a multi-dimensional and complex concept, but an understanding of it is central if a brand is to fulfill its competitive potential.[41] Branding guru David Aaker defined "brand equity" as "a set of brand assets linked to a brand name and symbol, which add to the value provided by a product or service."[42]

As defined above, brand equity is a multi-dimensional and complex concept, but its understanding remains central to a brand fulfilling its competitive potential.[43] The complexity of the concept is evident in the diverse range of interpretations and attempted definitions put forth by both academics and professionals. In this chapter, two representative frameworks are discussed: Keller's Customer-Based Brand Equity (CBBE) Model and Aaker's Brand Equity Model.

Customer-Based Brand Equity Model

Renowned branding expert Kevin Keller developed the CBBE brand equity model, focusing on four essential aspects of brand perception and consumer attitudes: brand identity, brand meaning, brand response, and brand relationship. These elements directly address the key questions pertaining to how consumers perceive a brand and their associated attitudes toward it:[44]

- Brand identity ("Who are you?"): To establish robust brand equity, it is necessary to strategically develop a brand that stands out in consumers' minds, enhancing its identity and salience.
- Brand meaning ("What are you?"): The company's communication of its brand values plays a crucial role in shaping brand equity. It is vital to effectively convey both the performance aspects, such as meeting customer needs; and the imagery elements, which include developing the brand's personality and overall image to meet customers' psychological needs.

- Brand response ("What about you?"): Consumers' responses to a brand are influenced by their emotions and perceptions, particularly regarding the brand's perceived quality and credibility. To effectively manage brand response, managers should strive to establish expertise in their industry, communicate clear brand values, and better fulfill consumer needs compared to competing brands.
- Brand relationships ("What about you and me?"): Brand equity can be enhanced by fostering a strong connection or resonance between a brand and its customers, which is demonstrated by indicators like repeat purchases and active engagement across various marketing channels.

Brand Equity Model

David Aaker proposed a simple framework that features the key components of brand equity—brand awareness, perceived quality, brand association, and brand loyalty (Figure 6.15):[45]

- Brand awareness: Brand awareness concerns the extent to which a brand is recognized and known by consumers. A brand with strong brand equity will be easily recalled and recognized when consumers are searching for a specific product. This is also referred to as "brand salience," as the brand holds a prominent position in consumers' minds.
- Perceived quality: This aspect focuses on the brand's reputation for delivering high-quality products and providing a superior customer experience. The emphasis is placed on overall product quality rather than specific features, and consumers are often willing to pay a premium for brands known for their exceptional quality compared to other alternatives.
- Brand association: Brand association covers all the elements related to a brand that evoke positive or negative emotions and perceptions. These include the functional, social, and emotional benefits associated with the brand. In a broader sense, it encompasses the overall image and attributes that consumers associate with the brand. If consumers predominantly associate positive attributes with the brand, this indicates high brand equity.
- Brand loyalty: This is the extent to which consumers exhibit a strong commitment and preference for a particular brand, leading them to make repeat purchases and resist switching to competitors. Strong brand loyalty ensures stability and consistency for the business, allowing it to capture a larger market share.

FIGURE 6.15 Aaker's Brand Equity Model.

6.5.3 Brand Loyalty

Brand loyalty is the positive association and dedication that customers have toward a specific product or brand.[46] These loyal customers consistently make repeat purchases, even in the face of efforts by competitors to attract them away. Companies invest significant resources in customer service and marketing initiatives to establish and maintain brand loyalty for their products.

Loyalty can be measured through the frequency of repeat purchases. However, Keller argues that repeat buying alone does not necessarily indicate either high customer loyalty or high customer satisfaction. Customers can make repeat purchases and feel satisfied without demonstrating genuine loyalty to the product, brand, or organization. True loyalty goes beyond having a positive attitude toward the brand and requires deeper emotional connections that fully satisfy customer needs.

In other words, brand loyalty is a direct measure of customers' willingness to remain committed to a specific brand.[47] Aaker suggests that the price premium is the primary indicator of brand loyalty and the most effective measure of brand equity. Loyal customers act as a defense against potential competitors and reduce the threat of substitutes. Additionally, loyalty allows companies to respond to market innovations and creates a protective barrier against price-focused competitors. Therefore, brand loyalty is a fundamental dimension in the brand equity model, according to Aaker.

Strong brands consistently win the "moment of truth"—the moment when customers or users engage with a brand to develop or alter their perception of that specific brand.[48] The first moment of truth occurs when customers choose the brand over competitors, while the second occurs when customers experience the brand and find it consistent with the promised brand image. The third moment of truth occurs when consumers provide feedback or react to a brand, product, or service, thus becoming brand advocates who share their experiences through word of mouth.[49] Throughout the process, trust plays a significant role, as credibility is earned during these moments of truth.

Brand Community

A brand community is a self-selected group of individuals who share common values, standards, and representations, forming a unique culture.[50] The term "brand community" was introduced by Albert Muniz Jr. and Thomas C. O'Guinn. They defined "brand community" as "a distinct, non-geographically bound community formed by a structured set of social relationships among individuals who are passionate about a particular brand."[51] The Harley Owners Group (HOG) is a representative example of brand communities. HOG is a group of Harley-Davidson motorcycle owners who come together to form a community centered around their love for the brand. It provides a platform for Harley-Davidson enthusiasts to connect, share experiences, and engage in activities related to the brand. It provides a sense of exclusivity and belonging, as individuals feel connected to a likeminded group of enthusiasts who understand and appreciate their passion for Harley-Davidson motorcycles. HOG also plays a role in enhancing brand loyalty and advocacy.

The concept of a brand community focuses on the connections among consumers. Members of a brand community feel a sense of belonging and form emotional connections with each other and the brand. The community is characterized by a shared

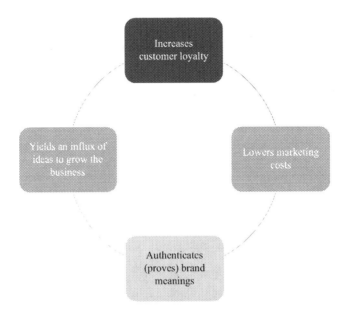

FIGURE 6.16 Benefits of a Strong Brand Community.

consciousness, rituals, traditions, and a sense of moral responsibility. When consumers identify with a brand and its values, they voluntarily join the brand community, seeking emotional support, a connection to their individual identity, and a shared culture.

A strong brand community can increase customer loyalty, lower marketing costs, authenticate brand meanings, and influx ideas for business growth (Figure 6.16):

- Increasing customer loyalty: A strong brand community can create a sense of connection among customers, increasing their loyalty to the brand. Customers who feel a sense of community with other loyal customers of the brand are more likely to remain loyal to the brand in the future.
- Lowering marketing costs: When customers feel a strong connection to a brand, they are more likely to share information about the brand with others through word-of-mouth marketing. This can help reduce the need for expensive advertising campaigns and other forms of traditional marketing.
- Probing brand meanings: A strong brand community can help authenticate a brand's meanings and values. When customers share their experiences and opinions about a brand with others in the community, it can help a company reinforce and authenticate the brand's values and meanings.
- An influx of ideas for business growth: Customers who are passionate about a brand are willing to share their ideas and suggestions for new products or services, which can help fuel innovation and growth for the company.

6.5.4 Brand Leverage

A brand leverage strategy involves using the established reputation of a brand to support the introduction of a new product in a related category (Figure 6.17).[52] This strategy

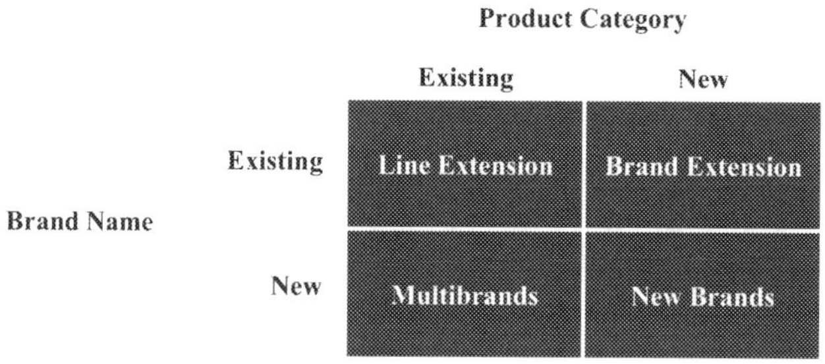

Product Category

		Existing	New
Brand Name	Existing	Line Extension	Brand Extension
	New	Multibrands	New Brands

FIGURE 6.17   Line Extension and Brand Extension.

leverages the positive associations consumers have with the brand, allowing them to transfer their trust and familiarity to the new product. This instant recognition and association with quality can encourage consumers to try the new product, leading to a successful market entry.

To ensure the success of brand leverage, it is crucial to maintain consistent quality across all product categories and limit expansion to related categories. This prevents brand dilution and minimizes the risk of disappointing brand-loyal consumers. By focusing on related categories, the brand can avoid direct competition and create a more effective branding strategy.

While brand leverage offers advantages such as cost savings in brand development and increased efficiency in manufacturing, it also presents challenges. The failure of new products can potentially harm the reputation of the parent brand, and diversification may result in higher manufacturing and inventory costs. Therefore, it is essential to carefully select and manage the introduction of new products to maintain brand integrity and maximize the benefits of brand leverage.

Line Extension

A product line extension aims to leverage an established brand to introduce a new product within the same product category.[53] The new product may have slight variations in aspects such as flavor, color, form, or ingredients.

For example, Coca-Cola has introduced various line extensions to cater to different consumer preferences. Examples include Diet Coke and Coca-Cola Zero. These variations were developed to offer low-sugar or low-calorie options to appeal to health-conscious consumers while leveraging the popularity and recognition of the original Coca-Cola brand.

In the MEI, several well-known companies have successfully employed brand line extension strategies. Apple has also used brand line extensions to introduce new products that are variations on its core product offerings. For example, the company introduced the iPhone SE, a smaller and less expensive version of its flagship iPhone line; and the iPad Mini, a smaller and more affordable version of its iPad tablet.

Disney has produced live-action adaptations of classic animated films like *The Lion King* and *Aladdin*, as well as new spinoff TV shows and movies featuring popular

196 Marketing Management

characters like *Frozen* and *Toy Story*. Similarly, Marvel—a Disney subsidiary—has created new characters and franchises within its larger superhero universe.

Brand Extension

"Brand extension" refers to the use of an established brand name on a new product or within a different product category.[54] This strategy capitalizes on the existing brand equity to introduce a new offering. By leveraging the loyalty and trust of current customers, companies aim to generate interest and acceptance of the new product under the familiar brand umbrella. Successful brand extensions can lead to expanded customer bases, increased sales, and improved profitability.

Brand extensions enable companies to diversify their product offerings and gain a competitive edge by leveraging the recognition and reputation of their existing brand. The established brand serves as a powerful marketing tool, reducing the need for extensive promotional efforts for the new product.

Brand extension can be applied to different product categories. For example, Dove—originally a soap brand—has successfully extended its presence into other personal care categories, such as deodorants, shampoos, and conditioners. Red Bull was originally an energy drinks brand and has ventured into extreme sports events, music festivals, and media production, including films and TV shows. Google—originally known for its search engine—has ventured into various non-advertising areas, including the Play Store, Chromebooks, Google Apps, and the Google Cloud Platform.

Different from line extension, brand extension can be a risky strategy, for the following reasons:

- Lack of fit: If the new product or service is not closely aligned with the existing brand, it can be challenging to convince customers to make the connection.
- Overextension: If a brand extends into too many categories or markets, it can become diluted and lose its distinctiveness. This can make it difficult to differentiate the brand from competitors, losing customer loyalty.
- Negative association: If the new product or service is associated with negative publicity or experiences, this can reflect poorly on the existing brand. For example, if a well-known food brand launches a new product line that is found to be contaminated or unsafe, this could damage its reputation.
- Cannibalization: If the new product or service competes with existing products or services under the same brand, this can lead to cannibalization of sales. This can be especially problematic if the new product or service is less profitable than existing products or services.

When brand extension fails, it can be costly for the company in terms of lost revenue and damage to its reputation. Companies should carefully examine the potential risks and rewards of brand extension before launching new products or services under an existing brand. Before launching a new product, brand managers must keep in mind their target audience and consider which products fit well under their company's brand.

Marketing Management **197**

Case Studies

The TKTS Theater Centers in New York City's Broadway and London's West End

The TKTS Theater Centers in NYC's Broadway and London's West End offer discounted same-day performance tickets using price discrimination strategies. These renowned booths—established in 1973 and 1980, respectively—have significantly contributed to theater growth and tourism. By adjusting prices based on demand, time of day, and theater popularity, these centers optimize revenue generation for theaters in the areas. This approach benefits both price-sensitive customers seeking discounts and those willing to pay higher prices for convenience. It enhances accessibility to live performances and bolsters the vitality of the theatrical arts. The TKTS Theater Centers are iconic symbols of theater accessibility and cultural enrichment in these two world-famous cities.

More case details for classroom use are available. Please check the book webpage at www.routledge.com/9781032221212 for more information.

Red Bull's Brand Leverage Strategy

Red Bull, a dominant energy drink brand, has employed a successful brand leverage strategy by extending its product lines into diverse categories. Utilizing its strong brand equity and customer loyalty, Red Bull aims to enter new markets and reduce reliance on a single product segment. This approach diversifies revenue streams and introduces new offerings under the trusted Red Bull brand. Examples like Red Bull TV, Red Bull Records, and Red Bull Racing demonstrate the effectiveness of this strategy. Careful alignment with core values and quality standards is vital for maintaining brand integrity. The Red Bull case underscores the significance of robust brand identity and thoughtful analysis when embarking on brand extensions.

More case details for classroom use are available. Please check the book webpage at www.routledge.com/9781032221212 for more information.

Review

- This chapter begins by introducing the marketing paradigm (6.1). This section discusses the customer-centric marketing concept and how it aims to maximize profits through customer satisfaction. It also articulates the concept of the customer as someone who interacts with the company by custom, believes in the company, praises the company, and preaches about the company.
- The next section stresses the critical importance of comprehensively examining both macro and microenvironments to gain a clear understanding of market dynamics (6.2).

198 Marketing Management

Macroenvironment factors include demographic, economic, technological, political, and social components. Microenvironment factors encompass various aspects, such as competitors and customers. 3C analysis is highlighted as an essential framework that analyzes customers, competitors, and corporation.

- The chapter then moves to the STP strategy (6.3), a strategic framework comprising segmentation, targeting, and positioning. The necessity of market segmentation is underlined, detailing the process of dividing a diverse market into homogenous and manageable groups based on a spectrum of characteristics, such as geography, demographics, psychographics, and behavioral factors. After segmenting the market, the company targets specific segments based on its strengths and the market attractiveness of the segment. Finally, the company strategically positions its offerings to resonate with the preferences of the target segment, establishing a unique market space.
- The next section articulates the 4 P marketing mix: product, price, place, and promotion (6.4). Each element of the marketing mix is dissected in detail, including the strategies and considerations associated with them. Companies utilize the marketing mix to evaluate key aspects essential to their business, such as understanding customer expectations, assessing the alignment of their product or service with those expectations, gauging the perceptions of their offering in the market, differentiating themselves from competitors, and establishing effective customer interactions.
- The final section of the chapter outlines how companies manage a brand in a complex, dynamic market (6.5). It describes different aspects of brand management, including building and leveraging brand equity, fostering brand loyalty, and managing brand communities. Further, strategies like brand leveraging, line extensions, and brand extensions are discussed with real-life examples from renowned companies. The chapter emphasizes the critical role a strong brand plays in a company's success and discusses the potential pitfalls of poor brand management.

Discussion Questions

1 How has the shift toward the marketing paradigm changed how companies interact with customers? What challenges and opportunities does this shift present to companies?
2 Why is marketing analysis crucial for a company's success? Provide an example of a business that thrived or failed due to its marketing analysis.
3 Discuss the importance of the STP strategy in today's diverse and dynamic marketplace.
4 How has the digital transformation affected the traditional marketing mix? How should companies develop and implement their marketing strategies in the digital era?
5 How can a company leverage its brand equity and loyalty to enhance its market position? Provide an example of a brand that effectively leverages its brand equity and loyalty.
6 What are the potential risks and downsides of brand extension? Can you cite a real-world example where a brand extension backfired and explain what the company could have done differently?

Further Reading

- Bitran, G. R. and Hoech, J. (1990) "The humanization of service: Respect at the moment of truth." *MIT Sloan Management Review*, 31(2), pp. 89–97.
- Broniarczyk, S. M. and Alba, J. W. (1994) "The importance of the brand in brand extension." *Journal of Marketing Research*, 31(2), pp. 214–228.
- Dholakia, U. M. (2016) "A quick guide to value-based pricing." *Harvard Business Review,* August 9, 2016. https://hbr.org/2016/08/a-quick-guide-to-value-based-pricing.
- Elliott, R. H., Rosenbaum-Elliott, R., Percy, L. and Pervan, S. (2015) *Strategic brand management.* Oxford: Oxford University Press.
- Fournier, S. and Lee, L. (2009) "Getting brand communities right." *Harvard Business Review*, 87(4), pp. 105–111.
- Van Waterschoot, W. and Van den Bulte, C. (1992) "The 4 P classification of the marketing mix revisited." *Journal of Marketing*, 56(4), pp. 83–93.

References

1. "Definitions of marketing" (2023) *American Marketing Association.* www.ama.org/the-definition-of-marketing-what-is-marketing/.
2. "The marketing concept" (no date) *Northern Arizona University.* www2.nau.edu/~rgm/ha400/class/professional/concept/Article-Mkt-Con.html.
3. Avlonitis, G. J. and Gounaris, S. P. (1999) "Marketing orientation and its determinants: an empirical analysis." *European Journal of Marketing*, 33(11/12), pp. 1003–1037.
4. Kotler, P., Rackham, N. and Krishnaswamy, S. (2006) "Ending the war between sales and marketing." *Harvard Business Review*, 84(7/8), p. 68.
5. Nwankwo, S. (1995) "Developing a customer orientation." *Journal of Consumer Marketing*, 12(5), pp. 5–15.
6. Barrington, R. (2021) "The impact of micro and macro environment factors on marketing." *Oxford College of Marketing Blog.* https://blog.oxfordcollegeofmarketing.com/2014/11/04/the-impact-of-micro-and-macro-environment-factors-on-marketing/.
7. Aguilar, F. (1967) *Scanning the business environment.* New York: Macmillan.
8. "PESTEL Analysis - Industry Research" (no date) *Washington State University Libraries.* https://libguides.libraries.wsu.edu/c.php?g=294263&p=4358409.
9. "3Cs Model (3C analysis business model)" (no date) *Web Analytics Consultants Association.* www.waca.associates/en/web-analytics-dictionary/3cs-model/.
10. Yankelovich, D. and Meer, D. (2006) "Rediscovering market segmentation." *Harvard Business Review*, 84(2), pp. 122–131.
11. Twin, A. (2023) "Marketing in business: Strategies and types explained." *Investopedia.* www.investopedia.com/terms/m/marketing.asp.
12. "Definitions of marketing" (no date) *American Marketing Association.* www.ama.org/the-definition-of-marketing-what-is-marketing/.
13. Van Waterschoot, W. and Van den Bulte, C. (1992) "The 4 P classification of the marketing mix revisited." *Journal of Marketing*, 56(4), pp. 83–93.
14. "Promotion marketing" (no date) *Association of National Advertisers.* www.ana.net/content/show/id/brand-activation-promotion-marketing.
15. Hester, B. (2019) "Marketing strategy: Forget the 4 P's! what are the 4 C's?" *CATMEDIA The Agency.* https://catmediatheagency.com/4-ps-of-marketing-strategy/.
16. Orth, U. R. and De Marchi, R. (2007) "Understanding the relationships between functional, symbolic, and experiential brand beliefs, product experiential attributes, and product schema: advertising-trial interactions revisited." *Journal of Marketing Theory and Practice*, 15(3), pp. 219–233.
17. Schmitt, B. (1999) "Experiential marketing." *Journal of Marketing Management*, 15(1–3), pp. 53–67.

18 Midgley, D. F. (1983) "Patterns of interpersonal information seeking for the purchase of a symbolic product." *Journal of Marketing Research*, 20(1), pp. 74–83.

19 Levitt, T. (1965) "Exploit the product life cycle." *Harvard Business Review*, 43(6), pp. 81–94. https://hbr.org/1965/11/exploit-the-product-life-cycle.

20 Dean, J. (1976) "Pricing policies for new products." *Harvard Business Review*, 54(6), pp. 141–153. https://hbr.org/1976/11/pricing-policies-for-new-products.

21 "What is cost plus pricing: Advantages & disadvantages" (2021) *Price Intelligently by Paddle*. www.priceintelligently.com/blog/bid/161014/Cost-Plus-Pricing-101-The-Necessities-and-Your-Pricing-Strategy.

22 "Competitive pricing: Pros and cons of competition-based pricing" (2022) *Price Intelligently by Paddle*. www.priceintelligently.com/blog/bid/161610/competitor-based-pricing-101-the-necessities-and-your-pricing-strategy.

23 Dholakia, U. M. (2016) "A quick guide to value-based pricing." *Harvard Business Review*, August 9, 2016. https://hbr.org/2016/08/a-quick-guide-to-value-based-pricing.

24 Spann, M., Fischer, M. and Tellis, G. J. (2015) "Skimming or penetration? Strategic dynamic pricing for new products." *Marketing Science*, 34(2), pp. 235–249.

25 Spann, M., Fischer, M. and Tellis, G. J. (2015) "Skimming or penetration? Strategic dynamic pricing for new products." *Marketing Science*, 34(2), pp. 235–249.

26 Varian, H. R. V. (1989) "Chapter 10" Price discrimination." In R. Schmalensee and R. Willig (eds.) *Handbook of industrial organization.* Amsterdam, Netherlands: North Holland Publisher, pp. 597–654. www.sciencedirect.com/science/article/pii/S1573448X89010137.

27 Anderson, E. T. and Dana Jr, J. D. (2009) "When is price discrimination profitable?" *Management Science*, 55(6), pp. 980–989.

28 Barone, A. (2023) "Digital marketing overview: Types, challenges, and required skills." *Investopedia*. www.investopedia.com/terms/d/digital-marketing.asp.

29 "Digital marketing mix & the 4Ps: An integrated marketing approach for business professionals" (2020) *Tower Marketing*. www.towermarketing.net/blog/digital-marketing-mix-4ps/.

30 Luenendonk, M. (2019) "Marketing mix: Promotion in four P's." *Cleverism*. www.cleverism.com/promotion-four-ps-marketing-mix/.

31 "How to establish a promotional mix" (no date) Edward Lowe Foundation. https://edwardlowe.org/how-to-establish-a-promotional-mix/.

32 Laman, L. (2022) "How 'The Blair Witch Project' changed movie marketing." *Collider*. https://collider.com/blair-witch-project-marketing-campaign/.

33 DiChristopher, T. (2016) "Deadpool's secret weapon: A viral social media campaign." *CNBC*. www.cnbc.com/2016/02/07/deadpools-secret-weapon-a-viral-social-media-campaign.html.

34 Godin, S. (2009) "Define: Brand." *Seth's Blog*. https://seths.blog/2009/12/define-brand/.

35 "Definitions of marketing" (2023) *American Marketing Association*. www.ama.org/the-definition-of-marketing-what-is-marketing/.

36 Andrivet, M. (2023) "What Is Branding?', *The Branding Journal*. www.thebrandingjournal.com/2015/10/what-is-branding-definition/.

37 Aaker, D. A. (1992) "The value of brand equity." *Journal of Business Strategy*, 13(4), pp. 27–32.

38 Ghodeswar, B. M. (2008) "Building brand identity in competitive markets: A conceptual model." *Journal of Product & Brand Management*, 17(1), pp. 4–12.

39 Elliott, R. H., Rosenbaum-Elliott, R., Percy, L. and Pervan, S. (2015) *Strategic brand management.* Oxford: Oxford University Press.

40 "Definitions of marketing" (2023) *American Marketing Association*. www.ama.org/the-definition-of-marketing-what-is-marketing/.

41 Williams, A. (2021) "What is brand equity?" *The Branding Journal*. www.thebrandingjournal.com/2021/02/brand-equity/.

42 Aaker, D. A. (2009) Managing brand equity. New York: Simon and Schuster.

43 Williams, A. (2021) "What is brand equity?" *The Branding Journal*. www.thebrandingjournal.com/2021/02/brand-equity/.

44 Keller, K. L. (2012) *Strategic brand management: Building, measuring, and managing brand equity.* 4th edn. Boston, MA: Pearson Education.

45 Williams, A. (2021) "What is brand equity?" *The Branding Journal*. www.thebrandingjournal.com/2021/02/brand-equity/.

46 Broniarczyk, S. M. and Alba, J. W. (1994) "The importance of the brand in brand extension." *Journal of Marketing Research*, 31(2), pp. 214–228.

47 van Haaften, R. (no date) "2.1.5 Brand loyalty." *Rovaha: Marketing, Strategy and Management*. www.van-haaften.nl/branding/corporate-branding/113-brand-loyalty.

48 Bitran, G. R. and Hoech, J. (1990) "The humanization of service: Respect at the moment of truth." *MIT Sloan Management Review*, 31(2), pp. 89–97.

49 Blackshaw, P. (2006) "The third moment of truth." *ClickZ*. www.clickz.com/the-third-moment-of-truth/67161/

50 Fournier, S. and Lee, L. (2009) "Getting brand communities right." *Harvard Business Review*, 87(4), pp. 105–111.

51 Muniz Jr, A. M. and O'Guinn, T.C. (2001) "Brand community." *Journal of Consumer Research*, 27(4), pp. 412–432.

52 "Building your brand with brand line extensions" (no date) *Iowa State University Extension and Outreach*. www.extension.iastate.edu/agdm/wholefarm/html/c5-53.html.

53 Mason, C. H. and Milne, G. R. (1994) "An approach for identifying cannibalization within product line extensions and multi-brand strategies." *Journal of Business Research*, 31(2–3), pp. 163–170.

54 Broniarczyk, S. M. and Alba, J. W. (1994) "The importance of the brand in brand extension." *Journal of Marketing Research*, 31(2), pp. 214–228.

7

CUSTOMER RELATIONSHIP MANAGEMENT IN MEDIA AND ENTERTAINMENT ORGANIZATIONS

Outline

Overview	202
7.1 CRM Framework	203
7.2 Customer Acquisition	212
7.3 Customer Retention	217
7.4 Customer Expansion	221
7.5 Managing Customer Misbehavior	228
Case Studies	230
Review	231
Discussion Questions	232
Further Reading	232
References	232

Intended Learning Outcomes

- Define and explain the concept and core activities of customer relationship management (CRM).
- Compare and analyze different CRM activities in the dynamic CRM framework.
- Identify and evaluate real CRM activities in the media and entertainment industry (MEI).

Overview

CRM is the process of building, retaining, and expanding long-term partnerships between a company and its customers based on mutual trust.

DOI: 10.4324/9781003271222-10

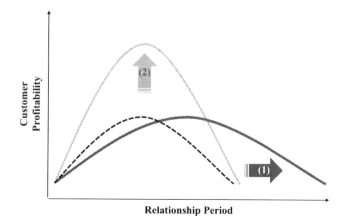

FIGURE 7.1 CRM Strategies: Increasing Customer Profitability and Extending the Relationship Period.

The two main generic CRM strategies involve increasing customer profitability and extending the customer relationship period:

- Increasing customer profitability: This approach identifies the most profitable customers and finds ways to increase their spending with the company. This might involve offering personalized promotions or discounts, cross-selling or up-selling additional products or services, or providing exceptional customer service that encourages customers to continue doing business with the company.
- Extending the customer relationship period: This strategy builds long-term customer relationships by providing ongoing value and support. This might involve providing personalized communication or content, offering loyalty rewards or benefits, or creating a community through which customers can connect with the company.

The specific strategies a company chooses will depend on its goals and the needs of its customers; but in most cases, combining the two strategies will be key in any CRM practices (Figure 7.1). That said, the overarching goal of CRM is to build solid and ongoing relationships with customers that benefit both the customer and the company.

7.1 CRM Framework

7.1.1 The Concept of the Customer in CRM

Customers are essential because they drive revenues; businesses cannot continue to exist without them.[1] As discussed in Chapter 6, the terms "customer" and "consumer" are almost synonymous and are often used interchangeably.

In CRM, three classes of customers can be identified: "customers," "identified customers," and "core customers" (Figure 7.2). "Customers" are similar to "consumers," defined as the individuals or businesses that consume or use goods and services. "Identified customers" are a subset of customers whose details have been acquired by a

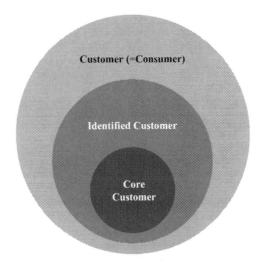

FIGURE 7.2 The Concept of the Customer in CRM.

company. Finally, "core customers" are a company's most important customers, distinguished by their long-term value to the company.[2]

7.1.2 Identifying Core Customers

Managers recognize the need to manage different groups of customers, defined by loyalty, profitability, and other factors. CRM is the art of attracting and retaining profitable customers.

A customer is considered profitable when the long-term revenue stream they generate exceeds the costs incurred by the company in attracting, retaining, and serving them by an acceptable margin. For example, according to the 80/20 rule, the top 20% of customers can potentially generate up to 80% of a company's profits.

In a seminal *Harvard Business Review* article published in 1990, Frederick F. Reichheld and W. Earl Sasser examined the efforts of service companies to satisfy their customers.[3] They discovered that successful companies aimed to achieve zero defections among their customer base, highlighting the risks associated with losing core customers.

Reichheld and Sasser emphasized the significant impact customer defections can have on a company's bottom line, often outweighing factors such as scale, market share, and unit costs which are typically associated with competitive advantage. They revealed that as the duration of a customer's relationship with a company increases, so too do the profits. Their research demonstrated that a mere 5% increase in core customer retention can see profits increase by between 25% and 125%.[4]

In addition to increased brand loyalty, long-term customers help reduce operating costs due to their familiarity with the company, which facilitates more efficient and effective service. Core customers are also willing to pay premium prices for products or services, and can serve as excellent brand advocates by recommending the brand to friends and family.[5]

Meanwhile, customer acquisition has become increasingly expensive, due to the availability of multiple media options, technological advancements, and hardware expenses, among other things. Additional data on core customers and profitability further supports

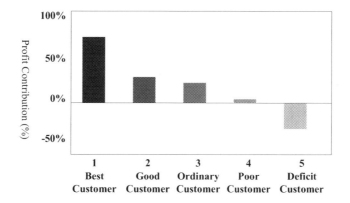

FIGURE 7.3 Profit Contribution by Customer Types: An Example.

these findings.[6] Core customers generate profits for a brand, while acquiring new customers drains financial resources. As a customer's relationship with the brand continues, their engagement frequency increases, leading to higher profits. When considering the profits to be gained from reduced operating costs, referrals, and premium pricing, the true value of a core customer becomes evident (Figure 7.3).

Given these compelling insights, it is important to allocate sufficient resources to retain the core customer base. Core customers not only provide profitable revenue streams for companies, but also serve as the foundation for future growth.[7] The key lies in focusing on core customer retention while simultaneously increasing the frequency of customer engagement.

7.1.3 Customer Value to Customer Equity

Customer Value Creation

Customers seek to maximize value. They form value expectations and act on them. Among different alternatives, they buy from the company that offers the greatest customer perceived value.

Customer perceived value = total customer benefits − total customer cost

"Customer perceived value" refers to the assessment made by potential customers regarding the overall benefits and costs of a particular offering in comparison to alternative options.[8]

"Total customer value" refers to the monetary value perceived by customers, covering the economic, functional, and psychological benefits expected from a market offering. This value is influenced by various factors, such as the product, service, people, and image associated with the offering.[9]

"Total customer cost" refers to the perceived expenses associated with obtaining, using, maintaining, owning, and disposing of an offering. These can include monetary expenses, time investment, energy exertion, and psychological considerations.

206 Marketing Management

To deliver high customer value, companies must focus on their value proposition, which encompasses the entirety of benefits promised to customers. This extends beyond the core positioning of the offering. Additionally, the value delivery system encompasses the entire range of experiences that customers encounter throughout the process of obtaining and using the offering.

Customer Satisfaction

"Satisfaction" refers to an individual's experience of contentment when evaluating the perceived performance or outcome of a product in relation to their expectations.[10] A customer's choice to remain loyal or defect is determined by the cumulative effect of numerous interactions with the company.

To track customer satisfaction, companies can monitor the customer loss rate, contact customers who have stopped buying, and learn why this happened.[11] In addition to tracking customer value expectations and satisfaction, companies must monitor their competitors' performance.

Customer Loyalty

"Customer loyalty" refers to the extent of customer commitment and attachment toward a specific brand, company, or product.[12] It represents the customer's inclination to repeatedly choose the same brand or company for future purchases, even when faced with competitive alternatives. Loyalty indicates the customer's ongoing preference and trust in the brand, fostering a long-term relationship and potential advocacy.

Why is customer loyalty so important?

Loyal customers tend to make repeated purchases over an extended period, which generates a steady revenue stream for the business. They often spend more per transaction and have a higher lifetime value compared to new or occasional customers. Businesses can also reduce their costs by targeting their existing loyal customer base with personalized campaigns rather than allocating resources toward broad customer acquisition initiatives. Loyal customers are more likely to recommend the brand to others. They become brand advocates, spreading positive word of mouth and influencing the purchasing decisions of people around them. This organic promotion can result in new customer acquisitions at a lower cost and with a higher level of trust. Finally, they are more willing to pay a premium for products or services from a brand they trust and have a positive relationship with. This reduces the need for businesses to engage in price wars or constant price reductions to attract customers, resulting in improved profit margins (Figure 7.4).

How can customer loyalty be measured at a company level? The Net Promoter Score (NPS) is a representative metric to measure customer loyalty and satisfaction. It was first introduced by Fred Reichheld, a Bain & Company consultant, in 2003.[13] The NPS is based on the simple question: "How likely are you to recommend our product or service to a friend or colleague?"

Customers are asked to respond to this question on a scale of 0–10, with 0 being "Not at all likely" and 10 being "Extremely likely." Based on their responses, customers are classified into three categories:

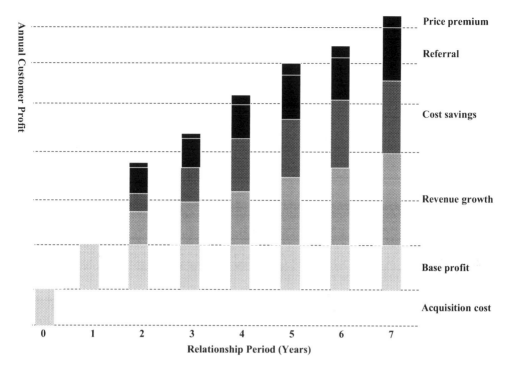

FIGURE 7.4 How Customer Loyalty Contributes to Profitability.

- Promoters (score 9–10): These customers express high levels of satisfaction with the product or service and are highly likely to recommend it to others.
- Passives (score 7–8): These customers are satisfied with the product or service but may not necessarily recommend it to others.
- Detractors (score 0–6): These customers are dissatisfied with the product or service and are unlikely to recommend it to others.

The NPS is calculated by subtracting the percentage of detractors from the percentage of promoters (Figure 7.5). The resulting score ranges from −100 to +100, with a higher score indicating a more positive customer experience, greater customer satisfaction, and, ultimately, stronger customer loyalty.

The NPS is widely adopted as a metric due to its simplicity, ease of comprehension, and ability to provide a rapid overview of customer satisfaction. Businesses utilize it to pinpoint areas that require improvement and monitor shifts in customer sentiment over time.[14] However, the NPS should not be used in isolation and should be combined with other metrics and qualitative feedback to gain a more comprehensive understanding of customer satisfaction.[15]

According to Reichheld's study, the average NPS across over 400 companies in 28 industries was just 16%.[16] Top performers had an NPS of 75%–80%

Top performers in any industry or market typically record higher NPS because they better understand their customers' needs and can meet or exceed those needs consistently. This leads to greater customer satisfaction and loyalty, which in turn translates into

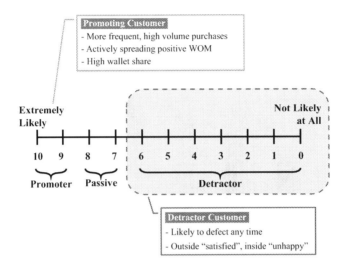

FIGURE 7.5 How to Calculate Net Promoter Score.

higher NPS. Common characteristics of the top performers with the highest NPS include the following:[17]

- They have a customer-centric culture, prioritizing customer satisfaction and loyalty as key business objectives. They focus on understanding and meeting customer needs, and they encourage their employees to go above and beyond to exceed customer expectations.
- They offer high-quality products that meet or exceed customer expectations regarding quality, reliability, and functionality. This leads to high levels of customer satisfaction and loyalty.
- They provide exceptional customer service, which is responsive, helpful, and empathetic. They can resolve customer issues quickly and effectively.
- They actively seek out customer feedback and use it to improve their products, services, and customer experience. They take customer complaints seriously and use them as an opportunity to learn and improve.

Customer Lifetime Value

"Customer lifetime value" (CLV) refers to the net present value of the future profits expected over the customer's lifetime purchases. In other words, it is the total value a customer represents to a company. CLV calculations provide a formal quantitative framework for planning customer investment and help marketers adopt a long-term perspective.

CLV is an important metric for businesses because it helps them understand the long-term value of a customer to their business. By calculating CLV, companies gain valuable insights into the optimal amounts to allocate toward customer acquisition and retention efforts. This serves as a guiding factor in devising effective marketing and sales strategies, as well as making informed decisions regarding product development and customer service enhancements. Key reasons why CLV is important include the following:

- By understanding the long-term worth of a customer, companies can determine how much they should invest in acquiring new customers. This knowledge helps optimize marketing and advertising expenditures to attract valuable customers.
- CLV can also guide customer retention strategies. Companies can focus on providing exceptional customer service, improving the quality of their products or services, and developing loyalty programs that incentivize customers to continue doing business with them.
- CLV is useful for identifying high-value customers and cross-selling or upselling them on additional products or services. By maximizing the value of each customer, companies can drive revenue growth and increase profitability.
- CLV can help companies allocate resources more effectively. By focusing on high-value customers, companies can prioritize investments in the products, services, and customer experiences likely to drive the most significant returns.

Figure 7.6 summarizes the process of how customer value creation leads to customer equity, increasing CLV.

Customer CLV is calculated as the difference between the *customer intrinsic value* and the *acquisition, development*, and *retention* costs.

The "customer intrinsic value" is the total amount of money a customer is expected to spend on a company's products or services over the entire duration of their relationship, minus the cost of the resources required to provide those products or services to the customer. It considers factors such as the frequency of purchases, the average purchase amount, and the length of the customer relationship.

"Acquisition, development, and retention costs" are the total cost incurred by a company in acquiring, developing, and retaining a customer over their entire lifetime relationship. They include the cost of marketing and advertising, sales efforts, product

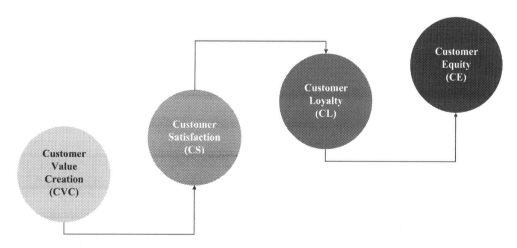

FIGURE 7.6 Customer Value Creation to Customer Equity.

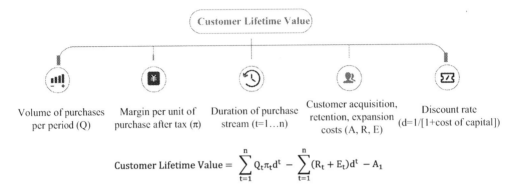

FIGURE 7.7 CLV Calculation.

development, customer service, and other expenses related to building and maintaining customer relationships.

By subtracting the acquisition, development, and retention costs from the customer's intrinsic value, companies can determine the total value of a customer to their business.

In sum, we can calculate customer equity through the following equation (Figure 7.7):

CLV = [Customer intrinsic value] − [acquisition, retention, and expansion costs]

CLV Exercise

- Customer intrinsic value
  - Purchase per year (Q): $2,000
  - Margin rate (π): 10%
- Acquisition cost (A)
  - $500
- Retention & expansion cost (R + E)
  - $100 per year
- Other assumptions
  - 10-year relationship (t)
  - No discount rate (d)
  - Purchase per year, margin rate, and all costs are fixed.

Based on the conditions above, calculate the customer equity of this customer.[18]

7.1.4 Dynamic CRM Framework

A dynamic CRM framework is a strategic approach that focuses on managing and improving the relationship between a company and its customers throughout their entire customer journey, from initial customer acquisition to retention and expansion (Figure 7.8).[19] It is an ongoing process involving continuous interactions and customer feedback, which allows companies to adapt and adjust their approach to meet their evolving needs:

- Customer acquisition: This is the process of attracting new customers. This stage involves attracting new customers to a company's products or services. The goal is to build a customer base that is likely to be profitable in the long term. Companies use various marketing and sales strategies to create awareness and interest in their products and services, and to convert potential customers into paying customers.
  In this stage, companies need information about the customers, such as profile information and the initial transaction history of the customer. The main tasks are to recruit and register the customer.
- Customer retention: Customer retention is the ability of a company to retain its customers over a specified period. Once a company has acquired customers, the next stage is to keep them engaged and satisfied to encourage repeat purchases and long-term loyalty. This involves providing excellent customer service, personalized experiences, and targeted marketing and communication efforts. The goal is to build a strong relationship with the customer that will increase their lifetime value and reduce churn.
  In this stage, companies need information based on customer value analysis. Companies can analyze information on the products and services that customers prefer and how the customer relationship has been built up.
- Customer expansion: This involves increasing the lifetime value of existing customers via increased loyalty, additional purchases, and more. This final stage involves expanding the relationship with existing customers by encouraging them to purchase additional products or services or to refer new customers to the company. This requires

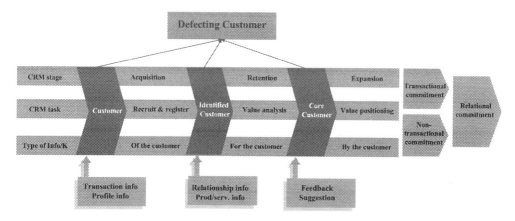

FIGURE 7.8 Dynamic CRM Framework.

212 Marketing Management

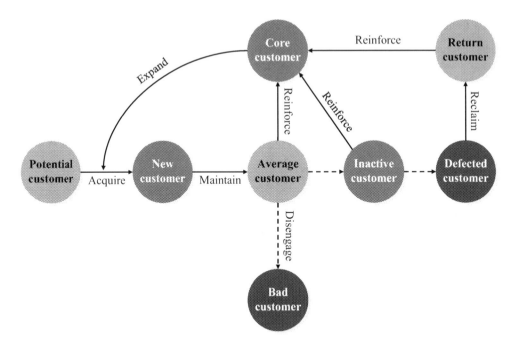

FIGURE 7.9 The CRM Framework.

a deep understanding of the customer's needs, preferences, and behaviors, and effective cross-selling and upselling strategies. The goal is to maximize the value of each customer and increase their contribution to the company's bottom line.

In this stage, companies will get feedback or suggestions from their core customers. The main task is to position more customized customer value and improve customer satisfaction and loyalty.

Throughout the CRM process, companies will build relational commitment between them and their customers while minimizing defections at each stage of the process.

In other words, CRM can aid in acquiring new customers from potential customer pools. Once these newly acquired customers have been retained, they have the potential to become average customers. Through CRM activities that strengthen the customer relationship, average customers can then transition into core customers. However, it is essential to address the risk of defection for average customers and implement strategies to regain their loyalty. Furthermore, disengaging from unprofitable customers is crucial to improve overall profitability. Lastly, core customers play a significant role in expanding the customer base as they act as brand advocates, promoting the company to others.

Figure 7.9 illustrates the CRM framework.

7.2 Customer Acquisition

7.2.1 The Concept of Customer Acquisition

Customer acquisition is the process of gaining new customers.[20] This involves efforts to convince individuals to purchase a company's products or services. The process guides consumers through the marketing funnel, from gaining brand awareness to making a purchase decision. The cost of acquiring new customers is a crucial metric for evaluating the profitability associated with each new customer gained.[21]

Customer acquisition is vital as it generates recommendations, enhances brand awareness, drives sales, and opens up new business opportunities. Acquiring a new customer often leads to an exploration of other offerings of the business. If the customer continues to find value, they are likely to recommend the business to others, thereby expanding the customer base. As the customer base grows, word about the business spreads, heightening brand awareness. This in turn fuels sales growth, enabling the business to introduce new products or services or expand into new markets.

A well-defined vision is the foundation for a successful customer acquisition strategy. Clearly defined end goals and aspirations are crucial. It is important to delve deeper into the vision and establish specific revenue targets, support systems, and desired profitability levels.

Identifying the target audience is another vital aspect of the strategy. The core customer base will vary across industries. For some consumer products companies, the target audience may be broad, while others catering to niche markets will have a more defined customer profile. It is important to understand who is purchasing your products or services and position your business as the solution to their needs. Consider their preferences, hobbies, and other products or services they consume and tailor your marketing approach accordingly.

Profitability is the ultimate goal upon which all other objectives rely. It is essential to focus on attracting quality customers who will contribute to the profitability of the business. Understanding and maximizing profitability is vital in order to identify potential core customers.

In addition, attracting customers through opinion leadership is important in customer acquisition because it allows businesses to harness the influence and persuasive power of these individuals, leverage word of mouth, and gain valuable feedback and insights.[22]

Environmental factors should be considered in customer acquisition. For example, the business setting—that is, business-to-business or business-to-consumer—is a key consideration, as CRM approaches will differ in terms of customer complexity, relationship depth, sales processes, and communication channels.[23] Also, product characteristics and competition level in the market may affect the company's CRM approach. For example, when products are complex, technical, or highly customized, the CRM approach often focuses on providing in-depth product knowledge, technical support, and ongoing assistance to ensure customer success. In highly competitive markets, where customers have numerous alternatives, companies may need to differentiate themselves by focusing on exceptional customer service, personalized experiences, and value-added offerings.

Figure 7.10 summarizes the process of identifying and managing core customers.

7.2.2 Customer Acquisition: Practices

How to Acquire Potential Core Customers?

The rules of thumb that can help identify the "right customer" for a business include the following:

- Inherently loyal: The right customer is inherently loyal to the business, meaning they are naturally inclined to stay with it over the long term. This type of customer is

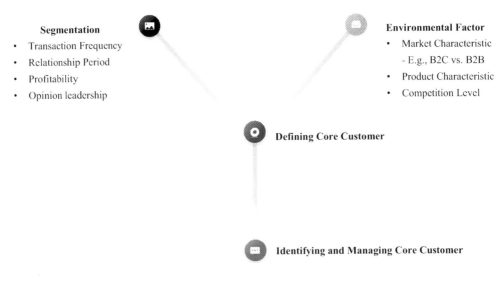

FIGURE 7.10 Identifying and Managing Core Customers.

valuable because they are less likely to be swayed by competitors and are more likely to recommend the business to others. They are also more inclined to make repeated purchases from the business, fostering a stable and profitable long-term relationship.
- Predictable: The right customer is also characterized by predictability in their behavior. This enables the business to anticipate their needs and preferences, allowing for customized products and services.
- Relationship oriented: The right customer is relationship oriented and prefers stable, long-term relationships with the business. This type of customer values trust, communication, and personalized attention, and is willing to invest in a relationship with the business over time. By building solid relationships with these customers, businesses can create a foundation for sustainable growth and success.
- Service oriented: Finally, the right customer is more sensitive to service than price. This means they value the quality of service they receive from the business and are willing to pay a premium. By providing exceptional service and support to these customers, businesses can differentiate themselves from competitors and create a loyal customer base.

By building long-term relationships with these customers, businesses can create a sustainable core customer base that drives growth and success over time.

In terms of practices, companies should consider different segmentation criteria. Profitability is one: identifying customers who spend more and pay more promptly while requiring less service. Recency, frequency, and monetary analysis or CLV analysis can be used for this purpose too. Fit is another important criterion: companies should customize their offerings to fit customer needs. More fitting customers will find these products and services more valuable.

Customers can be acquired through various marketing tactics, digital channels, and strategies (both on and offline).

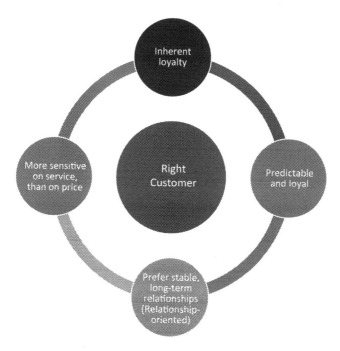

FIGURE 7.11 The Right Customer: Rules of Thumb.

Three Approaches to New Customer Acquisition

There are three generic approaches to acquiring new customers (Figure 7.12):

- Registering, inquiring, and responding to customers through advertising and promotion: This approach leverages various advertising and promotional channels—such as

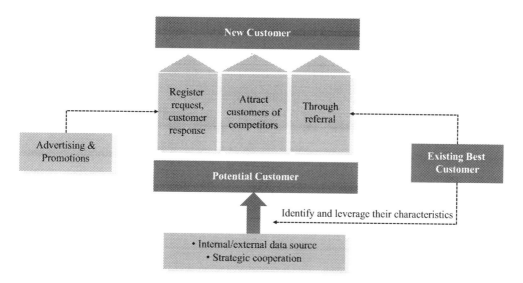

FIGURE 7.12 New Customer Acquisition.

216 Marketing Management

social media, email marketing, and paid search—to reach potential customers and encourage them to register, inquire, or respond to a specific call to action. This approach is often used for businesses with a broad target audience and that want to generate leads or build awareness of their products or services.

- Attracting and acquiring competitors' customers: This approach targets customers already buying from competitors and seeks to persuade them to switch to your business. This can be done through targeted advertising or promotional offers that highlight the unique value proposition of your business or products. It requires a deep understanding of your target audience and the competitive landscape, and may require significant investment in marketing and advertising.
- Leveraging word of mouth and referrals from existing best customers: This harnesses the power of customer advocacy by encouraging existing customers to refer their friends and family to your business. It may involve referral programs or exceptional customer service that inspires customers to share their positive experiences with others. This approach is often highly effective because it relies on the trust and credibility of existing customers to attract new customers. Moreover, businesses can analyze and utilize the characteristics of existing core customers to target potential new customers.

Businesses can obtain data on potential customers from internal and external sources based on strategic alliances. For example, businesses can use web analytics to track and analyze the behavior of visitors to their websites, including demographics, interests, and behavior. Businesses can also purchase data from third-party data providers, which can provide information on potential customers. Existing customers can refer their friends and family to the business, providing valuable data on potential customers.

One alternative is to acquire new customers through collaboration with other players in relevant industries. A customer share map is a tool used by businesses to collect data on their potential customer base and identify opportunities for growth and expansion.

For example, movie theater businesses can obtain potential customer data from a customer share map perspective by collaborating with other players in relevant industries to identify and target new customer segments (Figure 7.13). Potential strategies include the following:

- Partner with local restaurants: Movie theaters can partner with nearby restaurants to offer discounts or promotions to customers who visit both businesses. This can help the theater identify potential customers interested in dining out and entertainment.
- Connect with local event organizers: Movie theaters can partner with local event organizers to promote movie screenings as part of larger community events, such as festivals or concerts.
- Use social media: Movie theaters can use social media platforms like Facebook or Twitter to promote their events and engage with potential customers. By targeting ads to specific demographic groups or interests, the theater can identify and attract potential customers most likely to be interested in their offerings.

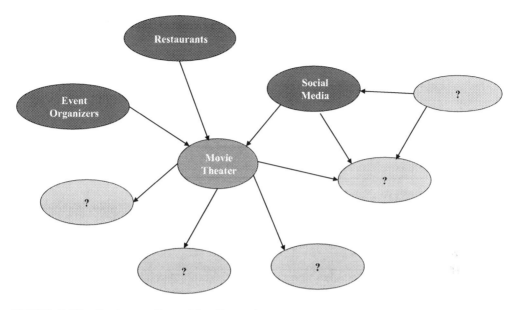

FIGURE 7.13 Customer Share Map Example.

7.3 Customer Retention

7.3.1 The Concept of Customer Retention

"Customer retention" refers to the ability of a company or product to retain customers over a specified period.[24]

High customer retention signifies that customers tend to continue purchasing or remain loyal to the product or business rather than defecting to competitors or discontinuing transactions. Businesses strive to minimize customer defections and enhance customer retention. The process of customer retention begins with the initial interaction between an organization and a customer and continues throughout the duration of their relationship. Successful retention efforts take into account the entire lifecycle of the customer. The ability of a company to attract and retain new customers is influenced by factors such as the quality of its products or services, how it caters to existing customers, the perceived value customers derive from using the solutions, and the reputation it builds within the marketplace.

Effective customer retention goes beyond meeting customer expectations. It aims to generate loyal brand advocates by exceeding customer expectations. By prioritizing customer loyalty, businesses place customer value at the core of their strategies rather than solely focusing on maximizing profits and shareholder value. Customer retention serves as a significant predictor of a company's financial success, as is evident in both accounting and stock market metrics.

Why is customer retention so important?

Research shows that the cost of acquiring new customers can be up to five times higher than the cost of satisfying and retaining existing customers.[25] It takes much greater effort to induce satisfied customers to switch from their current suppliers. The customer profit rate tends to increase over the life of the retained customer, but the average company

218 Marketing Management

TABLE 7.1 Importance of Customer Retention

Customer equity aspect	*Customer relationship/interaction aspect*
• Increases customer base and relationship period.	• Enables in-depth understanding of customers.
• Cost goes down as the relationship period increases.	• Strengthens customer relationships.
• Profit goes up as the relationship period increases.	• Increases customer loyalty.
→ Customer equity increases.	→ Core customer base expands.

loses 10% to 25% of its customers each year.[26] Thus, a reduction in the customer defection rate can significantly increase profits, given the high cost of new customer acquisition.

Given the importance of customer retention, there are four significant benefits of customer retention:

- Customer loyalty: Current customers already trust your brand, making it easier to make them repeat customers.
- Brand ambassadorship: Loyal customers act as vehicles of brand sentiment and customer acquisition via word-of-mouth marketing (e.g., testimonials and referrals).
- Cost savings: Repeat customers trust the brand, so there is no need for an extensive retention marketing strategy or advertising spend (versus new customers that require extensive spending to create brand sentiment and trust).
- Improved profitability: Satisfying new and repeat customers sustains loyalty and increases the bottom line. Happy customers tend to make repeat purchases over a more extended period.

When measuring customer retention, it is important to distinguish between behavioral intentions and actual customer behaviors. Behavioral intentions serve as indicators of customer retention since they are strong predictors of future behaviors.[27] Customers expressing stronger repurchase intentions toward a brand or company are more likely to exhibit corresponding behaviors. Repurchase intentions and behaviors can be measured in various ways, as discussed in multiple award-winning articles within the marketing field. Customer satisfaction plays a significant role in predicting both customer repurchase intentions and actual repurchase behaviors.[28]

Measurement of customer retention can typically be obtained through scale items included in customer surveys, while retention behaviors require secondary data sources such as accounting measures of purchase volume and frequency.

Customer retention helps facilitate the growth and stabilization of your customer base and company revenue.[29] By consistently delivering value, companies fulfill their brand promises, which elevates credibility, trust, and brand sentiment.

Table 7.1 illustrates the importance of customer retention.

7.3.2 Customer Retention: Practices

As previously mentioned, retaining customers is essential to build a successful business. Here are some strategies that can help companies retain customers:

- Recognition and registration: Companies can encourage customers to register for an account or loyalty program, which allows them to track their purchases and preferences. This information can be used to provide personalized recommendations and promotions.
- Coupons: Offering coupons or discounts to customers can incentivize them to make repeat purchases. These can be distributed through email campaigns, social media, or other channels.
- Frequency-based redemption: Rewarding customers for making repeat purchases, such as through a "Buy 10 get one free" program, can encourage them to continue doing business with the company.
- Mileage-based redemption: Similar to frequency-based redemption, companies can offer rewards or benefits based on the amount of money spent or the number of points earned through purchases.
- Needs-based offer and promotion: Providing personalized offers and promotions based on customers' preferences and needs can make them feel valued and encourage them to continue doing business with the company.
- After-purchase follow-ups: Following up with customers after a purchase to ensure their satisfaction and offer assistance if needed can help build a positive relationship and encourage repeat business.

"Rule of Two" in Customer Retention

The "Rule of Two" in CRM refers to converting a customer's first purchase into a second purchase. This strategy recognizes that the second purchase is often the most important in building a long-term relationship with the customer.

It aims to get customers to make that second purchase as quickly as possible after their first purchase. This might involve offering personalized recommendations or promotions based on the customer's first purchase or providing exceptional customer service that makes the customer feel valued and encourages them to return.

By focusing on the second purchase, companies can build a more loyal customer base and increase customer lifetime value. It is just one strategy in a broader CRM approach that aims to build solid and lasting relationships with customers and create a positive customer experience at every stage of the customer journey.

Loyalty Program

A loyalty program is a CRM strategy designed to incentivize customers to continue doing business with a company by offering rewards or benefits for their loyalty.[30] The initial objective of a loyalty program is often to collect data on customer purchase patterns, which can be used to personalize offers and promotions.

The most common loyalty program proposition is to offer customers the ability to earn points or rewards for their purchases, which can be redeemed for future benefits such as discounts, free products or services, or exclusive experiences. This proposition is simple and easy to understand, and it encourages customers to continue making purchases to accumulate points and reach the next reward level.

220 Marketing Management

TABLE 7.2 Loyalty Programs

Initial objectives	• Collecting data on purchase patterns. • A simple proposition: earn points for future value. • Examples include trading stamps and coupons, and airline frequent flyer programs.
Benefits	• Be the key drivers for enhancing customer experience. • Pinpoint individual buying patterns and predict future behavior.
Mistakes to avoid	• Don't create a new commodity. • Don't reward disloyalty or volume over profitability. • Don't promise what you can't deliver.

Examples of loyalty programs include trading stamps and coupons, and airline frequent flyer programs. Frequent flyer programs offer points or miles for flights, which can be redeemed for free flights, upgrades, or other benefits. Other loyalty programs include hotel loyalty programs, credit card rewards programs, and customer appreciation events or offers.

Loyalty programs can be a powerful tool for building customer loyalty and increasing lifetime value. By giving customers tangible benefits for their loyalty, companies can continue building relationships with them while collecting valuable data on customer behavior and preferences.

Loyalty programs are important for several reasons (Table 7.2). First, they can be a key driver in enhancing customer experience by providing personalized and relevant rewards and benefits that improve customer satisfaction and loyalty.

Second, they can help businesses pinpoint individual buying patterns and preferences and track customer interactions and feedback. This data can be used to identify opportunities for improvement, refine marketing strategies, and predict future behavior.

Third, loyalty programs can help businesses increase lifetime value by encouraging repeat purchases and higher spending. By providing incentives and rewards for customer loyalty, businesses can reduce customer churn and retain customers over time.

Finally, these programs can also help the business create advocates who are more likely to recommend its products or services to others. Businesses can foster a sense of loyalty and advocacy among customers.

When implementing loyalty programs, there are several mistakes that businesses should avoid:

- Don't create a new commodity: Rather than introducing completely novel offerings, loyalty programs should enhance the value proposition of existing products or services, creating additional incentives and benefits for loyal customers. This approach allows businesses to capitalize on their core competencies and expertise while providing added value to their loyal customer base. Furthermore, building on existing products and services ensures consistency and coherence in the overall customer experience, reinforcing the brand identity and strengthening customer trust.
- Don't reward disloyalty or favor volume over profitability: Loyalty programs should reward genuinely loyal customers, not just those who make frequent purchases or buy in high volume. Additionally, rewards should be focused on profitability rather than just increased sales volume.

- Don't promise what you can't deliver: Loyalty programs should be transparent and deliver on their promises. Overpromising and underdelivering can lead to disappointment and frustration among customers, damaging the relationship and decreasing loyalty.

As in other industries, loyalty programs can be a valuable tool for media and entertainment companies, as they can help build long-term relationships with customers and encourage repeat business. Moreover, by gathering data on customer preferences and behavior, businesses can use loyalty programs to tailor their offerings to better meet customer needs and preferences. For example, many movie theaters offer loyalty programs that reward customers with points or discounts for each ticket purchased. Some programs also offer perks such as free concessions, priority seating, or exclusive screenings.

7.4 Customer Expansion

7.4.1 The Concept of Customer Expansion

Customer expansion involves expanding the lifetime value of existing customers via product adoption, increased loyalty, additional purchases, and more.[31] Common customer expansion strategies include cross-selling and upselling. Customer expansion is significantly more cost effective than acquisition and can help companies sustain long-term growth when buying power decreases.

Businesses invest significant resources in acquiring new customers and driving revenue growth. However, there are many cost-effective strategies that can maximize the potential of existing customers. By focusing on customer expansion, companies can create value for existing customers, encouraging them to increase their purchases and engage with the product or service on a more regular basis. Successful implementation of customer expansion strategies not only leads to higher sales volume and profits but also helps retain existing customers, thereby eliminating the need for costly customer acquisition efforts.

To boost revenues, it is essential to prioritize a seamless customer experience, enhance customer satisfaction, and provide additional value to clients. Offering upgraded product versions, complementary products, or additional features for subscription-based services can capture users' attention and further engage them.

7.4.2 Customer Expansion: Practices

Identify, Transform, and Expand

Customer expansion starts with identifying and transforming identified customers into core customers.

To identify core customers, businesses can take the following steps:

- Segment customers based on behavior, demographics, and psychographics. This can help identify groups of customers with similar characteristics and needs.
- Calculate customer loyalty based on factors such as repeat purchases, customer satisfaction, and customer referrals.

- Determine customer profitability by analyzing the revenue generated by each customer, as well as their cost of acquisition, servicing, and retention.
- Assess customer fit by evaluating how well each customer's needs and preferences align with the business's offerings, values, and brand.
- Analyze the data to identify customers who are highly loyal and profitable, and who fit with the business. These are the core customers most likely to drive long-term growth and success.

By using loyalty, profitability, and fit as criteria to identify core customers, businesses can develop targeted strategies to deepen relationships with these customers, increase their value, and attract similar customers in the future.

Once potential core customers have been identified, companies should seek to transform them into core customers. Strategic management of the "moment of truth" is key to customer expansion. The "moment of truth" refers to any customer interaction with a business that can influence their perceptions of the brand.[32] Businesses can create positive experiences that foster customer loyalty and advocacy by strategically managing these moments of truth.

Companies can strategically manage their moment of truth through different approaches, such as personalized interactions, service recovery, positive employee interactions, scenario-based customer experience management, and education and empowerment of employees (Figure 7.14):

- Personalized interactions: Companies can use customer data to personalize interactions and make them more memorable. For example, a hotel might use customer data to customize room amenities and provide personalized recommendations for nearby attractions or restaurants.
- Service recovery: When things go wrong, companies can use service recovery strategies to turn negative moments of truth into positive ones. This might involve offering a sincere apology, providing a discount or free service, or going above and beyond to solve the problem.
- Positive employee interactions: Employees play a critical role in creating positive moments of truth, and companies can invest in training and development to ensure

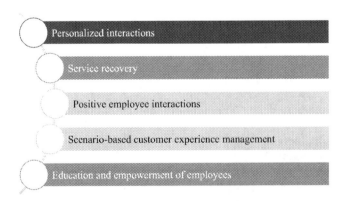

FIGURE 7.14 Strategic Management of Moment of Truth.

that employees are equipped to provide exceptional service. For example, a retail store might train employees to greet customers warmly and offer assistance without being pushy.
- Scenario-based customer experience management: Scenario-based customer experience management involves anticipating and addressing customer needs at different touchpoints of their journey with the business. Businesses can create a seamless and personalized experience that drives loyalty and satisfaction by designing scenarios that meet customer needs.
- Education and empowerment of employees: By providing employees with the knowledge, skills, and resources to deliver exceptional customer service, businesses can create a customer-centric culture that inspires loyalty and advocacy. This includes training employees on handling difficult situations, empowering them to make decisions, and rewarding them for delivering outstanding customer experiences.

Make Existing Customers More Profitable

Customer expansion is about making core customers more profitable. Increasing the revenue per customer is an effective way to increase CLV (Figure 7.15).

Ways to increase revenue and profit per customer include the following (Figure 7.16):

- Cross-selling: Offer related products or services to customers who have already purchased. For example, if a customer has bought a pair of shoes, you could offer them a matching handbag or socks.
- Upselling: Offer higher-priced versions of the products or services that a customer is considering. For example, if a customer is considering a basic model of a product, offer them a premium version with more features.
- Extending customer duration: Companies can aim to increase the time customers spend using their products or services. This can lead to higher revenue per customer as customers make repeat purchases or renew subscriptions. For example, by providing

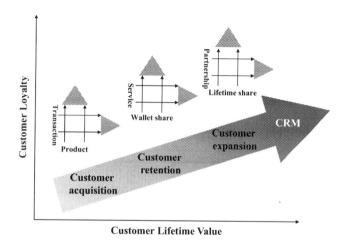

FIGURE 7.15 Customer Lifetime Value and Customer Loyalty.

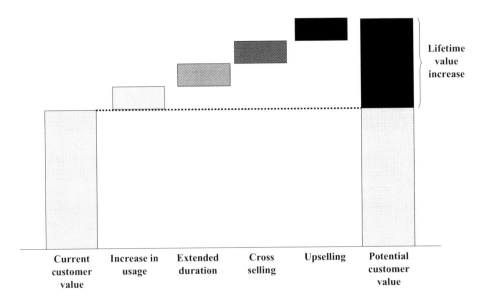

FIGURE 7.16 How to Increase Customer Lifetime Value.

personalized recommendations and content, media and entertainment companies can increase customer satisfaction and encourage them to continue using their products or services. Also, when customer duration is extended, there are many drivers to decrease customer management costs.

Upselling and cross-selling are the two main customer expansion strategies.

Upselling

Upselling is the process of enticing customers to enhance their purchases by upgrading a product or service or adding complementary features.[33] Typically, the promoted items are higher-priced products or add-ons that contribute to an increased total order value.

Similar to cross-selling, upselling typically occurs in the part of the buyer's journey where they have added something to their cart or initiated checkout and are more receptive to final sales efforts. As the customer has likely already researched the product, they may have considered the upgrade or add-on, which should increase the likelihood of them ultimately deciding to make the switch at the last minute (Figure 7.17).

Upselling is a common tactic that companies use to get customers to buy more of their products or services. Upselling is a common technique used in the MEI. For example, movie theaters employ different upselling practices to increase revenue per customer. Examples include the following:

- Premium seating: Many movie theaters have premium seating options, such as VIP or reclining seats, offering more comfort and amenities than regular seats. By upselling premium seating options, movie theaters can increase revenue per customer.

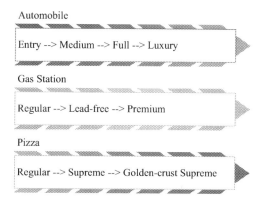

FIGURE 7.17 Examples of upselling.

- Concessions: Concessions such as popcorn, candy, and soda are a significant source of revenue for movie theaters. Theaters can increase revenue per customer by upselling customers to larger sizes or premium options such as gourmet popcorn or craft soda.
- 3D or IMAX screenings: Movie theaters often offer 3D or IMAX screenings of popular movies. By upselling customers to these premium screening options, theaters can increase revenue per customer.
- Merchandise: Many movie theaters sell merchandise such as t-shirts, hats, or posters related to popular movies. By upselling customers these items, theaters can increase revenue per customer and provide a souvenir of their movie-going experience.

Cross-Selling

Cross-selling encourages customers to purchase additional products or services to the original items they intended to purchase.[34] The cross-selling items frequently complement each other, providing customers with a stronger incentive to purchase both items together.

When a customer adds an item to their cart or proceeds to the checkout process, they are implicitly expressing their intention to make a purchase as an active customer. At this stage in the buyer's journey, businesses frequently employ cross-selling techniques, such as recommending a related product or offering a discount when two items are purchased together.

Cross-selling and upselling share a common objective, which is to encourage customers to make additional purchases. However, they differ in their approaches to achieving this goal.

Upselling aims to increase CLV by persuading customers to spend more on an upgraded or premium version of a product or service they already use. Cross-selling accomplishes this by enticing customers to pay more for a complementary product that enhances their initial purchase.

There are different approaches to cross-selling:

- Association analysis: This involves identifying products that are frequently purchased together by analyzing customer transaction data. For example, airlines may use

226 Marketing Management

association analysis to identify customers who purchase airline tickets and hotel rooms together and then offer them package deals or discounts on future purchases.

- Sequence discovery: This identifies products frequently purchased in a specific order by analyzing customer transaction data. For example, a retailer may discover that customers who purchase a jacket in the fall will likely purchase a long coat in winter and use this information to promote long coats to customers who have recently purchased a jacket.
- Market basket analysis: This involves analyzing customer transaction data to identify products frequently purchased together in a single transaction. For example, Wal-Mart famously used market basket analysis to discover that customers who purchased diapers were also likely to purchase beer and used this information to strategically place beer displays near the diaper section of their stores.
- Collaborative filtering: This employs customer data to identify products that are commonly purchased by customers with similar preferences. Leading online platforms like Amazon utilize collaborative filtering techniques to provide personalized recommendations to customers based on their browsing and purchase history (item-based), as well as the historical preferences of other customers with similar tastes (user-based).

Collaborative filtering is a popular technique used by many media and entertainment companies to recommend products to customers based on their browsing and purchasing history and the history of customers with similar preferences. Examples of collaborative filtering in action include the following:

- Netflix: Netflix uses collaborative filtering to recommend TV shows and movies to its subscribers.[35] When you watch a show or movie on Netflix, the platform uses algorithms to analyze your viewing history and the viewing history of other subscribers with similar preferences. Based on this information, Netflix generates personalized recommendations for each subscriber.
- Spotify: When using Spotify for music streaming, the platform employs algorithms to examine your listening history alongside the listening habits of other users who share similar preferences.[36] Using this data, Spotify creates customized playlists and recommendations tailored to each individual user.
- YouTube: By analyzing your viewing history as well as the viewing patterns of other users who exhibit similar preferences, YouTube's algorithms generate personalized video recommendations for each user.[37] YouTube continuously refines its recommendation system through continuous feedback loops and user feedback. The platform collects user interactions, such as likes, dislikes, and watch time, to improve the accuracy and relevance of its recommendations. User feedback and explicit signals help the system understand individual preferences and refine the collaborative filtering algorithms accordingly.[38]

Upselling versus Cross-Selling

The objective of upselling is to enhance the overall value of a transaction by persuading customers to invest in a pricier or upgraded variant of a product or service they are already considering purchasing. The focus is on offering customers a better version of the

Customer Relationship Management **227**

TABLE 7.3 Differences between Upselling and Cross-Selling

	Upselling	*Cross-selling*
Aim	Boost the overall value of the transaction by persuading customers who are already interested in making a purchase to opt for a higher-priced or upgraded version of the product or service.	Increase the total transaction value by persuading customers to purchase additional products or services that complement or enhance the product they are already interested in buying.
Focus	Offer the customer a better version of the product or service they are already interested in rather than trying to sell them something entirely new.	Offer the customer something new that complements or enhances the product they are already interested in, rather than trying to sell them a more expensive version of the same product.
Practice/ example in the MEI	Offer the customer a premium ticket package that includes additional perks like early access, exclusive seating, or complimentary concessions.	Offer the customer a merchandise bundle that includes a t-shirt, poster, and soundtrack album to complement the movie or concert they attend.

product or service they are already interested in, rather than trying to sell them something entirely new.

Upselling involves persuading customers to pay more for added features, benefits, or quality improvements. An example of upselling in the MEI could be offering customers a premium ticket package with additional perks like early access, exclusive seating, or complimentary concessions.

The aim of cross-selling is to increase the total transaction value by persuading customers to purchase additional products or services that complement or enhance the product they are already interested in buying rather than trying to sell them a more expensive version of the same product.

Cross-selling involves suggesting related or complementary products or services that the customer may be interested in buying. An example of cross-selling in the MEI could be offering customers a merchandise bundle that includes a t-shirt, poster, and soundtrack album to complement the movie or concert they are attending.

Table 7.3 summarizes the differences between upselling and cross-selling.

Build a Partnership with Customers

Finally, customer expansion aims to build a long-term, two-way partnership between the company and its core customers. Building a partnership with customers is a great way to increase their loyalty and lifetime value.

Companies can create an online and offline community through which customers can interact with them and with each other. This could be an online forum or an in-person event. They may encourage core customers to share their experiences, ask questions, and provide feedback. This community can be used to provide members with exclusive content, promotions, and rewards. Furthermore, companies can leverage social media platforms to engage with customers and create a two-way dialog. They can respond to

FIGURE 7.18 Customer Expansion Steps.

comments and questions, share user-generated content, and conduct polls and surveys to gather feedback.

More importantly, core customers can participate in the development of new products and services. By involving customers in the product development process, companies can ensure that their products meet their needs and preferences. This can be done through beta testing, surveys, or focus groups. They can also use this opportunity to build customer relationships and create a sense of ownership and loyalty.

"Prosumers"—also known as "producer-consumers"—are individuals who both produce and consume media content.[39] They can be a valuable asset to the MEI, as they can create authentic content that engages and resonates with their peers. For example, prosumers can create user-generated content that can be leveraged by media and entertainment companies. Companies can encourage prosumers to create content related to their products or services and use this to promote their brand. This can be done through social media contests, influencer partnerships, or a platform where users can upload their content.

Media and entertainment companies can also collaborate with prosumers to create content. For example, a prosumer who owns a popular YouTube channel can collaborate with a media company to create a video series or a podcast. This can help the company reach a new audience and provide the prosumer exposure and opportunities to work with established companies.

Prosumers can also provide valuable feedback and insights to media and entertainment companies. They are often early adopters of new technologies and can provide insights into what works and what doesn't. Companies can engage with prosumers through surveys and focus groups, or by inviting them to be beta testers for new products or services.

Moreover, prosumers passionate about a brand can become brand ambassadors. They can promote the brand on social media, blogs, and other platforms. This can be done through influencer partnerships or by providing prosumers exclusive access to products or services.

By creating partnerships with core customers through these methods, companies can build stronger relationships, increase loyalty, and gain valuable feedback and insights to improve their products and services (Figure 7.18).

7.5 Managing Customer Misbehavior

As discussed, identifying and managing core customer groups are key activities of CRM. That said, it is important for businesses to carefully select their customer base to ensure that they are working with customers who are aligned with their goals and values, and

Customer Relationship Management **229**

TABLE 7.4 Two Types of Customer Groups to Avoid

Customers without a fit with your firm	*Customers with behavioral problems*
• Have needs that exceed your firm's capabilities. • Do not have enough credit history.	• Generate negative value for your firm (e.g., breach of rules, illegal behavior). • Demand extra resources. • Generate negative word of mouth.

who will ultimately contribute positively to their business. Types of customer groups that businesses should generally try to avoid include the following (Table 7.4):

- Customers without a fit with the company: These customers have needs that go beyond what the company can offer or do not have enough credit history to engage with the business. Working with these customers can lead to frustration and dissatisfaction on both sides, as their needs cannot be met, and the company may struggle to provide the necessary resources to support them. It is important to carefully evaluate whether a potential customer is a good fit for the company before engaging with them.
- Customers with behavioral problems: These customers may generate negative value for the company through illegal behavior or may require extra resources to manage. These customers can drain the business, in terms of both the resources required to manage them and the negative word of mouth they may generate. It is important to carefully consider whether the potential benefits of working with these customers outweigh the potential risks and costs. Generally, it is best to avoid customers with behavioral problems, as they are unlikely to be a good fit for the business in the long run.

When dealing with "bad" customers, businesses may employ two approaches (Table 7.5).

First, companies may try to discourage negative behaviors through a variety of means, including:

- training and assigning special customer agents to handle demanding customers and de-escalate tense situations;
- making negative history data readily available to agents so they can be aware of past issues and respond appropriately;
- establishing clear rules and procedures for automatic disassociation, such as a "three strikes" policy, and notifying customers of these rules in advance; and

TABLE 7.5 How to Manage "Bad" Customers

Discourage the negative behavior	*Disengage from the customer gracefully*
• Train and assign special customer agents. • Make ready and share the negative history data. • Establish and notify customers in advance of the rules and procedures for automatic disassociation (e.g., "three strikes"). • Refer cases to a third-party evaluator.	• Raise prices and fees (but fairly!). • Introduce alternative product/service providers that can better meet their expectations. • Invite their natural enemies as guests.

230 Marketing Management

- referring the case to a third-party evaluator, such as a mediator or arbitrator, to help resolve any disputes.

Second, companies can disengage with "bad" customers in a respectful and professional way by:

- raising prices or fees in a fair and transparent manner to discourage the customer from continuing to do business with the company;
- introducing alternative products or service providers that may better serve the customer's needs; and
- inviting natural "enemies" of the customer, such as competitors or other companies they have had negative interactions with, to offer them alternative options.

Through these approaches, companies can avoid confrontations or negative customer feedback while freeing up resources to focus on more positive relationships. Ultimately, the approach chosen will depend on the situation's specific circumstances and the business's goals.

Case Studies

Starbucks Rewards: How to Best Engage Customers with a Loyalty Program

Starbucks Rewards, which was launched in 2009 to enhance customer loyalty, has thrived as a remarkable loyalty program. With 28.7 million active members as of October 2022, it has significantly boosted Starbucks' growth and profitability. This program employs a hybrid structure, combining points (Stars) and a tiered system (Green and Gold) to offer benefits like free items, birthday treats, and more. The mobile app engages customers and allows easy ordering and rewards tracking; while gamification elements and social features build excitement and word-of-mouth promotion. The app's data-driven personalization builds emotional connections and retention. Starbucks' well-designed, customer-centric loyalty program represents the positive impact of loyalty programs on business growth.

More case details for classroom use are available. Please check the book webpage at www.routledge.com/9781032221212 for more information.

Customer-centric Strategy of Zappos: "Deliver WOW through Service"

Online shoe and clothing retailer Zappos is renowned for its exceptional customer service and unique company culture. Founded in 1999 and acquired by Amazon in 2009, Zappos' "Deliver WOW through service" mission underpins its customer expansion strategy, cultivating loyalty and positive brand perception. With a focus on customer satisfaction, Zappos empowers employees to autonomously address needs and fosters a deep customer-centric culture. This strategy, combined with a strong emphasis on employee wellbeing, has earned Zappos a reputation for exceptional customer care and a positive workplace culture. Many notable cases represent Zappos' commitment to empathy, personalized experiences, and compassionate support to customers.

More case details for classroom use are available. Please check the book webpage at www.routledge.com/9781032221212 for more information.

Review

- CRM is the process of building, retaining, and expanding a long-term partnership between a company and its customers based on mutual trust. It drives companies to create customer value and transform it into customer equity (7.1). A dynamic CRM framework is a strategic approach that focuses on managing and improving the relationship between a company and its customers throughout their customer journey, from initial customer acquisition to retention and expansion.
- Customer acquisition is the initial step for any business, setting the tone for the customer relationship (7.2). Companies should segment their market based on demographics, psychographics, behavior, and geography to acquire customers effectively and then target the most promising segments. They can leverage existing core customer groups to attract new customers. This strategy, combined with a commitment to understanding customer needs and delivering value, can lead to successful customer acquisition.
- Customer retention keeps existing customers engaged and satisfied, leading to higher loyalty and profitability (7.3). Companies can leverage customer data to gain insights into customer behavior and preferences, and can use these insights to customize their offerings and improve customer satisfaction. Companies can increase customer lifetime value and profitability by focusing on customer retention.
- Customer expansion involves finding opportunities to expand relationships with core customers (7.4). This can be achieved through upselling and cross-selling strategies, which aim to increase the total transaction value by convincing customers to purchase a premium version of a product or service or to buy additional products or services that complement their original purchase. Building partnerships with customers is emphasized by creating online and offline communities and involving customers in developing new products and services.
- Customer determent management addresses the need for businesses to carefully select their customer base to ensure they work with customers that align with their goals and values (7.5). It also provides strategies for managing customers who may not fit well or exhibit problematic behaviors. The two approaches are discouraging negative behaviors and disengaging from "bad" customers gracefully. These strategies ensure that companies do not waste valuable resources on problematic customers and can focus on cultivating more constructive customer relationships.

232 Marketing Management

Discussion Questions

1 How can media and entertainment companies effectively implement a CRM strategy? What unique challenges might they face due to the nature of the MEI?
2 Discuss some innovative strategies companies can use to acquire new customers in the digital market.
3 How can companies balance the need for customer retention with the ongoing requirement for customer acquisition? Discuss the potential challenges and solutions.
4 Explore the concept of customer expansion in the context of the MEI. What are some novel ways companies in this industry can upsell or cross-sell to their existing customers?
5 Discuss the strategies of discouraging negative behaviors and disengaging gracefully in the context of the MEI. How can media and entertainment companies handle these difficult situations while maintaining their brand reputation?
6 Reflect on the overall CRM strategy. How does the interaction of the key components contribute to an effective CRM practice? How should companies balance and prioritize these different components?

Further Reading

- Buttle, F. and Maklan, S. (2019). Customer relationship management: Concepts and technologies. London: Routledge.
- Churchill Jr., G. A. and Surprenant, C. (1982). "An investigation into the determinants of customer satisfaction." Journal of Marketing Research, 19(4), pp. 491–504.
- Oliver, R. L. (1999). "Whence consumer loyalty?" Journal of Marketing, 63(4), 33–44.
- Reichheld, F. F. (2003) "The one number you need to grow." Harvard Business Review. 81(12), pp. 46–55. https://hbr.org/2003/12/the-one-number-you-need-to-grow
- Goodrow, C. (2021). "On YouTube's recommendation system." YouTube Official Blog. https://blog.youtube/inside-youtube/on-youtubes-recommendation-system/.

References

1 Kenton, W. (2023) "Customer: Definition and How to Study Their Behavior for Marketing." *Investopedia.* www.investopedia.com/terms/c/customer.asp.
2 "Core customers" (no date) *Oxford Reference.* www.oxfordreference.com/display/10.1093/oi/authority.20110803095638976;jsessionid=8EDF23E6FD9E951CD1827F017E26A03F?rskey= 49966 C&result=17.
3 Reichheld, F. F. and Sasser, W. E. (1990) "Zero defections: Quality comes to services." *Harvard Business Review*, 68(5), pp. 105–111. https://hbr.org/1990/09/zero-defections-quality-comes-to-services.
4 Reichheld, F. F. and Sasser, W. E. (1990) "Zero defections: Quality comes to services." *Harvard Business Review*, 68(5), pp. 105–111. https://hbr.org/1990/09/zero-defections-quality-comes-to-services.
5 "Brand advocates drive word of mouth" (no date) *Branding Strategy Insider.* https://brandingstrategyinsider.com/brand-advocates-drive-word-of-mouth/.
6 Light, L. (2022) "The undeniable value of core customers." *Branding Strategy Insider.* https://brandingstrategyinsider.com/the-undeniable-value-of-core-customers/.
7 Light, L. (2022) "Turnaround strategy begins at the core." *Branding Strategy Insider.* https://brandingstrategyinsider.com/turnaround-strategy-begins-at-the-core/.

8 Yang, Z. and Peterson, R. T. (2004) "Customer perceived value, satisfaction, and loyalty: The role of switching costs." *Psychology & Marketing*, 21(10), pp. 799–822.

9 Asgarpour, R., Hamid, A. B., Sulaiman, Z. and Asgari, A. (2014) "A review on customer perceived value and its main components." *Global Journal of Business and Social Science Review*, 2(2), pp. 1–9.

10 Churchill Jr., G. A. and Surprenant, C. (1982) "An investigation into the determinants of customer satisfaction." *Journal of Marketing Research*, 19(4), pp. 491–504.

11 Hill, N. and Alexander, J. (2017) *The handbook of customer satisfaction and loyalty measurement.* London: Routledge.

12 Oliver, R. L. (1999) "Whence consumer loyalty?" *Journal of Marketing*, 63(4), pp. 33–44.

13 Reichheld, F. F. (2003) "The one number you need to grow." *Harvard Business Review,* 81(12), pp. 46–55. https://hbr.org/2003/12/the-one-number-you-need-to-grow.

14 Baehre, S., O'Dwyer, M., O'Malley, L. and Lee, N. (2022) "The use of Net Promoter Score (NPS) to predict sales growth: Insights from an empirical investigation." *Journal of the Academy of Marketing Science*, 50(1), pp. 67–84.

15 Schulman, K. and Sargeant, A. (2013) "Measuring donor loyalty: Key reasons why Net Promoter Score (NPS) is not the way." *International Journal of Nonprofit and Voluntary Sector Marketing*, 18(1), pp. 1–6.

16 "How to achieve an NPS score of 60" (2018) *Billi UK.* www.billi-uk.com/news/how-to-achieve-an-nps-score-of-60/.

17 Alex (2022) "What do companies with high Net Promoter Score have in common?" *Retently.* www.retently.com/blog/companies-high-nps/.

18 Customer intrinsic value: $2,000 ×10% x 10 years = $2,000; acquisition cost: $500; retention and expansion cost: $100 ×10 years = $1,000 [$2,000 – ($500 + $1,000) = **$500**].

19 Park, C.-H. and Kim, Y.-G. (2003) "A framework of dynamic CRM: Linking marketing with information strategy." *Business Process Management Journal*, 9(5), pp. 652–671.

20 Leblo, C. (2022) "The four pillars of customer acquisition strategy." *Forbes*, August 15, 2022. www.forbes.com/sites/forbesbusinesscouncil/2022/08/15/the-four-pillars-of-customer-acquisition-strategy/?sh=1c2dd5ec3218 (Accessed: 20 February 2023).

21 Kumar, V., Pozza, I. D., Petersen, J. A. and Shah, D. (2009) "Reversing the logic: The path to profitability through relationship marketing." *Journal of Interactive Marketing*, 23(2), pp. 147–156.

22 Risselada, H., Verhoef, P. and Bijmolt, T. (2016) "Indicators of opinion leadership in customer networks: self-reports and degree centrality." *Marketing Letters*, 27(3), pp. 449–460.

23 Ata, U. Z. and Toker, A. (2012) "The effect of customer relationship management adoption in business-to-business markets." *Journal of Business & Industrial Marketing*, 27(6), pp. 497–507.

24 Vroman, H. W. (1996) "Book review: The Loyalty Effect: The Hidden Force Behind Growth, Profits, and Lasting Value." *Academy of Management Perspectives*, pp. 88–90.

25 Kumar, S. (2022) "Customer retention versus customer acquisition." *Forbes*, December 12, 2022. www.forbes.com/sites/forbesbusinesscouncil/2022/12/12/customer-retention-versus-customer-acquisition/?sh=7d0ca2121c7d

26 McCain, A. (2023) "28 critical customer retention statistics [2023]: Average customer retention rate by industry." *Zippia.* www.zippia.com/advice/customer-retention-statistics/

27 Martin, D., O'Neill, M., Hubbard, S. and Palmer, A. (2008) "The role of emotion in explaining consumer satisfaction and future behavioural intention." *Journal of Services Marketing*, 22(3), pp. 224–236.

28 Wen, C., Prybutok, V. R. and Xu, C. (2011) An integrated model for customer online repurchase intention. *Journal of Computer Information Systems*, 52(1), pp. 14–23.

29 Schmidt, M., Patel, N. and Williams, J. (2020) "Customer recommendations have only a small business impact for big brands." *Forrester.* www.forrester.com/report/customer-recommendations-have-only-a-small-business-impact-for-big-brands/RES175429?ref_search=0_1687451315812.

30 Zineldin, M. (2006) "The royalty of loyalty: CRM, quality and retention." *Journal of Consumer Marketing*, 23(7), pp. 430–437.

31 Brown, A. (2022) "Your complete guide to customer expansion in 2023." *Northpass.* www.northpass.com/blog/your-complete-guide-to-customer-expansion-in-2023.

32 Moran, G., Muzellec, L. and Nolan, E. (2014) "Consumer moments of truth in the digital context: How 'search' and 'e-word of mouth' can fuel consumer decision making." *Journal of Advertising Research*, 54(2), pp. 200–204.

33 Aydin, G. and Ziya, S. (2008) "Pricing promotional products under upselling." *Manufacturing & Service Operations Management*, 10(3), pp. 360–376.

34 "Differences between cross-selling and upselling" (2020) *Adobe Experience Cloud Blog*. https://business.adobe.com/blog/basics/difference-between-cross-selling-and-upselling.

35 Zhou, Y., Wilkinson, D., Schreiber, R. and Pan, R. (2008) "Large-scale parallel collaborative filtering for the netflix prize." In *Algorithmic Aspects in Information and Management: 4th International Conference*, AAIM 2008, Shanghai, China, June 23–25, 2008. Proceedings 4 (pp. 337-348). Berlin/Heidelberg, Germany: Springer.

36 Jacobson, K., Murali, V., Newett, E., Whitman, B. and Yon, R. (2016) "Music personalization at Spotify." In *Proceedings of the 10th ACM Conference on Recommender Systems* (pp. 373–373). New York: ACM.

37 Covington, P., Adams, J. and Sargin, E, (2016) "Deep neural networks for YouTube recommendations." In *Proceedings of the 10th ACM Conference on Recommender Systems* (pp. 191–198). New York: ACM.

38 Goodrow, C. (2021) "On YouTube's recommendation system." *YouTube Official Blog*. https://blog.youtube/inside-youtube/on-youtubes-recommendation-system/.

39 Ritzer, G., Dean, P. and Jurgenson, N. (2012) "The coming of age of the prosumer." *American Behavioral Scientist*, 56(4), pp. 379–398.

MODULE IV
Digital Business and Management

8

THE VALUE OF INFORMATION TECHNOLOGY IN BUSINESS AND MANAGEMENT

Outline

Overview	237
8.1 The Digital Revolution	238
8.2 IT Value in Business and Management	244
8.3 Online Platforms	250
8.4 E-business	254
8.5 Mobile Business	260
Case Studies	264
Review	264
Discussion Questions	265
Further Reading	265
References	266

Intended Learning Outcomes

- Describe the major technological and economic trends in digitization.
- Identify the fundamental values of information technology (IT) in business and management.
- Articulate the impact of these trends and values on organizations.
- Describe the unique features of online platforms, e-business, and mobile business.

Overview

This chapter explores how digital technologies are transforming existing businesses and creating new business opportunities:

DOI: 10.4324/9781003271222-12

- Digital technologies have reshaped business operations and spawned new business models by dramatically improving efficiencies and enabling the development of innovative products and services.
- Information technology (IT) is highlighted as a strategic asset in the digital age which is essential for data-driven decision-making, process optimization, and innovation.
- Online platforms play a vital role in marketing, sales, and the creation of dynamic online communities, enhancing business-customer engagement.
- E-business is a representative example that highlights the impact of the internet on business activities. Topics discussed include the advantages of e-business, the emergence of new models like online marketplaces, and the shift in competitive dynamics.
- The final section of this chapter details the rise of mobile business, underscoring the convenience it offers to customers and the real-time engagement and personalized marketing opportunities it provides for businesses.

8.1 The Digital Revolution

8.1.1 Analog vs. Digital Signals

Analog and digital signals are two types of signals used to transmit information from one place to another. The main difference between analog and digital signals is how they are processed and transmitted (Figure 8.1).[1]

Analog signals vary over time and can take on any value within a given range. For example, an analog signal could be the sound wave produced by a musical instrument or the voltage signal produced by a microphone.

Analog amplifiers are devices that amplify an analog signal, a continuous signal that varies over time. Analog amplifiers work by taking an input signal and amplifying it by a specific factor, thereby increasing its amplitude without altering its waveform. This can be

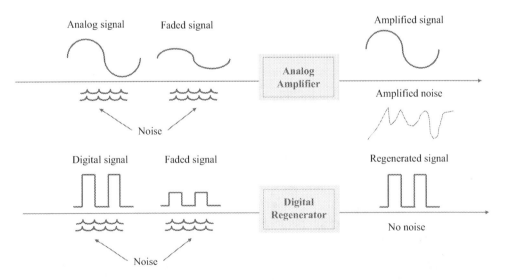

FIGURE 8.1 Analog versus Digital Signals.

useful in situations where the analog signal is weak or needs to be boosted to a certain level for processing or transmission.

Digital signals, on the other hand, are discrete signals that are represented by a series of 1 s and 0 s. They are generated by a process called sampling, which involves measuring the analog signal at regular intervals and assigning each measurement a binary code. These binary codes are then transmitted as a sequence of bits.

Digital regenerators are devices that regenerate a digital signal. Digital regenerators work by taking a digital input signal and re-timing it to remove any timing errors or distortions that may have occurred during transmission. This can be useful when the digital signal has been degraded or corrupted during transmission, such as in long-distance communication or noisy environments.

Digital regenerators play a critical role in maintaining the integrity and quality of digital signals during transmission. By removing timing errors and distortions, digital regenerators ensure that the digital signal accurately represents the original data and can be correctly interpreted by digital devices and systems.

One of the main advantages of digital signals over analog signals is that they are less susceptible to noise and distortion during transmission, which makes them more reliable and consistent. Digital signals can also be processed and manipulated using digital signal processing techniques, which enables a wide range of applications, including audio and video compression, data compression, and encryption.

These advantages of digital signals are the main drivers of digitization and digitalization.

8.1.2 Digitization and Digitalization

Digitization

"Digitization" is the process of converting analog information into digital format, which can then be processed, transmitted, and stored using digital devices and systems. Digitization creates a digital representation of physical objects or attributes.[2] In other words, digitization involves converting something non-digital into a digital representation or artifact. Digitization is foundational. This is the connection between the physical world and software. It is an enabler for all the processes that provide business value because of the need for consumable data.

Digitalization

On the other hand, "digitalization" involves creating and executing "changes associated with the application of digital technology in all aspects of human society."[3] "Digitalization" refers to enabling or improving processes by leveraging digital technologies and digitized data. Therefore, digitalization presumes digitization.

Digitalization deals with an organization's data and information resources through dedicated tools and techniques. It has changed the way employees interact with one another, their places of employment, their work objectives and goals, and how they perform their tasks. Digitalization increases productivity and efficiency while reducing costs. Digitalization improves existing business processes but does not change or transform them.

Digital Transformation

Digital transformation is business transformation enabled by digitalization.[4] The essence of digital transformation is the changing of business processes through digitalization technologies.

In recent years, there has been a trend toward digitizing all dimensions of human experiences, including things, tools and work, time and space, relationships, and even familiar products and services (Figure 8.2):

- Things: The digitization of things has begun through the integration of physical objects with digital technology such as sensors, wireless communication, and cloud computing. This enables objects to be tracked, monitored, and controlled remotely, increasing efficiency and productivity.
- Tools and work: Digitization has transformed how we work by enabling remote collaboration, virtual meetings, and online learning. Digital tools such as project management software, communication platforms, and cloud storage have made it easier to work remotely and to collaborate with others in real time. This has led to greater flexibility and efficiency in the workplace.
- Time and space: The digitization of time and space has made it possible to connect with others and access information from anywhere in the world. This has led to a blurring of boundaries between physical and virtual spaces and has enabled new forms of communication and collaboration. For example, social media platforms and video conferencing tools have made it possible to connect with others regardless of physical location.
- Relationships: Digitization has dramatically changed how we communicate and interact. Social media platforms, messaging apps, and online dating sites have made it easier to connect with others and build new relationships.
- Familiar products and services: The digitization of many familiar products and services, such as music, movies, and retail shopping, has led to new experiences and greater convenience for consumers. Digital platforms such as streaming services and online marketplaces have made it easier to access and purchase products and services worldwide.

FIGURE 8.2 Digitalization of Experiences.

The Value of Information Technology **241**

Through digitization, unrelated things become connected. For example, the Nike+iPod Sports Kit, announced in May 2006, is an activity tracker device developed through a collaboration between Nike and Apple.[5] It measures and records the distance and pace of a walk or run. The Nike+iPod consists of a small transmitter device attached to or embedded in a shoe, which communicates with either the Nike+ Sportband or a receiver plugged into an iPod device. This combination of unrelated things has opened up new experiences for those who love music and sports.

Many other digital applications have also transformed the way we live our daily lives. For example, shopping cart analysis is a digital application that allows retailers to analyze customers' shopping behavior. With this technology, retailers can track what items are being purchased, how frequently, and at what time of the day or week. This information can help retailers make better business decisions and provide a more customized and personalized service to customers.

Virtual reality (VR) and augmented reality (AR) are digital applications that have revolutionized how we experience things. With VR, we can enter a completely immersive digital environment that simulates reality; while with AR, we can overlay digital information onto the real world. These technologies have transformed how we interact with entertainment, education, and social media.

The Internet of Things connects everyday objects to the internet. This technology allows devices like home appliances, cars, and wearables to collect and share data, enabling us to make better decisions about our daily lives, such as when to turn on or off our air conditioning.

The Industrial Revolution and the Digital Revolution

The Industrial Revolution was a period of rapid and profound change that brought about new technologies, industries, and ways of life.[6] It was characterized by visible changes to the physical landscape, such as the development of factories, railroads, and large-scale manufacturing.

In contrast, the digital revolution has been more gradual and less visible, with its impact driven more by information and communication technology.[7] The digital revolution has transformed the way we access and share information, communicate with each other, and conduct business. It has enabled us to connect and collaborate in real time across borders and time zones. It has also created new jobs and disrupted traditional industries, such as retail and publishing.

The digital revolution has also changed the rules of competition and the relationships among players as new players enter the market and disrupt established industries. It has created new industries, such as the digital goods market (e.g., music, movies), and new marketplaces (e.g., online marketplaces like Amazon and Alibaba), transforming how we consume and do business (Figure 8.3).

8.1.3 Digitalization in Business and Management

Cases in the Music Industry and Publishing Industry

How can digital technologies transform businesses? IT and associated technologies (e.g., the internet) are making, driving, and facilitating profound changes in important business

242 Digital Business and Management

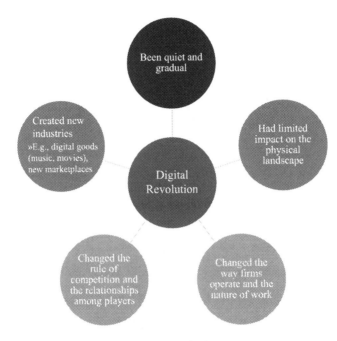

FIGURE 8.3 Characteristics of the Digital Revolution.

processes. To avail of the advantages of digital technologies, an organization must transform existing business activities and processes, both internal and external to the organization.

The music industry is a prime example of how innovation can bring about swift and profound changes, rendering established industry practices and competencies outdated.[8] The pre-internet music industry relied heavily on its capacity to control physical distribution channels. However, with the advent of the internet, the significance of physical music distribution has significantly diminished, compelling major music companies to undergo substantial reinvention in order to adapt and thrive.

The music business has undergone significant transformations due to advancements in digital technologies. The introduction of digital recording hardware and software revolutionized the recording process, making it more cost effective and user friendly. Additionally, compact discs emerged as a consumer-friendly format, promising enhanced audio quality while reducing manufacturing and distribution expenses.

Initially, digital technologies fueled growth in the music industry, but the emergence of Napster marked a major turning point.[9] The rapid advancement of the internet facilitated the seamless sharing and downloading of music online, rendering traditional methods obsolete. File-sharing platforms enabled users to acquire almost any desired song free of charge, which significantly impacted the music industry's revenue.

In response to this upheaval, paid digital distribution platforms like iTunes emerged, revolutionizing the monetization of digital downloads. Additionally, streaming services such as Spotify have further transformed the way people consume music. While these platforms now dominate music industry sales, revenue levels have not fully recovered to pre-Napster era levels.

Digitalization has also transformed the publishing industry, with the rise of digital platforms and online content leading to significant changes in how publishers operate.

The development of digital tools and platforms has enabled publishers to create and distribute content in digital formats, such as e-books, audiobooks, and digital magazines. This has expanded publishers' reach and made it easier to distribute content to a global audience.

Relatedly, digital platforms such as Amazon, Apple, and Google Play have disrupted the traditional distribution model of the publishing industry, providing a platform for publishers to reach a wider audience and sell their content directly to consumers. Moreover, the rise of digital subscription models such as Netflix and Spotify has led to the development of similar models in the publishing industry. Publishers increasingly offer digital subscription services, allowing readers to access a range of content for a monthly fee.

More importantly, the introduction of self-publishing platforms such as Amazon's Kindle Direct Publishing has enabled authors to bypass traditional publishers and distribute their content directly to readers.[10] This has led to the democratization of the publishing industry, with more opportunities for independent authors to reach a wider audience.

How Digitalization Transforms Business and Management

How does digitalization lead to the transformation of business enterprises? Digitalization has transformed businesses' operations and has led to various benefits and opportunities, including the following:

- Low transaction and coordination costs: Digital technology has reduced the cost of transactions and coordination between different parties, enabling businesses to operate more efficiently and cost effectively. This is achieved through digital platforms, automation, and data analytics that streamline processes and reduce the need for manual intervention.
- Location independence: Digitalization enables businesses to operate from anywhere globally, with employees and customers in different locations. This has opened up new markets and opportunities for businesses and has enabled greater flexibility and agility in responding to changing market conditions.
- Organizational flattening/flexibility: Digitalization has flattened the traditional hierarchy of organizations, enabling greater flexibility and agility in decision-making and operations. This is achieved through digital platforms and tools that facilitate collaboration and communication across different levels of the organization.
- Decentralization/empowerment: Digital technology has enabled greater decentralization and empowerment within organizations by giving employees access to data and tools that enable them to make decisions and take action autonomously. This has led to more significant innovation and creativity and improved employee engagement and satisfaction.
- Collaborative work and teamwork: Digitalization has facilitated greater collaboration and teamwork by providing employees with tools and platforms that enable them to work together seamlessly, regardless of geographical location or time zone. This has led to improved productivity, efficiency, innovation and creativity.

244 Digital Business and Management

8.2 IT Value in Business and Management

8.2.1 Data, Information, and More

Data, information, and knowledge are closely related concepts but have different meanings and implications, as follows (Figure 8.4):[11]

- "Data" refers to raw facts, figures, and statistics that have not been organized or analyzed. Data is usually not very useful, as it lacks context and meaning. For example, a list of numbers or letters is considered data.
- "Information" is data that has been processed and organized in a meaningful way to provide context, relevance, and significance. Information gives meaning to data and helps us understand its significance. For example, data becomes information if you organize the list of numbers or letters from the previous example and give it context, such as labeling the numbers or letters with specific categories.
- "Knowledge" is the understanding, comprehension, and insight that can be derived from information. Knowledge results from processing and analyzing information, enabling us to make decisions, solve problems, and take action. For example, if you have a deeper understanding of the meaning behind an organized list of numbers or letters and know how to use that understanding to make a decision or take action, that constitutes knowledge.

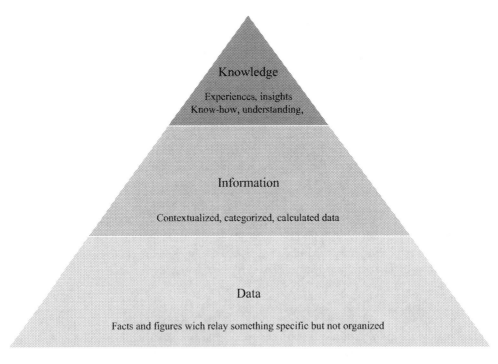

FIGURE 8.4 Data, Information, and Knowledge.

8.2.2 Information Technology and Information Systems

So, what are IT and information systems (IS)? IT is the hardware and software a business uses to achieve its objectives. IS are the interrelated components that manage information to support decision-making and control and help with analysis, visualization, and product creation. Simply put, IT is used to build IS (Figure 8.5).

IS isn't simply technology. People and organizations play an important role—information about an organization and its surrounding environment influences how IS works. Feedback is output returned to appropriate people or activities in the organization to evaluate and refine the input.

Enterprise resource planning (ERP) is a representative form of IS in a business setting because it provides a comprehensive suite of integrated software applications that helps organizations manage their core business processes in real time.[12] ERP systems automate and integrate various back-office functions, including accounting, inventory management, order processing, human resources, and customer relationship management (CRM).

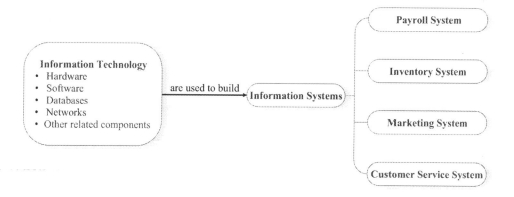

FIGURE 8.5 Information Technology and Information Systems.

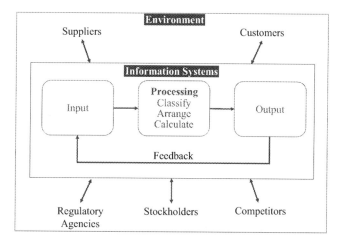

FIGURE 8.6 Concept of Information Systems.

246 Digital Business and Management

ERP systems are designed to provide a centralized view of an organization's data and operations, allowing decision-makers to access up-to-date information on all aspects of the business. This centralized view improves organizational efficiency by streamlining processes, eliminating redundant data entry, and providing a single source for all business data.

In addition to providing operational efficiency, ERP systems facilitate better decision-making by providing real-time data and analysis. This allows managers to quickly identify trends, track performance, and make informed decisions based on accurate and timely information.

Traditional views of ERP systems tend to focus on the technical aspects of the software and its ability to manage business processes. These views prioritize efficiency, standardization, and control to maximize productivity and minimize costs. The traditional view also places a heavy emphasis on the software's performance to serve each function of an enterprise, such as manufacturing systems and accounting systems.

In contrast, integrative views of ERP systems take a more holistic approach that considers the impact of the software on the entire organization, including its culture, people, and processes.[13] Integrative views focus on aligning the ERP system with the organization's strategy and goals and fostering collaboration and innovation among different departments and stakeholders. The integrative view recognizes that an ERP system can have a transformative effect on an organization, and that successful implementation requires a broad-based approach involving technical experts, business leaders, users, and stakeholders (Figure 8.7).

Cloud computing and business analytics are other examples of IS becoming increasingly important in business settings.

Cloud computing is an IS that enables users to access computing resources, such as servers, storage, and applications, over the internet (Figure 8.8).[14] Cloud computing allows businesses to store and process data remotely, reducing the need for on-premises infrastructure and increasing scalability and flexibility. Cloud computing services can be classified into three categories: infrastructure as a service, platform as a service, and software as a service. Examples of cloud computing platforms include Amazon Web Services, Microsoft Azure, and Google Cloud.

Business analytics is an IS that uses data analysis techniques to extract insights from large amounts of data.[15] These insights can help businesses make informed decisions, identify opportunities for improvement, and gain a competitive advantage. Business analytics can analyze data from various sources, including social media, customer interactions, and internal business processes. Examples of business analytics tools include Tableau, Microsoft Power BI, and Google Analytics.

8.2.3 Business Value of IT/IS

Businesses invest in IT/IS to achieve six essential business objectives (Figure 8.9):

- Operational excellence: IT/IS can help organizations improve operational efficiency, reduce costs, and optimize business processes. For example, businesses can use ERP systems to automate manufacturing and supply chain processes or CRM systems to streamline their sales and marketing operations.

The Value of Information Technology **247**

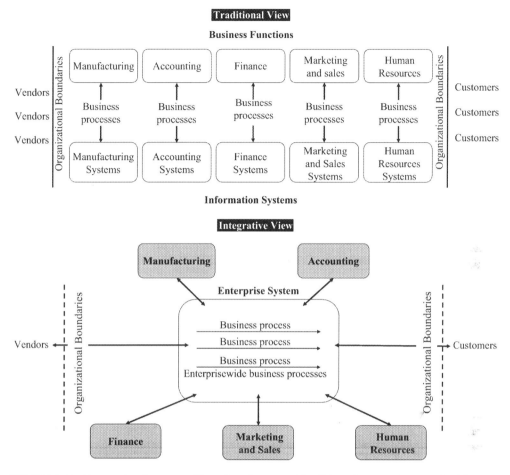

FIGURE 8.7 Enterprise Resource Planning Systems: Traditional versus Integrative Views.

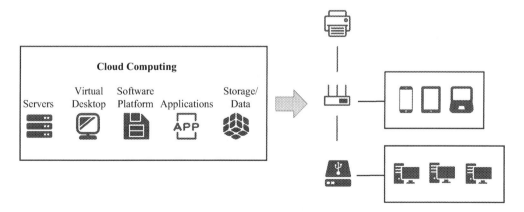

FIGURE 8.8 Cloud Computing.

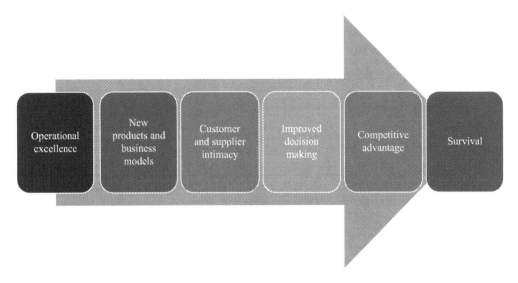

FIGURE 8.9 Why Invest in IT and IS?.

- New products and business models: IT/IS can enable organizations to develop new products and services and create new business models. For example, companies can use data analytics and market research to identify new customer needs and preferences and then use this information to develop new products or services.
- Customer and supplier intimacy: IT/IS can help businesses build stronger relationships with their customers and suppliers by providing personalized experiences and tailored services. For example, businesses can use CRM systems to track customer interactions and preferences or supplier relationship management systems to effectively manage their supplier networks.
- Improved decision-making: IT/IS can provide businesses with real-time data and analytics to help them make better decisions. For example, businesses can use business intelligence tools to analyze sales data and identify trends or use predictive analytics to forecast demand and optimize inventory management.
- Competitive advantage: IT/IS can provide businesses with a competitive advantage by enabling them to differentiate themselves from their competitors. For example, businesses can use e-commerce platforms to reach new customers and markets or social media to engage with customers and build their brands.
- Survival: Finally, businesses invest in IT/IS to ensure survival in an increasingly competitive and rapidly changing business environment. Without suitable IT/IS systems and capabilities, businesses may struggle to keep up with the pace of change and may even risk being left behind by their competitors.

IT can provide strategic value by affecting competition in three interrelated ways.[16] First, IT changes industry structure and, in so doing, alters the rules of competition. All components of the Five Forces Model are affected by the advancement of IT. As

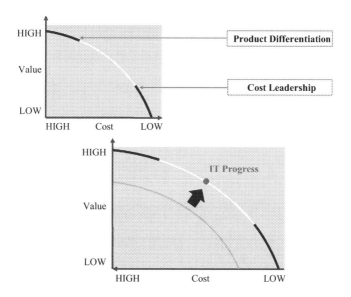

FIGURE 8.10 Productivity Frontier and Strategic Benefits of IT and IS.

technology progresses, traditional industry structures can undergo substantial transformations, leading to new rules of competition.

Second, IT creates a competitive advantage by giving companies new ways to outperform the competition. The value chain model thus changes dramatically. This may include leveraging data analytics for strategic decision-making, adopting advanced automation technologies, or implementing cutting-edge CRM systems.

Figure 8.10 shows the strategic benefit of IT in enhancing competitive advantages. There is a trade-off between low costs and high value. At a fixed level of production technology, when a firm increases product value, it also increases the cost. Top performers in the market aim to generate the maximum outputs given the trade-off relationship, named the "productivity frontier."[17] This is a concept that illustrates the maximum output or production level an economy can achieve with given resources and technology.

Progress in IT shifts the productivity frontier by:

- increasing the product value deliverable at the same cost level;
- lowering the cost level of delivering a specific product value; and
- introducing new levels of product value (Figure 8.10).

Finally, IT can spawn whole new businesses. By capitalizing on emerging technologies and digital innovations, entrepreneurs can introduce revolutionary products and services that cater to evolving consumer demands. Startups and established companies alike are embracing IT-enabled solutions to create novel business models and explore untapped markets. We can identify many examples of IT-enabled new products and services in the media and entertainment industry (MEI), such as online streaming platforms and e-sports.

250 Digital Business and Management

The continuous integration of IT in business strategies not only changes industry landscapes and fosters competitiveness but also paves the way for continuous innovation and the exploration of uncharted territories.

8.3 Online Platforms

8.3.1 The Concept of Online Platforms

Online platforms and their associated ecosystems are the dominant organizational forms of the digital age.[18] Online platforms help create digital value that underpins current and future economic growth. The role of online platforms is key in delivering benefits to consumers and businesses. Online platforms bring together consumers and producers, facilitating trades that otherwise would not happen.

In a nutshell, online platforms are digital services that facilitate interactions via the internet between two or more distinct but interdependent sets of users, either businesses or individuals. They provide a structure that utilizes the low search costs of digital technologies to generate efficient matches between globally connected users. Examples of such online platforms include online marketplaces, app stores, social media, and platforms for the collaborative economy.

Online platforms also facilitate innovation by enabling third-party firms, such as software developers, to build enormous quantities of complementary products or services. For example, online platforms such as Apple's iOS and Google's Android provide business opportunities for millions of application developers, facilitating the development of apps that they can distribute globally through app stores.

Online platforms make significant investments in research and development (R&D). Amazon, Alphabet, Microsoft, and Apple all feature among the top companies for global spending on R&D. These high levels of investment are likely to deliver significant benefits for these businesses, their consumers, and society.

Regardless of the sectors they serve and the range of activities they enable, online platforms exhibit shared economic, business, and governance traits when it comes to generating and retaining value.[19]

8.3.2 Types of Online Platforms

There are three different types of platforms, which can be divided into two broad types and a combined hybrid type, depending on how they create value—transaction platforms, innovation platforms, and hybrid platforms:[20]

- Transaction platforms: These facilitate transactions between many individuals and organizations that otherwise would have difficulty finding or transacting with each other, and that capture and transmit data, including personal data, over the internet (e.g., Tmall, Google Search, Amazon Marketplace). These organizations reduce search and other transaction costs for billions of users, customers, and providers.
- Innovation platforms: These serve as a technological building block on top of which innovators can develop complementary products or services (e.g., iOS, Google Android, Linux).

The Value of Information Technology **251**

- Hybrid platforms: These combine the characteristics of innovation platforms and transaction platforms. Google, Amazon, Microsoft, Apple, and Facebook are all hybrid platforms.

Online platforms can also be classified into four types based on their business models:[21]

- Omni-channel model: This model provides customers access to products across multiple channels, including physical and digital channels, giving them greater choice and a seamless experience.
- Ecosystem driver model: Some companies—such as Amazon, Fidelity, Aetna,
- Apple, and Microsoft—establish an ecosystem by creating relationships with other providers that offer complementary (or sometimes competing) services. Ecosystem drivers provide a platform for participants to conduct business; the platform can be more or less open. For example, Google has a very open platform, while Apple's is more closed.
- Modular producer model: Modular producers like PayPal provide plug-and-play products or services that can adapt to various ecosystems.
- Supplier model: Suppliers have at best partial knowledge of their end consumers and typically operate within the value chain of another large company. Companies that sell electronic goods through retailers (e.g., Sony) or mutual funds through brokers (e.g., Vanguard) are suppliers.

8.3.3 Benefits and Risks of Online Platforms

Benefits

Online platforms provide multiple benefits for both businesses and consumers.[22]

First, online platforms have the advantage of breaking down geographical barriers, enabling businesses to operate across traditional borders to varying degrees. Online marketplaces and app stores, in particular, offer a key benefit by allowing businesses to reach a wider and more diverse customer base.

Second, online platforms have a significant impact on the cost structures of businesses. By leveraging platforms, companies can potentially reduce costs—especially those associated with targeted search efforts. However, the effect on operating costs varies depending on available alternatives. While some sellers on online platforms may prefer direct selling to avoid platform fees, it is generally more cost effective to use online platforms compared to traditional brick-and-mortar stores.

Third, platforms provide support for new and diverse types of businesses seeking funding. They open up access to a market of investors with various motivations for providing financial support. The reduction of geographical limitations also enhances the viability of unique businesses by expanding their potential customer reach. For example, crowdfunding platforms play a crucial role in broadening the funding market and attracting different types of investors to back various projects.[23] This newfound accessibility to funding can be especially beneficial for projects with uncertain returns on investment, such as those primarily focused on artistic or cultural endeavors. Consequently, platforms enable projects that might not have qualified for traditional financing to become viable ventures.

252 Digital Business and Management

Risks

The rise of online platforms has also created different dimensions of risks.

First, the continuous collection and analysis of quantified data by online platforms raise privacy concerns that can affect individual users and have broader implications for society.[24] The potential consequences of users engaging with seemingly "free" digital services while unknowingly being manipulated toward platforms' goals have become a major concern.

Second, the influence of digital platforms on the news media has come under intense scrutiny.[25] Beyond the spread of fake news, these platforms have deeply disrupted the news and journalism ecosystem. The traditional business model of news has been severely affected, leading to reduced incentives for producing original reporting. Furthermore, platform algorithms tend to prioritize sensational and dynamic content, impacting the quality of news consumption.

Third, social risks associated with digital platforms involve environmental concerns such as climate and health. The rise of ride-sharing services, for example, has led to significant increases in vehicles on city streets, resulting in more traffic congestion and increased pollution and carbon emissions. Additionally, the dominance of these platforms may reduce the use of eco-friendly public transportation options, exacerbating environmental challenges.[26]

8.3.4 Impacts of Online Platforms

Effects on Employment

In the platform economy, a diverse range of new job opportunities has emerged. These jobs can be classified into two main categories: on-demand work and crowd work.[27] These roles are organized through digital platforms, which include various apps and websites, and are characterized by their focus on short-term engagements, often referred to as the "gig economy."[28] While these jobs are facilitated digitally, on-demand work involves offline tasks that require a physical presence in specific geographical locations, such as cleaning, ride-sharing, deliveries, caregiving, and maintenance. On the other hand, crowd workers utilize online platforms to offer virtual services to clients without the need for in-person interactions.

Supporters of platform work highlight that it provides opportunities for many individuals who might otherwise struggle to secure employment. Conversely, critics argue that it exposes workers to the risk of being terminated without recourse or explanation. The available evidence indicates that both viewpoints hold some truth. For advocates, the benefits of platform work include the ability to work from home, flexible hours, low entry barriers, the option to skip unpaid training, and reduced susceptibility to social biases. These aspects enable more people—especially those facing traditional barriers to employment—to enter the labor market with greater ease.

On the other hand, the non-standard nature of platform employment also means that workers can be dismissed rapidly. The platform economy operates on demand, driven by consumer demand and management decisions. While it opens doors to more work opportunities, it can also lead to swift worker removal when necessary.

In the MEI, "gig" workers play a crucial role in producing and distributing content.[29] They offer flexibility and specialized expertise, allowing companies to access talent for specific projects without committing to long-term employment contracts. This workforce includes a wide range of roles, including actors/actresses, musicians, photographers, writers, graphic designers, and other creative professionals. They collaborate with multiple clients simultaneously, allowing them to diversify their portfolio and gain valuable experience across various projects.

Platforms and digital marketplaces have facilitated the growth of the gig economy in the MEI, making it easier for freelancers to find opportunities and connect with potential clients globally.

However, it also comes with its challenges. Gig workers may experience income instability and may not enjoy the benefits typically associated with traditional employment. Additionally, competition can be intense and negotiating fair compensation for their services can be challenging. There is an ongoing discussion around labor rights, worker protections, and fair compensation for gig workers in the MEI. Advocacy for better working conditions, legal protections, and benefits for gig workers is gaining momentum, with the aim of ensuring their wellbeing while preserving the flexibility and opportunities that the gig economy provides.

The COVID-19 Pandemic and Online Platforms

During the global recession triggered by the COVID-19 pandemic, online platform companies not only displayed resilience but emerged as prominent beneficiaries of the widespread shift toward remote work, social distancing, and online shopping.[30]

Amid the economic turmoil caused by the pandemic, digital technologies emerged as a vital element of economic and social resilience. By enabling businesses and governments to continue their operations during lockdowns, digital technologies enabled faster economic responses to the crisis.[31] Evidence indicates that the COVID-19 crisis triggered significant changes in the use of digital technologies by individuals, businesses, and governments. For example, online shopping, videoconferencing, and telework experienced surges; and governments expedited the digitalization of public services. The COVID-19 pandemic also had a significant impact on various aspects of the MEI.[32] Physical location-based businesses that rely on synchronous content delivery were adversely affected by the outbreak, while online businesses based on platforms largely benefited from government-enforced lockdowns. The profits and market capitalization of digital companies providing in-demand services during lockdowns reached record levels, surpassing those of other companies by a significant margin.

Indeed, online marketplaces were already experiencing rapid growth before the COVID-19 crisis. With innovative use of user data and large network effects, they had captured a growing share of activity in various sectors, such as retail marketplaces, accommodation, transport, restaurants, and increasingly business-to-business and professional services. Their rapid rise has raised concerns across multiple policy areas, including competition, labor market regulation, privacy, and consumer protection.[33] Understanding the increased reliance on online platforms during the pandemic is important, as there is no recent historical parallel from which to draw insights.

8.4 E-business

8.4.1 The Concept of E-business

In 1994, IBM—in collaboration with ad agency Ogilvy & Mather—leveraged its extensive background in IT solutions and knowledge to position itself as a frontrunner in internet-based business operations. This strategic move was reflected in the adoption of the term "e-business" to promote IBM's capabilities in this emerging field.[34] In October 1997, following comprehensive global market research, IBM initiated its e-business campaign with an impactful eight-page spread in the *Wall Street Journal*. The purpose of this initiative was to introduce the concept of e-business to the public and highlight IBM's expertise and leadership in this rapidly evolving domain.

Companies must understand the nature of e-business and how it can facilitate operations and growth. For businesses that want to grow, e-business can help them do so by using the internet and online technologies to improve operational efficiencies, enhance strategic competencies, and thus increase customer value.[35a]

"E-commerce" refers to the marketing, sale, and purchase of goods and services online—in other words, to the use of the internet to transact business or conduct digitally enabled transactions. It generates revenue, which e-business does not. E-commerce has been the fastest-growing form of retail trade globally. It began in the early 1990s and has since grown exponentially. While many early companies failed, many survived and have seen revenues soar.

Every internet business is either pure-play or brick-and-click. A pure-play business, such as Amazon or Zappos, has an online presence only and uses the capabilities of the internet to create a new business. Brick-and-click businesses, such as Barnes and Noble, combine physical and online presence, using the internet to supplement their existing businesses.

Pure e-commerce, partial e-commerce, and traditional commerce are distinguished by three dimensions: the nature of the product or service sold, the process involved, and the delivery agent or intermediary (Figure 8.11).[35b] In traditional commerce, all dimensions are physical; whereas in pure e-commerce, all dimensions are digital. Partial e-commerce encompasses various possibilities that involve a mix of both digital and physical dimensions.

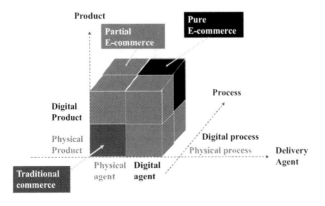

FIGURE 8.11 Pure vs. Partial E-commerce.

8.4.2 Characteristics of E-commerce

E-commerce possesses the following unique features which distinguish it from physical commerce:

- Ubiquity: Visitors and customers can access services anywhere, any time, on any device. This is also known as "omnichannel access."
- Global reach: E-commerce increases the access between a company and existing and potential customers through the internet.
- Universal standards: Features such as webpage design and payment are similar worldwide.
- Information richness: A company can use different types of media, including images and videos.
- Interactivity: E-commerce allows two-way communication between a company and customers, which was not possible through traditional channels.
- Information density: Information is more accurate and relevant to timeliness. This offers reduced costs and enhanced levels of service, increasing revenue.
- Personalization/customization: Personalization and customization involve creating or modifying an item using customer data to meet an individual's specific characteristics.
- Social technology: E-commerce has evolved to become much more social by allowing users to create and share content in the form of text, photos, and videos with their friends and the wider community.

Benefits

Digital markets allow for more transparency and access to information about products and services. This reduces the information asymmetry between buyers and sellers and makes it easier for buyers to compare prices and find the best deals. Additionally, digital markets reduce search costs, as buyers can easily search for products online; and transaction costs, as online transactions are often faster and cheaper than traditional transactions. Menu costs, or changing prices, are also reduced as digital markets allow for instant price changes.

In the traditional setting, sellers have more information on products than buyers. They can control price and thus also demand. However, in digital markets, buyers can also access a wealth of information about products and services, including customer reviews, ratings, and specifications. This reduces the information asymmetry and gives more bargaining power to buyers.

Digital markets also enable price discrimination, dynamic pricing, and disintermediation.

"Price discrimination" refers to charging different prices to customers based on their willingness to pay. Digital markets make it easier to implement price discrimination, as businesses can use data and algorithms to personalize prices.

Dynamic pricing is a strategy whereby businesses set flexible product or service prices based on current market demands. This allows businesses to adjust prices in real time to optimize revenue.

"Disintermediation" refers to eliminating intermediaries in the supply chain, such as wholesalers or retailers. Digital markets allow businesses to sell directly to consumers,

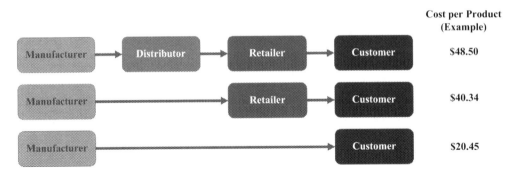

FIGURE 8.12 Disintermediation of E-commerce.

reducing the need for intermediaries. This can result in lower prices for consumers, as fewer intermediaries end up taking a cut (Figure 8.12).

Price Competition in E-commerce

During the early days of online markets, there was a prevailing sense of optimism regarding their potential to enhance fairness and competitiveness. In contrast to physical stores, consumers were presented with a multitude of options as they could effortlessly navigate through numerous websites with a simple click. This heightened level of accessibility was expected to foster fierce competition among online retailers, driving them to constantly strive to offer the lowest prices. Consequently, this heightened competition was anticipated to increase market efficiency and ultimately deliver significant benefits to consumers (Figure 8.13).

However, the initial promises made by online markets have fallen short of expectations. Instead of a landscape marked by fierce competition, a small number of retailers have come to dominate these markets.[36] While online prices occasionally offer a slight advantage over those in physical stores, this is not consistently the case. Furthermore, the prices of products can vary greatly across different online retailers, with instances where prices on platforms like Amazon fluctuate for a day and are sometimes significantly higher than the offline retail price.[37]

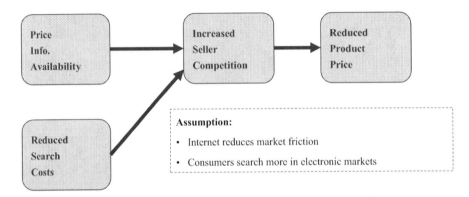

FIGURE 8.13 Reduced Price Hypothesis in E-commerce.

One notable trend in online markets is the increasing use of pricing algorithms by retailers.[38] A pricing algorithm is a computer program that independently adapts prices based on current and historical data related to demand, costs, and competitors' pricing. Instead of relying on human decision-making, computer programs now monitor market conditions and autonomously adjust prices in near real time. Initially, algorithms were mainly utilized in select industries, such as airline ticket pricing. However, with the emergence of online markets, there has been a significant expansion in the number of markets.

The simultaneous occurrence of such responsive pricing behavior and significant price discrepancies for identical products challenges the initial assumptions about competition in online markets. One would expect that greater pricing responsiveness would lead to intensified competition, but this has not been the case.

Long Tail in E-commerce

The idea of the "long tail" was introduced by Chris Anderson in the October 2004 issue of *Wired* magazine, suggesting that the online marketplace is shifting away from mainstream products and gravitating toward niche products (Figure 8.14).[39] As e-commerce continues to evolve, new retailers find it more feasible and cost-effective to concentrate on niche products within specific markets.

These goods can become profitable due to a shift in consumer preferences away from mainstream markets—a trend facilitated by the rise of online marketplaces. Consumers are increasingly moving toward niche products tailored to their needs rather than generic mass-produced items. They are also willing to pay more for quality niche products, which means smart retailers can increase their profitability by selling a smaller number of tightly focused long-tail products rather than trying to sell everything for everyone. Space is unlimited on digital platforms, allowing a wide array of products to be offered.

The cumulative demand for these less popular goods can rival that for mainstream products (Figure 8.15). While mainstream items may enjoy more attention through leading distribution channels and prominent shelf space, the high initial costs can impact overall profitability. On the other hand, long-tail goods have a relatively longer-lasting

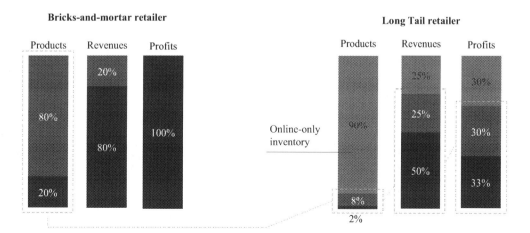

FIGURE 8.14 The Long Tail in E-commerce.

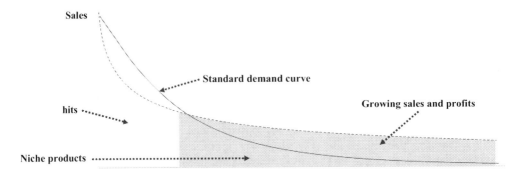

FIGURE 8.15 The Long Tail in Theory.

market presence and utilize alternative distribution channels, resulting in lower production and distribution expenses while remaining easily accessible for sale. Long-tail products also have lower marketing costs for the most part, increasing profitability even further.

E-commerce platforms can leverage the long-tail concept to provide customers with a vast array of choices, particularly in specific business categories. Companies like Netflix and Amazon have greatly benefited from this approach, offering products with zero inventory costs, such as online movies and e-books.

However, the abundance of choices in the long tail can sometimes overwhelm consumers, leading to the dilemma of excessive choice or the tyranny of choice. To harness the full potential of the long tail, e-commerce merchants must prioritize product discovery and make it relatively easy for customers. Personalization plays a vital role in this context, as customers often rely on recommendations from friends and other product users.

As the e-commerce industry matures, personalization and the long-tail approach are crucial strategies for effectively engaging customers and maximizing conversions. By tailoring offerings to individual preferences, companies can enhance the overall shopping experience and foster customer loyalty.

Long Tail versus Blockbusters in the MEI

The long-tail concept is applied in various marketplaces, including the MEI. Anderson supported this notion with concrete examples from Amazon, Netflix, and music service Rhapsody, highlighting that offering a wide range of choices to consumers, especially online, can lead to increased profitability.[40]

Contrary to the notion of the long tail, however, an *Economist* article titled "A World of Hits" presents a different perspective. The article asserts that in a world abundant with choices, blockbusters hold even greater significance.[41] It cited examples from the television industry, where top programs continue to perform well, often overshadowing lesser entertainment options. Similarly, the music industry relies heavily on "hits," as demonstrated by the albums occupying the number one spot, showing increased sales despite an overall decline in album sales. For example, managers at Spotify music service have disclosed that the most popular tracks on Spotify now account for 80% of streams. Spotify has more than 20 million tracks available, but one-fifth of them have never been played.[42]

This suggests that having more choice does not necessarily lead people to seek out more niche entertainment. Moreover, a study indicates that between 2004 and 2008, big studios found greater profitability in movies with budgets exceeding $100 million compared to cheaper films.[43]

The notion that the "tail" (i.e., niche products) is more important than the "head" (i.e., blockbuster products) may not be correct. Indeed, the tail is getting thinner and thinner, given that blockbuster products now dominate the market.[44]

These are compelling and tangible examples that demonstrate the continued relevance of the blockbuster. However, the long tail does not advocate that blockbuster products or services should be completely disregarded. Anderson also acknowledged that "hits" still matter in attracting customers to both online and offline platforms. Once customers are engaged, recommendation algorithms in online channels or trained personnel in offline channels can guide them toward other enticing products or services within the platform's offerings.

Looking ahead, a winning strategy for enterprises may involve a balanced approach, where a steady stream of profitable niche products and services complements a collection of blockbuster offerings. This "win-win" approach could prove to be effective in satisfying a diverse range of customer preferences and maximizing overall success.

Three Key Success Factors for E-commerce

Various factors can contribute to the success of an e-commerce business (Figure 8.16).

First, you should have a clear and persuasive business model, as this is essential for the success of an e-commerce business. The business model should outline the products or services, target audience, revenue streams, marketing strategies, and competitive advantages. The business model should also consider pricing, payment options, and shipping.

Second, you should have competitive technology, adding value for customers. This can include personalized product recommendations, easy navigation, fast and secure checkout, and mobile responsiveness. A seamless user experience can increase customer satisfaction, loyalty, and repeat business.

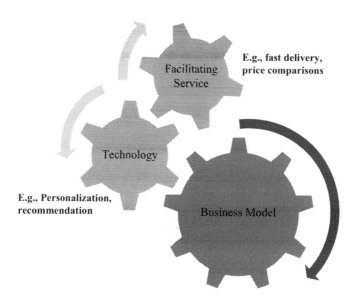

FIGURE 8.16 Key Success Factors of E-commerce.

260 Digital Business and Management

Finally, a series of facilitating services will enhance your competitive advantage. These could include customer support, easy returns, fast and reliable shipping, and secure payment options. These services can improve customer satisfaction, build trust, and differentiate your e-commerce business from its competitors.

8.5 Mobile Business

8.5.1 The Concept of Mobile Business

"Mobile business" is any transaction that occurs on a smartphone or tablet. Beyond retail use, mobile business touches other industries such as banking, healthcare, and construction.

There are nine forces shaping the "mobile economy."[45] Context examines the customer's thoughts; while location, time, and weather also matter. Salience, which pertains to the ranking of a product, is further crucial. Additionally, crowdedness, trajectory, social dynamics, and tech mix come into play in shaping the mobile business landscape.

Mobile Technology

"Mobile technology" refers to the technological capabilities that accompany users wherever they go. It consists of portable devices for two-way communication, computing, and networking technology that facilitate connectivity.[46] Mobile technology is primarily characterized by internet-enabled devices such as smartphones, tablets, and smartwatches.

The ubiquity of mobile technology in today's society is noteworthy. The wireless technologies that underpin communication networks for these devices allow for the exchange of voice, data, and mobile applications, contributing to the seamless functionality of mobile devices.

Types of mobile networks include WiFi, Bluetooth, and cellular networks:

- An abbreviation of "wireless fidelity," "WiFi" refers to the use of radio waves to connect devices to the internet through localized routers known as hotspots.[47] Unlike cellular networks, WiFi networks require the establishment of a WiFi connection for internet access. Most mobile devices have the capability to automatically switch between WiFi and cellular networks based on availability and user preference.
- Bluetooth is a specification within the telecommunications industry that enables the connection of devices over short distances using short-wavelength radio waves.[48] It allows for the convenient pairing of various devices such as headsets, speakers, phones, and more, facilitating seamless wireless communication between them.
- Cellular networks are radio networks that utilize distributed cell towers to enable mobile devices (e.g., cell phones) to switch frequencies automatically and maintain uninterrupted communication over large geographical areas. The switching capability of cellular networks allows them to accommodate numerous users across a limited number of radio frequencies. For example, 4 G—which stands for "fourth generation"—was the standard cellular service for wireless communication. It utilizes packet-switching technology, where data is organized into packets for transmission and reassembled at the destination. 4 G offers significant advancements over its predecessor, 3 G. The newer generation, 5 G, is even faster and is gaining widespread adoption. 5 G utilizes a range of aggregated

The Value of Information Technology **261**

frequency bands to unlock greater bandwidth, resulting in speeds around 20 times faster than 4 G.[49] This enables the delivery of larger amounts of data at higher speeds to multiple devices simultaneously. For example, when streaming videos to smartphones, 5 G significantly enhances the experience, making it ten times better not only for individual users but also for multiple users streaming videos concurrently.

8.5.2 Mobile Marketing and M-commerce

Mobile Marketing

"Mobile marketing" refers to marketing activities that promote products and services via mobile devices, such as tablets and smartphones.[50] Leveraging the capabilities of modern mobile technology, including location services, enables the customization of marketing campaigns based on an individual's geographical position.

Mobile marketing includes the utilization of technology to deliver personalized promotions of goods or services to users who are consistently connected to a network. Specifically, proximity systems and location-based services can notify users based on their geographical location or proximity to a service provider, offering valuable opportunities for personalized engagement.

Mobile marketing has emerged as an essential tool for businesses of all sizes, given the widespread adoption of mobile devices. The key stakeholders in this field are brands and the companies they represent through advertising, along with the service providers facilitating mobile advertising.

One significant behavior observed in mobile marketing is "snacking," where users briefly check in to media or messages on their mobile devices.[51] This inclination toward instant gratification provides marketers with multiple touchpoints for engagement.

The effectiveness of mobile marketing is influenced by the device being used, especially the screen size.[52] Smartphone users often find informative content most relevant, while iPad users are captivated by interactive advertising featuring visually appealing presentations and rich media, with the message of the content playing a secondary role.

In contrast to traditional marketing approaches, mobile marketing capitalizes on the fact that mobile device users carry their devices with them wherever they go. Leveraging location-based services, marketers can gather customer data and deliver targeted coupons, deals, or promotions based on the user's proximity to a store or frequently visited locations. This level of personalization enhances the effectiveness of marketing campaigns.[53]

Furthermore, mobile marketing offers exceptional cost effectiveness. There are diverse options available to suit any budget, and the impact it can deliver in relation to the cost is substantial.

However, privacy concerns arise regarding the utilization of data collected by mobile devices and the ethical implications of companies collecting such data without explicit consent.[54] This data, if mishandled or inadequately secured, can lead to identity theft or unsolicited spam. Additionally, the tracking of an individual's locations and movements may be perceived as an invasion of privacy.

M-commerce

"Mobile commerce," or "m-commerce," refers to the utilization of wireless handheld devices such as cellphones and tablets to facilitate the conclusion of various commercial

262 Digital Business and Management

transactions online. These encompass a wide range of activities, including the purchase and sale of products, online banking, and the convenient payment of bills.[55]

M-commerce is an increasingly large subset of e-commerce.[56] It offers a wide range of possibilities for conducting transactions, including banking, investing, and the purchase of books, plane tickets, and digital music. The rapid growth of m-commerce can be attributed to several factors, including the increased computing power of wireless handheld devices, the availability of numerous m-commerce applications, and the resolution of security concerns.

M-commerce transactions typically involve a few simple clicks, offering a streamlined experience compared to e-commerce transactions on tablets, laptops, or desktops that may require more time and navigation through a company's website.

The range of devices capable of facilitating mobile commerce is continuously expanding. Digital wallet services like Apple Pay and Google Pay enable customers to make in-store purchases in more convenient ways. Additionally, social media platforms such as Meta, Twitter, and Instagram have introduced "buy buttons" on their mobile platforms, enabling users to make direct purchases from retailers through these social media platforms.

The portability of mobile devices enables businesses to extend their reach to customers through mobile commerce. Retailers can send coupons and discounts directly to customers, facilitating personalized shopping experiences and strengthening the retailer-client connection. M-commerce apps equipped with Global Positioning Services capabilities assist customers in locating specific items within stores. Furthermore, m-commerce apps enhance security through multi-factor authentication, including biometric measures like fingerprints and retina scans.

8.5.3 Mobile Applications

A mobile application ("app") is a piece of software designed to run on a mobile device, such as a smartphone or tablet computer.[57] Apps are typically compact software units with limited functionalities—a concept popularized by Apple through its App Store, which offers a vast array of applications for iPhone and iPad devices.

Mobile apps provide specific and isolated functionalities such as games or productivity tools. While early mobile devices had limited hardware resources and lacked multitasking capabilities, the focused nature of apps has become desirable as it allows users to customize their devices' capabilities according to their preferences.

Initially, the simplest approach to mobile apps involved porting personal computer (PC)-based applications to mobile devices. However, as apps became more advanced, this method proved insufficient. A more sophisticated approach emerged, involving the development of apps specifically tailored to the mobile environment, leveraging advantages. For example, apps that utilize location-based features are purposefully designed with mobile usage in mind, considering the user's mobility and the absence of geographical constraints compared to PCs and laptops.

Apps can be broadly categorized into native apps and web apps.[58] Native apps are built for a specific mobile operating system, such as iOS or Android. They offer superior performance and a highly optimized user interface, often undergoing rigorous development and quality assurance processes before release.

The Value of Information Technology **263**

On the other hand, web apps require minimal device memory as they are accessed through a web browser. These apps rely on a stable internet connection and direct users to specific web pages where all information is stored in server-based databases.

In China, in addition to these two types of apps, a unique approach has emerged with the introduction of lightweight apps called WeChat Mini Programs (MPs), which are integrated into WeChat, the country's largest mobile messaging platform.[59] WeChat, developed by Tencent in 2011, is a free application that offers instant messaging services. WeChat introduced the MP feature in 2017, allowing third-party developers to create lightweight apps within the WeChat ecosystem.

The distinct advantage of MPs is that they provide an enhanced user experience without the need for installation. Users can access MPs directly within the WeChat app, eliminating the need for separate downloads and conserving storage space on their devices. Moreover, the development process for MPs is streamlined compared to that for native apps, avoiding complex procedures and reducing the time and effort required for deployment.

Since their launch, the popularity of WeChat MPs has soared. By 2021, over 3.5 million MPs had been developed, utilized by nearly 450 million daily active users, while the number of MP developers exceeded 3 million.[60] This highlights the widespread adoption and success of this lightweight app concept within the WeChat ecosystem.

There is a diverse range of app types available to users, each serving different purposes and catering to various needs:

- Gaming apps: These offer immersive gaming experiences similar to computer video games. They have gained significant popularity, accounting for approximately one-third of all app downloads and constituting three-quarters of all consumer spending in the app market.[61]
- Productivity apps: Designed to enhance business efficiency, these streamline tasks such as to-do-list management, work progress tracking, and more. They provide tools and features that help individuals and organizations optimize their workflow and enhance productivity.
- Lifestyle and entertainment apps: This category encompasses a broad range of apps that cater to personal lifestyle choices and socialization. These apps facilitate various activities, including dating, social media communication, and video sharing and streaming. Well-known examples include YouTube for video streaming, Instagram for social networking, and TikTok for short-form videos.
- M-commerce apps: With the rise of online shopping, m-commerce apps enable users to conveniently purchase goods and services through their mobile devices. These apps provide seamless browsing, secure transactions, and personalized shopping experiences.
- Travel apps: Designed to assist travelers, these offer a wide range of features such as tour and ticket bookings, navigation through maps and geolocation, travel diaries, and more. They help users plan, organize, and navigate their trips, enhancing their travel experiences.
- Utility apps: This category includes diverse apps that serve specific purposes, such as health apps for monitoring fitness and wellbeing, and barcode scanners for scanning product codes and accessing related information.

264 Digital Business and Management

Case Studies

Blockbuster versus Netflix: Dance with Digital Transformation

The competition between Blockbuster and Netflix highlights the transformative impact of digitalization on traditional business models. While Blockbuster, the incumbent, clung to its brick-and-mortar approach, Netflix adeptly embraced digital evolution, transitioning from DVD rentals to become a streaming giant. By leveraging technology, Netflix optimized user experiences and personalized content delivery, leading to the successful transition to a digital subscription-based model. This strategic shift not only generated sustainable revenue streams and cost efficiencies but also allowed Netflix to outpace Blockbuster. The key lesson here is that embracing digital transformation is crucial in adapting to evolving consumer behaviors, enhancing operational effectiveness, and ultimately thriving in the digital era.

More case details for classroom use are available. Please check the book webpage at www.routledge.com/9781032221212 for more information.

Baidu, Alibaba, Tencent: Digital Giants in China

Baidu, Alibaba, and Tencent stand at the forefront of China's tech industry. Baidu is the nation's foremost search engine; Alibaba dominates e-commerce through its vast online platforms; and Tencent operates leading social media and messaging apps. Their combined influence covers most domains, such as technology, entertainment, payments, and more. These firms are thriving due to China's extensive market, rapid digital adoption, and innovative tactics. Their integrated services have created a digital ecosystem that has transformed daily life. In response to regulatory shifts, these companies have adjusted their strategies to align with China's evolving tech scene while maintaining their essential role in shaping the nation's digital landscape.

More case details for classroom use are available. Please check the book webpage at www.routledge.com/9781032221212 for more information.

Review

- The advent of the digital revolution (8.1) has fundamentally transformed how businesses operate and has created new business models. Digital technologies have allowed businesses to streamline operations, enhance productivity, and deliver better customer value. Digital technologies have played a crucial role in this transformation, enabling businesses to be more effective and efficient in business processes and the development of innovative products and services that cater to specific customer needs.
- The value of IT in business and management (8.2) has become increasingly evident as organizations strive to stay relevant in a rapidly evolving digital landscape. IT has

emerged as a strategic asset that can facilitate business transformation and growth. It enables businesses to leverage data for decision-making, optimize business processes, enhance customer experiences, and foster innovation.

- Online platforms (8.3) have emerged as powerful tools for businesses to reach their target audience, engage with them, and provide personalized services. They have revolutionized how businesses market and sell their products and services. Online platforms have also facilitated peer-to-peer interactions and collaborations, creating vibrant online communities and ecosystems.
- E-business (8.4) uses the internet to conduct business activities, from marketing and sales to customer service. It provides businesses with numerous benefits, such as reduced operational costs, improved customer service, and access to a global market. E-business has also resulted in new business models like online marketplaces and sharing economy platforms. It has transformed the competitive landscape, with businesses now competing not only on price and quality but also on customer experience and digital capabilities.
- Mobile business (8.5) has gained immense popularity due to the proliferation of smartphones and the growing customer demand for convenience. It enables customers to access services anytime, anywhere, and on any device, enhancing their overall experience. For businesses, it provides opportunities for real-time engagement with customers, personalized marketing, and location-based services.

Discussion Questions

1 How has the digital revolution impacted traditional business models and practices? Provide specific examples of industries or businesses that the digital revolution has significantly transformed.
2 Discuss the value of IT in supporting better decision-making of business and management.
3 Online platforms have fundamentally transformed marketing strategies in the MEI. What key benefits and challenges do these platforms present to media and entertainment businesses?
4 E-business has enabled businesses to operate in a global marketplace. What implications does this have for competition and business growth?
5 M-commerce has changed how companies interact with customers. Discuss this shift's advantages and potential drawbacks for businesses and consumers in the MEI.
6 Looking forward, how do you see the digital revolution continuing to evolve and shape the business landscape in the MEI?

Further Reading

- Anderson, C. (2004) "The Long Tail." *Wired*, October 1. www.wired.com/2004/10/tail/.
- Marvin, G. (2013) "'Blockbusters": Why the long tail is dead and go-big strategies pay off." *MarTech.* https://martech.org/blockbusters-why-the-long-tail-is-dead-and-go-big-strategies-pay-off/.

266 Digital Business and Management

- Porter, M. E. and Millar, V. E. (1985). "How information gives you competitive advantage." *Harvard Business Review*, 63(4), pp. 149–160. https://hbr.org/1985/07/how-information-gives-you-competitive-advantage.
- Ryu, S. and Cho, D. (2022). "The show must go on? The entertainment industry during (and after) COVID-19." *Media, Culture & Society*, 44(3), pp. 591–600.
- Vallas, S. and Schor, J.B. (2020). "What do platforms do? Understanding the gig economy." *Annual Review of Sociology*, 46, pp. 273–294.
- Varnali, K. and Toker, A. (2010). "Mobile marketing research: The-state-of-the-art." *International Journal of Information Management*, 30(2), pp. 144–151.

References

1 Shanmugam, K. S. (1979) "Digital and analog communication systems." *NASA STI/Recon Technical Report A, 80*, p. 23225.
2 Gupta, M. S. (2020) "What is digitization, digitalization, and digital transformation?" *ARC Advisory Group.* www.arcweb.com/blog/what-digitization-digitalization-digital-transformation.
3 Parviainen, P. et al. (2022) "Tackling the digitalization challenge: How to benefit from digitalization in practice." *International Journal of Information Systems and Project Management*, 5(1), pp. 63–77.
4 Bloomberg, J. (2018) "Digitization, digitalization, and digital transformation: Confuse them at your peril." *Forbes*, April 29, 2018. www.forbes.com/sites/jasonbloomberg/2018/04/29/digitization-digitalization-and-digital-transformation-confuse-them-at-your-peril/?sh=6075e71f2f2c.
5 Apple (2006) "Nike and Apple Team Up to Launch Nike+iPod." www.apple.com/newsroom/2006/05/23Nike-and-Apple-Team-Up-to-Launch-Nike-iPod/.
6 Murr, K. B. (2019) "Talking about revolutions – from the industrial to the digital." *Europeana Pro.* https://pro.europeana.eu/post/talking-about-revolutions-from-the-industrial-to-the-digital.
7 Murr, K. B. (2019) "Talking about revolutions – from the industrial to the digital." *Europeana Pro.* https://pro.europeana.eu/post/talking-about-revolutions-from-the-industrial-to-the-digital.
8 Wikström, P. (2014) "The music industry in an age of digital distribution." In *Change: 19 Key Essays on How Internet Is Changing our Lives*. Nashville, TN: Turner, pp. 423–444. www.bbvaopenmind.com/en/articles/the-music-industry-in-an-age-of-digital-distribution/.
9 Reia, J. (2014) "Napster and beyond: How online music can transform the dynamics of musical production and consumption in DIY subcultures." *First Monday.*
10 Jacobs, D. L. (2014) "How to self-publish your book through Amazon." *Forbes*, April 25, 2014. www.forbes.com/sites/deborahljacobs/2014/04/25/how-to-self-publish-your-book-through-amazon/?sh=4d2c71c744d3.
11 Zins, C. (2007) "Conceptual approaches for defining data, information, and knowledge." *Journal of the American Society for Information Science and Technology*, 58(4), pp. 479–493.
12 Jacobs, F.R. (2007) "Enterprise resource planning (ERP)—A brief history." *Journal of Operations Management*, 25(2), pp. 357–363.
13 Al-Mudimigh, A., Zairi, M. and Al-Mashari, M. (2001) "ERP software implementation: an integrative framework." *European Journal of Information Systems*, 10(4), pp. 216–226.
14 Sadiku, M. N., Musa, S. M. and Momoh, O. D. (2014) "Cloud computing: opportunities and challenges." *IEEE Potentials*, 33(1), pp. 34–36.
15 Kohavi, R., Rothleder, N. J. and Simoudis, E., (2002) "Emerging trends in business analytics." *Communications of the ACM*, 45(8), pp. 45–48.
16 Porter, M. E. and Millar, V. E. (1985) "How information gives you competitive advantage. *Harvard Business Review*, 63(4), pp. 149-160. https://hbr.org/1985/07/how-information-gives-you-competitive-advantage.
17 Porter, M. E. (1996) "Operational effectiveness is not strategy" *Harvard Business Review*, 74(6), pp. 61–78.

18 Gawer, A. (2021) "Online platforms: Societal implications of the new dominant business models of the digital economy." *Governing Work in the Digital Age.* https://digitalage.berlin/wp-content/uploads/2021/09/HS_Brief-1_Gawer_final.pdf.

19 Kretschmer, T., Leiponen, A., Schilling, M. and Vasudeva, G. (2022) "Platform ecosystems as meta-organizations: Implications for platform strategies." *Strategic Management Journal,* 43(3), pp. 405–424.

20 Cusumano, M. A., Gawer, A. and Yoffie, D. B. (2019) *The business of platforms: Strategy in the age of digital competition, innovation, and power.* New York: Harper Business.

21 "The business of platforms: The platform business model to survive in an ecosystem driven economy" (no date) *Deloitte.* www2.deloitte.com/content/dam/Deloitte/za/Documents/financial-services/za-Article-1-The-business-of-platforms.pdf.

22 "Benefits of online platforms" (2015) *Oxera.* www.oxera.com/wp-content/uploads/2018/07/The-benefits-of-online-platforms-main-findings-October-2015.pdf.pdf.

23 Ryu, S. (2019) *Beauty of crowdfunding: Blooming creativity and innovation in the digital era.* London: Routledge.

24 Jiang, Z., Heng, C. S. and Choi, B. C. (2013) "Privacy concerns and privacy-protective behavior in synchronous online social interactions." *Information Systems Research,* 24(3), pp. 579–595.

25 Di Domenico, G., Sit, J., Ishizaka, A. and Nunan, D. (2021) "Fake news, social media and marketing: A systematic review." *Journal of Business Research,* 124, pp. 329–341.

26 Culiberg, B., Cho, H., Kos Koklic, M. and Zabkar, V. (2023) "From car use reduction to ride-sharing: The relevance of moral and environmental identity." *Journal of Consumer Behaviour,* 22(2), pp. 396–407.

27 "Online platforms: Economic and societal effects" (2021) *Panel for the Future of Science and Technology (STOA) | European Parliament.* www.europarl.europa.eu/stoa/en/document/EPRS_STU(2021)656336.

28 Vallas, S. and Schor, J. B. (2020) "What do platforms do? Understanding the gig economy." *Annual Review of Sociology,* 46, pp. 273–294.

29 Dolber, B., Rodino-Colocino, M., Kumanyika, C. and Wolfson, T. (eds.) (2021) "The gig economy: Workers and media in the age of convergence." London: Routledge.

30 "The role of online platforms in weathering the COVID-19 shock" (2021) *OECD.org.* www.oecd.org/coronavirus/policy-responses/the-role-of-online-platforms-in-weathering-the-covid-19-shock-2a3b8434/.

31 Gkeredakis, M., Lifshitz-Assaf, H. and Barrett, M. (2021) "Crisis as opportunity, disruption and exposure: Exploring emergent responses to crisis through digital technology." *Information and Organization,* 31(1), p. 100344.

32 Ryu, S. and Cho, D. (2022) "The show must go on? The entertainment industry during (and after) COVID-19." *Media, Culture & Society,* 44(3), pp. 591–600.

33 "The role of online platforms in weathering the COVID-19 shock" (2021) *OECD.org.* www.oecd.org/coronavirus/policy-responses/the-role-of-online-platforms-in-weathering-the-covid-19-shock-2a3b8434/.

34 Maddox, K. (2004) "IBM, Ogilvy celebrate 10 years." *Adage,* 4 June. https://adage.com/article/btob/ibm-ogilvy-celebrate-10-years/257702.

35a Pauley, M. (2015) "Chapter 16: E-business and E-commerce: The difference." In *Maritime Management: Micro and Small Businesses.* Charlottetown, CA: University of Prince Edward Island. https://pressbooks.library.upei.ca/smallbusinessmanagement/chapter/e-business-and-e-commerce/.

35b Choi, S. Y., Stahl, D. O., and Whinston, A. B. (1997) *The economics of electronic commerce.* Indianapolis, IN: Macmillan Technical Publishing.

36 Brown, Z. and MacKay, A. (2022) "Are online prices higher because of pricing algorithms?" *Brookings.* www.brookings.edu/research/are-online-prices-higher-because-of-pricing-algorithms/.

37 Cavallo, A. (2017) "Are online and offline prices similar? evidence from large multi-channel retailers." *American Economic Review,* 107(1), pp. 283–303.

38 Garbarino, E. and Lee, O. F. (2003) "Dynamic pricing in internet retail: effects on consumer trust." *Psychology & Marketing,* 20(6), pp. 495–513

39 Anderson, C. (2004) "The Long Tail." *Wired,* October 1. www.wired.com/2004/10/tail/.

40 Barsch, P. (2009) "Long tail vs. the blockbuster." *MarketingProfs*. www.marketingprofs.com/opinions/2009/22796/long-tail-vs-the-blockbuster.

41 "A world of hits" (2009) *The Economist,* November 26, 2009. www.economist.com/briefing/2009/11/26/a-world-of-hits.

42 Marvin, G. (2013) "'Blockbusters': Why the long tail is dead and go-big strategies pay off." *MarTech,* October 23, 2013. https://martech.org/blockbusters-why-the-long-tail-is-dead-and-go-big-strategies-pay-off/ (Accessed: 02 March 2023).

43 Marvin, G. (2013) "'Blockbusters': Why the long tail is dead and go-big strategies pay off." *MarTech,* October 23, 2013. https://martech.org/blockbusters-why-the-long-tail-is-dead-and-go-big-strategies-pay-off/ (Accessed: 02 March 2023).

44 Marvin, G. (2013) "'Blockbusters': Why the long tail is dead and go-big strategies pay off." *MarTech,* October 23, 2013. https://martech.org/blockbusters-why-the-long-tail-is-dead-and-go-big-strategies-pay-off/ (Accessed: 02 March 2023).

45 Morgan, J. (2017) "The rise of the mobile economy and what it means for our future." *Medium,* May 19, 2017. https://medium.com/jacob-morgan/the-rise-of-the-mobile-economy-and-what-it-means-for-our-future-5f5ba82c988f.

46 "What is mobile technology?" (no date) *IBM.* www.ibm.com/topics/mobile-technology.

47 Oswald, E. (2023) "What is Wi-Fi?" *US News & World Report.* www.usnews.com/360-reviews/privacy/what-is-wifi.

48 "What is mobile technology?" (no date) *IBM.* www.ibm.com/topics/mobile-technology.

49 Rao, S. K. and Prasad, R. (2018) "Impact of 5 G technologies on industry 4.0." *Wireless Personal Communications,* 100, pp.145–159.

50 Kenton, W. (2023) "Mobile marketing: Definition, how it works, and examples." *Investopedia,* February 27. www.investopedia.com/terms/m/mobile-marketing.asp.

51 Molyneux, L. (2018) "Mobile news consumption: A habit of snacking." *Digital Journalism,* 6(5), pp. 634–650.

52 Chae, M. and Kim, J. (2004) "Do size and structure matter to mobile users? An empirical study of the effects of screen size, information structure, and task complexity on user activities with standard web phones." *Behaviour & Information Technology,* 23(3), pp. 165–181.

53 Bernritter, S. F., Ketelaar, P. E. and Sotgiu, F. (2021) "Behaviorally targeted location-based mobile marketing." *Journal of the Academy of Marketing Science,* 49(4), pp. 677–702.

54 Varnali, K. and Toker, A. (2010) "Mobile marketing research: The-state-of-the-art." *International Journal of Information Management,* 30(2), pp. 144–151.

55 Bloomenthal, Andrew (2022) "Mobile commerce: Definition, benefits, examples, and trends." *Investopedia,* 24 March. www.investopedia.com/terms/m/mobile-commerce.asp.

56 "Mobile fact sheet" (2021) *Pew Research Center.* www.pewresearch.org/internet/fact-sheet/mobile/.

57 Rouse, M. (2020) "Mobile application." *Techopedia.* www.techopedia.com/definition/2953/mobile-application-mobile-app.

58 Ma, Y., Liu, X., Liu, Y., Liu, Y. and Huang, G. (2017) "A tale of two fashions: An empirical study on the performance of native apps and web apps on Android." *IEEE Transactions on Mobile Computing,* 17(5), pp. 990–1003.

59 Ryu, S., Cheng, K. and Schreieck, M. (2022) "User value perception of native apps versus mini programs: A means-end theory approach." *Journal of Service Management Research,* 6(3), pp. 167–180.

60 "Leveraging WeChat mini programs for enhanced brand engagement and independence" (2023) *Daxue Consulting.* https://daxueconsulting.com/wechat-mini-programs-2020-report/.

61 "Distribution of worldwide consumer spending on mobile apps and games from 2017 to 2022" (2023) *Statista.* www.statista.com/statistics/510043/app-store-app-and-gaming-revenue-share/.

9

THE DIGITALIZATION OF THE MEDIA AND ENTERTAINMENT INDUSTRY

Outline

Overview	269
9.1 Digital Media and Entertainment	270
9.2 Social Media and the Creator Economy	275
9.3 Open Innovation	283
Case Studies	289
Review	291
Discussion Questions	292
Further Reading	292
References	292

Intended Learning Outcomes

- Understand the meanings and implications of digitalization in the media and entertainment industry (MEI).
- Articulate the business and management of social media and the recent boom in the creator economy.
- Understand the concept and applications of open innovation, crowdsourcing, and crowdfunding.

Overview

This chapter examines the significant impact of digitalization on the MEI.

- Digitalization has democratized content creation and distribution, allowing individuals to become content producers; and has led to a shift in business models from traditional advertising to diverse revenue streams like subscriptions and freemium services.

DOI: 10.4324/9781003271222-13

270 Digital Business and Management

- Social media platforms have enabled content creators to monetize their work and influence by providing tools that facilitate direct financial transactions and by challenging conventional concepts of celebrity.
- The role of open innovation in the MEI includes using collective intelligence and creativity for product development and marketing, enhancing engagement, and reducing risks.
- Crowdsourcing and crowdfunding have introduced new ways to gather ideas, feedback, and financial support, shifting the power dynamics in the creation and financing processes.

9.1 Digital Media and Entertainment

9.1.1 Digital Transformation in the Media and Entertainment Industry

The digital transformation of the MEI is accelerating exponentially. New tools and formats are fueling innovation, including subscription-based services, curation, and personalization using cutting-edge technologies. Year after year, digital revenues account for an increasing share of the industry's total revenues.

Digital media has become a transformative force in the MEI, revolutionizing how companies, creators, and consumers interact with content. This has led to a significant restructuring of business models in the music, television, film, and publishing sectors.

One notable change concerns how content is distributed and disseminated. Most media and entertainment entities now utilize digital and social media platforms to reach their audiences. Creators have also embraced these platforms to engage directly with their fans, building more intimate and interactive relationships. By the end of 2021, fixed broadband had reached 1 billion households and there were approximately 4.3 billion unique mobile internet users worldwide.[1] As of early 2023, people were spending an average of three hours and 15 minutes per day engaging with media on mobile devices.[2]

Streaming services have made content such as TV shows and movies accessible on-demand through various electronic devices. Viewers can now watch their favorite shows and films at their convenience. Similarly, newspapers, magazines, books, and other publications have adapted to the digital era by offering content on smartphones and tablets, providing a more accessible and portable reading experience.

PricewaterhouseCoopers has predicted that digital sources will generate almost 62% of the estimated $2.6 trillion revenues of the global MEI in 2023.[3] It is thus clear that the digital transformation is sweeping the MEI and equipping it with greater resilience and opportunities for growth.

While traditional cinema and TV have experienced significant declines, companies that have embraced the digital transformation have thrived. In 2018, the number of TV viewers in the United States dropped to 297.7 million, while the number of over-the-top (OTT) viewers increased to 198.6 million.[4] Meanwhile, TV's share of total US media ad expenditure dropped from 33.9% in 2017 to 31.6% due to the rise in digital video consumption.[5]

On the other hand, subscription video-on-demand and OTT video services such as Netflix and Amazon Prime Video are projected to reach more than twice as many people as the box office in 2024.[6] Internet advertising is also holding its own compared to print, which was hit hard during the COVID-19 pandemic.

The opportunities for global growth are one of the gifts that digital transformation has given the MEI. China is expected to enjoy the greatest revenue growth in the coming years, which is forecast to exceed that of the United States for the first time by 2024.[7]

It is vital for the MEI to keep up with the digital transformation. But while some media and entertainment companies have been exploring how to leverage the new digital landscape for the better part of a decade, others are still struggling to catch up.

Consider the news industry as an example. Despite the industry's efforts, there has been only a marginal rise in the number of readers opting to pay for online news. Moreover, most of those paying for online news have just one subscription. Additionally, in certain countries, most people prefer to allocate their limited budgets to entertainment media rather than news. However, companies can overcome these challenges by harnessing the potential of personalization to boost consumer and subscription-based revenues.

Screen-based entertainment has now eclipsed traditional TV and movies.[8] The challenge for streaming platforms and studios lies in attracting and retaining the younger generations who have been raised with smartphones, social media, and videogames. These modern media provide immersive, interactive, and socially integrated experiences, making it essential for the MEI to adapt and cater to the preferences of this tech-savvy audience.

Social media in particular has seen significant expansion and evolution. It now delivers finely tuned, personalized feeds of various types of content—including images, videos, music, news, and gaming—to billions of users. In addition, top social media services have ventured into retail, leveraging influencers and the creator economy to enhance engagement and drive purchasing behavior.[9]

Over time, gaming has transcended borders and reached people of all age groups.[10] While gaming initially began as a solitary experience, it has evolved into a highly social activity. Games companies have adapted their strategies to monetize various aspects of gaming, including subscriptions, in-game purchases, and extensible games that function more like services. Moreover, they have embraced the social dimension of gaming by incorporating multiplayer features, branded content, and virtual goods to enhance the overall gaming experience.

9.1.2 Growth in the Mobile Entertainment Sector

The MEI has undergone a revolution due to advances in mobile devices and apps. It seems inevitable that mobile devices will predominate as the primary means of media and entertainment consumption.

Each year, the number of people consuming media primarily through mobile devices continues to rise.[11] According to a 2020 survey by Statista, 43% of participants preferred to use mobile devices to consume content; although television remained the leading choice, with 58%.[12] However, the margin between the two is likely to narrow over time, especially among the younger demographic. Given the increasing numbers of consumers going mobile, various content platforms are benefiting from this shift.

The future for mobile entertainment looks promising, given that multiple drivers are facilitating its growth. First, mobile devices such as smartphones and tablets offer a level of convenience that traditional forms of entertainment simply cannot match. Mobile entertainment content is widely available and easily accessible to a large portion of the

272 Digital Business and Management

global population. Users can enjoy a wide range of content—including music, videos, games, and social media—with just a few taps on their mobile screens.

Second, mobile entertainment platforms are using sophisticated algorithms to personalize content recommendations based on user preferences, behavior, and interests. This personalized approach enhances the user experience, providing content that aligns with individual tastes and increases engagement. Similarly, other advancements in mobile technology—such as faster network speeds (e.g., 5 G technology) and graphics processing units—have significantly enhanced the quality and variety of mobile entertainment content.

Third, many mobile entertainment apps incorporate interactive elements such as gaming, live streaming, and social networking features. This interactivity creates a more engaging and immersive experience, encouraging users to spend more time on the platform and fostering a sense of community among users. This also encourages social interaction, allowing users to connect with others around the world who share similar interests. This social aspect enhances the overall entertainment experience and creates a sense of belonging within the online community.

For example, popular video-sharing app TikTok allows users to create, share, and discover short-form videos, which typically last 15 to 60 seconds.[13] This format is perfect for mobile consumption, given the limited attention span of users, and allows for quick and easy engagement. The platform quickly gained immense popularity, especially among younger audiences, for its fun and creative approach to video content. TikTok was designed and optimized for mobile devices from the start, making it seamless and convenient to use on mobile devices. Most importantly, TikTok's recommendation algorithm has played a critical role in its success. By analyzing user behavior and preferences, the service delivers personalized content to each individual user, resulting in a highly engaging experience.

As another example, prominent digital music, podcast, and video service Spotify is widely regarded as one of the most popular mobile entertainment platforms. With a vast collection of over 100 million tracks and 5 million podcast titles, it has become a preferred destination for both artists and consumers.[14] Users can follow friends, artists, and influencers on Spotify. This creates a social network within the platform, and allows users to stay updated on the music preferences and playlists of the people they follow. Spotify also enables users to create collaborative playlists where multiple people can contribute and add songs. This feature fosters collaboration, allows friends to curate playlists together, and makes the music listening experience more communal and interactive.

9.1.3 The Subscription-Based Model as a Main Stream of Revenue

In the past, media monetization primarily relied on paid advertising, encompassing various forms such as television commercials, magazine ads, sponsored columns in newspapers, and radio commercials. However, with the emergence of the subscription economy, the MEI is gradually shifting its focus from ad revenue models to consumer revenue models.[15]

Traditional advertising revenues have fallen due to ad blockers, cord-cutting, and ad fatigue.[16] Subscription-based models provide a more stable and predictable source of income for media and entertainment companies, reducing their reliance on ad revenue.

Consumers are increasingly favoring on-demand and personalized content experiences. Subscription-based services offer the convenience of accessing a vast library of content—including movies, TV shows, music, and more—without the need for individual purchases. Subscription-based models allow companies to gather valuable data on consumer preferences and viewing habits. This helps them curate personalized content recommendations, enhancing the user experience and fostering customer loyalty. Moreover, streaming services have invested heavily in producing exclusive and original content to differentiate themselves from competitors. Consumers are enticed to subscribe to platforms that offer unique, high-quality content that is not available elsewhere.[17]

The transformation of the MEI has just begun and continues to evolve. While the subscription economy has made significant strides, there is still plenty of room for growth. Companies are actively exploring methods to attract, convert, and retain subscribers. The impact of the subscription economy is not limited to giants like Netflix and Spotify; and it spans various sectors of the MEI, including print media. For example, the *New York Times* has experienced substantial growth in digital subscriptions over the years. As of the second quarter of 2021, the company had over 8 million digital-only subscribers, surpassing its print subscriber base.[18]

Numerous print media companies have also placed their digital publications behind paywalls. As paywalls become more common, we can anticipate more sophisticated and dynamic implementations in predicting the likelihood of a visitor becoming a paying subscriber.[19] For example, by analyzing previous on-site behavior, publishers can determine the amount of free content to show before the paywall is presented.

However, with the growth of digital advertising in recent years, ad revenue remains crucial to the media industry. While Google, Meta (formerly Facebook), and other social media platforms continue to dominate the ad market due to their advanced targeting capabilities, media advertising nonetheless retains a prominent position. As is the case for many digital transformations, the shift in revenue streams is expected to occur gradually.

9.1.4 Personalization as a Core Element of the Transformation

In today's media landscape, technology, data, and personalization have become essential tools and strategies for media executives. However, the true drivers of digital transformation are the increasing expectations of users and the indispensable focus on delivering the best possible user experience.

The MEI is undergoing a rapid transformation due to the rise of personalization and curation. The goal is no longer to optimize a single experience but rather to tailor millions of individualized experiences for users.

Popular platforms such as YouTube, Facebook, Google, Amazon, Twitter, Netflix, and Spotify rely heavily on algorithms to curate and recommend content to users. These platforms have finetuned their user interfaces and recommendation engines to provide content that aligns precisely with users' interests and preferences.[20]

To this end, a combination of data from diverse sources—including user data, content-related information, and machine learning techniques—is harnessed to deliver relevant content to individuals. By leveraging this data-driven approach, the accuracy of content recommendations is significantly enhanced, resulting in the more efficient and effective distribution of content.[21]

274 Digital Business and Management

Until recently, the content experience across different platforms was mostly uniform for all users. Whether a news article, live video, or TV series episode, the same content was recommended to each viewer, resulting in a standardized experience for all. The concept of smart content seeks to revolutionize this approach by tailoring the content experience to each individual viewer, reader, or listener. With smart content, the actual content changes based on the viewer's unique identity and preferences.

Early adopters of this personalized approach have already been making waves in the industry. For example, popular platform TikTok curates content through short videos and audiovisual sequences which are skillfully ordered by sophisticated algorithms. As a result, each user receives a distinctive, personalized compilation of content based on their viewing history and user profile.

Another significant player in this space is Netflix, which has ventured into interactive content with shows like *Black Mirror: Bandersnatch*.[22] In these episodes, users' choices directly influence the content, shaping the dialog and storyline according to their decisions. The pursuit of innovative content experiences continues, as demonstrated by Netflix's *Love, Death & Robots* series, which experiments with episode order, providing different users with varying sequences of episodes for a more personalized viewing experience.[23]

9.1.5 The Emergence of New Entertainment Experiences

Content creators now have a wide array of tools to produce and distribute diverse content, leading to transformative changes in how we engage with entertainment. The impact of technology goes beyond facilitating leisure and fun; it also fosters enhanced learning experiences, making knowledge more accessible and enjoyable.

The gaming industry and game-related content, such as live streams and videos, are competing for people's attention in the vast entertainment landscape. These activities have evolved into highly social experiences for numerous gamers. One survey update indicates that 65% of respondents identify as frequent gamers, immersing themselves in gaming activities at least once a week across a range of devices, including smartphones, consoles, tablets, portable gaming devices, and computers.[24] Notably, Gen Zs and millennials are among the most avid gamers, dedicating approximately 13 to 14 hours per week to gaming pursuits.

Additionally, gaming has emerged as a significant generator of user-generated content on social media and streaming platforms. According to the same survey, 45% of frequent gamers regularly watch other users' gameplay streams; 38% stream their own gameplay; and 49% engage with gaming-related videos—such as tips, cheats, and tutorials—on a monthly basis.[25] This burgeoning variety of activities exemplifies the thriving content ecosystem that surrounds the gaming industry and highlights the strong social appeal gaming holds for a wide audience.

Moreover, over half of the gamers surveyed emphasized the importance of positive interactions with fellow players and the ability to personalize their in-game characters or avatars, which significantly enhances the gaming experience. Other key factors include the option to communicate with other players and the opportunity to play games online with friends. Gaming companies have effectively transformed into immersive and interactive social media platforms, catering to the expectations of a generation that grew up immersed in digital networks and interactive entertainment.

In response to these evolving trends and consumer expectations, gaming providers have proactively developed unique and immersive gaming experiences to keep players engaged and socially connected. As younger generations continue to embrace interactive entertainment and social media as integral aspects of their lives, gaming companies are actively meeting their expectations, providing dynamic, social gaming experiences that resonate with their audience.

9.2 Social Media and the Creator Economy

9.2.1 The Concept of Social Media

The term "social media" encompasses the websites and applications that enable people to interact and share information and various forms of user-generated content online.[26] Examples include:

- social networking sites (Facebook, WeChat, Twitter, Weibo);
- blogs (WordPress);
- video-sharing sites (YouTube, Bilibili, TikTok);
- photo-sharing sites (Instagram);
- crowdsourcing (Wikipedia, Mechanical Turk);
- user reviews (Amazon, Yelp, Douban);
- streaming sites (Twitch, AfreecaTV); and
- social bookmarking (Pinterest).

Why do people use social media? One study identified ten reasons for using social media (Figure 9.1), as follows:[27]

- Social interaction: Social media provides a virtual space for individuals to connect with friends, family, and acquaintances, fostering social relationships and reducing feelings of isolation.

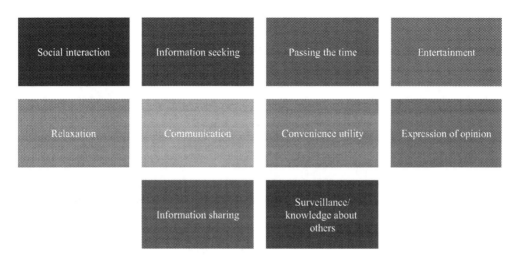

FIGURE 9.1 Reasons for Using Social Media.

276 Digital Business and Management

- Information: Users turn to social media platforms to access real-time news updates, discover relevant information, and stay informed about current events, trends, and topics of interest.
- Passing the time: Social media offers an engaging and entertaining way to fill leisure moments, making it a popular go-to activity during free time.
- Entertainment: From engaging videos to humorous memes and attention-grabbing stories, social media platforms offer an endless stream of entertainment content, serving as a constant source of amusement and enjoyment.
- Relaxation: Social media allows users to unwind and de-stress by immersing themselves in pleasant, visually appealing, emotionally positive content.
- Communication: As a powerful communication tool, social media enables users to easily and instantly connect with others across distances, fostering meaningful interactions and maintaining relationships.
- Convenience of access: Social media platforms streamline daily activities, providing users with a convenient way to access services, connect with businesses, and stay updated on offers and promotions.
- Expressing opinions: Users utilize social media to share their thoughts, beliefs, and perspectives, which fosters a sense of self-expression and enables them to engage in conversations around shared interests or causes.
- Information sharing: Social media serves as a platform for individuals to share valuable knowledge, experiences, and expertise, contributing to a collaborative, learning-driven online community.
- Knowledge of others: Social media allows users to observe the activities and lives of others, satisfying our human curiosity for insights into the lives of friends, celebrities, and public figures.

Social media influences how people communicate, inform and entertain themselves, and connect with others globally. These multifaceted motivations continue to shape the role of social media as an essential aspect of our lives on both a personal and societal level.

Benefits

Social media has changed how we interact with each other. It allows us to discover what is happening in the world in real time, connect and keep in touch with friends, and access endless amounts of information. Social media has helped many individuals find common ground with others online, making the world seem more approachable.

According to one survey, the use of social media correlates to having more friends and more diverse personal networks, especially in emerging economies.[28] For many teenagers, friendships can begin virtually, with 57% of teens making a friend online.[29]

Businesses are also using social media marketing to target consumers on their phones and computers, building loyal fanbases and creating a culture behind their brands.

Social media offers several key benefits for businesses, such as facilitating time-efficient communication and cost-effective marketing, and fostering valuable customer relations:

- It enables companies to connect with their target audience and build meaningful relationships with customers. By engaging directly with customers through social media platforms, businesses can gain valuable insights into their preferences and opinions.

- It serves as a powerful tool for brand exposure, enabling businesses to introduce their brand to a wider audience. Through regular updates and engaging content, companies can create brand awareness and establish a presence in the digital landscape.
- It provides a platform for customers to provide feedback about a brand and its products, and services. This feedback is essential for businesses in improving their offerings and enhancing customer satisfaction.
- It acts as a test audience, allowing companies to gauge the response to new products or marketing campaigns before a full-scale launch. This enables businesses to finetune their strategies to ensure a more successful outcome.

Most importantly, word of mouth through social media platforms is a significant benefit for business. Before social media, information was communicated through traditional, one-way media. However, social media circulates and diffuses information dynamically and simultaneously.[30]

Disadvantages

Despite the advantages, however, social media may not suit every business. The potential disadvantages of social media include the following:[31]

- It takes additional resources and time to effectively manage and maintain a social media presence. Social media demands active daily monitoring and engagement with the audience.
- Companies may be exposed to unwanted or inappropriate behavior on social media platforms. Dealing with online trolls, spam, or abusive comments can be challenging and time-consuming.
- Relatedly, there is a risk of negative feedback, information leaks, or hacking. Social media platforms are susceptible to security breaches, which can compromise sensitive data and damage a brand's reputation.
- Finally, the potential for false or misleading claims could threaten businesses. Such claims can fall under consumer law regulations and may lead to legal consequences, including fines—especially if misleading information is posted about competitors' products or services.

Table 9.1 summarizes the benefits and disadvantages of social media for business purposes.

TABLE 9.1 Benefits and Disadvantages of Social Media for Business

Benefits	Disadvantages
<ul><li>Connects businesses with their audience.</li><li>Builds brand exposure.</li><li>Gathers feedback.</li><li>Acts as a test audience.</li><li>Amplifies word of mouth.</li></ul>	<ul><li>Demands additional resources and active monitoring.</li><li>Risk of unwanted behavior, negative feedback, and information leaks.</li><li>Potential for legal consequences due to false or misleading claims.</li></ul>

Key Elements of Successful Social Media Initiatives

Given the benefits and potential disadvantages of social media, companies should exercise caution in planning and implementing their social media strategy. In developing a successful digital and social media strategy, businesses should consider the "4Ms" of mission, market, message, and medium (Figure 9.2):

- Defining a clear mission is key. Businesses should identify the specific goal they aim to achieve through their digital and social efforts—whether that be increasing brand awareness, driving website traffic, boosting sales, or enhancing customer engagement.
- Next, it is essential to understand the target market. Companies should identify their audience considering demographics, interests, and behaviors; and should determine the stage of the customer journey at which they wish to impact their audience—whether that be attracting new prospects, nurturing leads, or retaining existing customers.
- Once the mission and market have been established, crafting the right message becomes pivotal. Companies must convey a consistent and compelling message that aligns with their brand identity and resonates with the target audience. The message should address customer pain points, highlight unique value propositions, and prompt the desired actions.
- Selecting the most effective medium is equally important. With numerous digital, social, and mobile channels available, businesses must carefully choose the platform that best aligns with their goals and resonates with their target market. The chosen medium should offer the greatest potential for reaching and engaging with the intended audience.

9.2.2 Social Media in the Media and Entertainment Industry

Social media platforms have a significant impact on the MEI.[32] Facebook, Instagram, and Twitter have transformed how people interact with entertainers, significantly impacting artists' recognition and income-generating opportunities.

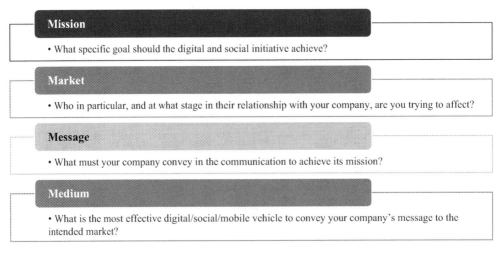

FIGURE 9.2 The 4Ms of Social Media Strategy.

First, real-time interactions are now possible between fans and their beloved celebrities. Users of platforms like Instagram can instantly view updates shared by specific artists they follow—for example, a new photo or song. Fans can leave comments on the posts and artists, in turn, can respond directly to their comments. Similarly, entertainers can leverage Twitter to share updates about events; and their dedicated fans can show their love and admiration by sending direct messages or replying to their tweets. This heightened level of engagement strengthens the connection between celebrities and their followers.

Second, the rise of social media has revolutionized the process of celebrity-making. These platforms have propelled many individuals to fame and given them significant influence over consumers' brand preferences. Such endorsements often bring substantial financial rewards, with these personalities earning millions for promoting major events or new merchandise.

Social media followings have also become crucial for celebrities seeking new opportunities and projects. Producers and industry players are keen to collaborate with personalities who can effectively promote their films or products on these platforms, ultimately driving sales and increasing exposure for their projects.

Third, social media has evolved into more than just a means of communication and interaction; it has also become a platform for earning money. One striking example of this phenomenon is the rise of YouTube millionaires who achieve wealth and success by producing short video clips that attract substantial numbers of views.

In the pre-digital era, artists faced the demanding task of releasing albums and embarking on global tours to promote their work. This process was both time-consuming and costly. In contrast, contemporary top singers now leverage platforms like Spotify, Instagram, and YouTube to create and promote their albums, effectively monetizing their creative endeavors in a more efficient and accessible manner.

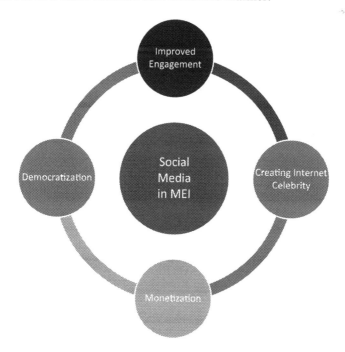

FIGURE 9.3 How Social Media Impacts the Media and Entertainment Industry.

280 Digital Business and Management

Finally, the path to celebrity status has become more democratic and accessible. Gone are the days when becoming a celebrity required close industry connections or a studio recording deal. Today, anyone can win fame by releasing their music or content on social media platforms.

Why Social Media Has Become a Primary Source of Entertainment

The introduction of social media has revolutionized the MEI. In the past, all entertainment sources were controlled by a single entity, leaving little room for public influence. However, social media has transformed this landscape, giving people a significant say in the content they consume.

As the Internet offers an endless array of entertainment options through search engines and social media platforms, streaming has become the new norm for watching movies and TV shows. Traditional TV is becoming outdated as social media establishes itself as an essential component of the MEI. Social media enriches the consumer experience and adds value to the overall entertainment journey.

Social media offers a uniquely valuable and captivating entertainment experience, setting it apart from other forms of entertainment. Its engaging, fast-paced, straightforward nature makes it incredibly enjoyable and addictive.[33] Social media also has a profound impact on our thinking, behaviors, and decision-making, influencing everything from the TV series we binge-watch to the movies we stream, the books we read, and the music we listen to.[34]

Social media not only influences our entertainment choices, but also affects how we share our opinions and how the MEI responds to consumer feedback. Content creators play a crucial role in curating playlists and driving the popularity of shows, movies, books, and songs. They set trends and become trusted sources of honest opinions, recommendations, and reviews, thus shaping the entertainment landscape as we know it.

The integration of entertainment and social media has given audiences a stronger voice in the MEI, leading to increased accountability for the brands using these platforms. However, this also presents challenges for businesses to navigate. Ignoring or mistreating customers can have severe repercussions as negative word of mouth can spread quickly, leading to a loss of customers and reputational damage.

Social media has a significant influence on the MEI and can impact businesses and even blockbuster movie productions. To adapt to this changing landscape, companies must rethink their strategies and learn how to harness the power of social media effectively.

9.2.3 The Changing Landscape of Streaming Services

Streaming services such as Netflix, Hulu, and Disney+ have changed how we consume entertainment content. Instead of waiting for new episodes of our favorite TV shows to be screened or movies to be released in theaters, we can now watch them whenever and wherever we want.

Streaming services have also given independent filmmakers and creators more opportunities, as they can now reach a wider audience through these platforms. Social media provides a platform for creators to promote their work and connect with audiences. This has led to the emergence of new voices and perspectives in the MEI, making it more inclusive and diverse than ever before.

The Impact on Traditional Media

Social media has changed how we consume and engage with entertainment content.[35] The MEI has always relied on its audience to promote its content, but social media has amplified this to a new level. With the ability to easily share and access user-generated content, audiences can connect and share their favorite forms of entertainment with friends and family.

One of the most significant ways in which social media has impacted the MEI is through the rise of influencers. Influencers have large followings on social media platforms such as Instagram, TikTok, and YouTube. They can reach millions with just one post, and their opinions and recommendations hold considerable weight with their followers.

Players in the MEI have taken notice of this and have begun to incorporate influencers into their marketing strategies. Musicians, actors, and filmmakers now collaborate with influencers to promote their projects and gain a wider audience. This has changed how entertainment content is marketed, with social media becoming the primary platform for reaching potential audiences.

With the rise of streaming services and user-generated content, traditional media has had to adapt to stay relevant. This has led to an increase in the number of TV shows and movies released directly on streaming services, bypassing traditional theaters and TV networks altogether.

Social media has also greatly impacted how traditional media is marketed. Instead of relying on traditional methods such as billboards, TV commercials, and magazine ads, marketers are now turning to social media as the primary platform through which to reach their audiences:

- Movie and TV: Studies have shown that social media directly impacts the popularity of films and television shows. Platforms such as TikTok are compelling, as they break new trends and allow users to interact with their favorite shows and movies in a unique way. Shows like *Squid Game* serve as remarkable examples of the power of social trends on streaming platforms. These shows, released on different streaming services, achieved immense popularity thanks to the virality of social trends that emerged shortly after their release.

  The COVID-19 pandemic also had a significant impact on the MEI, and particularly on movie theaters, which were forced to close. As a result, streaming services had to adapt and premiere new films directly on their platforms. In this new landscape, streaming services rely heavily on the hype generated by social media users and content creators to drive up streams and enhance the overall success of new shows and movies.

- Publishing: #BookTok is a popular trending hashtag on TikTok that suggests which books people should consider reading at any time. #BookTok is a community through which book lovers around the globe share images of their esthetically pleasing bookshelves and must-read recommendations.

282 Digital Business and Management

Bookstores have acknowledged the significant marketing potential of TikTok. The recent surge in book sales can be largely attributed to the virality of #BookTok. A prime example is Madeline Miller's *The Song of Achilles*, which became a *New York Times* bestseller a decade after its initial publication in 2011. This tremendous resurgence in popularity is primarily due to the widespread hype the book garnered through TikTok.

- Music: TikTok directly impacts global music charts and how streaming platforms bring new songs and playlists to listeners. Trending TikTok and Reels songs find new fans no matter what their release date. Aspiring artists know that having a trending song on social media can be a gamechanger. As streaming services create playlists of trending songs, this has helped propel the careers of artists.

9.2.4 The Creator Economy and Social Media

For over a decade, we have witnessed the rapid rise of "creators"—alternatively known as "content creators," "influencers," "YouTubers," "vloggers," "live streamers," "key opinion leaders," and "*wang hong*" (in Chinese).[36] The term has emerged as the industry's designated descriptor for social media users who are adept at utilizing various platforms to engage in media entrepreneurship on a global scale.[37] *Forbes'* annual list of the most successful creators extends across multiple content verticals to include entertainers, game players, beauty vloggers, and toy unboxers.[38] These examples represent only a fraction of the widespread global phenomenon of online cultural producers who skillfully blend traditional and modern media practices, entrepreneurship, creative work, and user engagement.

Creators have emerged organically across various platforms, availing of network effects and diverse technological and commercial opportunities to establish their own distinctive media brands. The global landscape of social media platforms continues to evolve, offering a wide array of modalities such as text, images, audio, video on demand, and live streaming. This dynamic environment includes first-generation platforms like Twitter, Facebook, and YouTube; mobile apps such as Instagram, TikTok, and Snapchat; and live streaming platforms like Twitch and YouNow. In China, the *wang hong* industry is even more competitive, with advanced and well-integrated commercial features on platforms like Bilibili, Douyin, Xiaohongshu (Red), and WeChat.

While the creator economy is difficult to measure in scale and influence, it has seen the revenues of creators grow exponentially. One report suggests that 15 million online creators are generating revenue off social media platforms in the US alone.[39]

The creator economy is likely to continue to evolve and grow in the coming years, driven by ongoing advancements in digital technologies and the changing preferences and behaviors of consumers. Three trends and developments will likely shape the creator economy in the coming years:

- The rise of niche creators: As the creator economy becomes more crowded and competitive, creators may need to concentrate on cultivating specialized audiences and catering to distinct interests or demographics. This may result in the emergence of novel platforms and communities centered on niche content and specific audiences.

- The evolution of monetization models: Creators may explore innovative ways to monetize their content beyond traditional advertising and sponsorships. These could include exploring new avenues in e-commerce, like selling digital products or services or venturing into the realm of blockchain and cryptocurrency technologies to establish new revenue streams.
- The importance of community and engagement: Creators may increasingly prioritize the establishment of robust communities and close audience engagement to stand out from their rivals and establish a more sustainable business. This could involve leveraging social media, online forums, and other platforms to connect with fans and followers, forging deeper connections with them.

9.3 Open Innovation

9.3.1 The Concept of Open Innovation

According to Joseph Schumpeter, innovation ("in" ["manner"] + "nov" [*novitas*/new]) comes about through new combinations made by entrepreneurs, resulting in:

- a new product;
- a new resource/process;
- the opening of a new market; or
- a new way of organizing business.

Traditionally, closed innovation has been the prevailing approach in various domains. Successful historic cases include the chemicals industry in Germany and later in the US; the pioneering work of Edison and General Electric in the rise of electrification; the impactful influence of Rockefeller and Standard Oil; and the remarkable scientific achievements during World War II.

Companies that adopt the closed innovation paradigm base their activities on the idea that efficient innovation involves specific control over the innovation process and everything that comes with it. They believe that they should develop their ideas internally and produce and promote their products by themselves.

This paradigm prevailed until the end of the 20th century, when the so-called "knowledge economy" emerged. This is also when the idea of intellectual work and intellectual property (IP) became more popular.

The problems with the closed innovation paradigm included significant expenses and low efficiency of R&D investments. Difficulties in protecting knowhow and IP also drove the need for a new innovation paradigm.

The concept of open innovation—first proposed by theorist Henry Chesbrough in 2003—asserts that sharing ideas and collaborating both internally and externally deliver better outcomes than closed innovation.[40] Open innovation has rapidly become an engine of revenue growth and business performance. Organizations that embrace open innovation have a higher revenue growth rate than those that do not.[41]

Open innovation uses purposive inflows and outflows of knowledge to accelerate internal innovation and expand the markets for the external use of innovation.[42]

Key concepts within open innovation include transcending firm boundaries, fostering collaboration both within and outside the organization, and effectively managing the external processes of innovation.

284 Digital Business and Management

TABLE 9.2 Principles of Closed vs. Open Innovation

Closed innovation	*Open innovation*
• The smart people in the field work for us.	• Not all smart people work for us.
• If we discover it ourselves, we go to market first.	• We don't have to originate the research to profit from it.
• If we are the first to commercialize an innovation, we will win.	• Building a better business model is more important than getting to market first.
• If we create the best ideas in the industry, we will win.	• We will win if we make the best use of both internal and external ideas.
• We should control our IP so our competitors can't profit from our ideas.	• We should profit from others' use of our IP and vice versa.

The main differences between the two paradigms concern how companies deal with idea generation and how products are brought to market (Table 9.2).[43a]

Open innovation aims to improve the four crucial rates below which collectively influence the effectiveness and efficiency of the whole innovation process (Figure 9.4):[43b]

- the rate of introducing new ideas into the firm (R1);
- the rate of developing ideas (R2);
- the rate of commercializing and marketing ideas (R3); and
- the adoption rate (R4).

R1 represents the speed and frequency at which innovative concepts and proposals are generated—whether internally through R&D departments or externally through collaboration with partners, customers, and even competitors. Emphasizing open ideation channels and encouraging a culture of idea-sharing can accelerate the influx of new concepts into a company's innovation pipeline.

Subsequently, R2 comes into play. This gauges how swiftly ideas progress from concept to a refined and viable stage where they are ready for further evaluation and testing. Engaging cross-functional teams, promoting rapid prototyping, and tapping into external expertise can all bolster R2. This may expedite the evolution of promising ideas into tangible prototypes or proofs of concept.

Moving along the open innovation journey, R3 becomes instrumental in turning innovations into marketable products or services. Collaboration with external partners such as suppliers, distributors, or even startups can streamline the commercialization process and enhance market penetration. Furthermore, the utilization of external marketing channels, including influencer partnerships and social media collaborations, can amplify the visibility and reach of new offerings.

Ultimately, R4 determines how rapidly customers and end users embrace the innovations yielded by the open innovation efforts. Fostering strong customer engagement, conducting user testing and feedback sessions, and tailoring products or services to meet specific customer needs can drive a higher adoption rate.

The successful implementation of open innovation programs can be hindered by three major obstacles:[44]

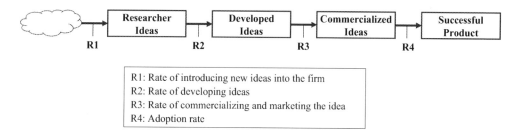

FIGURE 9.4 Open Innovation System Dynamics.

- Managing IP issues and legal risks: Companies adopting open innovation face challenges related to IP rights and legal risks. Disputes over IP can discourage outside innovators from submitting their ideas, and receiving companies may face potential litigation risks. To overcome this, it is crucial to design an open innovation program that carefully controls the type and amount of information submitted, alleviating the concerns of small innovators while mitigating the risk of legal disputes. Implementing an automated system to guide submitters on what information to disclose and documenting communications between corporations and inventors can help manage costs and liabilities effectively.
- Processing ideas efficiently: The success of an open innovation program can lead to a high volume of idea submissions, making it challenging to review and decide on which to pursue in a timely manner. Without a well-defined strategy, the process may become disorganized, leading companies to abandon their open innovation efforts. To address this, a structured screening process should be established to filter and manage all submissions, allowing for the quick and efficient evaluation of ideas. Criteria for scoring and ranking submissions based on business value, regulatory considerations, market opportunities, and manufacturing requirements can assist in separating potential winners from less promising ideas. Automation of this process enhances efficiency and reduces time to market, ultimately increasing the return on innovation.
- Establishing an efficient internal structure: A successful open innovation program requires an effective internal structure to solicit and review ideas and communicate with innovators in a timely manner. This structure—which usually involves a combination of people and technology—ensures that the best ideas are evaluated and promoted within the organization while also safeguarding against IP litigation. Dedicated portals can formalize and standardize the submission process, giving external ideas an equal footing within the organization. Furthermore, such portals discourage individuals from submitting confidential information through uncontrolled channels, minimizing the legal risks.

There are several other difficulties in managing open innovation, including the task of finding genuine partners that are trustworthy and cooperative. Moreover, the increased management demands, coupled with slow and intricate processes, can further complicate matters. One crucial aspect that requires careful consideration is risk assessment, particularly when it comes to issues like free riding and the potential cost of failure.

286 Digital Business and Management

Another noteworthy hurdle in open innovation is the lack of sufficient research and the absence of established best practices and standardized procedures. Addressing these challenges and implementing countermeasures to overcome them will be essential for the successful management of open innovation programs.

9.3.2 Crowdsourcing: The Wisdom of Crowds

Crowdsourcing is a process whereby companies or institutions outsource tasks that were once performed by employees to an undefined network of people through an open call. This involves gathering work, information, or opinions from a large group of individuals who submit their contributions via the Internet, social media, and mobile apps.[45]

Some participants in crowdsourcing work as paid freelancers, while others volunteer to perform smaller tasks. The concept of "prosumers" is essential to crowdsourcing and refers to consumers who engage in various management activities by blurring consumer and business roles, including design, development, production, promotion, and service.

The appeal of crowdsourcing for businesses is that it enables them to access a diverse pool of talent around the world without incurring the standard overhead costs associated with in-house employees. Companies can reach people globally and tap into a vast array of skills and expertise.

One of the most successful crowdsourcing projects is the Netflix Prize, which was launched in 2006.[46] Netflix offered a $1 million prize to anyone who could improve its recommendation algorithm by at least 10% accuracy. The competition was open to all and attracted thousands of entries from teams and individuals worldwide. Participants were provided with a large dataset of anonymous movie ratings from Netflix customers and were tasked with developing algorithms to predict which movies customers might enjoy based on their viewing history and ratings. A team of researchers eventually won the Grand Prize in 2009 with an algorithm that improved Netflix's recommendation accuracy by 10.06%.[47]

Benefits

Crowdsourcing offers several benefits for businesses (Figure 9.5):

- Enhanced scalability: Scaling can be a complex challenge for businesses, especially when dealing with large projects and limited resources. Crowdsourcing offers an effective solution by dividing tasks into smaller portions that can be completed by remote workers at their own convenience. This flexibility is a major factor that drives businesses toward crowdsourcing.
- Bridging of the knowledge gap: Companies may not always have all the resources they need. Crowdsourcing affords them access to individuals with specialized skill sets that may not be readily available within the organization. This is invaluable for projects or issues that demand unique expertise or skills.
- Accelerated processes: Crowdsourcing enables businesses to complete tasks faster than if they relied on a single employee or a limited team. By breaking down projects into smaller components and distributing them among a larger group of workers, efficiency and speed are significantly increased. Overall, crowdsourcing presents a more streamlined approach to work.

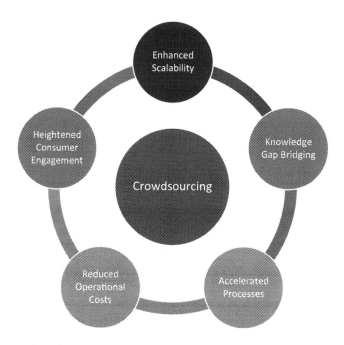

FIGURE 9.5 Benefits of Crowdsourcing.

- Reduced operational costs: One major advantage of crowdsourcing is its cost-effectiveness. When a group of people collaborate digitally to complete tasks, businesses can bypass many of the typical operational costs associated with in-house employees, including overhead expenses related to office space and salaries. Additionally, faster turnaround times may lead to increased profits, depending on the nature of the project.
- Heightened consumer engagement: Involving consumers in crowdsourcing efforts can lead to exceptional levels of engagement. Unlike traditional marketing approaches, which often have limited impact, involving consumers in solving specific problems or contributing valuable data about a brand captures their attention and interest. This level of engagement is often highly sought after by companies and can be achieved through well-executed crowdsourcing initiatives.

Disadvantages

However, crowdsourcing is not a cure-all for companies in seeking to reduce their workload and searching for the next groundbreaking idea. First, the results can easily be skewed depending on the crowd that is sourced. A lack of confidentiality or ownership of ideas is another critical concern. Finally, there is a risk that the company may miss out on the best ideas, talent, or direction, causing it to fall short of its goal or purpose.

Types of Crowdsourcing

Companies are utilizing crowdsourcing in different ways to bolster their product offerings, obtain consumer data to steer future product decisions, and much more.[48]

288 Digital Business and Management

Many companies utilize crowdsourced data and tasks to enhance their product offerings. A wide variety of creative crowdsourcing platforms provide different designs for logos, websites, ads, product packaging, and so on. 99Designs is one of the best known.

Some companies even use crowdsourcing to form the backbone of their products or to serve as a differentiator. For example, Threadless is an e-commerce website based in Chicago, founded in 2000. Threadless designs are generated and selected by an online community through a voting process. Numerous designs are submitted weekly and subjected to a public vote. At the end of the week, the staff review the top-scoring designs and approximately 10 designs are chosen based on average score and community feedback. These selected designs are then printed on clothing and other products, which are sold globally through online stores and retail outlets. Similarly, Lego Digital Designer collects unique design products from users and orders the necessary parts. The top user designs are selected through an annual competition for retail production and sales.

Another common type of crowdsourcing concerns open-source software, which allows developers to access the source code and modify and improve it as they see fit. Ultimately, this enables many people to analyze the code and utilize their unique skill sets to improve it. Examples of open-source software include the Linux operating system and Firefox browsers.

Another example of effective crowdsourcing is Amazon Mechanical Turk, which provides solutions for tasks such as data entry, transcription, content creation, user studies, and more. Workers from all over the world log onto Mechanical Turk to perform these "human intelligence tasks." The platform allows projects to be divided into micro-tasks and supports various types of projects. It is most suitable for relatively straightforward tasks and user surveys rather than creative or innovation-based work. Requesters have the flexibility to set the desired rate per task and can exercise some control over the types of workers who respond to their tasks.

9.3.3 Crowdfunding

Crowdfunding is a way of sourcing funds to support individuals, charities, or startups. Many creators have become accustomed to using crowdfunding to raise capital. This technique allows anyone to engage people interested in their ideas and raise capital without pitching to large investors, banks, or other gatekeepers that might withhold funding.

Crowdfunding has sparked significant changes in various sectors, particularly in creativity and innovation.[49] It has become a catalyst for fostering creativity and generating solutions to longstanding financing problems in diverse fields.

Crowdfunding platforms offer reasonable fees for their services, making them stand out from other forms of financing, including traditional sources. Many crowdfunding campaigns have gone on to raise thousands, and sometimes even millions, of dollars. Examples of successful products that began as crowdfunded projects include the Oculus virtual reality headset and the Pebble Watch.

Today, creators from diverse domains have expanded opportunities to secure funding, validate their ideas, build communities, and pursue long-term careers and businesses through crowdfunding. The benefits are substantial: some creators obtain funding to distribute their products, while others attract attention from valuable business partners.

Many creators appreciate the freedom from external controls that institutional sponsors might impose on their work. Furthermore, crowdfunding can serve as a launchpad for new ventures and nonprofit organizations, helping them take their first steps toward success. Additionally, creators can generate sustainable revenue from their projects, making crowdfunding an essential driver for their continued creative endeavors.

Crowdfunding impacts creativity and innovation in the MEI in the following ways:

- Addressing the lack of financing channels: Crowdfunding proves more effective than traditional financing methods in promoting ideas and engaging potential contributors. Successful campaigns have an immediate impact on revenue, freeing creators from the burdens of pursuing external financing. Collaborators also benefit, as they are compensated for their creative contributions.
- Validating creativity and innovation: Crowdfunding provides a platform for creators to validate and refine their ideas through immediate feedback from potential contributors. This process serves as an opportunity for brainstorming and focus group interviews, enabling creators to refine and improve their concepts.
- Creating a supportive community: Crowdfunding attracts contributors who are motivated not only by financial returns but also by the desire to support and build relationships with creators. These early adopters become devoted advocates, generating momentum for creators both during and after the campaign. Their support and sharing on social networks contribute to the success of crowdfunding campaigns.
- Securing creative independence: Crowdfunding empowers creators to bring their ideas to life without compromising their creative freedom. Unlike other financing channels, crowdfunding allows creators to maintain complete control over their work, which is essential to taking risks and accelerating creativity and innovation.

Crowdfunding has become a popular financing option in the MEI, from music singles to feature films. Popular crowdfunding platforms include Indiegogo and Kickstarter; while some of the best crowdfunding platforms specialize in helping creators (Patreon), consumer-goods startups (Circle), movie producers/distributors (Seed&Spark), and fashion designers (BetaBrand).

Case Studies

Spotify: The Digitalization of Music Consumption

Spotify, the pioneering digital music streaming platform founded in 2006, has transformed music consumption through its "freemium" ("free" + "premium") subscription services. It rapidly expanded globally by offering free access with ads and premium subscriptions with benefits like ad-free unlimited music and offline playback. Despite early hurdles (e.g., relating to royalties and competition), Spotify thrived by introducing novel features such as personalized music recommendations driven by advanced algorithms, diverse subscription plans, and a user-friendly interface across multiple devices. It has enjoyed success by

290 Digital Business and Management

catering to varied user preferences, enhancing music discovery, and reshaping the digital music landscape.

More case details for classroom use are available. Please check the book webpage at www.routledge.com/9781032221212 for more information.

New York Times: **The Transformation to a Digital Subscription Model**

The *New York Times* achieved a remarkable business transformation by embracing a digital subscription-based model to counter the challenges of the digital revolution. Battling declining print readership and ad revenue, it invested in quality journalism and user experience. It launched digital subscriptions in 2011, initially offering limited free access and later requiring subscriptions for full content. Despite initial doubts, this strategy paid off, as expanded digital offerings like apps and podcasts resulted in substantial subscriber growth. Digital subscriptions quickly gained traction, exceeding 8.2 million in total by late 2021. This success has stemmed from significant investment in top-notch journalism, an emphasis on a seamless user experience, and the strategic use of data analytics to enhance content and engagement strategies. This shift from ad dependency has allowed the *New York Times* to thrive and set a blueprint for the industry's revitalization in the digital age.

More case details for classroom use are available. Please check the book webpage at www.routledge.com/9781032221212 for more information.

Threadless: **Crowdsourcing Ideas and Designs**

Founded in 2000, Threadless has revolutionized the custom t-shirt industry through crowdsourcing. Designers submit designs via an online platform, with users voting on their favorites. The chosen designs are manufactured, marketed, and shipped by Threadless, which compensates designers with royalties. The company also collaborates with major brands. This innovative approach taps into a wide creative network and promotes engagement and community. Threadless's unique model produces high-quality, diverse products by combining creative talent, user involvement, and brand partnerships in a successful and engaging business venture.

More case details for classroom use are available. Please check the book webpage at www.routledge.com/9781032221212 for more information.

BTS: **Managing Fans and Influencers in Social Media**

South Korean boy band BTS has achieved stardom by masterfully managing fans and influencers on social media. Through interactive engagement on platforms like Twitter and

Instagram, along with live events and the promotion of user-generated content, BTS has cultivated an intensely loyal fanbase known as the ARMY. This sense of belonging has also been nurtured by the incorporation of fan-created art into their official merchandise. BTS's social media presence also extends beyond entertainment, as they use their platform to advocate for social causes, such as the Love Myself campaign with UNICEF. This fusion of fan connection and impactful activism has propelled BTS to fame and positioned them as a potent force for positive global transformation.

More case details for classroom use are available. Please check the book webpage at www.routledge.com/9781032221212 for more information.

Review

- This chapter discusses the transformation of the MEI through digitalization (9.1). The democratization of content creation and distribution has empowered individuals to become producers, not just consumers. Content creators now have unprecedented opportunities to engage audiences with audiences through various platforms. The digitalization trend has also reshaped business models in the MEI, which have shifted from traditional advertising-based models to diverse revenue streams such as subscription models and freemium services.
- Social media platforms have provided creators with tools to monetize their content and influence (9.2). Platforms have given creators more control over revenue by introducing features that facilitate direct financial transactions between creators and followers. The rise of influencers has also put conventional concepts of celebrity to the test, as influencers are often perceived as more relatable and authentic.
- Open innovation, which leverages the collective intelligence and creativity of a diverse pool of people, has been a driving force in the MEI (9.3). Companies have utilized open innovation successfully, inviting consumers to propose and evaluate new product ideas. Platforms facilitate collaboration between brands and creative professionals. This approach can bring fresh perspectives, enhance engagement, and reduce the risks associated with product development and marketing activities.
- Crowdsourcing and crowdfunding are crucial trends in the digitalization of the MEI. They introduce novel ways to harness collective efforts and resources. Crowdsourcing solicits ideas and feedback from a large group, while crowdfunding seeks financial contributions to support a cause or project. These models have democratized the creation and financing processes, transferring power to the crowd.
- Finally, a range of cases have illustrated the impact of digitalization in the MEI. Spotify has revolutionized music consumption with its freemium service model and vast music library. The *New York Times*, faced with a decline in print readership, has shifted to a digital subscription model. Threadless crowdsources ideas and designs. BTS expertly manages fans and influencers on social media. Each case underscores how digitalization has disrupted established industries and created new business opportunities.

Discussion Questions

1 How has digitalization promoted the democratization of content creation and distribution in the MEI? Discuss whether digitalization has empowered individuals to become producers and creators, not just consumers.

2 How has the rise of the creator economy disrupted the traditional landscape of the MEI? Can you identify the challenges that this development presents for traditional companies?

3 Discuss the impact of open innovation on the MEI. How can companies effectively use open innovation to gain competitive advantage and enhance user engagement?

4 Discuss the advantages and drawbacks of leveraging crowdfunding in growing businesses in the MEI. Why could it be a more appropriate service for businesses in the MEI?

5 Given the *New York Times*' successful shift to a digital subscription model, do you think it would be feasible for all print media organizations to do likewise? What are the potential challenges of this transition and how can they be overcome?

6 BTS's management of fans and influencers on social media has been highly effective. Discuss the role of social media in shaping the success of creators.

Further Reading

- Chesbrough, H. W. (2003). *Open innovation: The new imperative for creating and profiting from technology*. Cambridge, MA: Harvard Business Press.
- Cho, D. and Ryu, S. (2021). "BTS: Success and risk with fans and influencers on social media." *Ivey Case Studies,* 9B21E010. London, ON: Ivey Publishing.
- Cunningham, S. and Craig, D. (2019). *Social media entertainment: The new intersection of Hollywood and Silicon Valley.* New York: New York University Press.
- Kaplan, A. M. and Haenlein, M. (2010). "Users of the world, unite! The challenges and opportunities of social media." *Business Horizons,* 53(1), pp. 59–68.
- Ryu, S. (2022). "ByteDance: TikTok and Douyin in online streaming wars. SAGE Business Cases Originals. London: SAGE Publications.
- Ryu, S. (2019). *Beauty of crowdfunding: Blooming creativity and innovation in the digital era.* London: Routledge.
- Shapiro, R. and Aneja, S. (2019). "Taking root: The growth of America's new creative Economy." *Re:Create.* https://www.recreatecoalition.org/wp-content/uploads/2019/02/ReCreate-2017-New-Creative-Economy-Study.pdf

References

1 "The state of mobile internet connectivity 2022." (2022) *GSM Association.* https://www.gsma.com/r/wp-content/uploads/2022/12/The-State-of-Mobile-Internet-Connectivity-Report-2022.pdf.

2 Howarth, J. (2023) "Time spent using smartphones (2023 statistics)." *Exploding Topics.* https://explodingtopics.com/blog/smartphone-usage-stats#top-smartphone-stats.

3 "Global Entertainment and media outlook 2019-2023" (no date) *PwC.* https://mediaoutlook.pwc.com/dist/assets/pdf/Take-a-Tour-Outlook-2019.pdf.

4 Insider Intelligence. (2018) "US TV Ad Spending to Fall in 2018: Digital video continues double-digit growth; OTT spend rises." *eMarketer,* March 28, 2018. www.insiderintelligence.com/content/us-tv-ad-spending-to-fall-in-2018.

5 eMarketer editors. (2018) "US TV ad spending to fall in 2018." *Insider Intelligence*. www.insiderintelligence.com/content/us-tv-ad-spending-to-fall-in-2018.
6 "Global entertainment and media outlook 2019-2023" (no date) *PwC*. https://mediaoutlook.pwc.com/dist/assets/pdf/Take-a-Tour-Outlook-2019.pdf.
7 "Global entertainment and media outlook 2019-2023" (no date) *PwC*. https://mediaoutlook.pwc.com/dist/assets/pdf/Take-a-Tour-Outlook-2019.pdf.
8 Westcott, K. et al. (2022) "2022 Digital media trends, 16th edition: Toward the metaverse." *Deloitte Insights*, March 28. www2.deloitte.com/us/en/insights/industry/technology/digital-media-trends-consumption-habits-survey/summary.html.
9 "2022 Digital media trends, 16th edition: Toward the metaverse" (2022) *Deloitte Insights*. https://www2.deloitte.com/za/en/insights/industry/technology/digital-media-trends-consumption-habits-survey/summary.html.
10 "2021 essential facts about the video game industry" (2021) *Entertainment Software Association*. www.theesa.com/resource/2021-essential-facts-about-the-video-game-industry/.
11 Bradley, D. (2022) "The mobile entertainment industry and its multi-billion dollar growth" *TIICKER*. www.tiicker.com/insights/the-mobile-entertainment-industry-and-its-multi-billion-dollar-growth.
12 "Devices used to watch online streaming videos in the United States as of the 4th quarter of 2020" (2020) *Statista*. www.statista.com/statistics/784383/online-video-devices-in-the-us/.
13 Ryu, S. (2022) "ByteDance: TikTok and Douyin in online streaming wars." SAGE Business Cases Originals. London: SAGE Publications.
14 "About Spotify" (2023) *Spotify*. https://newsroom.spotify.com/company-info/.
15 Kawashima, N., (2020) "Changing business models in the media industries." *Media Industries Journal*, 7(1). https://quod.lib.umich.edu/m/mij/15031809.0007.105/--changing-business-models-in-the-media-industries?rgn=main;view=fulltext.
16 Çelik, F., Çam, M.S. and Koseoglu, M. A. (2023) "Ad avoidance in the digital context: A systematic literature review and research agenda." *International Journal of Consumer Studies*. Forthcoming.
17 Tryon, C. (2015) "TV got better: Netflix's original programming strategies and the on-demand television transition." *Media Industries Journal*, 2(2).
18 Lee, E. (2021) "The New York Times reaches 8 million subscriptions." *The New York Times*, August 4,. www.nytimes.com/2021/08/04/business/media/nyt-new-york-times-earnings-q2-2021.html.
19 Wadbring, I. and Bergström, L. (2021) "Audiences behind the paywall: News navigation among established versus newly added subscribers." *Digital Journalism*, 9(3), pp. 319–335.
20 Koponen, J. (2019) 'Get ready for a new era of personalized entertainment', *TechCrunch*, 14 April. https://techcrunch.com/2019/04/13/get-ready-for-a-new-era-of-personalized-entertainment/.
21 Koponen, J. (2015) "The future of algorithmic personalization." *TechCrunch*, June 26. https://techcrunch.com/2015/06/25/the-future-of-algorithmic-personalization/.
22 Shieber, J. (2019) "Netflix is pursuing more interactive content, including, maybe, a rom-com." *TechCrunch*. March 13. https://techcrunch.com/2019/03/12/netflix-is-pursuing-more-interactive-content-including-maybe-a-rom-com/.
23 Liptak, A. (2019) "Netflix is experimenting with different episode orders for its new anthology show." *The Verge*, March 23. www.theverge.com/2019/3/22/18277634/netflix-love-death-robots-different-episode-orders-anthology-show.
24 Deloitte (2021) "Digital media trends: Online entertainment usage up." *The Wall Street Journal*. https://deloitte.wsj.com/articles/digital-media-trends-online-entertainment-usage-up-01638474446.
25 Deloitte (2021) "Digital media trends: Online entertainment usage up." *The Wall Street Journal*. https://deloitte.wsj.com/articles/digital-media-trends-online-entertainment-usage-up-01638474446.
26 Kaplan, A. M. and Haenlein, M. (2010) "Users of the world, unite! The challenges and opportunities of social media." *Business Horizons*, 53(1), pp. 59–68.
27 Whiting, A. and Williams, D. (2013) "Why people use social media: A uses and gratifications approach." *Qualitative Market Research: An International Journal*, 16(4), pp. 362–369.
28 Silver, L. and Huang, C. (2019) "Social media users more likely to interact with people who are different from them." *Pew Research Center*. www.pewresearch.org/internet/2019/08/22/social-media-users-more-likely-to-interact-with-people-who-are-different-from-them/.

29 Lenhart, A. (2015) "Teens, technology and Friendships." *Pew Research Center*. www.pewresearch.org/internet/2015/08/06/teens-technology-and-friendships/.

30 Winerman, L. (2009) "Social networking: Crisis communication." *Nature*, 457(7228), pp. 376–378. www.nature.com/news/2009/090121/pdf/457376a.pdf.

31 "Social media for business" (2023) *Australian Government*. https://business.gov.au/online/social-media-for-business.

32 Adzo, K. (2022) "How is digital media affecting the entertainment industry?" *Startup.info*, February 2. https://startup.info/how-is-digital-media-affecting-the-entertainment-industry/.

33 James, H. (2021) "The merging of social media and the entertainment industry." *Network Ustad.* https://networkustad.com/2021/10/20/the-merging-of-social-media-and-the-entertainment-industry/.

34 "The impact of social media and content creators on the entertainment industry" (2022) *Vamp*. https://vamp.com/blog/2022/05/13/the-impact-of-social-media-and-content-creators-on-the-entertainment-industry/.

35 Constantin (2023) "The impact of social media on the entertainment industry: How it's changing the game." *Entertainment Era*, January 24. https://entertainmentera.net/culture/the-impact-of-social-media-on-the-entertainment-industry/.

36 Craig, D. (2019) "Creator management in the social media entertainment industry." In Deuze, M. and Prenger, M. (eds.) *Making media: Production, practices, and professions.* Amsterdam, Netherlands: Amsterdam University Press, pp. 363–374. www.degruyter.com/document/doi/10.1515/9789048540150-027/html.

37 Cunningham, S. and Craig, D. (2019) *Social media entertainment: The new intersection of Hollywood and Silicon Valley.* New York: New York University Press.

38 Sternlicht, A. and Lucas, E. (2023) "Top creators 2022." *Forbes*, September 6, 2022. www.forbes.com/sites/alexandrasternlicht/2022/09/06/top-creators-2022/.

39 Shapiro, R. and Aneja, S. (2019) "Taking root: The growth of America's new creative economy." *Re:Create.* www.recreatecoalition.org/wp-content/uploads/2019/02/ReCreate-2017-New-Creative-Economy-Study.pdf.

40 "Open the door to open innovation" (no date) *IBM.* www.ibm.com/thought-leadership/institute-business-value/en-us/report/open-innovation.

41 "Extending digital acceleration" (no date) *IBM.* www.ibm.com/thought-leadership/institute-business-value/report/extending-digital-acceleration.

42 Chesbrough, H. W. (2003) "Open innovation: The new imperative for creating and profiting from technology." Cambridge, MA: Harvard Business Press.

43a "Open innovation - definitions, benefits and examples" (2020) *InnovatingSociety*. https://innovatingsociety.com/open-innovation-definitions-benefits-and-examples/.

43b Eldishnawy, M. (2013) Adapting Open Innovation In ICT Ecosystem Dynamics. Aalto University School of Electrical Engineering. https://www.slideserve.com/anthony-whitaker/adapting-open-innovation-in-ict-ecosystem-dynamics.

44 von Dyck, P. (2019) "Overcoming the challenges to successful open innovation." *Innovation Management.* https://innovationmanagement.se/2015/03/03/overcoming-the-challenges-to-successful-open-innovation/.

45 Hargrave, M. (2022) "Crowdsourcing: Definition, how it works, types, and examples." *Investopedia*, November 20. www.investopedia.com/terms/c/crowdsourcing.asp (Accessed: 06 March 2023).

46 Bennett, J. and Lanning, S. (2007) "The Netflix Prize." *Proceedings of the KDD Cup Workshop*. New York: ACM, pp. 3–6. www.cs.uic.edu/~liub/KDD-cup-2007/proceedings/The-Netflix-Prize-Bennett.pdf.

47 Fisher (2015) "The Netflix Prize: Crowdsourcing to improve DVD recommendations." *HBS Digital Initiative.* https://d3.harvard.edu/platform-digit/submission/the-netflix-prize-crowdsourcing-to-improve-dvd-recommendations/.

48 White, J. (2019) "What is crowdsourcing and how does it work? Definition and example." *TheStreet.* www.thestreet.com/personal-finance/what-is-crowdsourcing-15026002.

49 Ryu, S. (2019) *Beauty of crowdfunding: Blooming creativity and innovation in the digital era.* London: Routledge.

10

NEW TECHNOLOGICAL ADVANCEMENTS IN THE MEDIA AND ENTERTAINMENT INDUSTRY

Outline

Overview	295
10.1 5G Technology	296
10.2 Artificial Intelligence and Machine Learning	298
10.3 Blockchain	305
10.4 The Metaverse	315
Case Studies	319
Review	320
Discussion Questions	321
Further Reading	321
References	322

Intended Learning Outcomes

- Understand how technological innovations could advance the development of the media and entertainment industry (MEI).
- Explain key concepts and applications of emerging technological advancements in the MEI.
- Apply the key features of emerging technologies to the management of the MEI.

Overview

This chapter examines the impact of four cutting-edge technologies that are transforming the MEI:

- 5G technology is revolutionizing the MEI with its faster speeds and lower latency. It enhances productivity, enables immersive content, and creates new revenue streams. 5G technology also plays an important role in enabling other advanced technologies

DOI: 10.4324/9781003271222-14

296 Digital Business and Management

and applications, such as artificial intelligence (AI), virtual reality/augmented reality (VR/AR), the Internet of Things (IoT), real-time interactivity, improved streaming, cloud gaming, and virtual concerts.

- The paradigm shift introduced by artificial intelligence (AI) is affecting creativity, personalization, and efficiency. AI is transforming content creation, from streamlining workflows to generating AI-driven content, and is taking personalization and audience engagement to a new level.
- The diverse applications of blockchain include content distribution and consumption models. The emergence of non-fungible tokens (NFTs) has opened up new monetization avenues for artists and unique ownership experiences for audiences. This chapter also discusses the role of blockchain in protecting IP rights and fostering equitable distribution and revenue-sharing models.
- The metaverse is a new frontier, given its development by companies like Meta, Roblox, and Microsoft. This chapter explores how the metaverse is revolutionizing interactions, work, play, and learning through immersive digital experiences that transcend physical world limitations.

10.1 5G Technology

10.1.1 5G in the Business and Management Context

As discussed in Chapter 8, 5G is the latest iteration of wireless communication technology, which offers faster data transfer speeds, lower latency, and increased network capacity.[1]

5G has the potential to bring significant benefits to business and management. Most of all, with faster data transfer speeds and lower latency, 5G can enable businesses to connect more devices and people to their networks, improving productivity and efficiency. For example, 5G can support remote working, allowing employees to work from home with the same connectivity as they would have in the office.

Relatedly, with faster download and upload speeds, 5G can enhance the customer experience by enabling businesses to offer more immersive experiences, such as virtual and augmented reality. This can promote greater customer engagement and strengthen brand loyalty.

5G can also open up new revenue streams for businesses by enabling the development of new products and services. Businesses that adopt the technology early can gain a competitive advantage. Businesses can leverage 5G to offer real-time services like remote healthcare monitoring or logistics tracking.

More importantly, 5G technology is closely interrelated to other technological advancements, such as VR/AR, AI, cloud computing, big data analysis, and the IoT (Figure 10.1).[2]

For example, 5G's capabilities are essential for delivering immersive VR/AR experiences. Users can stream high-quality VR/AR content without lag or buffering, enabling them to enjoy more immersive and realistic experiences. 5G technology also makes it possible to transmit large amounts of data quickly and reliably, which is crucial for AI and big data applications. AI-powered devices can send and receive data in real time, enabling them to make faster and more accurate decisions. Large-scale data can be

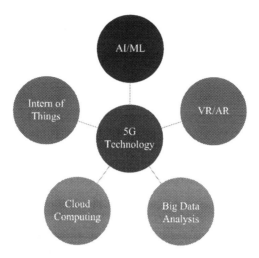

FIGURE 10.1 5G Technology and Interrelated Technological Advancements.

transmitted and processed in real time, enabling businesses to make faster decisions based on up-to-date data insights.

With 5G, these technologies can achieve their full potential, enabling businesses to make faster decisions, reduce costs, and improve efficiency. As a result, 5G is expected to play a critical role in driving the next wave of technological innovation and digital transformation.

10.1.2 The Impact of 5G Technology on the Media and Entertainment Industry

The impact of 5G technology on the MEI is significant, as it enables faster and more reliable connectivity and provides new opportunities for content delivery and consumption.

The key impacts of 5G on the MEI include the following:

- Streaming video and audio content will be faster and more reliable. This means that consumers can enjoy high-quality, uninterrupted streaming of movies, TV shows, and music—even in areas with weak or congested networks.
- 5G enables the delivery of more immersive experiences, such as VR and AR. This opens up new opportunities for media and entertainment companies to create innovative and engaging content that leverages these technologies.
- Real-time interactivity between consumers and content creators becomes possible. For example, live events can be streamed in real time with interactive features that enable viewers to engage with the content and with other viewers.
- As streaming quality improves with 5G, consumers will demand higher-quality content, including 4 K and 8 K video, requiring media and entertainment companies to invest in creating high-quality content to meet these demands.

Ultimately, 5G creates new revenue opportunities for media and entertainment companies by delivering new services such as cloud gaming, virtual concerts, and live sports

298 Digital Business and Management

events. These new services can generate revenue from new audiences and offer new monetization opportunities for existing audiences:

- Cloud gaming: 5G's low latency and high-speed connectivity have paved the way for cloud gaming services, which stream games directly from remote servers to users' devices. This eliminates the need for powerful hardware and enables gaming on various devices, including smartphones and tablets.
- Virtual concerts and live sports events: 5G's capacity to handle large data volumes in real time is revolutionizing the live entertainment experience. Virtual concerts allow artists to perform remotely and audiences to interact and participate virtually. Relatedly, 5G-powered live sports streaming has elevated the fan experience. Viewers can access multiple camera angles, real-time stats, and interactive features, enhancing their engagement during sporting events.
- Enhanced AR experiences: 5G's increased network speed allows for more engaging and interactive ads, such as AR experiences, enabling advertisers to create immersive brand campaigns. 5G is fueling the development of AR applications in the MEI. With faster data transfer, AR apps can provide seamless experiences, such as interactive tours in museums or location-based AR games like Pokémon GO.

10.2 Artificial Intelligence and Machine Learning

10.2.1 The Concept of Artificial Intelligence

AI is based on the broader concept of machines that have the capacity to perform tasks in an intelligent manner.[3]

AI is commonly perceived as a tool to assist rather than replace human intelligence and creativity. While AI may struggle with practical, commonsense tasks, it excels at swiftly processing and analyzing vast amounts of data, surpassing the capabilities of the human brain.[4] AI software is designed to generate and present synthesized courses of action to human users, facilitating the evaluation of potential consequences for each choice. With AI, the decision-making process can be streamlined, providing valuable insights and aiding in the exploration of various outcomes.

AI has three generic objectives:[5]

- Process automation: The automation of digital and physical tasks—for example, transferring data from emails or call centers into customer relationship management systems.
- Cognitive insight: The use of algorithms to detect patterns and interpret their meanings—for example, the personalized targeting of digital ads.
- Cognitive engagement: The engagement of employees and customers using different AI applications—for example, intelligent agents (or chatbots) that offer customer service.

Although the widespread acceptance of AI in modern society is relatively recent, the concept itself is not new. While the idea dates back to 1956, bringing it to life as a technological reality has taken decades of dedicated effort and progress.[6] AI is now revolutionizing how businesses interact with customers, enabling faster and more efficient processes.

Artificial Intelligence is not new

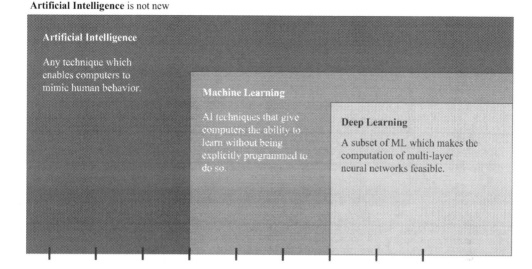

FIGURE 10.2 Artificial Intelligence, Machine Learning, and Deep Learning.

AI technologies have unlocked new possibilities for businesses and organizations by developing different subsets and subfields, from predictive analytics and deep learning to chatbots and image recognition. For example, the terms "machine learning" (ML) and "deep learning" (DL) are used interchangeably in explaining the concept (Figure 10.2).[7]

ML is a subset of AI that covers the development of algorithms and statistical models that enable computers to learn and improve from data without being explicitly programmed to do so. ML algorithms learn patterns and insights from data, allowing them to make predictions or take actions without explicit instructions. This is achieved by training models using labeled or unlabeled data; the models are then used to make predictions or decisions on new, unseen data. ML is widely used in applications such as image and speech recognition, natural language processing, fraud detection, and recommendation systems.

DL is a subfield of ML that focuses on developing and training artificial neural networks inspired by the human brain's structure and functioning. DL models, known as "deep neural networks," consist of multiple layers of interconnected artificial neurons. These networks can learn hierarchical representations of data, enabling them to extract complex features and patterns from large amounts of unstructured data. DL has achieved remarkable success in areas such as computer vision, natural language processing, speech recognition, and autonomous vehicles.

10.2.2 The Roles of Artificial Intelligence in Business

AI is used in a variety of ways in business. Businesses now engage with AI regularly in one way or another, and AI is rapidly upending almost all business activities in all industries. Popular business uses include automation, data analytics, and natural language processing (NLP):[8]

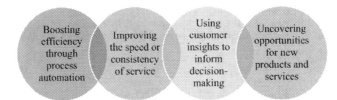

FIGURE 10.3 The Business Benefits of AI.

- Automation: AI has automated monotonous tasks, allowing employees to focus on more valuable and strategic work, reducing errors, and enhancing overall efficiency.
- Data analytics: AI's ability to identify novel patterns and connections in data has empowered organizations to gain previously unattainable insights, leading to better decision-making and improved performance.
- NLP: This has improved accessibility for individuals with disabilities, particularly those with hearing impairments, and has made search engines smarter and chatbots more effective at providing assistance.

There are many ways in which businesses can use AI, with a primary focus on driving growth and enhancing overall performance. As companies embrace AI and ML, they are discovering innovative ways to optimize various aspects of their operations, ultimately leading to improved business performance (Figure 10.3).[9]

First, AI can significantly enhance operational efficiency by automating various business processes. For example, in customer service, AI chatbots can handle routine inquiries and provide immediate responses. This automation streamlines workflows, reduces manual labor, and improves overall efficiency.

Second, AI can greatly improve the speed and consistency of service delivery. For example, ride-sharing apps use AI algorithms to match drivers with passengers efficiently, optimizing routes and reducing waiting times. AI can enhance consistency by providing standardized responses and actions based on predefined rules. This ensures that customers receive consistent service quality regardless of the specific agent or location they interact with.

Third, AI enables businesses to gather and analyze vast amounts of customer data, providing valuable insights for decision-making. E-commerce platforms leverage AI to analyze customer browsing and purchasing patterns, allowing them to personalize product recommendations and tailor marketing campaigns. AI-powered analytics tools can identify trends, preferences, and behaviors, enabling businesses to make data-driven decisions and improve customer satisfaction. Companies like Netflix and Spotify use AI to analyze user preferences and consumption patterns to recommend new content.

Finally, AI can assist in identifying market gaps and uncovering opportunities for new products and services. AI algorithms can detect emerging needs and preferences by analyzing customer feedback, social media trends, and market data. This helps businesses stay innovative, develop targeted offerings, and gain a competitive edge in the market.

Other business applications of AI include the detection of fraud and spam, speech-to-text tools, intelligent personal assistants (e.g., Siri, Alexa), sales forecasting, and real-time price optimization.[10]

10.2.3 Artificial Intelligence in the Media and Entertainment Industry

The practical applications of AI in the MEI continue to grow. Given the remarkable achievements realized through the deployment of AI and ML on social media platforms to provide personalized video and image content, the discussion now revolves around the possibility of integrating AI into the film and TV industry. Broadcasters, streamers, studios, and other entities are exploring how AI can enhance their ability to cater to audience preferences and deliver tailored content.[11]

AI in the MEI was worth $13 billion in 2022.[12] This substantial growth has been driven by the need for production companies, streaming platforms, distributors, and exhibitors to gain a deeper understanding of their audiences. By doing so, they can refine their focus on delivering content that aligns precisely with viewers' preferences, ultimately impacting their overall performance and bottom line.

Throughout the history of cinema and TV, finding a winning content formula has been challenging. Entities have struggled to understand what viewers truly want and what will become a hit. Top actors and actresses and a blockbuster budget are not always a formula for success, and the MEI is fraught with significant risk and pressure for platforms and studios. However, the advent of AI is set to change the guessing game that the MEI has grown accustomed to.

One "classic" example is AI-based recommendation systems, such as Netflix's use of personalized thumbnails.[13] Recommendation engines are part of nearly every service. Massive volumes of rich content can be monetized with increasing flexibility and agility, but only if AI can empower us to manage, manipulate, and store it at scale.[14] For example, the BBC has used AI/ML techniques to combine a linear program output and the associated metadata to segment programs into individual stories, which can be searched for, found and made available on web pages.[15] This allows stories to be recombined into personalized and potentially interactive experiences.

Advancements in AI technology have brought about new tools and applications that enhance decision-making and performance in the MEI. Film analytics software such as Cinelytic and Scriptbook has emerged as a valuable resource in mitigating uncertainty and improving film performance.[16]

Cinelytic, for example, leverages algorithms and data analytics to provide insights and recommendations on various aspects of the film industry.[17] One of its key functionalities is the ability to make casting recommendations based on various factors, including actors' popularity, previous box office successes, and audience demographics. By analyzing vast amounts of data, Cinelytic aims to assist filmmakers and studios in making informed decisions regarding casting choices, which can significantly impact a film's commercial success.

Cinelytic and similar film analytics software also endeavor to predict box office results using advanced predictive modeling techniques. By analyzing historical data, market trends, and various external factors, these tools attempt to forecast a film's potential financial performance. This helps stakeholders such as producers and distributors make strategic decisions regarding marketing budgets, release dates, and distribution strategies.

Beyond film analytics, AI has also found application in music composition within the MEI.[18] AI-powered systems can analyze vast music libraries, identify patterns, and generate original compositions based on specific criteria or styles. This technology enables

302 Digital Business and Management

composers and musicians to explore new creative avenues and streamline the music production process.

10.2.4 The Emergence of Generative Artificial Intelligence in the Media and Entertainment Industry

In November 2022, OpenAI—an AI startup backed by Microsoft—introduced a chatbot model called ChatGPT.[19] This was designed to simulate human language behavior and interact naturally with users. It is an optimizing large language model which interacts with users in a conversational way. ChatGPT quickly gained popularity due to its ability to provide high-quality answers and efficiently retrieve information. It also showcases strong language organization skills that have exceeded user expectations.

"Generative AI" refers to algorithms like ChatGPT that can generate new content across various formats, such as audio, code, images, text, simulations, and videos.[20] Although ChatGPT is not the first generative AI system to be developed—or even the first from OpenAI—it represents a significant advancement in generative AI technology. Generative AI is a ground-breaking technology that utilizes a DL approach known as "generative adversarial networks" to create original content.

AI researchers have trained large-scale neural networks through vast online training data. Traditional AI systems are typically trained for specific applications, resulting in models with limited scope to migrate to other contexts ("small models"). This process often involves extensive manual parameter adjustments and the input of labeled data, leading to reduced efficiency in AI research and development and high costs. In contrast, large models are trained using self-supervised learning on extensive unlabeled datasets. These models can then be finetuned or undergo secondary training with minimal data to adapt to new application scenarios, providing a more efficient and cost-effective approach.

The application of generative AI is extensive, including dialog, content creation, customer service and so on. Generative AI, represented by ChatGPT, has demonstrated its advantages in several business areas, including marketing, operations, IT, and human resources (HR).[21] Table 10.1 presents generative AI's business applications in different management domains.

In addition to text-based generative AI applications, there is a corresponding field of graphic generative AI. For example, Dall-E—also released by OpenAI—is an AI program capable of generating graphics based on DL models.[22] This innovative AI program can generate graphics based on user input and requirements. By providing textual descriptions and specifying desired graphic styles, users can prompt Dall-E to swiftly produce corresponding images, even if the descriptions are fantastical or imaginative. The extraordinary capabilities demonstrated by Dall-E have fueled a rapid expansion of the concept of generating graphics through textual descriptions.

As expected, different types of generative AI have the potential to revolutionize the MEI by transforming domains such as content creation, personalization, and audience engagement:

- Generative AI could play a pivotal role in automating various aspects of content creation, such as writing, music composition, and visual effects. For example, language

TABLE 10.1 The Business Applications of Generative AI

Marketing and sales	Operations	IT/engineering	Risk and legal	HR	Utility/employee optimization
• Write marketing and sales copy, including text, images and video. • Create product user guides for industry-dependent offerings. • Analyze customer feedback by summarizing and extracting important themes from online text and images. • Improve salesforce by flagging risks, recommending next interactions and so on. • Improve sales support through chatbots that help potential clients understand and choose products.	• Create or improve customer support chatbots. • Identify production errors, anomalies, and defects. • Streamline customer service by automating processes and increasing agent productivity. • Identify clauses of interest.	• Write code and documentation. • Automatically generate or auto-complete data tables while providing contextual information. • Generate synthetic data to improve the training accuracy of ML models with limited unstructured input.	• Draft and review legal documents. • Summarize and highlight changes in large bodies of regulatory documents. • Answer questions from large volumes of legal documents.	• Assist in creating interview questions for candidate assessment. • Provide self-serve HR functions such as employee onboarding or automated Q&As.	• Optimize communication among employees. • Create business presentations based on text prompts, including visualization from text. • Synthesize summaries. • Enable search and question answering on companies' private knowledge data. • Automate accounting by sorting and extracting documents.

models such as OpenAI's ChatGPT assist in generating scripts, articles, and other written content. AI-powered systems compose original music pieces, create soundtracks, and remix existing songs. Also, DL algorithms streamline visual effects creation in movies, TV shows, and videogames, generating realistic graphics and automating tedious tasks. Generative AI is a creative tool, collaborating with human creators to produce innovative content across various media. Collaborative efforts between AI and human creators have become prevalent, with AI systems assisting in ideation and prototyping, and enhancing the creative process.

- Generative AI enhances personalization and recommendation systems. Generative AI applications can analyze user preferences based on user interactions and provide personalized recommendations for movies, music, and articles. AI-powered chatbots engage users in interactive conversations, answer queries, and simulate characters from movies, games, and TV shows. Virtual assistants like Alexa understand natural language and generate human-like responses. Generative AI will continuously improve personalized recommendations, tailoring content to individual interests and preferences.

- Generative AI contributes to interactive and immersive media experiences. AI-generated virtual environments, characters, and objects enhance audience experiences, enabling interactive storytelling and immersive gaming. Relatedly, generative AI facilitates user-generated content creation. For example, while critical ethical concerns exist, AI-generated "deepfakes" creatively mimic a person's appearance and voice for entertainment. Moreover, generative AI automates video editing, retouching, and color grading, empowering content creators to enhance their work. Advancements in real-time rendering and AI processing enable interactive experiences, such as live-generated graphics and personalized narratives.

The future holds immense potential for AI-driven advancements that will reshape how content is created, personalized, and experienced in this ever-evolving landscape. However, while generative AI offers exciting possibilities, addressing ethical considerations—including bias, privacy, and consent—is crucial to ensure the responsible and inclusive use of these technologies in the MEI:[23]

- AI algorithms trained on biased or unrepresentative datasets can perpetuate and amplify existing media and entertainment content biases. This can result in the reinforcement of stereotypes, discrimination, or the exclusion of certain groups. Relatedly, AI-generated content can potentially manipulate and influence audience perceptions and emotions. This also raises concerns about the potential for exploitation or psychological harm.

- Data and copyright protection is another critical issue. Generative AI requires access to large datasets, including personal information, to create content. This raises concerns about privacy and data protection, as personal information used in training models could be at risk of exposure or misuse. Generative AI also has the potential to generate content that closely resembles existing works, raising concerns about copyright infringement. Media producers and artists may face challenges protecting their original creations as AI algorithms can create derivative works that blur the lines of ownership and originality. Also, determining responsibility and accountability for AI-generated content becomes challenging. The attribution of generated content to the responsible AI system or its developers can be crucial in determining the legal, ethical, or social implications arising from the content.

- Most importantly, generative AI in media creation can have implications for creative professionals, including writers, musicians, and visual artists.[24] It may raise questions about the value of human creativity and the potential displacement of human workers by AI-generated content.

10.3 Blockchain

10.3.1 The Concept of Blockchain

Blockchain technology has emerged as one of the foundational technologies in the new era of "Industry 4.0" and "Web 3.0."[25] Blockchain technology has the potential to transform the business world and the functioning of the economic system. It offers numerous possibilities for existing businesses to flourish and entirely new ones to emerge; but it is also significantly disrupting traditional industries.

The adoption of blockchain can provide several benefits to businesses, including enhanced security for transactions, reduced errors, improved organizational functions and procedures, and fraud prevention. One notable feature of blockchain technology is the smart contract, which can be applied to transactions involving the movement of resources such as finance, materials, and people. This application enables effective tracking, visibility, security enhancement, and cost reduction in overall business processes.

Blockchain technology is a distributed and decentralized ledger that facilitates secure and transparent transactions without intermediaries. Transactions are recorded in a series of blocks in a digital ledger, with each block containing a cryptographic hash of its predecessor, forming a chain of interconnected blocks. This design ensures the integrity and immutability of the recorded transactions, making it extremely difficult to alter or tamper with the data once it has been added to the blockchain.

Initially introduced in 2008 as the underlying technology of Bitcoin, a decentralized digital currency, blockchain technology has since gained in popularity across various industries, including finance, healthcare, logistics, and real estate.[26]

The functioning of blockchain technology relies on the distribution of a copy of the ledger across a network of participating computers known as nodes. Each node possesses a copy of the ledger and can validate and verify transactions within the network. Complex algorithms are utilized to verify the authenticity of transactions; once verified, the transactions are then recorded on the blockchain.

By eliminating the need for intermediaries like banks or financial institutions to verify transactions, blockchain's decentralized nature reduces costs, shortens transaction times, and enhances overall efficiency (Figure 10.4).[27] Moreover, the transparency inherent in blockchain technology enables users to track the history of transactions, facilitating the tracing of fund sources and preventing fraudulent activities.

The concept of blockchain is built on five fundamental principles (Figure 10.5):[28]

- Blockchain operates on a distributed database, where every participating party has full access to the entire database. Instead of relying on a centralized authority or server, the data is stored and replicated across multiple nodes in the network. This distributed

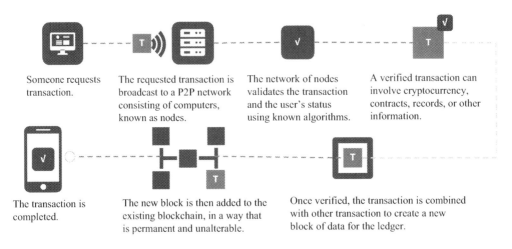

FIGURE 10.4 How Blockchain Works.

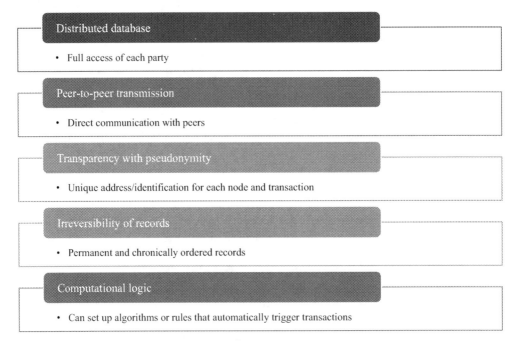

FIGURE 10.5 The Five Basic Principles of the Blockchain Concept.

nature ensures that no single entity controls the entire database, enhancing transparency and reducing the risk of data manipulation or loss.
- In a blockchain network, participants can directly communicate with each other, forming a peer-to-peer network. This enables seamless and efficient data transmission between nodes without intermediaries. Through peer-to-peer communication, participants can validate and verify transactions, establish consensus, and maintain the integrity of the blockchain.

New Technological Advancements **307**

- Blockchain provides transparency by allowing every transaction to be recorded on the public ledger. Each node and transaction within the network is associated with a unique address or identification, providing transparency while maintaining pseudo-nymity. While the real-world identities behind these addresses are often anonymous or represented by cryptographic keys, the traceability of transactions promotes account-ability and trust within the system.
- Once a transaction is recorded on the blockchain, it becomes virtually immutable and permanent. The records are stored in chronological order, forming a chain of blocks linked through cryptographic hashes. This irreversible nature of blockchain records ensures the integrity of the data, creating a high level of trust and eliminating the need for intermediaries to enforce transaction validity.
- Finally, blockchain technology enables the utilization of smart contracts, which are self-executing contracts with predefined rules and conditions embedded within the blockchain. These contracts automatically enforce transactions when certain condi-tions are met. Through smart contracts, blockchain facilitates the automated and secure execution of agreements, leading to more efficient business processes and reducing the need for manual intervention.

The key components of blockchains include the following (Table 10.2):[29]

- Shared ledger: A shared ledger is a database distributed across a network of nodes. Each node has a copy of the ledger and can verify and validate transactions. This ensures that the ledger is tamper-proof, as the network will reject any attempt to modify or alter the ledger.
- Smart contract: A smart contract is a self-executing contract that automates verifying and executing transactions. Smart contracts are coded using a programming language; and once the conditions specified in the contract are met, the contract is automatically executed. This reduces the need for intermediaries such as lawyers or notaries to verify and execute contracts, saving time and reducing costs.
- Privacy: Privacy is a critical component of blockchains, ensuring that sensitive data is kept confidential and secure. In a public blockchain, transactions are transparent and visible to everyone, which may not be suitable for all transactions. On the other hand, private blockchains provide a higher level of privacy and restrict access to authorized parties.
- Trust: Trust is a critical component of blockchains, ensuring that transactions are valid and verified. Trust is established through a consensus mechanism, which is the process

TABLE 10.2 The Key Components of Blockchain Systems

Component	Description
Shared ledger	An append-only distributed system of records shared across the business network that provides transaction visibility to all involved participants.
Smart contract	Business terms are embedded in the transaction database and executed with the transactions to which they apply.
Privacy	Transactions are reliable and authenticated verifiably.
Trust	Relevant participants endorse transactions.
Transparency	All participants in the network are aware of all transactions that impact them.

308 Digital Business and Management

by which the network of nodes agrees on the state of the blockchain. This consensus mechanism ensures that all nodes in the network agree on the order and validity of transactions, maintaining the integrity and security of the blockchain.

- Transparency: Transparency is another essential component of blockchains, as it allows users to track the transaction history, making it easier to trace the source of funds and prevent fraudulent activities. In a public blockchain, all transactions are visible and transparent, which increases accountability and reduces the potential for fraudulent activities.

10.3.2 The Roles of Blockchain Technology in Business

Due to its various applicative and useful features, blockchain technology offers many opportunities to transform how businesses function.[30]

For example, the utilization of blockchain platforms enables the management of various elements of the marketing mix. This technology facilitates customized promotion by eliminating intermediaries and reducing unnecessary costs. Advertising can target specific segments, while the sales process can be automated and monitored in real time, ensuring greater transparency. Blockchain facilitates disintermediation and enables the faster and more cost-effective delivery of marketing communications. Digital marketing and email marketing, as part of the marketing communications mix, can become more effective and less susceptible to fraud.

The features of blockchain—such as anonymity, immutability, transparency, privacy, and security—address consumers' concerns. With blockchain, personal data can be tokenized and directly sold to marketers by customers, eliminating the need for intermediaries. These tokens can be converted into loyalty points or rewards, allowing for special promotions and customized offerings to selected users. Tokenization enhances customer engagement by integrating all loyalty points under one platform. It enables transparent tracking and monitoring of customer interactions and transactions with the brand. This approach reduces unnecessary communication and spam, reducing the risk of fraud.[31]

The implementation of smart contracts brings customers and marketers closer, streamlining processes and making market surveys more cost-effective for companies. All types of communications, including rewards, can be directly conveyed and transferred to customers' wallets. Direct access to customer profiles by marketers reduces costs and enhances the operational efficiency of marketing campaigns.

Blockchain technology has wide-ranging applicability in the field of finance. It has also found utility in financial reporting, auditing, and assurance, with numerous firms and regulators developing blockchain platforms worldwide.

Reliability and security are paramount for accounting. The greater the reliability of financial reporting, the more efficient financial markets can become. This reliability also benefits auditors by reducing the time required to verify the accuracy of accounting information.

The implementation of blockchain technology in financial processes and systems can mitigate the risks associated with financial fraud and cyberattacks. The tamper-proof nature of blockchain provides robust security and defense against such threats. Additionally, blockchain serves as a foundation for smart contracts, offering opportunities

10.3.3 Blockchain Applications in the Media and Entertainment Industry

Companies in many industries have been exploring the possible benefits of blockchain technology. But what positive or negative impacts will blockchain have on existing media and entertainment value chains? Will it help create opportunities to generate more revenue streams and develop new products and services?

Blockchain can transform how media content such as music, videos and other entertainment is delivered, consumed and paid for.[32] Current systems were not designed to manage complex, personalized content and service bundles. Managing digital rights, royalty collections, and transactions among many intermediaries is challenging in today's digital ecosystems. With its shared ledger approach, blockchain can help improve the supply chain and decrease copyright infringements in the MEI by enhancing transparency and security. For example, it may decrease copyright infringements in music streaming, where publishers and songwriters regularly accuse music streaming providers of not paying them all they are entitled to.[33]

Greater transaction transparency in advertising helps eliminate waste by better identifying which intermediaries are taking a cut of the advertiser's budget at each step in the process.[34] Blockchain enhances ad targeting, ensuring more pertinent and timely ads reach the right audience, thereby streamlining ad frequency and boosting revenue.

Major players in the MEI have begun exploring blockchain technology. For example, Spotify acquired blockchain startup Mediachain Labs with the aim of enhancing the technology that connects artists and rights holders to the tracks available on the platform.[35]

Improving Processes in the Media Supply Chain

The digitization of the MEI has led to the emergence of complex ecosystems with multiple stakeholders, presenting new challenges related to trust, transparency, efficiency, performance, quality control, and security. These challenges affect content creators, brands, advertisers, and the overall integrity of financial transactions in the industry.

One significant challenge is ensuring fair and timely royalty settlements for content creators. Traditional supply chains have become convoluted, making it difficult for creators to verify if they have received their rightful royalties. In some cases, creators must wait for extended periods—ranging from months to years—to receive their payments. This lack of transparency and delayed compensation can hinder creators' motivation and financial stability.

Similarly, brands and advertisers face difficulties in verifying the accuracy and fairness of financial transactions. They need assurance that their advertising budgets are not being depleted through fraudulent activities, and that their ads are being displayed on reputable platforms as intended. The lack of transparency in the advertising ecosystem poses risks to brands, leading to concerns about the effectiveness of their marketing campaigns and the proper allocation of resources.

310 Digital Business and Management

Blockchain technology offers solutions to these challenges, particularly through smart contracts. Smart contracts provide modularity, allowing different aspects of media and entertainment operations to be streamlined. This modularity brings cost-efficiency, speed, reliability, scalability, and transparency to various processes within the industry. Smart contracts enable automated and self-executing agreements, ensuring that royalty payments are distributed fairly and on time. They also provide an audit trail of transactions, creating a comprehensive and immutable record of financial activities.

Furthermore, blockchain's cryptographic algorithms enhance security by protecting sensitive information and preventing tampering or unauthorized access. This added layer of security builds trust among stakeholders and fosters a more transparent and accountable environment for financial transactions.

Creating Blockchain-Enabled Services and Revenue Opportunities

Blockchain technology offers more than just process improvements in existing media supply chains. It also provides opportunities to develop new functionality and deliver value-added digital services that cater to the evolving expectations of both content creators and consumers.[36]

One notable example is the use of blockchain-enabled micropayments.[37] By leveraging cryptocurrencies and blockchain technology, micropayments for low-priced content—such as individual song tracks, articles, or pictures—become more feasible. Unlike traditional payment systems, which impose disproportionate fees on low-value transactions, blockchain-based micropayments allow for seamless and cost-effective transactions, boosting revenue for creators and encouraging consumers to engage with more affordable content.

Blockchain can also enhance audience targeting by delivering content and ads that are more relevant and timely. By leveraging blockchain's transparent and immutable nature, consumer preferences and behavior can be securely recorded and analyzed. This data can be used to personalize content recommendations and ads, improving the overall customer experience. Additionally, with AI, blockchain technology can optimize campaign outcomes by effectively identifying and targeting specific audience segments.

Other potential blockchain applications in the MEI include content distribution, revenue assurance, and the handling of customer personal data. Blockchain can streamline content distribution by providing a decentralized and secure platform for digital rights management, ensuring that content is distributed to authorized channels and protecting against unauthorized use. It can also enhance revenue assurance by providing transparent and auditable records of transactions, reducing the risk of revenue leakage and improving financial accountability.

Furthermore, blockchain technology can address privacy concerns associated with customer personal data. With the implementation of regulations like the General Data Protection Regulation,[38] protecting customer data and ensuring compliance have become paramount. Blockchain's decentralized and immutable nature can enhance data protection, giving users more control over their personal information and enabling transparent and auditable data-handling practices.

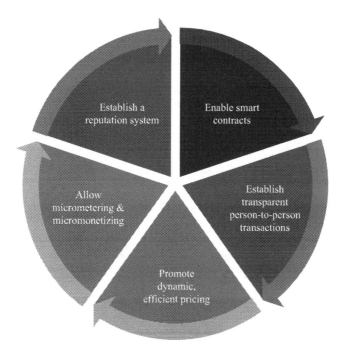

FIGURE 10.6 New Blockchain Application for Creators in the MEI.

New Blockchain Applications for Creators

New blockchain applications present innovative solutions to empower creators and protect their rights (Figure 10.6):[39]

- Transparent person-to-person transactions: Blockchain provides a decentralized and transparent ledger that records all transactions. This eliminates the need for intermediaries such as record labels or distributors, and allows artists to engage in direct person-to-person transactions. Artists can directly sell their work, negotiate licensing agreements, and distribute content, ensuring transparency and reducing the risk of revenue leakage.
- Smart property: Blockchain enables the tracking and enforcing of rights for digital content creators such as music, video, books, articles, and art. Through blockchain's transparent and immutable nature, creators can establish proof of ownership and maintain a record of their IP rights. This allows for greater control over their creations and safeguards against unauthorized use or infringement. Blockchain technology also allows for digital content to be published and distributed at predefined times and prices. Content creators can set specific release dates and pricing tiers for their work, ensuring controlled and timely distribution.
- Micropayments (micrometering and micromonetizing): Blockchain facilitates micropayments using cryptocurrencies, allowing users to make small, frictionless transactions to access and purchase individual content. For instance, users can buy a single song, video, or news article using cryptocurrency tokens. This enables creators to

312 Digital Business and Management

monetize their work on a granular level, providing a direct and efficient payment mechanism that eliminates intermediaries and reduces transaction costs.

- Smart contracts: Blockchain-based smart contracts automate the enforcement of license terms and enable seamless financial transactions between content creators and consumers. Smart contracts are self-executing agreements that automatically trigger predefined actions when specific conditions are met. In the MEI, smart contracts can ensure that creators receive fair compensation for using their content by automatically dispensing payments based on predetermined terms and conditions. Blockchain can facilitate revenue sharing among multiple contributors to a piece of content. For example, a collaborative song can be released on a blockchain-based platform, and the platform can automatically split the revenue generated among the artists involved, ensuring fair compensation for each contributor.
- Dynamic, efficient pricing: Blockchain technology enables dynamic pricing models based on supply and demand. Artists can leverage blockchain-based platforms to set flexible pricing for their work, adjusting prices in real time based on market conditions and consumer preferences. This fosters efficient pricing strategies and ensures artists receive appropriate compensation for their creations.
- Establishment of a reputation system: Blockchain-based platforms can establish reputation systems that track and verify the reputation and credibility of artists. These systems provide a trust mechanism for consumers, enabling them to make informed decisions when engaging with artists or purchasing their works. Artists with a proven track record of delivering high-quality content and upholding their rights can build a strong reputation within the blockchain ecosystem, enhancing their visibility and opportunities.

New Business Models Enabled by Blockchain Technology

Blockchain technology has enabled the emergence of sustaining and disruptive business models in the MEI.[40] These models leverage the unique features of blockchain to revolutionize content monetization, IP protection, and the digitization of value chains (Table 10.3):

- Sustaining business models:

  - Protecting IP: Companies like Codex Protocol utilize blockchain to establish verifiable ownership and provenance of digital assets, including artworks, photographs, and other creative content. This helps protect the rights of creators and enables transparent transactions in the art and media industries.

TABLE 10.3 Blockchain-Enabled Business Models

Sustaining business models	Disruptive business models
Smart property (e.g., Codex Protocol)	Blockchain-based social networks (e.g., Steemit)
Smart contracts (e.g., PeerTracks: immediate royalty payments through smart contracts)	Micrometering and micropayments (e.g., ArtBloc)
Playing and trading	One-stop content shops (e.g., Musicoin)

- Digitizing the music value chain: Using smart contracts, platforms like PeerTracks enable immediate royalty payments to musicians.[41] These smart contracts automatically distribute payments based on pre-defined terms, eliminating the need for intermediaries and ensuring faster and more transparent revenue streams for artists.
- Playing and trading: Blockchain-based platforms allow users to trade and own virtual assets within digital ecosystems. These assets can include in-game items, virtual real estate, or collectibles. Blockchain ensures secure ownership and facilitates peer-to-peer transactions, creating new opportunities for gamers and collectors.

- Disruptive business models:

  - Blockchain-based social networks: Platforms like Steemit use blockchain-based social networks that reward creators and curators with cryptocurrency based on the quality and popularity of their content. This incentivizes users to contribute to and engage in the platform's ecosystem.[42]
  - Micrometering and micropayments: ArtBloc, for example, leverages blockchain technology to enable micropayments for digital art, allowing creators to receive fair compensation for their work, even for low-priced pieces.[43]
  - One-stop content shops: Platforms like Musicoin aim to create comprehensive ecosystems that provide artists with tools for content creation, distribution, and monetization. These platforms leverage blockchain technology to offer transparent and decentralized solutions, giving creators more control over their work and financial outcomes.

10.3.4 Non-Fungible Tokens: A Gamechanger

NFTs are unique and indivisible digital tokens on the Ethereum blockchain.[44] In the crypto world, tokens can be either fungible or non-fungible. Fungible tokens, like currency, are interchangeable, as another identical unit can replace one unit. In contrast, NFTs are distinct and cannot be substituted by any other token. NFTs have gained popularity for representing various items like collectibles, digital art, sports memorabilia, virtual real estate, and in-game assets. NFTs represent exclusive digital assets. The uniqueness and ownership of NFTs can be verified; and NFTs can be utilized across different applications and easily traded on secondary markets. These features present new possibilities for use cases and business models.

The mainstream attention toward NFTs intensified when artist Beeple sold his digital artwork *Everydays: The First 5000 Days* for $69 million in collaboration with Christie's auction house.[45] The demand for rare and limited tokenized items continues to attract artists, celebrities, and creators, who are launching diverse NFT projects to cater to the growing interest in this asset class. NFTs are proving their utility beyond art by revolutionizing fundraising and audience engagement and fueling the fan economy within the MEI.

NFTs serve as proof of ownership for various digital items, including artworks, videos, profile pictures, and in-game assets. The gaming industry is particularly active in the NFT market, with games like *Axie Infinity* incorporating NFTs for in-game assets and experiences. This intersection of NFTs and gaming is driving innovation and growth within the broader NFT market.

314 Digital Business and Management

While some perceive NFTs as a passing trend, others recognize the potential for a new revenue stream and are eager to participate. Many stakeholders—both within and outside of the MEI—are skeptical, making comparisons with the dot.com boom and bust. Nonetheless, the technology has numerous other applications that the MEI is beginning to explore. Consequently, influential players in the industry are minting and acquiring NFTs, ensuring their involvement in this emerging market.

Advantages

The advantages of NFTs open up new avenues for various use cases and innovative business models:

- NFTs contribute to marketplace efficiency by digitizing physical assets. This transformation streamlines processes, eliminates intermediaries, enhances supply chains, and strengthens security. For example, in the art world, NFTs enable artists to connect directly with their audiences, bypassing costly agents and cumbersome transactions. The digitization of artwork improves authentication and reduces costs. Furthermore, NFTs have broader applications beyond marketplaces, potentially serving as effective tools for managing sensitive data and records for individuals and organizations. For instance, converting physical passports into distinct NFTs could significantly streamline travel management and identification, resulting in significant time and cost savings.
- NFTs facilitate the fractionalization of ownership for physical assets. Traditional ownership fragmentation of assets like real estate, artworks, and fine jewelry is challenging. With NFTs, dividing a digitized version of a building or a prized piece of jewelry among multiple owners becomes much easier. Digitization expands the market for such assets, enhancing liquidity and increasing prices. At an individual level, NFTs enhance the construction of financial portfolios, enabling greater diversification and precise position sizing. Unlike traditional investments like stocks and bonds, NFTs possess unique qualities and advantages that are only starting to be fully understood. However, ownership of NFTs carries its own set of risks.
- NFTs are created and stored using blockchain technology, a tamper-proof and decentralized system of recording information. The blockchain ensures each NFT has a distinct record of authenticity and ownership, safeguarding against mishandling and theft. Once data is added to the blockchain, it becomes immutable, preserving the scarcity and authenticity of each NFT and instilling confidence in the market.
- NFTs specifically applied in the digital arts domain bring additional benefits. They empower artists by allowing global access to their work through various marketplaces, with minimal or no cuts taken by galleries or agents. This wealth creation potential provides artists with a direct connection to their customers, documented on the blockchain for transparency. Such transparency fosters viral communities and fan engagement, enabling authentic dialog between creators and buyers on social platforms.

Uncertainties and Risks

As an emerging technological application, NFTs present some inherent uncertainties and risks:

- Most significantly, NFTs possess certain characteristics that include illiquidity and volatility. As the market for NFTs is still in its early stages of development, it lacks sufficient liquidity, making it challenging to trade these assets due to the limited number of potential buyers and sellers. Additionally, the prices of NFTs can experience high levels of volatility, further complicating their trading dynamics, especially during market distress.
- Despite the integrity of the blockchain, NFTs can be susceptible to fraudulent use. Recent reports from artists have brought to light instances where their works were found for sale as NFTs on online platforms without their consent. This undermines the intended purpose of NFTs, which is to authenticate physical works of art through unique tokens, guaranteeing ownership of the original artwork. The problem arises when someone creates a digital copy of the original work, attaches a token, and sells it on a virtual marketplace. In such cases, the token becomes associated with a fraudulent reproduction, disconnected from the original artwork.
- NFTs can have a detrimental impact on the environment.[46] Creating blockchain records requires a substantial amount of computing energy, sparking a growing debate about the long-term environmental harm caused by this process. Estimates suggest that if the current rate continues, the carbon emissions from mining cryptocurrencies and NFTs will surpass those generated by the entire city of London in the coming years.[47] The proponents of blockchain argue that NFTs are facilitating a reduction in pollution by transforming global marketplaces and reducing the need for travel and office space utilization.

10.4 The Metaverse

10.4.1 The Concept of the Metaverse

Another key element of Web 3.0 that has recently captured the attention of the media and investors alike is the "Metaverse"—a term that has taken on many meanings, but with common themes around virtual and immersive experiences, online communities and the creator economy.[48]

The metaverse and NFTs are two important components of Web 3.0. The metaverse can be understood as a virtual reality space in which people can engage in various activities. NFTs, on the other hand, represent unique digital assets and can be seen as commodities in the metaverse and in real-life scenarios. These elements add depth and richness to the Web 3.0 experience, creating new possibilities for interaction and transactions.

The concept of the metaverse is evolving and its specific form is not yet well defined. The metaverse encompasses parallel virtual spaces in which people interact and create, transcending physical limitations. For example, in the context of cryptocurrency builders, the "metaverse" refers to a collection of interconnected virtual worlds built on blockchain

316 Digital Business and Management

technology, leveraging open and interoperable systems. These virtual environments allow for NFT assets to be utilized across different worlds and games, such as avatars, virtual clothing, and other items.

The metaverse has a rich history. The concept originated in Neal Stephenson's science fiction novel *Snow Crash* in the early 1990s and attracted attention through the emergence of games such as *Second Life* in 2003.[49] It gained renewed attention through industry analyst Matthew Ball's essays on the concept. It saw increased interest after the initial public offering (IPO) of Roblox in March 2021,[50] followed by Facebook's name change to Meta to align with its vision of the metaverse.[51] The COVID-19 pandemic accelerated the development of online virtual technologies, leading to the rapid integration of the metaverse into various aspects of our lives.

The value of the metaverse market may reach $783.3 billion in 2024, compared to $478.7 billion in 2020, with an annual growth rate of 13.1%.[52] Early leaders like *Roblox*, Microsoft's *Minecraft*, and Epic Games' *Fortnite* have garnered significant attention and user bases in the emerging race for metaverse dominance. These platforms have successfully created immersive virtual environments that engage millions of users worldwide. Several game makers have already demonstrated their ability to attract large and active user bases in online gaming titles. These companies possess strong foundations and can leverage their existing services to tap into the growing metaverse demand.

To capture a share of the metaverse market, game developers and social networking companies have the opportunity to enhance their offerings. They can introduce additional social features that foster virtual interactions, enabling users to connect and collaborate within the virtual space. Moreover, incorporating user-generated content as a prominent aspect of their experiences could further attract users and drive engagement. By empowering users to create and share their content, these companies can tap into the creativity and enthusiasm of their user communities.

The metaverse encompasses seven layers that contribute to its functionality and user experience (Figure 10.7):[53]

- Infrastructure: The foundation of the metaverse relies on robust infrastructure such as 5G networks and cloud technologies. These technologies ensure high bandwidth and ample storage capacity to support the seamless operation of virtual worlds.
- Human interfaces: Devices like mobile phones, wearables, and other hardware act as the gateways through which users access and engage with the metaverse. These devices provide users with the necessary interfaces and functionalities to navigate virtual environments. Examples include VR headsets like Oculus Quest and AR glasses like Microsoft HoloLens, enabling users to immerse themselves in interactive metaverse experiences.
- Decentralization: The metaverse embraces decentralized technologies to establish a more democratic structure and protect user account assets. AI, blockchain, NFTs, and other decentralized mechanisms ensure transparency, security, and ownership rights within the metaverse. Blockchain-based virtual worlds like Decentraland utilize decentralized governance and immutable ownership records to empower users in the virtual realm.

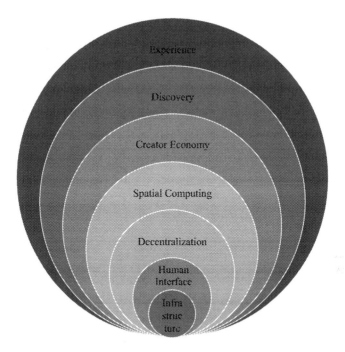

FIGURE 10.7 The Seven Layers of the Metaverse.

- Spatial computing: Spatial computing technologies—including 3D graphics, VR, AR, and extended reality—enhance the immersive experiences within the metaverse. These technologies enable users to perceive and interact with virtual objects and environments in a more natural and intuitive manner. Games like *Minecraft* employ spatial computing to create dynamic and interactive virtual worlds that users can explore and shape.
- Creator economy: The metaverse fosters a thriving creator economy in which individuals can generate and monetize their content using the tools and technologies provided. Platforms like *Roblox* and *Fortnite* offer creation tools that allow users to build virtual experiences, games, and digital assets. Creators can earn revenue through in-game purchases, virtual item sales, and monetization opportunities, thus incentivizing users to spend more time in the metaverse and contribute to its ecosystem.
- Discovery: Discoverability is crucial in the metaverse, as it introduces users to new experiences and connects them with relevant content. Various mechanisms, such as recommendation algorithms and social discovery features, help users navigate vast virtual landscapes and find engaging activities.
- Experience: The ultimate purpose of the metaverse is to offer diverse and immersive experiences to users. These include interactive games, live music performances, social gatherings, virtual conferences, and more. For instance, metaverse platforms like *Fortnite* and *Roblox* have hosted virtual concerts with musicians like Lil Nas X and Travis Scott performing live in the virtual world, attracting millions of participants and blurring the boundaries between real-world entertainment and metaverse experiences.

318 Digital Business and Management

10.4.2 The Business Applications of the Metaverse

Many businesses are starting to explore the potential uses of the metaverse:[54]

- Marketing campaigns: Companies can use the metaverse to host virtual events such as conferences, trade shows, and product launches. This allows participants to attend from anywhere in the world and interact with each other in a more immersive environment. Relatedly, the metaverse can also be used for advertising purposes, such as creating virtual billboards or sponsoring virtual events. This allows businesses to reach a wider audience and create more engaging advertising experiences.
- Virtual merchandise: Companies can showcase their products in a more engaging and interactive way. For example, a car manufacturer could create a virtual showroom where customers can interact with the cars and customize them to their liking. It can also create virtual merchandise and collectibles that fans can purchase and display in their virtual spaces. Retailers can use the metaverse to create virtual stores where customers can browse and purchase products. This can be especially useful for businesses that operate in niche markets or have limited physical locations.
- Virtual offices: Businesses can use the metaverse to create virtual offices where employees can work and collaborate in a virtual environment. This can be especially useful for remote teams, as it can help to create a sense of community and collaboration.

The metaverse presents an innovative platform for unprecedented audience engagement. Providing highly immersive experiences transports users to new digital worlds and facilitates exciting interactions with content. The metaverse fosters enhanced interactivity, enabling more personalized and engaging experiences. Additionally, as a global platform, the metaverse connects audiences worldwide, allowing content creators and brands to broaden their reach and forge connections with diverse audiences. Consequently, the metaverse offers valuable opportunities for monetization, including virtual merchandise and advertising in virtual spaces, thereby creating new revenue streams for content creators and brands.

However, there are several challenges to leveraging the metaverse in business and management:

- The technology for creating and operating in the metaverse is still evolving and technical limitations must be addressed. For example, the metaverse can be slow or laggy, detracting from the user experience.
- There is currently a lack of standardization and interoperability between different metaverse platforms. This makes it difficult for users to move between different platforms and for businesses to create a presence across multiple platforms.
- While the metaverse is a virtual world, it is still subject to real-world security risks. There are concerns about data privacy and security in the metaverse—mainly in relation to personal information and financial transactions. More importantly, there is a lack of governance and regulation around it. This can create uncertainty for businesses operating in the metaverse and can complicate legal and regulatory issues.
- Finally, although the metaverse has the potential to be a highly engaging and immersive platform, there are concerns about accessibility and inclusivity. For example, some users may not have access to the necessary hardware or software to participate in the metaverse, and there may be barriers to entry for people with disabilities.

10.4.3 The Metaverse in the Media and Entertainment Industry

The metaverse holds great promise for the MEI, due to its ability to revolutionize how content is created, distributed, and consumed.[55]

Most of all, the metaverse offers immersive and interactive experiences beyond traditional media forms. It allows users to step into virtual worlds and engage with content in a more engaging and participatory manner. In the same vein, it fosters social connections and community engagement on a global scale. Users can interact with each other, collaborate, and share experiences within virtual environments. This opens up opportunities for new forms of social entertainment and shared experiences.

The metaverse enables seamless integration across multiple platforms and devices, allowing users to access and engage with content from various entry points. This cross-platform compatibility enhances reach and accessibility, breaking down barriers between different media formats and devices.

From the creation and production perspective, the metaverse provides creators with a new canvas for storytelling and expression. It enables them to explore innovative formats, blending gaming, storytelling, and social interaction elements. VR experiences like those created by Oculus Studios and independent developers push the boundaries of traditional media, allowing users to be fully immersed in captivating narratives.

The metaverse also introduces new avenues for monetization and revenue generation. Through virtual economies, users can purchase virtual goods, accessories, and experiences, creating a thriving marketplace for digital assets. Companies can monetize their content through virtual events, advertising, and partnerships. Examples include the following:

- Virtual concerts and events: The metaverse can host virtual concerts and other entertainment events that allow fans to interact with each other and the performers in a simulated environment.
- Film and television: The metaverse can be used to create interactive film and television experiences that allow viewers to participate in the story and make decisions that impact the outcome of the narrative.
- Gaming and e-sports: The metaverse is an ideal platform for gaming and e-sports, as it allows players to compete and collaborate in a simulated environment that is not limited by physical space.

Case Studies

Two Worlds of NFTs: CryptoPunks and Bored Ape Yacht Club

The NFT landscape features two groundbreaking projects: CryptoPunks and Bored Ape Yacht Club (BAYC). Larva Labs' CryptoPunks pioneered algorithmically generated pixel art in 2017, with each of the 10,000 unique NFTs boasting distinct attributes. Yuga Labs introduced BAYC in 2021, offering programmatically unique Bored Ape NFTs. BAYC holders enjoy exclusive access and IP rights. These projects have revolutionized the art world by securing digital art creation, ownership, and exchange through blockchain technology. NFTs' scarcity and capacity to facilitate the monetization of art have inspired traditional art

320 Digital Business and Management

institutions to explore blockchain integration, potentially transforming the dynamics of the art industry.

More case details for classroom use are available. Please check the book webpage at www.routledge.com/9781032221212 for more information.

Roblox: A Metaverse Platform for Game Design and Play

Roblox, established in 2006, has evolved into a metaverse platform where users can both play and create games. Enjoying rapid growth, it reached 202 million monthly active users in April 2021 and achieved a remarkable valuation of $68 billion after its IPO in 2021. *Roblox* empowers users to craft, explore, and engage in diverse virtual spaces powered by in-game currency Robux. The platform has even hosted virtual concerts with top artists such as Lil Nas X and Zara Larsson, amassing huge audiences. Its success lies in fostering creativity, social interaction, and an immersive gaming experience. Its growth has cemented its role as a pioneering influence in the development of the metaverse.

More case details for classroom use are available. Please check the book webpage at www.routledge.com/9781032221212 for more information.

Microsoft's Journey in the Gaming World: From Xbox to *Minecraft*

Microsoft's journey into the gaming world is defined by its ownership of Xbox and the popular game *Minecraft*. Xbox—an influential gaming brand—has gained prominence for its immersive gaming experiences based on consoles, applications, and networks. Microsoft's metaverse ambitions are evident in its Microsoft Teams platform and CEO Satya Nadella's commitment to gaming. *Minecraft*, acquired by Microsoft in 2014 for $2.5 billion, is a sandbox game cherished for its creative possibilities. Microsoft envisions *Minecraft* as a metaverse contributor that offers expansive virtual experiences. Microsoft's $70 billion acquisition of Activision Blizzard has reinforced its dedication to the metaverse by enabling accessible content and community engagement across devices. These strategic steps underline Microsoft's commitment to gaming and its role in shaping the future of the metaverse.

More case details for classroom use are available. Please check the book webpage at www.routledge.com/9781032221212 for more information.

Review

- This chapter explores the profound impact of four transformative technologies on the MEI: 5G technology, AI, blockchain, and the metaverse. Each technology brings unique capabilities and potential for shaping the future of the MEI.

- 5G is a transformative force for the MEI (10.1). Its faster speeds and lower latency benefit businesses and the MEI. It improves productivity, offers immersive content, and creates new revenue streams. It also drives innovation in AI, VR/AR, and the IoT. In the MEI, it enables real-time interactivity and better streaming, opening up new revenue opportunities through cloud gaming and virtual concerts.
- AI has catalyzed a paradigm shift in the MEI, fostering creativity, personalization, and efficiency (10.2). It can transform content creation, from streamlining workflows to creating entirely AI-driven content. AI-based content creation tools, such as generative AI, can revolutionize the MEI by transforming domains such as content creation, personalization, and audience engagement.
- The potential applications of blockchain in the MEI are numerous, creating new models for content distribution and consumption (10.3). One notable development is the rise of NFTs, which allow artists and creators to monetize their work in new ways and provide audiences with unique ownership experiences. The transparency, immutability, and decentralization of blockchain also protect IP rights. Blockchain also provides more equitable content distribution and revenue-sharing models.
- The metaverse represents a new frontier for the MEI (10.4), facilitated by advances in AI, VR/AR, and blockchain. It is revolutionizing the way people interact, work, play, and learn. Companies like Meta, Roblox, and Microsoft are developing their visions of the metaverse, creating immersive digital experiences that transcend the limitations of the physical world.

Discussion Questions

1 Which aspects of 5G technology could transform business activities in the MEI? How does this transformation affect customer experiences?
2 In what ways can AI further revolutionize the content creation process in the MEI? What are some of the potential challenges that might arise?
3 How can blockchain technology, particularly NFTs, disrupt traditional models of content distribution and consumption? What potential legal, ethical, and practical issues should be considered?
4 How do you envision the metaverse's role in shaping the future of the MEI? What opportunities and challenges does it present?
5 Considering the cases of Meta, Roblox, and Microsoft, how are leading technology companies leveraging AI, blockchain, and the metaverse to innovate their businesses?
6 How might the intersection of AI, blockchain, and the metaverse continue to shape the future of the MEI? What implications might these technologies have for businesses, consumers, and policymakers?

Further Reading

- De Cremer, D., Bianzino, N. M., and Falk, B. (2023) "How generative AI could disrupt creative work." *Harvard Business Review*, April 13, 2023. https://hbr.org/2023/04/how-generative-ai-could-disrupt-creative-work.

322 Digital Business and Management

- Dutra, A., Tumasjan, A. and Welpe, I. M. (2018) "Blockchain is changing how media and entertainment companies compete." *MIT Sloan Management Review*, September 11, 2018. https://sloanreview.mit.edu/article/blockchain-is-changing-how-media-and-entertainment-companies-compete/
- Tapscott, D. and Tapscott, A. (2017) "Blockchain could help artists profit more from their creative works." *Harvard Business Review*, March 22, 2017. https://hbr.org/2017/03/blockchain-could-help-artists-profit-more-from-their-creative-works.
- Takahashi, R. (2017) "How can creative industries benefit from blockchain?" *McKinsey & Company*, August 7, 2017. www.mckinsey.com/industries/technology-media-and-telecommunications/our-insights/how-can-creative-industries-benefit-from-blockchain
- Vincent, J. (2019) "Hollywood is quietly using AI to help decide which movies to make." *The Verge*, May 28, 2019. www.theverge.com/2019/5/28/18637135/hollywood-ai-film-decision-script-analysis-data-machine-learning

References

1 Rao, S. K. and Prasad, R. (2018) "Impact of 5G technologies on industry 4.0." *Wireless Personal Communications*, 100, pp. 145–159.

2 Zhang, Z., Wen, F., Sun, Z., Guo, X., He, T. and Lee, C. (2022) "Artificial intelligence-enabled sensing technologies in the 5G/Internet of Things era: From virtual reality/augmented reality to the digital twin." *Adv. Intell. Syst.*, 4: 2100228. https://doi.org/10.1002/aisy.202100228

3 Marr, B. (2016) "What is the difference between artificial intelligence and machine learning?" *Forbes*, December 6. www.forbes.com/sites/bernardmarr/2016/12/06/what-is-the-difference-between-artificial-intelligence-and-machine-learning/#337aac0b2742

4 Uzialko, A. (2023) "How artificial intelligence will transform businesses." *Business News Daily.* www.businessnewsdaily.com/9402-artificial-intelligence-business-trends.html.

5 Davenport, T. H. and Ronanki, R. (2018) 'Artificial Intelligence for the Real World', *Harvard Business Review*, January–February. https://hbr.org/2018/01/artificial-intelligence-for-the-real-world.

6 Eliaçık, E. (2022) "AI is the key to being a competitive business." *Dataconomy*, August 10. https://dataconomy.com/2022/08/artificial-intelligence-in-business/.

7 Berkman, J. (2017) "Machine learning vs. deep learning." *Oracle AI & Data Science Blog.* https://blogs.oracle.com/ai-and-datascience/post/machine-learning-vs-deep-learning.

8 Eliaçık, E. (2022) "AI is the key to being a competitive business." *Dataconomy*, August 10. https://dataconomy.com/2022/08/artificial-intelligence-in-business/.

9 "How do businesses use artificial intelligence?" (2022) *Wharton Online*, January 19. https://online.wharton.upenn.edu/blog/how-do-businesses-use-artificial-intelligence/.

10 "How do businesses use artificial intelligence?" (2022) *Wharton Online*, January 19. https://online.wharton.upenn.edu/blog/how-do-businesses-use-artificial-intelligence/.

11 Wilson, J. (2022) "Artificial intelligence, machine learning, and the future of entertainment." *Forbes*, December 6. www.forbes.com/sites/joshwilson/2022/12/06/artificial-intelligence-machine-learning-and-the-future-of-entertainment/?sh=383ab65f6de4.

12 Saha, S. (2022) "AI in media & entertainment market industry outlook (2022-2032)." *Future Market Insights*. www.futuremarketinsights.com/reports/aI-in-media-and-entertainment-market.

13 Barton, G. (2018) "Why your Netflix thumbnails don't look like mine." *Vox*, November 21. www.vox.com/2018/11/21/18106394/why-your-netflix-thumbnail-coverart-changes.

14 Bilow, S. (2022) "The ever-growing importance of AI and machine learning in media and entertainment." *SMPTE Motion Imaging Journal*, 131(3), p. 6.

15 Armstrong, M. et al. (2022) "Realizing additional value from linear content using metadata and automation." *SMPTE Motion Imaging Journal*, 131(3), pp. 8–16.

16 Vincent, J. (2019) "Hollywood is quietly using AI to help decide which movies to make." *The Verge*, May 28. www.theverge.com/2019/5/28/18637135/hollywood-ai-film-decision-script-analysis-data-machine-learning.

New Technological Advancements **323**

17 "Startup company Cinelytic uses algorithms to suggest who ought to be in movies" (2019) *CBS News*, June 10. www.cbsnews.com/news/can-ai-predict-box-office-gold-startup-company-cinelytic-uses-algorithms-to-suggest-who-ought-to-be-in-movies/.

18 Barreau, P. (2018) "How AI could compose a personalized soundtrack to your life." *TED*. www.ted.com/talks/pierre_barreau_how_ai_could_compose_a_personalized_soundtrack_to_your_life.

19 "Introducing ChatGPT" (2022) *OpenAI*. https://openai.com/blog/chatgpt.

20 Wiggers, K. and Stringer, A. (2023) "ChatGPT: Everything you need to know about the AI-powered chatbot', *TechCrunch*, May 31. https://techcrunch.com/2023/05/31/chatgpt-everything-you-need-to-know-about-the-open-ai-powered-chatbot/.

21 Chui, M., Roberts, R. and Yee, L. (2022) "Generative AI is here: How tools like CHATGPT could change your business." *McKinsey & Company*. www.mckinsey.com/capabilities/quantumblack/our-insights/generative-ai-is-here-how-tools-like-chatgpt-could-change-your-business.

22 "Dall·E now available without waitlist" (2022) *OpenAI*. https://openai.com/blog/dall-e-now-available-without-waitlist/.

23 Dwivedi, Y. K., Kshetri, N., Hughes, L., Slade, E. L., Jeyaraj, A., Kar, A. K., Baabdullah, A. M., Koohang, A., Raghavan, V., Ahuja, M. and Albanna, H. (2023) "So what if ChatGPT wrote it?" Multidisciplinary perspectives on opportunities, challenges and implications of generative conversational AI for research, practice and policy." *International Journal of Information Management*, 71, p. 102642.

24 De Cremer, D., Bianzino, N. M., and Falk, B. (2023) "How generative ai could disrupt creative work." *Harvard Business Review*, April 13. https://hbr.org/2023/04/how-generative-ai-could-disrupt-creative-work.

25 Pal, A., Tiwari, Chandan K. and Haldar, Nivedita (2021) "Blockchain for business management: Applications, challenges and potentials." *The Journal of High Technology Management Research*, 32(2), p. 100414.

26 Underwood, S. (2016) "Blockchain beyond bitcoin." *Communications of the ACM*, 59(11), pp.15–17.

27 "Making sense of bitcoin, cryptocurrency and Blockchain" (no date) *PwC*. www.pwc.com/us/en/industries/financial-services/fintech/bitcoin-blockchain-cryptocurrency.html.

28 Making sense of bitcoin, cryptocurrency and Blockchain" (no date) *PwC*. www.pwc.com/us/en/industries/financial-services/fintech/bitcoin-blockchain-cryptocurrency.html.

29 Takahashi, R. (2017) "How can creative industries benefit from blockchain?" *McKinsey & Company*. www.mckinsey.com/industries/technology-media-and-telecommunications/our-insights/how-can-creative-industries-benefit-from-blockchain.

30 Bai, C. A., Cordeiro, J. and Sarkis, J. (2020) "Blockchain technology: Business, strategy, the environment, and sustainability." *Business Strategy and the Environment*, 29(1), pp. 321–322.

31 Burnett, S. (2018) "Council post: Can Blockchain reinvigorate loyalty programs?", *Forbes*, December 11. www.forbes.com/sites/forbesagencycouncil/2018/12/11/can-blockchain-reinvigorate-loyalty-programs/?sh=78740a1b1456.

32 "Enforcing accountability in media: How blockchain technology can work for media and entertainment" (2018) *IBM*. www.ibm.com/downloads/cas/6146Z4JE.

33 Christman, E. D. (2015) "Publishers said to be missing as much as 25 percent of streaming royalties." *Billboard*, October 20. www.billboard.com/pro/publishers-songwriters-streaming-25-percent-royalties/.

34 Hickman, A. (2017) "Programmatic 'tech tax' costs 48 cents of every dollar - ANA study", *AdNews*, June 20. www.adnews.com.au/news/programmatic-tech-tax-costs-48-cents-of-every-dollar-ana-study.

35 Perez, S. (2017) "Spotify acquires blockchain startup Mediachain to solve music's attribution problem." *TechCrunch*, April 26. https://techcrunch.com/2017/04/26/spotify-acquires-blockchain-startup-mediachain-to-solve-musics-attribution-problem/.

36 Mangla, U. et al. (2018) "Blockchain could enforce accountability in media and entertainment." *IBM*. www.ibm.com/thought-leadership/institute-business-value/report/blockchain-me.

37 Khan, N., Ahmad, T. and State, R. (2019) "Blockchain-based micropayment systems: economic impact." *Proceedings of the 23rd International Database Applications & Engineering Symposium (IDEAS '19)*. Association for Computing Machinery, New York Article 45, 1–3.

324 Digital Business and Management

38 "General Data Protection Regulation (GDPR)" (no date) *Intersoft Consulting.* https://gdpr-info.eu/.

39 Takahashi, R. (2017) "How can creative industries benefit from blockchain?" *McKinsey & Company.* www.mckinsey.com/industries/technology-media-and-telecommunications/our-insights/how-can-creative-industries-benefit-from-blockchain.

40 Dutra, A., Tumasjan, A. and Welpe, I. M. (2018) "Blockchain is changing how media and entertainment companies compete." *MIT Sloan Management Review,* September 11. https://sloanreview.mit.edu/article/blockchain-is-changing-how-media-and-entertainment-companies-compete/.

41 Bartmann, J. (2018) "Peertracks aims for free, ad-free music streaming using blockchain tech." *Medium,* October 1. https://medium.com/@johnbartmann/peertracks-aims-for-free-ad-free-music-streaming-using-blockchain-tech-a830a0de76b4.

42 Tsui, E. (2018) "Buying art with bitcoin, authenticating it with blockchain – art world cottons on to cryptocurrencies." *South China Morning Post,* May 9. www.scmp.com/culture/arts-entertainment/article/2145222/buying-art-bitcoin-authenticating-it-blockchain-art-world.

43 Partz, H. (2019) "South Korean ArtBloc to sell David Hockney paintings via blockchain." *Cointelegraph,* August 31. https://cointelegraph.com/news/south-korean-artbloc-to-sell-david-hockney-paintings-via-blockchain.

44 "Non-fungible tokens (NFT)" (no date) *ethereum.org.* https://ethereum.org/en/nft/.

45 Silver, N. S. (2021) "The history and future of NFTs." *Forbes,* November 2. www.forbes.com/sites/nicolesilver/2021/11/02/the-history-and-future-of-nfts/?sh=502eb24a6a16.

46 Calma, J. (2021) "The climate controversy swirling around NFTs." *The Verge,* May 15. www.theverge.com/2021/3/15/22328203/nft-cryptoart-ethereum-blockchain-climate-change.

47 Hern, A. (2021) "Bitcoin rise could leave carbon footprint the size of London's." *The Guardian,* March 10, 2021. www.theguardian.com/technology/2021/mar/10/bitcoin-rise-could-leave-carbon-footprint-size-london.

48 Sheridan, E. et al. (2021) "Framing the future of web 3: Metaverse edition." *Goldman Sachs.* www.goldmansachs.com/intelligence/pages/gs-research/framing-the-future-of-web-3.0-metaverse-edition/report.pdf.

49 Ball, M. (2020) "The metaverse: What it is, where to find it, and who will build it." *MatthewBall.co.* www.matthewball.vc/all/themetaverse.

50 Liao, S. (2021) "Roblox, the game company made wildly popular by kids, goes public with $41 billion valuation." *The Washington Post,* March 11. www.washingtonpost.com/video-games/2021/03/11/roblox-ipo/.

51 "Introducing Meta: A social technology company" (2021) *Meta.* https://about.fb.com/news/2021/10/facebook-company-is-now-meta/.

52 "Metaverse may be $800 billion market, next tech platform" (2021) *Bloomberg.* www.bloomberg.com/professional/blog/metaverse-may-be-800-billion-market-next-tech-platform.

53 Radoff, J. (2021) "The metaverse value-chain." *Medium,* April 7. https://medium.com/building-the-metaverse/the-metaverse-value-chain-afcf9e09e3a7.

54 Alaghband, M. and Hackl, C. (2022) "What is the metaverse—and what does it mean for business?" *McKinsey & Company.* www.mckinsey.com/capabilities/mckinsey-digital/our-insights/what-is-the-metaverse-and-what-does-it-mean-for-business.

55 Law, M. (2023) "Entertainment industry continues to sound out the metaverse." *Technology Magazine,* March 13. https://technologymagazine.com/articles/entertainment-industry-continues-to-sound-out-the-metaverse.

MODULE V

New Business Models and Entrepreneurship

11

BUSINESS MODEL PLANNING IN THE MEDIA AND ENTERTAINMENT INDUSTRY

Outline

Overview	327
11.1 The Business Model as a Management Concept	328
11.2 Business Model Planning	332
11.3 Business Model Types	340
11.4 Business Model Innovation	343
Case Studies	346
Review	347
Discussion Questions	347
Further Reading	348
References	348

Intended Learning Outcomes

- Define the concept and elements of the business model.
- Classify and compare different types of business models in the media and entertainment industry (MEI).
- Analyze and explain the business model of a company.
- Apply the business model innovation framework to media and entertainment businesses.

Overview

This chapter provides an in-depth look at the business model as a vital management concept:

DOI: 10.4324/9781003271222-16

328 New Business Models and Entrepreneurship

- Business models are roadmaps that link value propositions, resources, and processes. They serve as a blueprint for a company's operations, competition, and value creation for stakeholders.
- The elements of a business model include value proposition, customer segments, channels, customer relationships, key resources, activities, partnerships, revenue streams, and cost structure. The interconnectedness of these components should be highlighted in serving customers and achieving business objectives.
- The structured development of a business model is critical, starting with value proposition and followed by revenue model, market opportunity, competitive environment, competitive advantage, market strategy, and organizational development. These processes come together to form a comprehensive model for value creation, revenue generation, and market success.
- Different types of business models may suit various objectives, industries, and market conditions, ranging from traditional brick-and-mortar models to modern online models like portals and platforms. This chapter offers insights into how to choose the right model based on strategic goals and specific contexts.
- Business model innovation in response to changing market dynamics and technological advancements is key to business success and sustainability. The process includes identifying opportunities, developing solutions, achieving product-market fit, and scaling operations.

11.1 The Business Model as a Management Concept

11.1.1 The Concept of a Business Model

The term "business model" describes "the logic of the firm, the way it operates, and how it creates value for its stakeholders." [1] It presents the system of how individual elements of a business fit together.

A business model focuses on designing a business to:

- fulfill customers' needs;
- generate a profitable revenue stream;
- create a sustainable competitive advantage; and
- offer growth opportunities to expand and thrive in the long term. [2]

While some people may mistake a business model for a strategy, these are distinct concepts. A business model revolves around the operations and structure of a firm, focusing on how it creates, delivers, and captures value. On the other hand, a strategy takes a broader perspective, encompassing the external environment in which the firm operates. It involves determining the markets to target, the investments to make, and the competitive approach to adopt.

A business model does not describe how a company deals with competition, for example. Instead, this is the task of strategy. A strategy defines the company's target markets, investment decisions, and competitive approach. Its ultimate objective is to establish a sustainable competitive advantage, ensuring the company's long-term success and distinctiveness in the marketplace. Selecting a suitable business model for competing in the marketplace is also a strategic task.[3] While business models and strategies differ in their functions and scope, they are inherently related.

In essence, leveraging a business model enhances decision-making for a business. Established companies benefit from improved decision-making concerning their future trajectory, while startups find it valuable in crafting effective solutions to meet customer needs and drive profitability. By employing the business model framework, entrepreneurs gain a profound understanding of the options and the strategic elements required to build a successful business.

Imagine a company that is seeking a suitable strategy to complement its cutting-edge technology. Beyond assessing the market landscape, including competitors and customer demands, the company must craft a business model that effectively harnesses the potential of this technology. Without a well-designed business model, the technology's value will remain untapped and underutilized.

One essential element of the business model is the value proposition.[4] This describes the company's products or services and explains why they appeal to customers or clients. The value proposition is strategically crafted to set the product or service apart.

A well-rounded business model for a new company should cover key elements such as projected startup costs, potential funding sources, target customers, marketing strategy, competitive analysis, and revenue projections. Moreover, it is essential to explore opportunities for collaboration with established companies.

To succeed, a business must effectively meet customer needs at a competitive and sustainable cost. As the business environment and market demands change, it is common for businesses to update their business models to remain relevant and agile.

Let's compare two music businesses, both engaged in selling music albums. Both companies generated $10 million in revenue and spent $7 million to purchase music albums, resulting in a gross profit of $3 million and a gross profit margin of 30%.

Company A recognized the potential of digital music streaming and shifted its focus away from the sale of physical albums. This strategic move positively impacted its business model as it eliminated the costs associated with purchasing physical albums and managing inventory, resulting in cost savings of $4 million. Consequently, Company A's new gross profit increased to $6 million and its margin rose to 60%.

On the other hand, Company B stuck with its traditional approach of selling physical albums, leading to higher costs and a lower gross profit margin. As a result, Company B started losing customers to the more innovative Company A. Company A's sales revenue remained the same; its forward-thinking business model allowed it to significantly reduce costs and outperform its competitor in the digital music market.

11.1.2 The Business Model Framework

William Sahlman, in his 1997 article "How to Write a Great Business Plan," identifies four key components of a business model (Table 11.1):[5]

- People: The team or individuals responsible for executing the business plan, including their skills, experience, and expertise.
- Opportunity: The problem or need in the market that the business seeks to address and the proposed solution.

TABLE 11.1 The Four Interdependent Factors Affecting Business Models

Factor	Content
People	• The founders starting and running the venture. • External parties providing key services or important resources.
Opportunity	• What to sell and to whom. • Whether the company can grow and how fast. • Who and what stands in the way of success.
Context: "big picture"	• Regulatory environment, demographic trends, inflation. • Factors that inevitably change but cannot be controlled.
Risk and reward	• All the things that can go wrong and right. • How the entrepreneurial team can respond.

- Context: The broader context in which the business operates, including market trends, competition, and regulatory environment.
- Risk and reward: The potential risks associated with the business and the potential rewards if successful.

Sahlman emphasizes that these components should be presented in a clear and concise manner in the business plan, highlighting how they work together to create a successful and sustainable business model.

From a different perspective, a business model consists of four interlocking components (Figure 11.1):[6]

- Customer value proposition: The unique value that a company delivers to customers, including the product or service offered, the price, the quality, the convenience, and the overall experience.

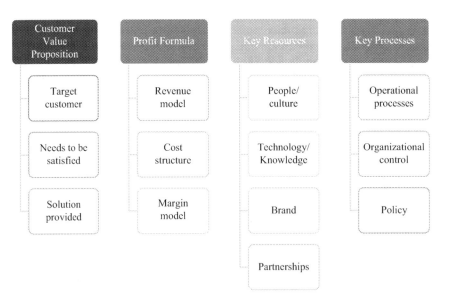

FIGURE 11.1 The Core Components of a Business Model.

Business Model Planning **331**

- Profit formula: How the company creates value by generating revenue and managing costs, including revenue, cost structure, and margin models.
- Key resources: The assets, capabilities, and competencies a company needs to create and deliver its value proposition, including physical, financial, human, and intellectual resources.
- Key processes: The company's operational and managerial processes to deliver its value proposition and manage its resources, including innovation, operations, and customer relationship management.

The interplay between these four components helps to create a coherent and sustainable business model that can deliver value to customers while generating profits for the company.

11.1.3 The Business Model Canvas: A Framework

The Business Model Canvas (BMC) tool helps companies visualize and organize their business model. Alexander Osterwalder and Yves Pigneur introduced it in their book *Business Model Generation.*[7]

The BMC is a one-page visual representation of the key elements of a business model, including the company's value proposition, target customers, revenue streams, key activities, resources, and partnerships (Figure 11.2). It consists of nine sections or building blocks that the business owner or team can fill in.

The researchers interpret business models as how companies create and capture value—how the value proposition takes shape and is subsequently monetized. To better define value creation and value capture, Osterwalder and Pigneur identified the nine elements that define a business model.[8]

The central aspect of a business model is the value proposition, which addresses customer demands and explains why a customer would choose one company over

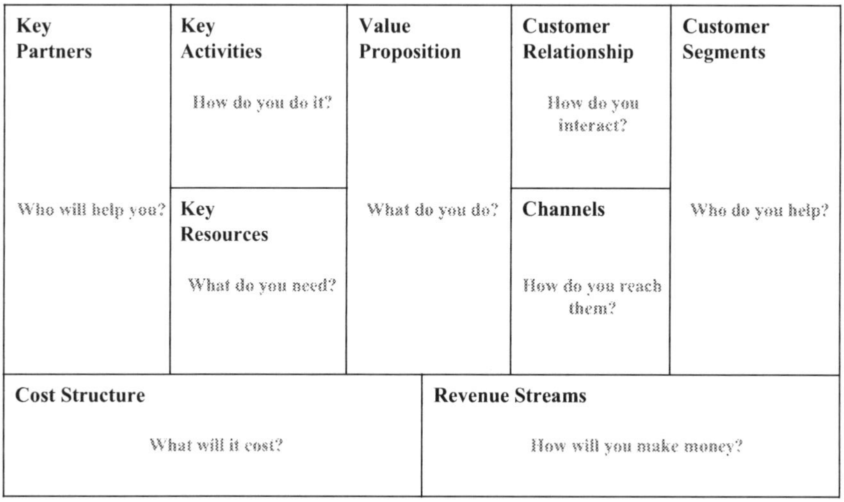

Key Partners	Key Activities	Value Proposition	Customer Relationship	Customer Segments
	How do you do it?		How do you interact?	
Who will help you?	**Key Resources**	What do you do?	**Channels**	Who do you help?
	What do you need?		How do you reach them?	
Cost Structure			**Revenue Streams**	
What will it cost?			How will you make money?	

FIGURE 11.2   The Business Model Canvas.

332 New Business Models and Entrepreneurship

another. Surrounding the value proposition are eight elements. Those on the left in Figure 11.2 are company-related aspects, while those on the right are customer-related aspects.

As highlighted by the authors, the key activities represent a company's fundamental tasks of creating a value proposition, attracting customers, and generating revenues. These tasks are made possible by a network of key partners, such as suppliers, joint ventures, and research and development (R&D) networks; and by key resources, including human, technological, informational, infrastructural, and financial resources.

As value creation incurs expenses, the cost structure accounts for all the costs associated with operating the business model, depicted in the last block on the left-hand side of the BMC.

On the right-hand side, customer segments and customer relationships define the specific groups of people a company aims to reach and the level of engagement between the company and its customers, respectively. Companies may target a single main customer segment or address different types of customers through various products and services.

Regarding customer relationships, companies can consider involving customers in the co-development of their offers and determine the level of service they should provide, ranging from tailored experiences to self-service options.

The channels allow a company to communicate with customers and deliver goods and services.

Finally, the revenue streams represent the turnover a firm generates—which, depending on the particular business model of a firm, can take the form of usage, subscription or licensing fees.

Some companies may even offer a service or product for free (or subsidize it) to one customer segment while gaining revenues from a different customer segment—for example, from advertisers. In this case, advertisers can be viewed as key partners and customers.

A company's unique strategy and market positioning influence the design of its business model elements. Every company has a distinct business model, whether consciously acknowledged or not, and shapes its own version of the generic business model. However, one shared characteristic among all companies is the interdependence of their business model elements. Even with a brilliant value proposition, a company cannot fulfill stringent customer demands without effective channels. Similarly, a company with a loyal customer base cannot thrive without a well-defined revenue logic. Changes or innovations in one business model element often lead to modifications in other elements.

11.2 Business Model Planning

To plan a business model, all companies or individuals should consider the following elements (Figure 11.3):[9]

- Value proposition: This is a statement that describes the unique benefits that a company's product or service provides to customers. It should address the target market's pain points or needs and differentiate the company from its competitors.

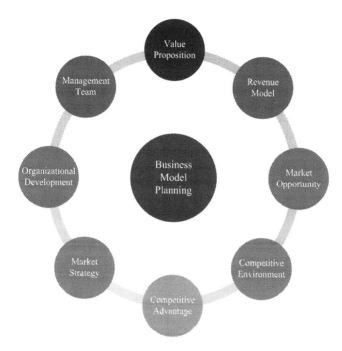

FIGURE 11.3 The Eight Elements of Business Model Planning.

- Revenue model: This outlines how a company plans to generate revenue from its product or service. It includes pricing strategies, sales channels, and other revenue streams such as subscriptions, licensing, or advertising.
- Market opportunity: This describes the size and growth potential of the target market, as well as any trends or opportunities that may exist. It should also include an analysis of customer demographics, behavior, and purchasing patterns.
- Competitive environment: This involves assessing the strengths and weaknesses of competitors in the market, including their product offerings, pricing strategies, marketing efforts, and market share. This analysis can help a company identify gaps in the market and develop a competitive advantage.
- Competitive advantage: A competitive advantage is a unique attribute or advantage that sets a company apart. It can be achieved through product differentiation, pricing, marketing, or operational efficiency. The company's competitive advantage should be clearly articulated in its business model.
- Market strategy: The market strategy outlines how a company plans to market and sell its products or services to its target market. It includes promotional tactics such as advertising, social media, public relations, and distribution channels (e.g., direct sales or e-commerce).
- Organizational development: This involves developing the organization's structure, culture, and processes to support the business model. It includes developing a team, establishing roles and responsibilities, and implementing policies and procedures.
- Management team: The management team executes the business plan and ensures the company achieves its goals. The team should have a strong track record of success and complementary skills and expertise to ensure that all aspects of the business model are covered.

334 New Business Models and Entrepreneurship

These eight key elements work together to create a comprehensive business model that outlines how the company plans to create value for customers, generate revenue, and succeed in the market.

11.2.1 Value Proposition

"Why should the customer buy from you?"

"Value proposition" refers to the unique value that a company's products or services provide to its customers—in other words, why customers would choose to buy from that company instead of its competitors.

Developing a clear and compelling value proposition is critical to the success of any business. This involves understanding the needs and wants of customers and designing products or services that meet those needs in a unique and valuable way.

Characteristics that enable a strong value proposition include the following:

- Unique features: Highlighting unique features of the product or service that differentiate it from competitors.
- Benefits: Demonstrating how the product or service will benefit the customer, such as by saving time or money, increasing productivity, or improving quality of life.
- Cost-effectiveness: Offering a cost-effective solution that provides value for the price.
- Personalization: Tailoring the product or service to the specific needs and preferences of the customer.
- Convenience: Offering a convenient and easy-to-use solution that makes the customer's life easier.

11.2.2 Revenue Model

"How will you earn money?"

The revenue model is how a company generates revenue from its products or services. In other words, it is a company's strategy or approach to generate income and sustain its operations.

Developing a clear and compelling revenue model is critical to the success of any business. This involves identifying the most profitable sources of revenue and designing a pricing strategy that maximizes profitability while meeting customers' needs.

Revenue models differ by industry. Some representative revenue models in the MEI include the advertising, subscription, transaction fee, and sales revenue models. The advertising and subscription revenue models are the two main approaches to generating revenue in the MEI.

The advertising revenue model involves generating revenue by displaying ads to customers. This model is commonly used by media and entertainment companies such as television networks, websites, and social media platforms—YouTube and Facebook are good examples. Revenue is generated by charging advertisers to display their ads to customers based on the number of views or clicks they receive. The advantage of this model is that it can be very profitable for companies with a large customer base and high traffic to their platforms. However, balancing the need for revenue with the desire to provide a good user experience can be challenging. Too many ads can be intrusive and lead to a negative customer experience.

The subscription revenue model generates revenue by charging customers a recurring fee for access to a product or service. Netflix and Pandora are representative examples. This model is commonly used by companies that offer ongoing services or content, such as streaming video services, music services, and software companies. The advantage of this model is that it provides a predictable and recurring source of revenue, which can be more stable than advertising revenue. However, attracting and retaining customers can be challenging, as customers may hesitate to commit to ongoing fees.

Both advertising and subscription revenue models can be effective in different contexts, depending on the business model and customer needs. For example, advertising may be more effective for companies with a large customer base and high traffic. On the other hand, subscription revenue may be more effective for companies with ongoing services or content. Ultimately, the choice between these revenue models depends on the specific needs and goals of the business.

In recent years, the "freemium" ("free" + "premium") revenue model has become popular among companies in the MEI. This unique revenue model combines two pricing tiers: a free version and a premium (paid) version of a product or service.[10] In this model, companies offer users a basic version of their product or service at no cost, allowing them to access and use it without any upfront payment. In some cases, it is paired with the advertising model.

The free version typically includes essential features that give users a taste of the product's capabilities and benefits. This approach helps attract a large user base and create a broad market presence. By offering a free version, the company aims to generate awareness, build trust, and acquire a large user base, which can later translate into potential paying customers.

Meanwhile, the company also provides a premium version with additional and more advanced features, services, or content that cater to users who require more features or value. These premium features often come with a subscription fee or a one-time payment. The premium version aims to cater to users who find value in the extra features and are willing to pay for an enhanced experience.

The freemium revenue model can be advantageous in multiple ways.[11] First, it allows companies to acquire a large user base, which can serve as a marketing asset for word-of-mouth referrals and user-generated content. Second, it helps users to become familiar with the product and its value before committing to a paid version, increasing the likelihood of conversions. Third, it provides an opportunity for upselling and cross-selling premium features to users already engaged with the free version.

However, it also comes with key challenges. One of the primary concerns is striking the right balance between the free and premium features to avoid cannibalizing the premium version.[12] Companies must ensure that the free version offers sufficient value to users without giving away too much to discourage them from upgrading to the premium version.

11.2.3 Market Opportunity

"Which market space do you intend to serve and what is its size?"

"Market opportunity" refers to the size of the potential market for a company's products or services and the opportunity for growth and profitability. This includes the

336 New Business Models and Entrepreneurship

potential market size, growth rate, and profitability of a particular market or customer segment.

Identifying and analyzing market opportunities is critical in developing a successful business model. This may involve conducting market research, identifying target customer segments, and understanding the needs and preferences of these customers. It also includes assessing the size and growth rate of the market and identifying any barriers to entry or other competitive factors that may impact the company's ability to succeed.

In summary, there are two main activities involved in identifying market opportunities:

- Identifying target customer segments: This involves identifying specific groups of customers who are likely to be interested in the company's products or services and understanding their needs and preferences.
- Assessing the market size and growth rate: This involves analyzing the size of the potential market, its growth rate and the potential for profitability.

11.2.4 Competitive Environment

"Who else occupies your intended market space?"

The competitive environment encompasses the external market factors that affect a company's ability to compete. These can include the number and strength of competitors, the level of rivalry in the market, the availability of substitute products or services, and the bargaining power of suppliers and customers.

A deep understanding of the competitive environment requires a thorough analysis of the market and competitors, the identification of key trends and drivers, and an understanding of how these factors will impact the company's ability to compete.

The activities involved in analyzing the competitive environment include:

- identifying key competitors in the market, both direct and indirect;
- analyzing the strengths and weaknesses of competitors, including their market position, product offerings, pricing strategies, and customer base;
- identifying key trends in the market, such as changes in consumer behavior, emerging technologies, or regulatory changes; and
- assessing the level of rivalry in the market, the threat of new entrants, the bargaining power of suppliers and customers, and the availability of substitute products or services.

11.2.5 Competitive Advantage

"What special advantages does your firm bring to the market?"

"Competitive advantage" refers to a company's unique advantage over competitors in the marketplace. This advantage can be derived from various factors, including technology, intellectual property (IP), brand reputation, cost structure, distribution network, or customer service.

Developing a solid competitive advantage consists of several key steps:

- analyzing the competitive landscape to understand competitors' strengths and weaknesses and identify areas where the company can differentiate itself;

- defining the unique value the company's products or services offer customers and how this value differs from competitors;
- identifying the factors critical to market success and understanding how the company can leverage its strengths to succeed;
- developing a sustainable competitive advantage over the long term that competitors cannot easily replicate; and
- continuously monitoring the competitive landscape and adjusting the company's competitive advantage to maintain its market position.

For example, first-mover advantage is a competitive advantage that a company secures by being a pioneer in a specific market or launching a novel product or service ahead of competitors.[13] Being a first mover allows a company to establish a strong position in the market ahead of its competitors, creating barriers to entry and setting the stage for long-term success.

When a company is the first to introduce a new product or service, it may face limited or no direct competition, allowing it to capture a significant market share and build brand recognition and customer loyalty. Additionally, being the first to enter a market enables a company to shape customer preferences and expectations. The first mover can set industry standards and define the features and benefits customers associate with that product or service. As a result, competitors that enter the market later may find it challenging to differentiate their offerings or meet customer expectations set by the first mover.

Furthermore, first-mover advantage can lead to economies of scale and cost advantages. As the market leader, the company can benefit from larger production volumes, lower costs per unit, and more efficient distribution channels. This cost advantage helps the first mover to price its products competitively, further consolidating its position in the market.

However, first-mover advantage is not guaranteed and may not always lead to success. There are inherent risks in being a first mover, such as higher R&D costs, uncertainty about customer acceptance, and the possibility of technological or market changes that could make the initial offering obsolete.

Competitors that enter the market later may also learn from the mistakes and successes of the first mover, allowing them to develop improved or more innovative products or services (i.e., "second-mover advantage").[14] As a result, first movers must continue to innovate and evolve to maintain their competitive advantage over time.

11.2.6 Market Strategy

"How do you plan to promote your products or services to attract your target audience?"

"Market strategy" refers to a company's plan or approach to market and sell its products or services to its target customers.

To develop a strong market strategy, a company should identify the specific customer segments it wants to target with its products or services. This requires a deep understanding of customers' needs, preferences, and behaviors.

The company should then position its product or service in the target segments. This involves defining the unique value proposition of the product or service and positioning it to differentiate it from competitors in the market.

338 New Business Models and Entrepreneurship

The next step involves developing different marketing strategies—such as pricing, distribution, and promotion—aligned with the target market and the company's positioning.

It is important to understand that even the best business concepts will fail if they are not properly marketed to potential customers.

11.2.7 Organizational Development

"What organizational structures within the company are required to carry out the business plan?"

"Organizational development" refers to the establishment and development of the organizational structure, systems, and processes needed to support the business model. It covers the design and implementation of the systems and processes needed to support the company's operations, including its financial management, sales, human resources (HR), and other functions. It also involves developing the organizational culture and values needed to support the business model and create a high-performing team.

Key elements of organizational development include the following:[15]

- Organizational structure: How the company is organized, including its departments, reporting lines, and decision-making processes. A well-designed organizational structure ensures the company can execute its business model effectively and efficiently.
- Organizational systems and processes: The tools and processes used to manage the company's operations, such as financial management, marketing, sales, and human resources. Developing efficient and effective systems and processes is essential to ensure the company can deliver its products or services in a timely and cost-effective manner.
- Organizational culture: The values, beliefs, and behaviors that shape the company's culture and how employees work together.[16] Developing a solid organizational culture that aligns with the company's values and goals is critical in building a high-performing team that can execute the business model effectively.
- HR development: The process of recruiting, training and developing employees to ensure they have the skills and knowledge needed to support the business model. Focusing on employee development is critical in attracting and retaining top talent and building a team to drive growth and innovation. As a company grows, talent acquisition and development move from generalists to specialists.

11.2.8 Management Team

"What kinds of backgrounds do the company's leaders have?"

The management team is responsible for leading and managing the company's operations. One of its main roles is to ensure the business model is executed effectively. A strong management team has market-specific knowledge and experience in implementing business plans, so it can make the business model work and give credibility to stakeholders.

A strong management team is essential to the success of any business, as it is responsible for setting the company's strategic direction and making key decisions that impact the company's growth and profitability.[17] The management team should have diverse skills and expertise that align with the company's goals and objectives:

- Strategic direction: The management team is responsible for setting the strategic direction of the company, which includes defining the company's goals, objectives, and overall vision.
- Decision-making: The management team is also responsible for making key decisions that impact the company's direction, such as determining which products or services to offer, which markets to target, and how to allocate resources. A strong management team with diverse skills and expertise is better equipped to make informed decisions that drive growth and profitability.[18]
- Talent development: The management team is responsible for hiring and developing employees, creating a culture of innovation and collaboration, and ensuring the company has the talent and resources to succeed.
- Operational efficiency: The management team manages day-to-day operations and ensures that the company runs efficiently and effectively.

11.2.9 Other Factors in Business Model Planning

Another critical factor in business model planning is raising capital. This is essential to cover initial expenses such as setting up, hiring staff, and marketing the business. Without sufficient capital, getting off the ground and achieving profitability may be difficult. It can also help businesses expand their operations and achieve their growth objectives.

Raising capital can additionally help businesses innovate and develop new products or services. This may require investment in R&D or the recruitment of specialized staff. Without sufficient capital, investing in innovation and staying ahead of competitors may be difficult.

There are many different sources of capital, including:[19]

- seed capital from friends and family;
- traditional startup financing sources, such as angel investors and venture capital firms;
- commercial banks; and
- new alternative sources such as crowdfunding (e.g., Indiegogo, Kickstarter) and accelerators (e.g., Y-combinator).

Timing is another critical factor in business model planning, as it can significantly impact a company's success and competitiveness in the market.[20] Most significantly, the right timing can help a company capitalize on emerging market opportunities. Being early to market with an innovative product or service can give a company first-mover advantage and establish it as a leader in the industry. On the other hand, entering the market too late (or too early) can result in missed opportunities and a more challenging path to gain market share.

Technology is constantly evolving and the timing of adopting new technologies can profoundly influence a company's competitiveness. Embracing the right technologies at the opportune moment can streamline operations, enhance efficiency, and elevate customer experiences. The ever-changing technological landscape and shifts in customer demand require companies to be agile in meeting altered customer needs and preferences

340 New Business Models and Entrepreneurship

promptly, enhancing their chances of success. Anticipating changes in customer behavior and tailoring offerings accordingly gives companies a competitive edge.

11.3 Business Model Types

11.3.1 Generic Business Model Examples

Various generic business models exist, each tailored to offer distinct values to its target customer segments. Moreover, technological advancements have facilitated the development of new business models in online business domains. Businesses may also use a combination of these models or develop a unique business model tailored to their specific market and customer needs:

- Brick-and-mortar sales: A brick-and-mortar business model involves operating a physical store or location where customers can visit and purchase products or services. Examples include retail stores and restaurants.
- E-tailers: These are online versions of traditional retailers. Sales of products and services are the primary revenue model. This can be done through a dedicated website or through platforms like Amazon or Etsy.
- Community providers (social network services): These create an online space where individuals with similar interests can interact, share content, and engage with each other. Examples include Facebook, Weibo, Twitter, and LinkedIn. Revenue models for such platforms are often hybrid, incorporating advertising, subscriptions, sales, transaction fees, and other revenue streams.
- Content providers: These provide digital content—such as news, music, videos, text, and artworks—on the internet. Their main revenue models are advertising, subscription, and sales of digital goods. The change of channels in providing content has dramatically impacted this business model—for example, the music industry has shifted from physical channels to online channels.
- Portal business: These businesses provide search plus an integrated package of content and services. Their main revenue models are advertising, referral fees, transaction fees, and subscriptions for premium services.
- Transaction brokers: These process online transactions for consumers. The primary value proposition for customers is saving time and money. The main revenues come from transaction fees. Industries using this model include financial services, travel services, and job placement services.
- On-demand: The on-demand business model provides customers with immediate access to a product or service whenever needed. Examples of on-demand-based businesses include ride-sharing services like Uber and Didi, and food delivery services like Grubhub and DoorDash.
- Market creators (platforms): These create a digital environment where buyers and sellers can meet and transact. This model facilitates transactions between individuals rather than between a company and a customer. The primary revenue sources are transaction fees and fees to merchants for access. The sharing economy (or on-demand economy) has promoted the rapid expansion of this business model. Platforms allow people to transact goods and services in a peer-to-peer setting (e.g., Airbnb, TaskRabbit).

11.3.2 The Platform Business Model in the Media and Entertainment Industry

Due to the distinctive attributes of the MEI, various business models have emerged in addition to the traditional advertising-based and subscription-based models. Different platform business models have become more prominent in recent years.

The Traditional Linear Pipeline Business Model versus the Platform Business Model

The linear pipeline and platform models are distinct business models with their own characteristics and strategies (Figure 11.4). On the one hand, the linear pipeline model is based on the sequential process of transforming inputs into outputs through a linear value chain. The goal is to optimize efficiency and reduce costs throughout the process. In this model, the company owns the entire value chain, from production to delivery and distribution; and the focus is on improving the efficiency of internal processes. This model is standard in manufacturing and traditional retail industries, where companies seek to minimize costs and increase production throughput.

On the other hand, the platform model is based on a network of interconnected participants, where value is created through interactions and exchanges between them.[21] In this model, the company provides a platform that connects buyers and sellers, service providers and consumers, or any other combination of participants. The company's role is to facilitate and orchestrate interactions between participants, while the participants themselves create and exchange value. Examples of companies that use this model include Uber, Airbnb, and Kickstarter.

The Competitive Advantages of the Platform Business Model

Platform companies are overtaking traditional incumbents such as banks and energy companies, for several reasons.[22]

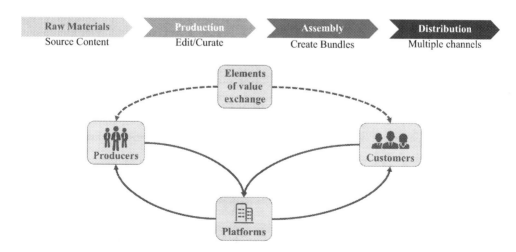

FIGURE 11.4 The Linear Pipeline Model versus the Platform Business Model.

342 New Business Models and Entrepreneurship

First, platform companies have a high potential for scalability since their products or services can be delivered at virtually no additional cost to many users. This means they can expand without incurring significant costs, making them attractive to investors. Moreover, they typically require less initial capital than traditional companies, maximizing potential profitability.

Second, platform companies create value by bringing together different participants in a network. As more participants join the network, the platform's value increases for all participants, creating a network effect.

Third, platform companies generate a large amount of data from users' interactions, which they can utilize to gain insights into consumer behavior and preferences. This data can be used to improve their products and services and to develop new revenue streams. With this approach, platform companies have disrupted traditional industries by providing more convenient and efficient alternatives. This disruption has created new markets and revenue streams, leading to rapid growth and market dominance.

Likewise, the platform business model has also transformed the MEI in several respects.[23] Platforms such as YouTube and Netflix have disrupted traditional distribution channels and eliminated the need for intermediaries like record labels, studios, and broadcasters. Indeed, disintermediation is a key aspect of how the platform business model has transformed the MEI. Traditionally, the MEI relied on intermediaries such as record labels, movie studios, and TV networks to distribute and market content to audiences. These intermediaries acted as gatekeepers, controlling access to distribution channels and deciding which content was produced and distributed to audiences.

The rise of platform businesses has disrupted this traditional model by enabling creators to reach their audiences directly, without intermediaries. These platforms have provided creators with direct access to global audiences and enabled them to distribute their content in a more democratic and open manner.

For example, YouTube allows anyone to create and distribute videos without going through traditional gatekeepers such as TV networks or film studios. This has enabled new types of content, such as user-generated content, which would not have been possible under the traditional model.

Similarly, Netflix has disrupted the traditional model of movie distribution by bypassing the theatrical release window and releasing movies directly on its platform. This has enabled filmmakers to reach global audiences without going through traditional distribution channels.

Platforms also allow creators and independent artists to showcase their work and reach a global audience, which was previously impossible. They have broken down geographical barriers and created new markets for media and entertainment.

Finally, platforms use data analytics to personalize content recommendations for users, improving the user experience and increasing engagement. They have further enabled new formats and genres of content, such as short-form videos and user-generated content, which have become increasingly popular. Relatedly, platforms have generated new revenue streams, such as advertising, subscriptions, and merchandise sales, leading to more revenue for creators and platform owners.

Business Model Planning **343**

11.4 Business Model Innovation

11.4.1 The Concept of Business Model Innovation

"Business model innovation" refers to creating, changing, or improving how a company creates and delivers value to its customers.[24] It involves exploring new ways to generate revenue, reduce costs, and differentiate from competitors through innovative business models.

Business model innovation is the process of discovering innovative ways to create value and increase profits by reimagining and transforming a company's capabilities and strategies.[25]

Business model innovation can involve changing the different components of a company's business model, such as its value proposition, target customers, distribution channels, revenue streams, and cost structure. It can also involve the combination of existing business models in new and innovative ways to create entirely new sources of value.

Business model innovation is important as it enables companies to stay agile and adapt to evolving markets, disruptive technologies, and emerging competitors. By challenging existing assumptions and exploring novel approaches, companies can discover new avenues for growth and gain a competitive edge. This process allows businesses to identify and seize fresh opportunities, ensuring continued relevance and success in dynamic environments. Examples of business model innovation include the following:

- Apple's introduction of the iPod and iTunes disrupted the traditional music industry by creating a new business model for selling digital music;
- Airbnb's introduction of the sharing economy model enabled homeowners to rent out their spare rooms and apartments to travelers; and
- Tesla's focus on electric vehicles and direct-to-consumer sales disrupted the traditional automotive industry by offering a new business model for sustainable transportation.

11.4.2 The Business Model Innovation Process

Business model innovation aims to strengthen competitive advantage and value creation by implementing cohesive changes to an organization's value proposition and operation model.[26] At the operation model level, the primary focus is on driving profitability and creating value by determining how to deliver the value proposition more effectively. The aim is to make informed decisions on operational aspects, enabling the organization to enhance its competitive position and foster sustainable growth.

Business model innovation is a deliberate process that transforms an existing business model into a novel one. It goes beyond introducing new products or services, although these might be part of the transformation. Various opportunities can be explored in the process of business model innovation. For example, companies can identify untapped customer opportunities with entirely new business models that can reshape the competitive landscape; or they can generate value by creating transformative and innovative business models that effectively, efficiently, and profitably fulfill customers' needs. Successful entry into emerging markets is another way to redesign business models that cater to the unique unmet demands of consumers in those markets.

Unlike other forms of innovation, changing the business model involves altering the fundamental principles that drive the company's operations. Most innovation is typically incremental, such as product innovation incorporating technology enhancements to improve performance or reduce costs. However, business model innovation reinvents the dominant logic of the business, transforming how value is created, delivered, and captured.[27]

The business model innovation process can be broken down into four steps, as follows (Figure 11.5):[28]

- Customer discovery: First, businesses must identify a specific customer segment with a well-defined problem. Businesses should profile customer demographics, psychographics, and behaviors to better understand their customers. They should also clearly articulate the problem their target customers face and define the essential jobs they need to be done.
- Problem and solution fit: This involves developing a solution that the target customers would be willing to pay for, ensuring that it is profitable and sustainable. Companies must create a compelling value proposition, carefully considering the "painkillers" (how they solve customers' primary pain) and "gain creators" (the extra value their solution provides compared to alternatives). Additionally, businesses should analyze the costs associated with implementing their solution and identify any potential unfair advantages they possess.
- Product market fit: As businesses move forward, they should verify the product market fit. This involves understanding the channels through which they can reach their target

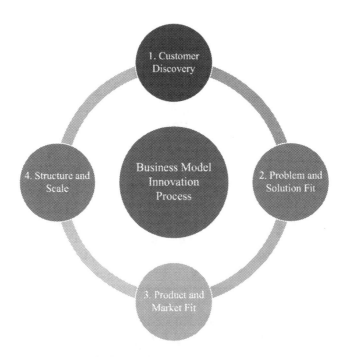

FIGURE 11.5 The Business Model Innovation Process.

customers for both sales and delivery of the solution. Companies should develop effective communication strategies to make their target audience aware of their solution and position their brand strategically compared to competitors. They should consider the overall customer experience, including post-purchase support and retention tactics. Furthermore, businesses should analyze the cost of customer acquisition and the potential lifetime value of each customer.

- Structure and scale: Finally, companies should address the structure and scale of their business model. They should determine the necessary resources—including people, time, and financial investments—required to support and scale their operations. Setting out key processes to streamline their business and ensure efficiency is crucial. Companies should also consider protecting their IP to safeguard their innovative ideas. Identifying potential partners and collaborations that can sustain and contribute to the growth of their business model is essential.

11.4.3 Business Model Innovation Outcomes

Business model innovation can transform how companies deliver value to their customers, creating novel revenue streams or distribution channels. Numerous case studies and examples demonstrate how new entrants have successfully disrupted and outperformed established companies by introducing innovative business models.[29]

Research consistently underscores the advantages of business model innovation, including improved corporate profits, enhanced growth, and increased market share.[30] It also brings about higher operational efficiency, effectiveness, and customer loyalty. Embracing innovative business models allows companies to reduce costs and gain strategic flexibility. Moreover, this approach empowers businesses to swiftly capitalize on emerging market opportunities and foster adaptability and scalability.

11.4.4 Digital Business Model Innovation

"Digital business model innovation" refers to leveraging digital technologies and strategies to transform how a company creates, delivers, and captures value in the digital era.[31]

There are four steps in innovating new digital business models:[32]

- Discovery: This involves identifying new opportunities for digital business models, including by researching emerging technologies, analyzing customer behavior, and identifying unmet needs in the market.
- Development: In this step, the focus is on creating and refining the new digital business model. This may involve developing prototypes, testing different approaches, and refining the value proposition, customer segments, revenue streams, and cost structure.
- Diffusion: Once the new digital business model has been developed, the focus shifts to diffusion. This covers launching the new model and promoting it to target customers. This step may include marketing campaigns, partnerships, and other strategies to build awareness and attract customers.
- Evaluation of impact: The final step is the evaluation of impact, including assessing the effectiveness of the new digital business model and measuring its impact on key metrics such as revenue, profitability, and customer satisfaction.

346 New Business Models and Entrepreneurship

This process is iterative and requires ongoing evaluation and refinement to ensure the new model is successful over the long term. Digital business model innovation allows companies to adapt to changing market dynamics, connect with digitally savvy customers, and unlock new growth opportunities. It requires a willingness to challenge existing norms, embrace digital disruption, and continuously evolve to meet the demands of the digital age.

Case Studies

What Happened to Apple between 2003 and 2007?

Between 2003 and 2007, Apple experienced an extraordinary growth phase: revenues skyrocketed from $6.2 billion to $24.6 billion, while net income surged from $0.2 billion to $3.5 billion. This growth was chiefly driven by the launch of the iPod and the arrival of iTunes in 2003, which revolutionized the digital music arena. By providing a legitimate and user-friendly music purchasing avenue, iTunes successfully countered rampant online piracy. The strategic synchronization of the iPod and iTunes created a profitable ecosystem and yielded more than $10 billion in revenue by 2007. Apple's adept negotiations with major record labels, integration of digital rights management, and introduction of individual track purchases empowered both consumers and musicians. This case exemplifies how an innovative product wrapped in a great business model can reshape industries and redefine consumption behaviors.

More case details for classroom use are available. Please check the book webpage at www.routledge.com/9781032221212 for more information.

HYBE: Business Model Innovation in the Media and Entertainment Industry

HYBE, formerly Big Hit Entertainment, has redefined the K-pop industry through its innovative digital business models. HYBE's ingenious approach spans fan engagement, content distribution, and revenue diversification. Weverse, a fan-centric platform, facilitates direct artist-fan interaction and thus enhances fan experiences. Through pioneering paid online concerts like Bang Bang Con: The Live, HYBE has attracted record-breaking global audiences and proved the viability of virtual performances. Diversifying its revenue streams, HYBE has expanded into merchandising, NFTs, and gaming, such as *Rhythm Hive*. By blending digital content, community-building, and diversified revenue sources, HYBE has shown how strategic innovation can reshape entertainment paradigms and has enhanced K-pop's global influence.

More case details for classroom use are available. Please check the book webpage at www.routledge.com/9781032221212 for more information.

Review

- This chapter examines the importance of the business model as a management concept (11.1). Business models act as a roadmap, linking the value proposition, resources, and processes. They serve as a blueprint for how a company operates, competes, and creates value for its stakeholders.
- Business model components (11.2) include value proposition, customer segments, channels, customer relationships, key resources, key activities, key partnerships, revenue streams, and cost structure. Each component of the business model is integral to the others. The components influence how a company serves its customers and achieves its desired outcomes.
- Business model planning is the structured process of creating a business model (11.3). Key elements of business model planning include value proposition, revenue model, market opportunity, competitive environment, competitive advantage, market strategy, and organizational development. These elements work together to create a comprehensive business model that outlines how the company plans to create value for its customers, generate revenue, and succeed in the market.
- Different types of business models exist based on different objectives, industries, and market conditions (11.4). These models range from the traditional brick-and-mortar type to more recent online business models like portals and platforms. Understanding the different types of business models gives businesses a clearer perspective on which model might be best suited to their strategic objectives and specific circumstances.
- This chapter also discusses the importance of business model innovation in changing market dynamics and technological advancements (11.5). Business model innovation is critical if organizations are to stay competitive, avoid disruption, and unlock new growth opportunities. The chapter explores the business model innovation process, including identifying new opportunities, developing solutions, achieving product-market fit, and scaling operations.

Discussion Questions

1 Why is understanding the concept of a business model crucial for managers and leaders in today's business environment?
2 Discuss the role of each business model component in creating and delivering value to customers.
3 What is the most important element of business model planning in the MEI? Provide examples of media and entertainment companies that have successfully created business models in response to market changes.
4 Discuss the factors a business should consider when choosing a specific business model.
5 Why is business model innovation important? How can companies leverage emerging technologies to innovate their business models?
6 Discuss the phases of digital business model innovation as highlighted in this chapter. Provide an example of a company in the MEI that has successfully transitioned through these phases.

348 New Business Models and Entrepreneurship

Further Reading

- Chesbrough, H. W. (2010) "Business model innovation: Opportunities and barriers." *Long Range Planning*, 43(2/3), pp. 354–363.
- Johnson, M. W., Christensen, C. M. and Kagermann, H. (2008) "Reinventing your business model." *Harvard Business Review*, 86(12), pp. 50–55.
- Kumar, V., (2014) "Making 'freemium' work. *Harvard Business Review*, 92(5), pp. 27–29.
- Magretta, J. (2002) "Why business model matters." *Harvard Business Review*, 80(5), pp. 86–92.
- Osterwalder, A. and Pigneur, Y. (2010) *Business model generation.* Hoboken, NJ: Wiley.
- Sahlman, W. A. (1997) "How to write a great business plan." *Harvard Business Review*, 75(4), pp. 98–108. https://hbr.org/1997/07/how-to-write-a-great-business-plan

References

1 Casadesus-Masanell, R. and Ricart, J. E. (2010) "From strategy to business models and onto tactics." *Long Range Planning*, *43*(2–3), pp. 195–215.
2 "What is a business model? Definition, explanation and 30+ examples you need to know" (no date) *GARY FOX.* www.garyfox.co/what-is-a-business-model/.
3 Voigt, K.-I., Buliga, O. and Michl, K. (2016) "The business model concept." In *Business model pioneers*. Cham, Switzerland: Springer, pp. 7–10. https://link.springer.com/chapter/10.1007/978-3-319-38845-8_2.
4 Kopp, C. M. (2023) "How companies makes money." *Investopedia.* www.investopedia.com/terms/b/businessmodel.asp.
5 Sahlman, W. A. (1997) "How to write a great business plan." *Harvard Business Review*, July–August. https://hbr.org/1997/07/how-to-write-a-great-business-plan.
6 Johnson, M. W., Christensen, C. M., and Kagermann, H. (2008) "Reinventing your business model." *Harvard Business Review*, December. https://hbr.org/2008/12/reinventing-your-business-model.
7 Osterwalder, A. and Pigneur, Y. (2010) *Business model generation: A handbook for visionaries, game changers, and challengers.* New York: Wiley & Sons.
8 Voigt, K.-I., Buliga, O. and Michl, K. (2016) "The business model concept." In *Business model pioneers*. Cham, Switzerland: Springer, pp. 7–10. https://link.springer.com/chapter/10.1007/978-3-319-38845-8_2.
9 Couturier, L. (2022) "8 key elements of a business model that you should understand." *StartUp Mindset.* https://startupmindset.com/8-key-elements-of-a-business-model-that-you-should-understand/.
10 Gu, X., Kannan, P. K. and Ma, L., (2018) "Selling the premium in freemium." *Journal of Marketing,* 82(6), pp. 10–27.
11 Seufert, E. B. (2013) *Freemium economics: Leveraging analytics and user segmentation to drive revenue.* Amsterdam: Elsevier.
12 Kumar, V. (2014) "Making 'freemium' work." *Harvard Business Review*, *92*(5), pp. 27–29.
13 Lieberman, M. B. and Montgomery, D. B. (1988) "First-mover advantages." *Strategic Management Journal*, 9(S1), pp. 41–58.
14 Hoppe, H. C. (2000) "Second-mover advantages in the strategic adoption of new technology under uncertainty." *International Journal of Industrial Organization*, 18(2), pp. 315–338.
15 Friedlander, F. and Brown, L. D. (1974) "Organization development." *Annual Review of Psychology*, 25(1), pp. 313–341.
16 Ouchi, W. G. and Wilkins, A. L. (1985) "Organizational culture." *Annual Review of Sociology*, 11(1), pp. 457–483.

17 Hambrick, D. C. (1987) "The top management team: Key to strategic success." *California Management Review*, 30(1), pp. 88–108.

18 Talke, K., Salomo, S. and Rost, K. (2010) "How top management team diversity affects innovativeness and performance via the strategic choice to focus on innovation fields." *Research Policy*, 39(7), pp. 907–918.

19 Klein, M., Neitzert, F., Hartmann-Wendels, T. and Kraus, S., (2019) "Start-up financing in the digital age: A systematic review and comparison of new forms of financing." *The Journal of Entrepreneurial Finance*, 21(2), pp. 46–98.

20 Vigroux, G. (2022) "Successful entrepreneurship: it's all about timing." *Forbes*, August 8, 2022. www.forbes.com/sites/forbesbusinesscouncil/2022/08/08/successful-entrepreneurship-its-all-about-timing/?sh=f352df5266a3.

21 Hsieh, Y.-J. and Wu, Y.-J. (2019) "Entrepreneurship through the platform strategy in the digital era: Insights and research opportunities." *Computers in Human Behavior*, 95, pp. 315–323.

22 Zhao, Y., Von Delft, S., Morgan-Thomas, A. and Buck, T. (2020) "The evolution of platform business models: Exploring competitive battles in the world of platforms." *Long Range Planning*, 53(4), p. 101892.

23 Gimpel, G. (2015) "The future of video platforms: Key questions shaping the TV and video industry." *International Journal on Media Management*, 17(1), pp. 25–46.

24 Massa, L. and Tucci, C. L. (2013) "Chapter 21: Business model innovation." In M. Dodgson, D. M. Gann, and N. Phillips (eds.) *The Oxford handbook of innovation management*. Oxford, UK: Oxford University Press, pp. 420–441.

25 "What is a business model? definition, explanation and 30+ examples you need to know" (no date) *GARY FOX*. www.garyfox.co/what-is-a-business-model/.

26 Baldassarre, B., Calabretta, G., Bocken, N. M. P. and Jaskiewicz, T. (2017) "Bridging sustainable business model innovation and user-driven innovation: A process for sustainable value proposition design." *Journal of Cleaner Production*, 147, pp. 175–186.

27 Chesbrough, H. (2010) "Business model innovation: opportunities and barriers." *Long Range Planning*, 43(2–3), pp. 354–363.

28 Bortolini, R. F., Nogueira Cortimiglia, M., Danilevicz, A. D. M. F. and Ghezzi, A. (2021) "Lean startup: A comprehensive historical review." *Management Decision*, 59(8), pp. 1765–1783.

29 Guldmann, E. and Huulgaard, R. D. (2020) "Barriers to circular business model innovation: A multiple-case study." *Journal of Cleaner Production*, 243, p. 118160.

30 Zhang, H., Xiao, H., Wang, Y., Shareef, M.A., Akram, M. S. and Goraya, M. A. S. (2021) "An integration of antecedents and outcomes of business model innovation: A meta-analytic review." *Journal of Business Research*, 131, pp. 803–814.

31 Trischler, M. F. G. and Li-Ying, J. (2023) "Digital business model innovation: Toward construct clarity and future research directions." *Review of Managerial Science*, 17(1), pp. 3–32.

32 Fichman, R. G., Dos Santos, B. L. and Zheng, Z. (2014) "Digital innovation as a fundamental and powerful concept in the information systems curriculum." *MIS Quarterly*, 38(2), pp. 329–354, A1–A15.

12

CREATIVE ENTREPRENEURSHIP

Outline

Overview	350
12.1 The Creative Economy and the Creative Industry	351
12.2 Entrepreneurs and Entrepreneurship	355
12.3 Different Types of Entrepreneurship	365
12.4 Creative Entrepreneurship: Theory and Practice	367
Case Studies	371
Review	372
Discussion Questions	373
Further Reading	373
References	373

Intended Learning Outcomes

- Understand the concepts of entrepreneurs and entrepreneurship.
- Explain and compare different types of entrepreneurship.
- Articulate the theories and practices of creative entrepreneurship.

Overview

This chapter explores the dynamics of the creative economy and entrepreneurship:

- The creative economy encompasses economic activities where creativity and intellectual capital are primary inputs, including the arts, music, design, and entertainment. The media and entertainment industry is a crucial part of the creative economy, focused on the creation and distribution of cultural goods and services.

DOI: 10.4324/9781003271222-17

- Entrepreneurship is the process of identifying opportunities, allocating resources, and creating value. This chapter examines the role of entrepreneurs in initiating and managing new ventures, the risks involved, and the unique characteristics and skills needed for successful entrepreneurship. The importance of entrepreneurial contexts and ecosystems is also highlighted.
- Various forms of entrepreneurship exist, including social entrepreneurship, aimed at solving social issues; and digital entrepreneurship, focused on digital platform-based business activities.
- Creative entrepreneurship combines creativity, innovation, and commerce to create new products, services, and business models, particularly in the cultural and creative sectors. This chapter outlines the challenges faced by creative entrepreneurs, such as balancing artistic and commercial values.

12.1 The Creative Economy and the Creative Industry

12.1.1 The Concept of the Creative Economy

The "creative economy" refers to an economic system in which creativity, innovation, and intellectual property (IP) are the key drivers of economic growth and development.[1] It is a concept that has gained popularity in recent years as countries worldwide have recognized the importance of creative industries in generating jobs and driving economic growth.

The main characteristics of the creative economy include the following (Figure 12.1):

- Reliance on creativity and innovation: Creative industries are characterized by their reliance on creativity, innovation, and IP. These industries are driven by the ability of

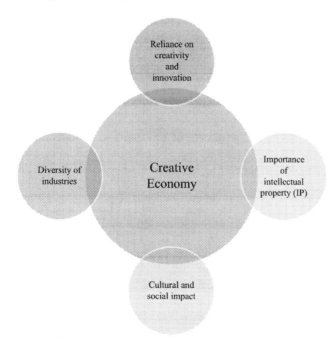

FIGURE 12.1 The Main Characteristics of the Creative Economy.

352 New Business Models and Entrepreneurship

individuals and organizations to create and develop new ideas, products, and services that are unique and valuable.

- Importance of IP: IP is a key asset in the creative economy, allowing businesses and individuals to protect and monetize their creations. It includes trademarks, copyrights, patents, and other forms of IP used to protect and monetize creative works.
- Cultural and social impact: The creative economy has a significant cultural and social impact, as it shapes how people think, feel, and interact with the world around them. Creative industries often reflect and shape cultural norms and values, and can profoundly impact social and political discourse.
- Diversity of industries: The creative economy includes many industries, including art, music, film, fashion, design, architecture, advertising, software development, and more. These industries are often interconnected, with businesses and individuals collaborating across sectors to create new products and services.

12.1.2 Creative Industries

Creative industries encompass various activities, products, services, and production processes, as well as workers and firms with diverse economic status.[2] The United Nations Conference on Trade and Development describes "creative industries" as those which create, produce and distribute products and services through relativity and intellect.[3] The UK Department for Digital, Culture, Media and Sport (DCMS) first categorized the relative industries under the following headings: "Advertising, Antiques, Architecture, Crafts, Design, Fashion, Film, Leisure Software, Music, Performing Arts, Publishing, Software, TV, and Radio."[4] This framework has been widely adopted by policymakers and academics since 1998 as a comprehensive descriptor of the creative industries. Ireland's Western Development Commission subsequently expanded the categorization of the DCMS model.[5] Each creative field is assigned to one or more categories, such as "creative expression," "creative application," and "creative technology" (Figure 12.2).[6]

From an academic viewpoint, the publication in 2000 of Richard Caves' work on creative industries, titled *Creative Industries: Contracts Between Art and Commerce*, was a significant milestone. The book attempts to characterize the specificities of these industries and the way they operate.[7]

In his book, Caves examines the economic and social aspects of industries that rely on creativity and IP, such as music, film, and publishing. He explores how these industries differ from traditional manufacturing industries and identifies several key features of creative industries (Figure 12.3).

One crucial observation highlighted by Caves is the presence of high fixed costs and low variable costs within creative industries. This implies that significant investments are required for the initial production and development of creative goods and services, while subsequent copies or distribution incur minimal expenses. This cost structure presents distinct challenges and opportunities for firms operating in creative sectors.

Furthermore, Caves emphasizes the pervasive presence of uncertainty and risk in creative industries. Given the subjective nature of esthetic preferences and the dynamic nature of consumer demands, predicting market reception and success is inherently challenging. This unpredictability necessitates adaptive strategies and a willingness to take calculated risks in these industries.

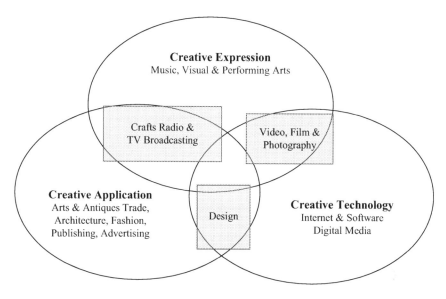

FIGURE 12.2 Categories of Creative Industries.

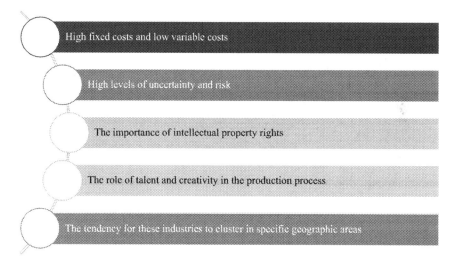

FIGURE 12.3 Key Features of Creative Industries.

IP rights emerge as a critical aspect within creative industries. Protecting and enforcing IP becomes essential to preserve the value of creative works and incentivize ongoing innovation. Securing copyrights, patents, and trademarks enables creators and firms to safeguard their creative outputs and derive economic value from their intellectual assets.

Caves also highlights the central role of talent and creativity in the production process of creative industries. The cultivation and utilization of artistic skills and innovative thinking become pivotal in delivering compelling and original content. The success of creative endeavors often hinges on the ability to harness and nurture talent, making human capital a critical factor.

Moreover, Caves observes a tendency for creative industries to cluster in specific geographical areas. These creative clusters—such as Hollywood for the film industry or Silicon Valley for the tech industry—foster synergies, knowledge spillovers, and collaboration among creative professionals. The concentration of resources and talent in these regions contributes to the vibrancy and dynamism of creative industries.

Caves argues that the traditional economic models used to understand manufacturing and other relevant industries are inadequate for understanding creative industries. He proposes new models that consider the unique characteristics of creative industries, such as the role of subjective preferences and esthetic standards in determining demand.

His work has significantly impacted the study of creative industries and has helped shape public policy and business strategies in these sectors. His ideas continue to be widely discussed and debated in academic and industry circles.

12.1.3 Creative Entrepreneurship in the Creative Economy

Given the characteristics of the creative economy, creative entrepreneurship is a key component of the creative economy, as it involves creating and developing new businesses in creative industries. Creative entrepreneurs are individuals who can identify opportunities in these industries and create innovative products, services, or business models that meet the needs of consumers.[8]

Creative entrepreneurship is critical in driving innovation, fostering new businesses, generating employment opportunities, and contributing to economic growth. It promotes creative and innovative ideas to initiate and expand ventures within creative industries such as art, music, design, film, and fashion. By leveraging their imaginative and enterprising skills in producing and distributing cultural goods and services, creative entrepreneurs play a crucial role in shaping and advancing the creative economy.

Creative entrepreneurs frequently devise fresh business models and approaches that challenge conventional practices. For example, they may leverage digital technologies to create novel music or film distribution channels, or adopt innovative marketing strategies to access untapped audiences. Such entrepreneurial activities pave the way for fresh avenues of growth and innovation within the creative economy.

Beyond its economic implications, creative entrepreneurship also contributes significantly to the cultural vibrancy of societies.[9] Creative entrepreneurs are at the forefront of cultural production, engendering novel forms of art, music, and design that reflect evolving consumer preferences and interests.

The integration of technology and digital platforms empowers creative entrepreneurs to reach a global audience and unlock new business prospects. This trend has catalyzed the emergence of numerous startups within creative industries and the expansion and adaptation of established enterprises in response to shifting market conditions. The utilization of technology enables creative entrepreneurs to transcend geographical boundaries, connect with a broader customer base, and seize opportunities for growth and innovation.

Creative entrepreneurship serves as a catalyst for driving economic progress, infusing vitality into cultural expression, and facilitating the evolution of the creative economy.

12.2 Entrepreneurs and Entrepreneurship

12.2.1 The Concept of Entrepreneurship

To understand the concept of creative entrepreneurship, it is essential first to understand the fundamental notion of entrepreneurship itself. The term "creative" serves as a modifier, refining and enhancing the core concept of entrepreneurship. However, without a clear understanding of entrepreneurship, the addition of creativity alone fails to yield substantial significance.

Entrepreneurship involves identifying new "means-ends relationships" and capitalizing on opportunities by establishing novel organizations to implement innovative ideas.[10] Innovations and fresh ideas are integral components of the entrepreneurial journey. The existing literature on entrepreneurship widely acknowledges that entrepreneurs exhibit distinct behaviors compared to managers.[11] Entrepreneurs establish an organization to exploit entrepreneurial opportunities and simultaneously shoulder the responsibility for its sustained existence. Conversely, managers typically assume the role of planning, organizing, and overseeing the operations of a pre-existing enterprise that is not their creation.

The word "entrepreneurship" has mixed connotations.[12] On the positive side, it signifies a distinctive, inherent ability to perceive and seize opportunities, merging innovative thinking with a singular resolve to conceive or introduce something novel to the world. On the negative side, "entrepreneurship" is an *ex-post* term because it takes time before the true impact of entrepreneurial activities becomes evident.

The history of entrepreneurship is rich and diverse, spanning centuries and continents. The term "entrepreneur" was officially coined by French economist Jean-Baptiste Say in the early 19th century, but the concept and practice of entrepreneurship have a much longer lineage.[13]

One of the earliest manifestations of entrepreneurship can be observed in the medieval guilds of Europe. These guilds were associations of craftsmen who joined forces to protect their trade secrets, ensure a stable supply of raw materials, and maintain quality standards. Many members demonstrated entrepreneurial skills within these guilds and successfully expanded their businesses beyond local boundaries, even venturing into international trade.

The era of exploration and colonization in the 16th and 17th centuries provided fertile ground for entrepreneurial endeavors. Wealthy merchants and investors financed expeditions to discover new trade routes and exploit the abundant resources of the New World. This period saw the rise of ambitious entrepreneurs who sought to profit from the trade in exotic goods, precious metals, and even the transatlantic slave trade.

The Industrial Revolution brought about a significant transformation in the landscape of entrepreneurship. Technological advancements and manufacturing processes revolutionized the production of goods on a mass scale. This era saw the emergence of large corporations and the establishment of new industries, such as textiles, steel, and railways. Entrepreneurs played a pivotal role in driving these industries and capitalizing on the opportunities presented by the changing economic landscape.

In the 20th century, Joseph Schumpeter significantly contributed to our understanding of entrepreneurship.[14] He viewed entrepreneurs as the catalysts of economic progress, driving the "creative-destructive process" of capitalism. Schumpeter believed that entrepreneurs were agents of change who introduced new technologies, products, and business models, revolutionizing industries and opening new markets. He emphasized the crucial role of entrepreneurship in driving innovation and propelling economies forward.

Schumpeter's concept of entrepreneurship highlights its transformative nature, characterized by the identification of commercial opportunities and the establishment of ventures to capitalize on them. Successful entrepreneurship sets in motion a chain reaction, inspiring and encouraging other entrepreneurs to build upon and propagate innovation. This process ultimately leads to "creative destruction," whereby established products, services, and business models become obsolete as the new ventures gain prominence.

While Schumpeter portrays entrepreneurs in heroic terms, his analysis acknowledges their place within a larger economic system. Entrepreneurs are seen as agents of change, capable of both disruptive and generative impacts on the economy. They introduce innovation, challenge existing norms, and play a critical role in shaping the evolution of industries and economies. Understanding the multifaceted nature of entrepreneurship helps us appreciate its historical significance and ongoing relevance in driving economic progress.

Indeed, starting a business is not the essence of entrepreneurship. Though other economists may have used the term with various nuances, the Schumpeter tradition that identifies entrepreneurs as the catalysts and innovators behind economic progress has served as the foundation for the contemporary use of the concept.

Peter Drucker, a renowned management thinker, emphasizes the entrepreneurial mindset as one that seeks and exploits change as an opportunity.[15] Drucker highlights that entrepreneurship goes beyond simply starting a business and extends to recognizing and capitalizing on opportunities for innovation and growth. He argues that not every new venture or organization can be considered entrepreneurial, as true entrepreneurship involves significant change and a commitment to exploiting it.

Drucker also emphasizes that entrepreneurship is not limited to profit-seeking endeavors. He points to examples such as the creation of modern universities and entrepreneurship in public service institutions as forms of innovation and change-oriented endeavors that fall within the scope of entrepreneurship.

In the 20th century, entrepreneurship became increasingly associated with innovation and the creation of new businesses, particularly in emerging fields like technology, biotechnology, and finance. Visionary entrepreneurs like Steve Jobs, Bill Gates, and Elon Musk exemplify the impact of entrepreneurship in new industries.

Howard Stevenson, a prominent entrepreneurship theorist, introduced the concept of resourcefulness as a defining characteristic of entrepreneurial management.[16] He highlights that entrepreneurs pursue opportunities without being constrained by their existing resources, leveraging the resources of others to achieve their objectives. This perspective expands the understanding of entrepreneurship beyond business startups and recognizes the importance of mobilizing resources to seize opportunities.

Entrepreneurship continues to play a critical role in the global economy. Entrepreneurs drive innovation by creating new products, services, and business models that meet evolving market needs. They also generate employment opportunities, contributing to economic growth and prosperity. Governments and businesses recognize the significance of fostering an entrepreneurial ecosystem to cultivate innovation, attract investment, and stimulate economic development.

12.2.2 Entrepreneurial Skills and Characteristics

The term "entrepreneurial skills" is used extensively in academia and business but often refers to different conceptualizations.[17] Entrepreneurship requires unique skills that enable individuals to identify and capitalize on business opportunities, as follows:[18]

- Creativity: Entrepreneurs must be able to generate new ideas and solutions to problems. They must be able to think outside the box and come up with innovative ways to differentiate themselves from their competitors. "Creativity" has been described as developing new methods instead of using standard procedures. In the literature, a distinction can be made between the four main components of creativity.[19]

  - Originality: The ability to produce new and unusual ideas (quality);
  - Fluency: The ability to produce a large number of ideas (quantity);
  - Flexibility: The ability to change between approaches; and
  - Elaboration: The ability to develop the amount of detail associated with the ideas.

- Risk-taking: Entrepreneurship involves taking risks and making decisions without complete information. Successful entrepreneurs are willing to take calculated risks and have the confidence to pursue their goals despite uncertainty. Risk-taking, in essence, involves acknowledging the prospect of an unsuccessful outcome of an endeavor that is usually associated with some negative implications.
- Problem-solving: This is an individual's capacity to engage in cognitive processing to understand and resolve problems where a solution is not immediately apparent. It includes the willingness to engage in such situations to achieve one's potential as a constructive and reflective citizen.
- Collaboration: This involves two or more people working together to achieve the same thing. People engaged in collaboration capitalize on one another's resources and skills (e.g., asking one another for information, evaluating one another's ideas, monitoring one another's work). Elements of collaboration emphasize the development of social skills to solve problems, innovate, manage emotions, and communicate.
- Persistence: Entrepreneurship can be a long and arduous journey. Setbacks and failures are inevitable. Successful entrepreneurs are resilient and persistent, are willing to learn from their mistakes, and keep pushing forward even when the going gets tough.
- Adaptability: The business environment constantly changes, and entrepreneurs must adapt to new challenges and opportunities. They must be flexible and able to pivot quickly to stay ahead of the curve.
- Leadership: Entrepreneurs must be able to inspire and motivate their teams to work toward a common goal. They need to communicate effectively, delegate tasks, and make difficult decisions when necessary.
- Financial management: Successful entrepreneurs need a solid understanding of financial management, including budgeting, forecasting, and cash-flow management. They must make sound financial decisions to support their businesses' growth and sustainability.
- Networking: Entrepreneurs must forge relationships with clients, suppliers, and relevant parties. Harnessing opportunities for teamwork and strategic alliances can catalyze business growth.

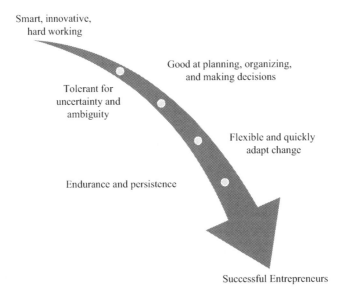

FIGURE 12.4 Common Traits of Successful Entrepreneurs.

- Time management: The entrepreneurial journey entails multitasking and balancing various obligations with scarce resources. Those who succeed are proficient at time management and prioritization, and know when to delegate duties to concentrate on high-priority objectives.

Successful entrepreneurs also possess common traits that contribute to their achievements (Figure 12.4).[20] These characteristics enable them to navigate challenges, seize opportunities, and create lasting impact in their respective fields. By examining these traits, we can gain insights into the qualities that set entrepreneurs apart.

First, successful entrepreneurs demonstrate intelligence and bring innovation to their industries. They can generate fresh ideas, challenge conventional thinking, and identify untapped opportunities. Their creative thinking and problem-solving skills enable them to develop ground-breaking products, services, and business models that disrupt the status quo.

Entrepreneurs also have exceptional planning, organizational, and decision-making skills. They have the foresight to set clear objectives, devise strategies, and allocate resources effectively. Through meticulous planning, they can navigate complexities, manage risks, and optimize outcomes. Moreover, their decisive nature allows them to make informed choices in uncertain scenarios, embracing calculated risks and adapting swiftly to changing circumstances.

Flexibility is another key trait possessed by successful entrepreneurs. They quickly adapt to new market trends, technological advancements, and evolving customer preferences. While remaining steadfast in their vision, they are open to feedback and willing to adjust their strategies to stay ahead of the curve. Simultaneously, entrepreneurs are known for their strong work ethic, dedicating themselves to their ventures and displaying resilience in the face of challenges.

Finally, successful entrepreneurs blend prudence, courage, hope, and faith in their actions. They carefully assess risks and take calculated steps, while displaying the courage to venture into uncharted territories. They maintain a sense of hope and optimism, even in the face of adversity, which fuels their determination and resilience. By combining prudence with a steadfast belief in their vision, entrepreneurs navigate challenges and persistently work toward realizing their aspirations.

12.2.3 Entrepreneurial Context and Ecosystems

The Entrepreneurial Context

The starting point for entrepreneurship, "entrepreneurial context" refers to the environment or circumstances in which an entrepreneur operates, including economic, social, cultural, and political factors that influence the opportunities and challenges they face.[21] For example, entrepreneurs in developed countries may have access to more resources, infrastructure, and support systems than those in developing countries. Entrepreneurs in high-tech industries may face different challenges and opportunities than those in traditional industries like agriculture or manufacturing.

Economic factors play a crucial role in the entrepreneurial context. These include the overall economic conditions of a country or region, such as gross domestic product growth, inflation rates, and availability of capital. Developed countries often provide entrepreneurs with a more favorable economic context, offering robust infrastructure, financial resources, and support systems. Conversely, entrepreneurs in developing countries may face limited access to capital, market size, and technological resources.

Social and cultural factors also contribute to the entrepreneurial context. Cultural attitudes toward entrepreneurship, risk-taking, and innovation can significantly impact the opportunities available to entrepreneurs. Societal support for entrepreneurial ventures, the level of acceptance of failure, and the prevalence of role models and mentors all shape the environment in which entrepreneurs operate.

Political factors, including government policies and regulatory frameworks, are key elements of the entrepreneurial context. Entrepreneur-friendly policies such as tax incentives, streamlined business registration processes, and IP protection can attract and support entrepreneurial activity. Conversely, excessive regulations, bureaucratic hurdles, and unstable political climates can pose significant challenges to entrepreneurs.

The entrepreneurial context is further influenced by industry-specific factors. Different industries have unique characteristics and dynamics that affect opportunities and challenges for entrepreneurs. High-tech industries, for example, may offer greater potential for innovation and scalability, but they also come with rapid technological advancements and fierce competition. On the other hand, traditional industries may provide more stable markets but require innovative approaches to stand out among established players.

Moreover, the competitive landscape, the availability of skilled labor, and market demand are additional components of the entrepreneurial context. Understanding the existing competition and the demand for products or services is crucial to identify market opportunities. Access to a skilled workforce and talent pool is essential for the success of entrepreneurial ventures, as it enables the realization of innovative ideas and effective business operations.

360 New Business Models and Entrepreneurship

Entrepreneurial Ecosystems

Entrepreneurial ecosystems have emerged as a powerful framework for understanding the complex and interconnected factors that foster entrepreneurial activity and promote economic growth. An entrepreneurial ecosystem encompasses the people, organizations, institutions, and resources within a specific geographical region or industry that collectively support and nurture entrepreneurship.[22]

At the heart of any entrepreneurial ecosystem are its people: the entrepreneurs themselves. These individuals have the drive, vision, and determination to create and grow innovative ventures. However, an entrepreneurial ecosystem goes beyond individual entrepreneurs. It recognizes the importance of the broader network of actors involved in the entrepreneurial process, including investors, mentors, educators, policymakers, and support organizations.

One critical characteristic of a thriving entrepreneurial ecosystem is a culture of trust and collaboration. Trust enables entrepreneurs and other ecosystem participants to interact, exchange ideas, and build relationships. Collaboration fosters the sharing of knowledge, resources, and experiences, leading to the creation of new opportunities and the acceleration of innovation.

A robust entrepreneurial ecosystem facilitates the seamless flow of talent, information, and resources. Entrepreneurs can readily access the skills and expertise they need at each stage of the development of their venture—whether technical expertise, business acumen, or marketing insights. Furthermore, information flows freely within the ecosystem, informing entrepreneurs about market trends, emerging technologies, and potential opportunities. Access to resources such as capital, infrastructure, and support services is crucial for entrepreneurs to overcome barriers and successfully navigate their entrepreneurial journeys.

By leveraging the interconnectedness and interdependence within the ecosystem, entrepreneurs can tap into a vast network of opportunities and leverage its collective knowledge and resources. This network effect creates synergies whereby the whole is greater than the sum of its parts. It enables entrepreneurs to achieve outcomes that would be challenging or impossible to accomplish in isolation.

Entrepreneurial ecosystems are not confined to specific geographical boundaries; they can exist at different levels, from local to regional to national and even global. Some ecosystems are industry-specific, focusing on particular sectors such as technology, biotech, or creative. Regardless of their scope, entrepreneurial ecosystems play a pivotal role in driving economic growth, innovation, and job creation.

Policymakers and stakeholders recognize the significance of entrepreneurial ecosystems and actively work to cultivate and strengthen them. They strive to create an enabling environment that supports entrepreneurship through policies and regulations that encourage innovation, attract investment, and promote entrepreneurship education and training. Additionally, they foster collaboration among various ecosystem stakeholders by establishing networks, incubators, accelerators, and other support mechanisms.

Daniel Isenberg, the founding executive director of the Babson Entrepreneurship Ecosystem Project at Babson College, has developed a framework for understanding entrepreneurial ecosystems, which includes the following key components (Figure 12.5):[23]

Creative Entrepreneurship **361**

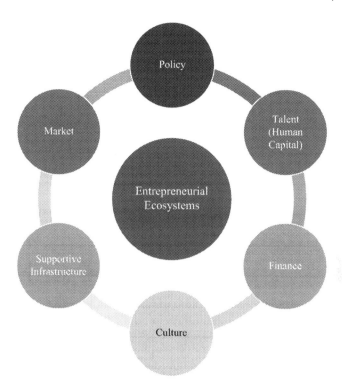

FIGURE 12.5 Entrepreneurial Ecosystems.

- Talent (or human capital): The talent component of an entrepreneurial ecosystem comprises the skills, knowledge, and expertise of the people who live and work within it. These include entrepreneurs, investors, educators, and other professionals who support the development of new businesses.
- Culture: This refers to the values, attitudes, and beliefs of the people who live and work within the entrepreneurial ecosystem. A culture of entrepreneurship is critical to the success of an ecosystem, as it encourages risk-taking, innovation, and the pursuit of opportunity.
- Finance: This comprises the financial resources available to entrepreneurs in an ecosystem, including seed funding, venture capital, and other investment forms. Access to capital is essential for entrepreneurs to launch and scale their businesses.
- Supportive infrastructure: This includes the physical and institutional structures needed to support entrepreneurship, such as incubators, accelerators, co-working spaces, and regulatory frameworks.
- Market: This is the demand side of entrepreneurship. A vibrant market with diverse customer segments and opportunities for growth is essential for entrepreneurial success. Market conditions such as consumer preferences, purchasing power, industry trends, and competition significantly influence the viability and scalability of entrepreneurial ventures.
- Policy: Policies and regulations established by governments at various levels significantly impact the entrepreneurial ecosystem. Supportive policies can create a conducive

362 New Business Models and Entrepreneurship

environment for entrepreneurship by reducing barriers to entry, providing tax incentives, offering funding opportunities, and promoting innovation. Government initiatives to improve education and skills development, protect IP rights, and streamline business regulations are examples of policies that can positively influence entrepreneurship.

A solid entrepreneurial ecosystem requires all of these components to be in place and to work together in a coordinated way. When these components are effectively aligned, they can create a virtuous cycle of entrepreneurship, whereby the success of one entrepreneur attracts more talent, capital, and support to the ecosystem, leading to even more entrepreneurship and innovation.

12.2.4 Entrepreneurial Outcomes

Entrepreneurial outcomes are the consequences of an entrepreneurial activity. There are several dimensions and types of entrepreneurial outcomes that can be measured and evaluated (Figure 12.6):

- Entrepreneurship can have personal impacts on the entrepreneurs themselves. These encompass psychological and social factors such as increased self-esteem, greater autonomy, and psychological resilience.[24] Entrepreneurship offers individuals greater control over their work and decisions, leading to a sense of autonomy. This autonomy can contribute to increased job satisfaction and overall wellbeing. It also provides a sense of personal fulfillment and satisfaction by allowing individuals to pursue their passions, create something meaningful, and make a difference in the world.[25] Entrepreneurs navigate their entrepreneurial journey through setbacks, failures, and uncertainties, developing psychological resilience and the ability to bounce back from adversity.[26]
- Entrepreneurship significantly impacts economic outcomes at various levels, from individual businesses to national economies.[27] Successful entrepreneurs who build scalable businesses accumulate substantial wealth through the growth and value of their enterprises. Entrepreneurship provides opportunities for individuals to generate income and improve their living standards. Relatedly, one of the primary economic outcomes of entrepreneurship is job creation. Entrepreneurs often start and grow businesses, leading to the employment of workers. Entrepreneurship plays a vital role in local and regional development by establishing businesses and attracting investments. Silicon Valley is a renowned example of entrepreneurship fostering regional development, driving technological innovation, and attracting talent and capital.[28]
- Innovation is a key driver of entrepreneurial success, and measuring innovation outcomes helps assess the extent to which entrepreneurial ventures contribute to advancements in products, services, and business models.[29] Entrepreneurs identify unmet needs or gaps in existing offerings and create innovative solutions. They also leverage emerging technologies to develop innovative products, processes, or business models. Entrepreneurship often disrupts traditional business models by introducing innovative approaches that challenge established norms and create new market opportunities. Disruptive business models redefine industry dynamics and can lead

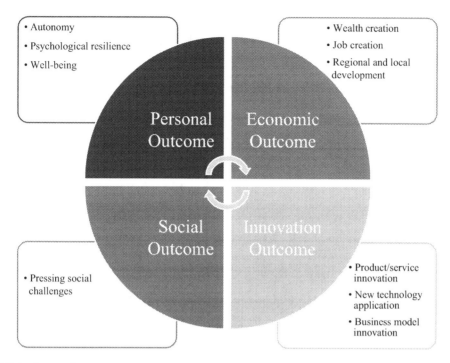

FIGURE 12.6 The Dimensions of Entrepreneurial Outcomes.

to significant changes in consumer behavior. For example, Netflix disrupted the home video industry by introducing a subscription-based streaming model, fundamentally changing how people consume entertainment at home.
- Finally, entrepreneurship can profoundly impact society, leading to social outcomes such as social innovation and environmental sustainability. These outcomes highlight the broader societal benefits generated by entrepreneurial ventures. Entrepreneurs can address pressing social challenges through innovative solutions. Social entrepreneurship, in particular, focuses on creating businesses that primarily aim to generate positive social or environmental impact.[30] These ventures tackle issues such as poverty, education, healthcare, and sustainability. They can improve access to essential goods and services in underserved or marginalized communities, promote renewable energy solutions, implement resource-efficient processes, and create businesses focused on environmental conservation.

12.2.5 Design Thinking and Entrepreneurship

Design thinking is a valuable approach to entrepreneurship, offering a systematic and human-centered way to address complex problems, uncover new opportunities, and foster innovation. Tim Brown, chief executive officer of IDEO, invented the concept and defines "design thinking" as a "human-centered and collaborative approach to problem-solving, using a design mindset to solve complex problems."[31] It goes beyond the traditional boundaries of design studios, finding applications in various domains, including business management, digital interactions, services, and social policy.

At its core, design thinking emphasizes understanding the human needs behind a product, method, process, or service. This customer-centric perspective is essential for entrepreneurs that wish to generate bold and innovative ideas. Entrepreneurs can create offerings that effectively meet the needs of target customers by deeply understanding them and their requirements. This approach allows entrepreneurs to view their business from the customer's perspective, enabling them to identify desires, discover unmet needs, and generate ideas that address them.[32]

The design thinking process typically consists of five essential steps, blending creative thinking, logical reasoning, and iterative testing to drive innovation.[33] These steps help entrepreneurs connect with customers, refine their offerings, and drive business growth. The key steps of the design thinking process are as follows (Figure 12.7):

- Observe and empathize: This initial step involves keen observation and an empathetic understanding of people's behaviors, wants, and needs. Entrepreneurs can gain deep insights into customers' challenges and aspirations by immersing themselves in their world. Through empathy, entrepreneurs develop a genuine connection with customers, which forms the foundation for meaningful problem-solving.
- Define the problem: After gathering information and insights, entrepreneurs reflect on these observations and identify the core problem they are seeking to address. By clustering and synthesizing the gathered data, they can distill the most significant problem to focus on. The emphasis is on framing the problem from a human-centered perspective, ensuring that it aligns with the needs and desires of the target customers.
- Ideate solutions: This phase encourages entrepreneurs to think creatively and generate various possible solutions. Brainstorming and ideation sessions allow for free-flowing creativity without judgment. Quantity is valued over quality at this stage, as it allows for the exploration of novel and unconventional ideas. The goal is to push boundaries and generate diverse potential solutions to the defined problem.
- Prototype: In this stage, entrepreneurs transform their selected ideas into tangible prototypes or representations of their solutions. Prototypes can be physical or digital, providing a means of visualizing the concept and communicating it to others. Through prototyping, entrepreneurs can gather feedback, test assumptions, and refine their ideas. The iterative nature of prototyping allows for continuous improvement and optimization of the solution.
- Test: The final step involves testing the prototypes with the target audience to gather valuable feedback and insights. By engaging users in the evaluation process, entrepreneurs can gauge the effectiveness of their solutions and make necessary adjustments. User feedback drives further refinement and ensures that the final product or service meets users' needs and expectations.

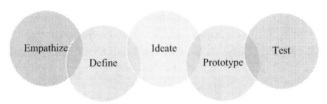

FIGURE 12.7 The Design Thinking Process.

Successful entrepreneurs leverage design thinking principles to drive growth and achieve their long-term goals. They combine novel ideas that address an unmet need or challenge and bring value to a large total addressable market. More importantly, they recognize that applying design thinking is not a "once-and-done" exercise, but rather a mindset that will position them for long-term success. Beyond the tools and techniques of design thinking is a passionate focus on human-centered design—a mindset that is inherent to successful entrepreneurs.[34]

12.3 Different Types of Entrepreneurship

12.3.1 Social Entrepreneurship

Social entrepreneurship encompasses distinct behaviors and characteristics crucial for driving social change and creating sustainable impact.[35] While not everyone is suited to social entrepreneurship, those with the necessary capabilities and temperament can play a transformative role in addressing societal challenges. It is important to recognize and encourage these exceptional individuals dedicated to creating positive social value.

In contrast to traditional entrepreneurship, social entrepreneurship requires a substitute for market discipline since the same mechanisms may not effectively address social issues. Therefore, any definition of "social entrepreneurship" should emphasize discipline, accountability, and value creation.

The following definition encapsulates the essence of social entrepreneurship.[36] "Social entrepreneurship" involves:

- adopting a mission that prioritizes creating and sustaining social value rather than solely focusing on private gain;
- identifying and pursuing new opportunities to advance that mission, continually seeking innovative ways to address social needs;
- engaging in a continuous process of adaptation, learning, and innovation, recognizing that the social landscape is dynamic and complex;
- taking bold and courageous actions, despite limited resources, to drive meaningful change and make a lasting impact; and
- demonstrating heightened accountability to the communities and stakeholders served, ensuring that outcomes align with the mission and deliver tangible benefits.

At the heart of social entrepreneurship lies a mission to create and sustain social value, which sets it apart from traditional business entrepreneurship and socially responsible businesses.[37] For social entrepreneurs, the social mission serves as the fundamental driving force. Unlike businesses that are solely focused on generating financial returns or satisfying consumer desires, social entrepreneurs prioritize social improvement as their primary goal.

While social entrepreneurs may incorporate profit-making and wealth creation into their models, these aspects are viewed as a means to achieve their social objectives rather than the end goal itself. Instead of measuring success solely by financial gains or customer satisfaction, social entrepreneurs gauge their impact by the extent of social transformation they bring about. They prioritize long-term social return on investment, seeking to create lasting societal improvements.

366 New Business Models and Entrepreneurship

In essence, social entrepreneurs are driven by a deep sense of purpose and a commitment to improving society. Their focus on creating and sustaining social value sets them apart, as they recognize that true success lies in the lasting impact they create rather than the mere satisfaction of immediate demands. By prioritizing social impact over financial gain, social entrepreneurs contribute to the wellbeing of communities and drive positive change in the world.

The recognition and relentless pursuit of new opportunities is another key characteristic of social entrepreneurs. They are uniquely able to perceive potential where others see challenges or problems. Their motivation goes beyond mere awareness of social needs or a sense of compassion. Instead, they have a clear vision of how to bring about improvement and are unwavering in their commitment to realizing that vision. Social entrepreneurs exhibit remarkable persistence in the face of obstacles and setbacks.

Embracing innovation also means accepting the inherent uncertainty and potential for failure that comes with it. Social entrepreneurs exhibit a high tolerance of ambiguity and are skilled in managing risks both for themselves and for others involved in their initiatives. They view the failure of a project not as a personal tragedy but as a valuable learning experience. Social entrepreneurs understand that failure can provide valuable insights and serve as a catalyst for future success. By treating failures as opportunities for growth and learning, they continually refine their approaches and increase their chances of making a lasting social impact.

In their resource strategies, social entrepreneurs explore various options, going beyond traditional philanthropy to embrace innovative approaches from the business sector.[38] They are not bound by sector norms or traditions and are willing to experiment with various resource models that align with and reinforce their social missions. These may include sustainable revenue models, social impact investing, or creative financing arrangements.

Moreover, ensuring the harmonious alignment of investor values and community needs is critical to the challenge. Social entrepreneurs strive to develop feedback mechanisms that reflect market dynamics, ensuring ongoing accountability and responsiveness to all stakeholders' expectations. They carefully assess their progress based on a comprehensive range of outcomes, including social impact, financial sustainability, and effective management practices. Instead of solely focusing on size, outputs, or processes, they emphasize the overall results and the extent to which they have tangibly improved the lives of their beneficiaries and the communities they serve.

Social entrepreneurs are change agents who drive reform and innovation in the social sector. They confront the root causes of social problems, pursue systemic changes, and aspire to create sustainable improvements that have the potential to impact society at large.

12.3.2 Digital Entrepreneurship

Digital entrepreneurship has emerged as a significant phenomenon facilitated by technological advancements—particularly the internet and information and communication technology. Business models have tilted dramatically toward entire digital environments. In addition to the new businesses created through the opportunities of digitalization, existing businesses have shifted from offline to online, establishing digital entrepreneurship as a novel form of entrepreneurial activity.[39] This encompasses entrepreneurial activities that involve the transfer of assets, services, or essential business components to the digital realm. This shift toward digital platforms encapsulates the essence of digital entrepreneurship.[40]

Various business models have emerged to cater to diverse market demands and capitalize on the unique advantages of digital platforms.[41] These include e-commerce ventures for online buying and selling; platform-based ventures, which enable different types of users to connect and facilitate transactions between them; software ventures, which focus on the development and marketing of digital applications; digital content and media ventures, centered on the creation and distribution of digital content; digital marketing ventures, which specialize in leveraging digital channels for promotional activities; and data analytics ventures, which harness the power of data-informed decision-making.

Central to digital entrepreneurship is the use of digital infrastructure and tools to pursue entrepreneurial opportunities. Digitalization has enabled businesses to digitize their assets, services, or core elements. This expansion of entrepreneurship into the digital domain represents a departure from traditional notions of entrepreneurship and encompasses a diverse and ever-evolving set of participants.

Digital entrepreneurs differ from their non-digital counterparts in various ways.[42] One key differentiating factor lies in their products, as digital entrepreneurs often provide intangible goods or digital solutions such as software applications, online services, or digital content. Additionally, their marketing activities differ, with digital entrepreneurs leveraging digital marketing strategies, social media platforms, and online advertising to reach their target audience. Furthermore, the digital nature of their ventures influences their workplaces: digital entrepreneurs often operate in virtual environments, leveraging remote work, online collaboration tools, and cloud-based systems to facilitate their operations. This departure from traditional brick-and-mortar establishments allows for flexibility, global reach, and scalability in their business models. This implies that digital entrepreneurs require both technical proficiency and business acumen—dual expertise that is not always readily available.

The relentless advancement of technology and the ever-changing landscape of the digital economy have sparked multiple iterations and transformations in the digital entrepreneurial process. Consequently, digital entrepreneurs face increasingly dynamic trajectories characterized by many activities that unfold within uncertain timeframes.[43]

12.4 Creative Entrepreneurship: Theory and Practice

12.4.1 Creative Entrepreneurship and Creative Entrepreneurs

"Creative entrepreneurship" is the practice of entrepreneurship in a creative industry.[44] It can be defined as creating or identifying an opportunity to provide a cultural product, service or experience, and bringing together the necessary resources to exploit this as an enterprise.[45] Creative entrepreneurs work in social, political, economic and artistic discourse.[46] There are various perspectives on the concept of creative entrepreneurs in the ongoing discussion surrounding the creative economy. These definitions may vary, but they all share a common focus on economic endeavors that cover the production of goods and services imbued with esthetic and symbolic value.[47] They confront substantial

368 New Business Models and Entrepreneurship

challenges in reconciling artistic and commercial ends, commercializing creative and cultural processes, and accessing the market.[48]

Creative entrepreneurship and traditional entrepreneurship share many similarities, but there are also several unique characteristics that set them apart.[49] First, creative entrepreneurship involves creating and promoting artistic or cultural products or experiences, such as music, film, design, or fashion. It is often driven by a desire to express oneself creatively and to create products or experiences that reflect the entrepreneur's unique vision or values. This means that creative entrepreneurs must have a deep understanding of the arts and cultural industries, and the ability to navigate the unique challenges of these fields.

Second, the boundaries between work and personal life are more fluid in creative entrepreneurship. Creative entrepreneurs may be passionate about their work and struggle to switch off from their creative pursuits. Creative entrepreneurs may be more willing to take risks or pursue unconventional ideas, even if they are not guaranteed commercial success. This can make it challenging to maintain a healthy work-life balance and may require creative entrepreneurs to find ways to integrate their interests and values into their business activities.

Thus, creative entrepreneurship involves a connection between entrepreneurial and creative skills. One must mediate between the complex creation process and exploitation of the commercial potential of cultural goods and services. The hardest challenge that a creative entrepreneur may face is managing the business at both levels: financial and creative.[50] Creative entrepreneurs must undertake a range of entrepreneurial tasks in a similar way to traditional entrepreneurs, including generating innovative ideas, identifying target markets, promoting their products or services, and recruiting talented individuals.

Moreover, to capture the interest of investors, creative entrepreneurs must exhibit a genuine commitment to establishing and growing their ventures. They must emphasize how the unique value of their creative content affords a competitive edge in the market. Additionally, the adoption of effective management practices is essential to ensure the long-term viability and success of their endeavors.

Finally, the contribution of creative entrepreneurship toward social innovation and inclusion is evident, as it creates sociocultural values and stimulates economic diversification.[51] The growing prominence of creative entrepreneurship in the economy reflects the changing dynamics of the workforce, the decline in traditional full-time employment and industry restructuring.

12.4.2 The Characteristics of Creative Entrepreneurs

Like any other entrepreneur, a successful creative entrepreneur must be willing to take risks, seize opportunities, and innovate to generate revenue. However, the main difference between creative entrepreneurs and traditional entrepreneurs is that the former prioritize self-fulfillment and personal expression over making money.[52]

Creative entrepreneurs prioritize ideas over data, akin to artists. What sets them apart from artists is their ability to recognize the value of ideas and methodologies, transforming them into culturally significant products or services. While their primary objective is to disseminate and promote culture, they also aim to generate profits through entrepreneurial principles which guide their organizational and managerial practices. Creative entrepreneurs encompass various roles, including creative service providers, creative content producers, creative experience providers, and innovative creators.

Creative entrepreneurs distinguish themselves by emphasizing ideation and applying entrepreneurial principles to leverage their creative endeavors. They share a common goal of nurturing and disseminating culture while also recognizing the economic potential of their activities. Unlike traditional artists, creative entrepreneurs actively seek to translate their ideas into tangible products or services that hold cultural significance and resonate with their target audience. Their entrepreneurial mindset guides them in organizing, managing, and monetizing their creative pursuits, ensuring their artistic endeavors align with cultural and commercial objectives.

There are three categories of competencies a creative entrepreneur must possess—besides personality factors like intrinsic motivation or decision-making capacities—to succeed (Figure 12.8):[53]

- Cultural competency: A vital component for creative entrepreneurs, this requires a deep understanding of the cultural context in which they operate. It includes possessing general knowledge and experience in the field of arts, such as understanding different art forms, historical and contemporary artistic movements, and cultural trends. For example, a creative entrepreneur in the music industry should have a comprehensive understanding of various music genres, industry trends, and audience preferences.
- Social competency: This plays a significant role in the success of creative entrepreneurs. It involves interpersonal skills such as empathy, effective communication, and the ability to build and maintain relationships with partners, collaborators, and employees. Creative entrepreneurs must be adept at working collaboratively with others, leading teams, and inspiring creativity within their networks. Strong social skills enable them to form connections, engage with stakeholders, and navigate the complex dynamics of the creative industry. For example, a fashion designer launching a clothing line must possess social competency to develop essential networks with fashion influencers, collaborate with suppliers and manufacturers, and build a loyal customer base.
- Business competency: Equally important for creative entrepreneurs, this encompasses a range of skills and knowledge related to marketing, sales, and managerial practices.

FIGURE 12.8 Three Key Competencies for Creative Entrepreneurs.

Creative entrepreneurs must understand effective marketing strategies to promote their products or services and reach their target audience. They should also possess sales skills to negotiate deals, secure partnerships, and generate revenue. Additionally, managerial skills are crucial for organizing and overseeing the operations of their creative ventures, ensuring efficient resource allocation, and fostering a productive work environment.

12.4.3 Types of Creative Entrepreneurs

There are four types of creative entrepreneurs, shedding light on the diverse approaches and characteristics of this unique group (Figure 12.9):[54]

- Creative constructionists: These are entrepreneurs who develop innovative ideas and create novel products or services. They are driven by a passion for exploration and experimentation, often pushing the boundaries of traditional artistic or creative practices. They may create tangible goods to sell to their audience, such as housewares, clothing, jewelry, paintings, or perfume.
- Creative opportunists: These are entrepreneurs who identify and seize opportunities in the creative industry. They are keenly aware of trends, consumer demands, and market gaps. These entrepreneurs quickly adapt and capitalize on emerging opportunities, leveraging their creativity to meet market needs and generate value. They create value by performing as curators. They collect and arrange creative products and find the balance between buying products and selling them to customers.
- Creative designers: These are entrepreneurs who excel in the esthetics and visual aspects of their creative endeavors. They possess a deep understanding of design principles, form, and function. These entrepreneurs often work in fields such as graphic design, web design, copywriting, photography, video production, and illustration, where their ability to create visually appealing and functional products is highly valued. Frequently, they leverage their creative skills for an hourly rate or on a per-project basis. They find clients online and in real life, and offer solutions to help grow other people's businesses and organizations.

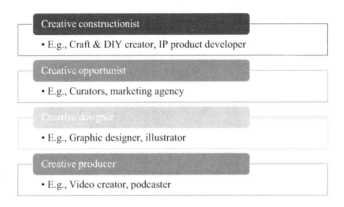

FIGURE 12.9 Types of Creative Entrepreneurs.

Creative Entrepreneurship **371**

- Creative producers: These are entrepreneurs who produce and distribute creative content. They have strong business acumen and the skills to manage the production process, coordinate resources, and effectively market and distribute their creative works. They may use various media, such as podcasts, videos, and web series. They produce engaging content that captivates their audience. Others use information to teach their followers—for example, a video of a new skill like how to cook a unique dish or a tutorial on how to grow an aspect of their business. They use a combination of blog posts, podcasts, and videos, giving away free content to build interest, authority, and trust. After building a solid relationship with their audience, they sell e-books, courses, and workshops to generate revenue.

Case Studies

Etsy: An Open Marketplace for Creative Entrepreneurs

Founded in 2005, Etsy has emerged as a leading online marketplace for handmade and vintage items, catering to 5 million creative entrepreneurs. Sellers can establish personalized shops, utilizing listing and transaction fees alongside useful analytics and marketing tools. Prioritizing sustainability and ethical production, Etsy empowers independent artists and makers to connect globally. Although its expansion into scaled manufacturing has sparked debate, Etsy remains a symbol of the maker movement and champions small businesses by nurturing creative entrepreneurship.

More case details for classroom use are available. Please check the book webpage at www.routledge.com/9781032221212 for more information.

Bilibili: A Community-driven Video Platform built on Professional User-Generated Content

Bilibili—a major Chinese video platform—is a hub for *anime*, comics, and games (ACG) culture with over 200 million users. It is renowned for professional user-generated content: high-quality user-made content akin to traditional media. ACG enthusiasts gather to share *anime*, *manga*, and gaming-related content, creating an interactive community through comments and live streams. The platform empowers creators with tools for crafting premium content and monetization. As Bilibili expands globally, its vibrant ACG-focused community continues to attract users from China and beyond.

More case details for classroom use are available. Please check the book webpage at www.routledge.com/9781032221212 for more information.

---

372 New Business Models and Entrepreneurship

Patreon: Subscription-Based Crowdfunding for Creators

Patreon, established in 2013 by musician Jack Conte and software developer Sam Yam, is a subscription-based crowdfunding platform that empowers creative entrepreneurs. As of late 2023, Patreon had attracted over 250,000 creators and 8 million patrons. It has helped creators to earn $3.5 billion in total since its launch in 2013. Creators provide exclusive content to patrons who pledge monthly support. Patreon's service fee (5% to 12%) is deducted from each pledge. This model grants creators autonomy, a direct fan connection, and a sustainable income stream that surpasses traditional funding avenues. Through its innovation, Patreon is revolutionizing creative entrepreneurship and enabling artists to flourish by fostering fan engagement and financial stability.

More case details for classroom use are available. Please check the book webpage at www.routledge.com/9781032221212 for more information.

Review

- This chapter begins by defining the concept of the creative economy and the creative industry (12.1). The creative economy encompasses all economic activities related to producing and distributing goods and services that use creativity and intellectual capital as primary inputs. It includes the arts, music, design, and entertainment sectors. These foster innovation and drive economic growth in developed and developing economies. The creative industry is a key component of the creative economy, which creates and distributes cultural goods and services.
- The role of the entrepreneur and the concept of entrepreneurship are discussed (12.2). "Entrepreneurship" is the process of identifying opportunities, allocating resources, and creating value. Entrepreneurs initiate, organize, and manage new business ventures, taking on risks and hoping for desired outcomes. Entrepreneurship requires unique characteristics and skills that enable individuals to identify and capitalize on business opportunities. Entrepreneurial context and ecosystems are important in promoting entrepreneurship in a region or a society.
- Different types of entrepreneurship are analyzed, encompassing multifaceted fields (12.3). They include social entrepreneurship, which seeks to solve social issues; and digital entrepreneurship, which involves business activities on digital platforms.
- The next section elaborates on the theory and practices of creative entrepreneurship (12.4). This unique form of entrepreneurship bridges creativity, innovation, and commerce to create novel products, services, or business models. Creative entrepreneurs operate in cultural and creative sectors, bringing artistic and innovative ideas to market and generating cultural, social, and economic value. They face unique challenges, like reconciling artistic value with commercial viability.
- The chapter provides practical examples of creative entrepreneurship, with case studies on popular platforms such as Etsy, Bilibili, and Patreon (12.5). These platforms offer avenues for creators to showcase their work, engage with audiences, and monetize their content.

Discussion Questions

1 How has the growth of the creative economy impacted traditional industries? What opportunities and challenges does this present for both sectors?
2 What are the roles of entrepreneurs and entrepreneurship in the economy? Discuss the unique skills and mindset needed for entrepreneurship.
3 Compare and contrast different types of entrepreneurship, such as social, digital, and creative entrepreneurship. How do their goals, methodologies, and impacts vary?
4 Discuss the challenges faced by creative entrepreneurs. How do these challenges differ from those faced by entrepreneurs in traditional industries, and how might creative entrepreneurs overcome these challenges?
5 Analyze one of the cases from this chapter. How does this platform facilitate creative entrepreneurship? What are the benefits and potential risks for creators using this platform?
6 Predict how the creative entrepreneurship landscape might change in the future. How would advancements in technology or shifts in consumer trends impact this field?

Further Reading

- Caves, R. E. (2002) *Creative industries: Contracts between art and commerce.* Cambridge, MA: Harvard University Press.
- Deresiewicz, W. (2015) "The death of the artist—and the birth of the creative entrepreneur." *The Atlantic*, January, 2015. www.theatlantic.com/magazine/archive/2015/01/the-death-of-the-artist-and-the-birth-of-the-creative-entrepreneur/383497/
- Martin, R. L. and Osberg, S. (2007) "Social entrepreneurship: The case for definition." *Stanford Social Innovation Review,* 5(2), pp. 28–39. https://ssir.org/articles/entry/social_entrepreneurship_the_case_for_definition
- Nambisan, S. (2017) "Digital entrepreneurship: Toward a digital technology perspective of entrepreneurship." *Entrepreneurship Theory and Practice*, 41(6), pp. 1029–1055.
- Ryu, S., Dutta, S., Bergen, M., and Zbaracki, M. (2023) "Patreon: A new service and pricing strategy for subscription-based crowdfunding." *Ivey Case Studies.* London, ON: Ivey Publishing.

References

1 "Creative Economy Programme" (no date) *UNCTAD.* https://unctad.org/topic/trade-analysis/creative-economy-programme (Accessed: 20 March 2023).
2 Chapain, C., Emin, S. and Schieb-Bienfait, N. (2018) "Cultural and creative entrepreneurship: Key issues of a still emergent research field." *Revue de l'Entrepreneuriat*, 17(1), pp. 29–37.
3 Dos Santos Duisenberg, E. et al. (2010) "The creative economy report 2010 — Creative economy: A feasible development option." *UNCTAD.* https://unctad.org/system/files/official-document/ditctab20103_en.pdf.
4 Higgs, P., Stuart C. and Hasan, B. (2008) *Beyond the creative industries: Mapping the creative economy in the United Kingdom.* London, UK: NESTA.
5 The Western Development Commission is a statutory body that was established in 1997 to promote social and economic development in the Western Region of Ireland (the counties of Donegal, Leitrim, Sligo, Mayo, Roscommon, Galway, and Clare).

374 New Business Models and Entrepreneurship

6 White, A. (2009) "A grey literature review of the UK Department for Culture, Media and Sport's Creative Industries Economic Estimates and Creative Economy research programme." *Cultural Trends*, 18(4), pp. 337–343.

7 Caves, R. E. (2002) *Creative industries: Contracts between art and Commerce*. Cambridge, MA: Harvard University Press.

8 Koch, F. et al. (2023) "Innovation in the creative industries: Linking the founder's creative and business orientation to innovation outcomes." *Creativity and Innovation Management*, 32(2), pp. 281–297.

9 Markusen, A. and Gadwa, A. (2010) "Creative placemaking" (White paper), *National Endowment for the Arts*. www.arts.gov/sites/default/files/CreativePlacemaking-Paper.pdf.

10 Dutta, D. K. and Crossan, M. M. (2005) "The nature of entrepreneurial opportunities: Understanding the process using the 4I organizational learning framework." *Entrepreneurship Theory and Practice*, 29(4), pp. 425–449.

11 Stewart, W. H. et al. (1999) "A proclivity for entrepreneurship: A comparison of entrepreneurs, small business owners, and corporate managers." *Journal of Business Venturing*, 14(2), pp. 189–214.

12 Val, E. et al. (2017) "A Design Thinking approach to introduce entrepreneurship education in European school curricula." *The Design Journal*, 20(sup1), pp. S754–S766.

13 Katz, Y. (2020) "Entrepreneurial science." *Political Concepts*, November 11. www.politicalconcepts.org/entrepreneurial-science-yarden-katz/.

14 Ziemnowicz, C. (2013) "Joseph A. Schumpeter and Innovation." In E. G. Carayannis (ed.) *Encyclopedia of creativity, invention, innovation and entrepreneurship*. New York: Springer, pp. 1171–1176.

15 Drucker, P. F. (2002) "The discipline of innovation." *Harvard Business Review*, August. https://hbr.org/2002/08/the-discipline-of-innovation.

16 Stevenson, H. H. (1983) "A perspective on entrepreneurship." *Harvard Business School Background Note* October (Revised April 2006), pp. 384–131.

17 Stuetzer, M. et al. (2013) "Where do entrepreneurial skills come from?" *Applied Economics Letters*, 20(12), pp. 1183–1186.

18 Martin, R. L. and Osberg, S. (2007) "Social entrepreneurship: The case for definition', *Stanford Social Innovation Review*, Spring. https://ssir.org/articles/entry/social_entrepreneurship_the_case_for_definition.

19 Gautam, S. (2012) "Creativity components." *The Creativity Post*, September 10. www.creativitypost.com/article/creativity_components.

20 Singh, H. R. and Ratvi, H. (2013) "Traits of successful entrepreneurs." *International Journal of Scientific Research*, 2(11), pp. 292–294.

21 Autio, E. et al. (2014) "Entrepreneurial innovation: The importance of context." *Research Policy*, 43(7), pp. 1097–1108.

22 "What are entrepreneurial ecosystems?" (no date) *Ewing Marion Kauffman Foundation*. www.kauffman.org/ecosystem-playbook-draft-3/ecosystems/.

23 Isenberg, D. (2011) "The entrepreneurship ecosystem strategy as a new paradigm for economy policy: Principles for cultivating entrepreneurship." *Babson Entrepreneurship Ecosystem Project*, Babson College, www.innovationamerica.us/images/stories/2011/The-entrepreneurship-ecosystem-strategy-for-economic-growth-policy-20110620183915.pdf.

24 Uy, M. A., Foo, M.-D. and Song, Z. (2013) "Joint effects of prior start-up experience and coping strategies on entrepreneurs' psychological well-being." *Journal of Business Venturing*, 28(5), pp. 583–597.

25 Baron, R. A. (2008) "The role of affect in the entrepreneurial process." *Academy of Management Review*, 33(2), pp. 328–340.

26 Hartmann, S. et al. (2022) "Psychological resilience of entrepreneurs: A review and agenda for future research." *Journal of Small Business Management*, 60(5), pp. 1041–1079.

27 Wennekers, S. and Thurik, R. (1999) "Linking entrepreneurship and economic growth." *Small Business Economics,* 13, pp. 27–56.

28 Lee, C.-M. et al. (eds) (2000) *The Silicon Valley Edge: a habitat for innovation and entrepreneurship*. Stanford, CA: Stanford University Press.

29 Shane, S. and Venkataraman, S. (2000) "The promise of entrepreneurship as a field of research." *Academy of Management Review*, 25(1), pp. 217–226.

30 Zahra, S. A. et al. (2009) "A typology of social entrepreneurs: Motives, search processes and ethical challenges." *Journal of Business Venturing*, 24(5), pp. 519–532.

31 Laverty, M. and Littel, C. (2020) "6.3 Design Thinking." In *Entrepreneurship*. Houston, TX: OpenStax, Rice University. https://openstax.org/books/entrepreneurship/pages/6-3-design-thinking.

32 "The design thinking process in entrepreneurship" (2020) *Voltage Control*. https://voltagecontrol.com/blog/the-design-thinking-process-in-entrepreneurship/.

33 Khalid, F. (no date) "How to use the design thinking process?" *DevTeam.Space*. www.devteam.space/blog/how-to-use-the-design-thinking-process-to-develop-a-product/.

34 "The design thinking process in entrepreneurship" (2020) *Voltage Control*. https://voltagecontrol.com/blog/the-design-thinking-process-in-entrepreneurship/.

35 Saebi, T., Foss, N. J. and Linder, S. (2019) "Social entrepreneurship research: Past achievements and future promises." *Journal of Management*, 45(1), pp. 70–95.

36 Dees, J. G. (2016) "The meaning of 'social entrepreneurship'." In Allhoff, F., Sager, A. and Vaidya, A. J. (eds.) *Business in Ethical Focus: An Anthology*, 2nd edn. Peterborough, ON: Broadview Press, pp. 160–167.

37 Zahra, S. A. et al. (2009) "A typology of social entrepreneurs: Motives, search processes and ethical challenges." *Journal of Business Venturing*, 24(5), pp. 519–532.

38 Wilson, F. and Post, J. (2013) "Business models for people, planet (& profits): Exploring the phenomena of social business, a market-based approach to social value creation." *Small Business Economics*, 40(3), pp. 715–737.

39 Hull, C. E. et al. (2007) "Taking advantage of digital opportunities: A typology of digital entrepreneurship." *International Journal of Networking and Virtual Organisations*, 4(3), pp. 290–303.

40 Antonizzi, J. and Smuts, H. (2020) "The characteristics of digital entrepreneurship and digital transformation: A systematic literature review." *Responsible Design, Implementation and Use of Information and Communication Technology*, 12066, pp. 239–251.

41 Kraus, S. et al. (2019) "Digital entrepreneurship: A research agenda on new business models for the twenty-first century." *International Journal of Entrepreneurial Behavior & Research*, 25(2), pp. 353–375.

42 Hull, C. E. et al. (2007) "Taking advantage of digital opportunities: A typology of digital entrepreneurship." *International Journal of Networking and Virtual Organisations*, 4(3), pp. 290–303.

43 Nambisan, S. (2017) "Digital entrepreneurship: Toward a digital technology perspective of entrepreneurship." *Entrepreneurship Theory and Practice*, 41(6), pp. 1029–1055.

44 Santos, B. et al. (2021) "Overview on creativity and entrepreneurship in creative industries." *E-Revista De Estudos Interculturais*, 3(9), pp. 1–14. www.iscap.pt/cei/e-rei/n9vol3/atas/Bárbara%20Santos_Óscar%20Bernardes_Vanessa%20Amorim_Orlando%20Rua_Overview%20on%20creativity%20and%20entrepreneurship%20in%20creative%20industries.pdf.

45 Rae, D. (2005) "Cultural diffusion: A formative process in creative entrepreneurship?" *The International Journal of Entrepreneurship and Innovation*, 6(3), pp. 185–192.

46 Kolsteeg, J. (2013) "Situated cultural entrepreneurship." *Artivate*, 2(1), pp. 3–13.

47 Smit, A. J. (2011) "The influence of district visual quality on location decisions of creative entrepreneurs." *Journal of the American Planning Association*, 77(2), pp. 167–184.

48 Henry, C. and de Bruin, A. (eds.) (2011) *Entrepreneurship and the creative economy: Process, practice and policy*. Cheltenham, UK: Edward Elgar Publishing.

49 Santos, B. et al. (2021) "Overview on creativity and entrepreneurship in creative industries." *E-Revista De Estudos Interculturais*, 3(9), pp. 1–14. www.iscap.pt/cei/e-rei/n9vol3/atas/Bárbara%20Santos_Óscar%20Bernardes_Vanessa%20Amorim_Orlando%20Rua_Overview%20on%20creativity%20and%20entrepreneurship%20in%20creative%20industries.pdf.

50 Bujor, A. and Avasilcai, S. (2016) "The creative entrepreneur: A framework of analysis." *Procedia-Social and Behavioral Sciences*, 221, pp. 21–28.

51 Chen, M.-H., Chang, Y.-Y. and Lee, C.-Y. (2015) "Creative entrepreneurs' guanxi networks and success: Information and resource." *Journal of Business Research*, 68(4), pp. 900–905.

52 Suwala, L. (2015) "Cultural entrepreneurship." In Wherry, F. F. and Schor, J. B. (eds.) *The Sage encyclopedia of economics and society*, Thousand Oaks, CA: SAGE Publications, pp. 513–515.

53 Engelmann, M., Grünewald, L. and Heinrich, J. (2012) "The new artrepreneur – how artists can thrive on a networked music business." *International Journal of Music Business Research*, 1(2), pp. 31–45.

54 Chen, M.-H., Chang, Y.-Y. and Pan, J.-Y. (2018) "Typology of creative entrepreneurs and entrepreneurial success." *Journal of Enterprising Communities: People and Places in the Global Economy*, 12(5), pp. 632–656.

INDEX

References to illustrations are in *italics*. References to tables are in **bold**.

5G technology: benefits 296; and impact on MEI 297–8; new revenue opportunities 297–8; related technological advancements 296–7, *297*

Aaker, David: brand equity model 191, *192*
Activision Blizzard 17, 18, 320
advertising: digital 273; subscription pricing, comparison 50–1, 272–3
advertising revenues: fall 272
Aladdin 195
algorithms: pricing 257
Alibaba: case study 264
Amazon: diversification 148–9
Amazon Mechanical Turk 288
Amazon Prime Video 270
Amazon Web Services 246
analog signals 238–9
analysis: external 130–3; internal 133–6; Porter's Five Forces Model 130–2, *130*, *133*; role 129–30; *see also* SWOT analysis
Anderson, Chris 257, 258
Anime 53
AOL: case study 115
Apple: case studies 115, 346; growth 346; portfolio 4–5
Apple Pay 262
apps: gaming 263; lifestyle/entertainment 263; m-commerce 263; productivity 263; travel 263; utility 263
artificial intelligence (AI) 11–12, 80; and automation 300; British Broadcasting Corporation (BBC), use 301; in business 299, 300, *300*; concept 298; context *299*; and data

analytics 300; in MEI 301–2; music composition 301–2; and natural language processing (NLP) 300; objectives 298; personalization 301; *see also* ChatGPT; deep learning (DL); generative AI; machine learning (ML)
artist management 78
assessment tasks (ATs) x, *xi*; types xii
augmented reality (AR) 241
authority concept 97
automation: and AI 300
Avatar 23, 54

Baidu: case study 264
balanced scorecard: organizational performance 104–5, *105*
benchmarking 95–6
bias 112
"big, hairy, audacious goals" (BHAGs) 127
Big Hit Entertainment *see* HYBE
Bilibili: case study 371
Black Panther 55
The Blair Witch Project 188
Blockbuster corporation: case study 116, 264
blockbusters 22–3; advantages 23; vs long tail 258–9
blockchain technology 12; applications for creators 311–12, *311*; benefits 305, 309–10; business models 312–13, **312**; business role 308–9; content distribution 310; data protection 310; dynamic pricing 312; in finance 308; and IP rights 311; key components 307–8, **307**; in MEI 309–13; micropayments 310, 311–12; personalization

378 Index

310; principles 305–7, *306*; reputation systems 312; security features 310; smart contracts 310, 311, 312; workings 305, *306*
Bluetooth 260
#BookTok: influence on book sales 281–2
Borden, Neil 173
Boston Consulting Group 142
brand: benefits 189–90, **190**; community 193–4, *194*; definition 188; identity 191; loyalty 193; name, and differentiation strategy 143–4; recognition, media franchise 41–2, **42**; reinforcement, promotion 187; scope 188–9; value of 189
brand equity: definition 191; model 192, *192*
brand leverage 194–5, *195*; brand extension *195*, 196; line extension 195–6, *195*
branding: impact 190–1; origins 189; strategic process 190
branding paradigm: vs hit paradigm 177, **177**
branding strategy: and hit marketing 177–8, *178*
Branson, Richard 148
British Broadcasting Corporation (BBC): use of AI 301
broadcast networks 14
broadcasters *see* commercial broadcasters; public service broadcasters
Brown, Tim 363
BTS band 16; case study 290–1
budgeting 96
business analytics 246
business model: concept 328; generic examples 340; interdependent factors 329–30, **330**; interlocking components 330–1, *330*; and management team 338; purpose 328–9; value proposition 329; *see also* platform business model; revenue model
Business Model Canvas (BMC) 331–2, *331*
business model innovation: concept 343; examples 343; importance 343; outcomes 345; *see also* digital business model innovation
business model innovation process: purpose 343; steps 344–5, *344*
business model planning: elements 332–4, *333*; raising capital 339; timing 339
business strategy: corporate strategy, comparison **138**; elements 137; generic type *140*, **146**; purpose 139, 328; and value-price-cost framework 139–40, **139**; *see also* corporate strategy
ByteDance: case study 28; *see also* TikTok

Call of Duty 18
Candy Crush Saga 17, 18
capabilities 134
capital: sources 339

case studies: Alibaba 264; AOL 115; Apple 115, 346; Baidu 264; Bilibili 371; Blockbuster 116, 264; BTS band 290–1; ByteDance 28; CJ E&M 154; Disney 115; Etsy 371; HYBE 346; *League of Legends* 56; LEGO 84; *Minecraft* 320; Netflix 84, 264; *New York Times* 290; News Corp. 153; NFTs 319–20; Patreon 372; Red Bull 197; *Roblox* 320; Spotify 289, 289–90; *Star Wars* 55; Starbucks 230; Tencent 264; Threadless 290; TikTok 28; TKTS Theatres Centers 197; Virgin Group 153–4; Vivendi 28; Walt Disney 27; Zappos 230–1
Caves, Richard 354; *Creative Industries: Contracts Between Art and Commerce* 352
celebrity: and social media 279
celebrity endorsement: and differentiation strategy 144
cellular networks 260–1
centralization: vs decentralization 97, 98
chain of command 97
change: Darwin on 130; *see also* organizational change
change agents: organizational change 111
ChatGPT: as generative AI 302
Chesbrough, Henry 283
Cinelytic software 301
CJ E&M: case study 154; corporate strategy 154; portfolio 5–6
cloud computing 246, *247*
Coca-Cola company: diversification 148
collaborative filtering: customer expansion 226
Collins, Jim & Porras, Jerry: *Built to Last: Successful Habits of Visionary Companies* 128
Columbia Pictures 148
Comcast: portfolio 5–6
commercial broadcasters 14
communication *see* organizational communication
community: and creator economy 283; and crowdfunding 289; engagement 84
competencies: business 369, *369*; creative entrepreneurs 369–70, *369*; cultural *36*, 369; social 369, *369*; transferring 148; *see also* core competence
competitive advantage *135*; development 336–7; first-mover advantage 337–8; forms 135; and strategic management 123
competitive environment 336
competitor intelligence 95
Condé Nast 15
conflict management: global teams 112
connectivity: and digitization 241
consumer demand: MEI 23–4; *see also* hedonic consumption

consumers: definition 165

core competence: key issues 134; leveraging 147; MEI examples 134

core customer 204–5, 213–14, *214*; in CRM 203, *204*; ideal 165–6; identification 221–2; satisfaction 206; types *205*

core values 127

corporate culture: and HRM 99

corporate governance 151

corporate strategy: business strategy, comparison **138**; CJ E&M 154; elements 138; purpose 146; *see also* business strategy

corporate vision 126–7, *127*; *see also* goals

corporation analysis: marketing analysis 170–1

cost 136

cost leadership strategy **146**; benefits 140; flexibility 140; purpose 140; risks 140

COVID-19: lockdown 12, 16, 21, 22, 270; and movie theaters 281; and online platforms 253

Crazy Rich Asians 55

create once, publish everywhere (COPE) 38; advantages of 40; National Public Radio (NPR) 40

creative entrepreneurs: characteristics 368–70; concept 367–8; constructionists 370, *370*; designers 370, *370*; key competencies 369–70, *369*; opportunists 370, *370*; producers *370*, 371; tasks 368; vs traditional entrepreneurs 368–9; types 370–1, *370*

creative entrepreneurship 357; activities 368; definition 367; economic diversification 368; sociocultural values 368; and work-life balance 368

creative independence: and crowdfunding 289

creative industries: categories 352, *353*; components 12; creative clustering 354; definition 352; IP rights 353; key features 352, *353*; risks 352

creative professionals: and generative AI 305

creative/creator economy: characteristics 351–2, *351*; and community 283; concept 351; entrepreneurship 354; and social media 282–3; trends 282–3

creativity: and economies of learning (experience curve) 143; entrepreneurship 357; *see also* organizational creativity

creators: emergence 282; niche 282; revenues 282

cross-selling: customer expansion 225–6; upselling, comparison 226, **227**

crowdfunding 26; and community 289; and creative independence 289; fan base 26; and MEI 289; Patreon 372; platforms 26, 288, 289

crowdsourcing: benefits 286–7, *287*; disadvantages 287; Threadless 290; types 287–8

cultural discount 57; definition 53; rate 54; theory 53–4

cultural intelligence 81

cultural premium 54–5, 57; examples 55

customer acquisition 230; concept 212–13; data sources 216; importance 213; new customers 215–16, *215*; and profitability 213; the right customer *215*; target audience 213

customer analysis: marketing analysis 170

customer equity: calculation *210*; and customer lifetime value (CLV) 209, *209*

customer expansion 221–8, 230; collaborative filtering 226; cross-selling 225–6; and "moment of truth" 222–3, *222*; partnerships 227–8, *228*; and profitability 223, *223*; steps 228; upselling 224–5, *225*; *see also* customer acquisition

customer lifetime value (CLV) 208–9; calculation *210*; and customer equity 209, *209*; and customer loyalty *223*; exercise on 210; importance 209; increasing *224*

customer loyalty: and CLV *223*; importance 206; measurement 206–7; Net Promoter Score (NPS) 206–7, *208*; and profitability *207*; *see also* core customer

customer misbehavior: customers to avoid 229, **229**; disengagement from 230; management of 229–30, **229**

customer relationship management (CRM) strategies 203, *203*, 230; framework 211–12, *211*, *212*

customer retention 230; benefits 218; importance 217–18, **218**; loyalty programs 219–20, **220**; measurement 218; practices 218–19; "rule of two" 219; *see also* core customer

customer share map: movie theaters *217*

customer value creation 205–6

Dall-E: graphic generative AI 302

The Dark Knight 54

Darwin, Charles: on change 130

data: definition 244, *244*

data analytics 80; and AI 300

data protection: blockchain technology 310

decision-making 90–1; and ERP 246; process 91–3, *92*, 116; teams 100

deep learning (DL) *299*; applications 299; deep neural networks 299; *see also* machine learning (ML)

departmentalization 97

design thinking: and entrepreneurship 363–5, *364*; steps 364, *364*

differentiation strategy **146**; advantages 144; and brand name 143–4; and celebrity endorsement 144; disadvantages 144–5; and guarantees 144; MEI 143–4; and packaging 144; and sponsorship 144

380 Index

digital business model innovation: development
345; diffusion 345; discovery 345; evaluation
of impact 345–6
digital marketing: personalization 26
digital media 10–11
digital music distribution 16
digital music market 329
digital regenerators 239
digital revolution: characteristics *242*; Industrial
Revolution, comparison 242; new
industries 241
digital signals 239; vs analog signals 238–9, *238*
digital subscriptions: *New York Times* 273
digital transformation 240; MEI 270–1; music
industry 21, 242; personalization 273–4
digitalization 239; benefits 243; of experiences
240; publishing industry 243
digitization 239; and connectivity 241
discrimination 113
Disney: case study 115
Disney + channel 25
distribution: diversification *25*; low marginal
cost 45–6; music industry 25; trends 24–5
distributors 185
diversification: Amazon 148–9; assessment of
business attractiveness 149–50, *149*; Coca-
Cola company 148; critical tests 147; News
Corp. 153; related 147–8; Starbucks 148, 149;
unrelated 148–50; Virgin Group 148, 153–4
diversity: aspects 112, *113*; and inclusion 84;
promotion of 113–14
Drucker, Peter: on entrepreneurship 356; and
MBO 68–9
Dungeon Fighter Online 18

e-business: concept 254
e-commerce: benefits 255–6; characteristics 255;
disintermediation 255–6, *256*; long tail 257,
257, 258; price competition 256; pure vs
partial 254, *254*; reduced price hypothesis
256; success factors 259, *259*;
see also blockbusters; m-commerce
e-sports industry 17–18
economic diversification: creative
entrepreneurship 368
economies of learning (experience curve) 142–3;
and creativity 143; MEI 143
economies of scale 141–2; calculation exercise
141–2; drivers 141; MEI 142; methods 141
economies of scope 148
ecosystems: entrepreneurship 360–1, *360*
Electronic Arts (EA) 18
enterprise resource planning (ERP) 245; and
decision-making 246; integrative vs
traditional views 246, *247*; purpose 246
entrepreneurs *see* creative entrepreneurs
entrepreneurship: concept 355; context 359;

in creative economy 354; and design thinking
363–5, *364*; digital 366–7; Drucker on 356;
ecosystems 360–2, *360*; history of 355; and
innovation 356, 362–3; leadership 357;
outcomes 362–3, *362*; and resourcefulness
356; Schumpeter on 355–6; skills needed
357–9, *358*; social 365–6; *see also* creative
entrepreneurship
environmental scanning 94–5
ethics 114
Etsy: case study 371
event management 78
Everydays: The First 5000 Days 12
experience goods: characteristics 46, 56;
examples 46; *see also* search goods

fan base 17; and crowdsourcing 26
fandom 52–3, 56; examples 53
Fayol, Henri: on management 64–6
FIFA 18
film: history of 9
film industry: studios 13
film production and distribution 13
film and video market: growth 19–20
flextime working 99
focus strategy **146**; advantages 145; types 145
Ford, Henry: and moving assembly line 67
forecasting 92; qualitative 95; quantitative 95
formalization concept 98
Fortnite 12, 316
Fox: portfolio 6
free-rider problem: public goods 48–9
freemium games 18

GameCube 18
games 11; *see also* mobile gaming; videogames
gaming industry 271; components 17; NFTs 313
Gantt charts: example 96, *96*
Gen Z: and identity 26; radical inclusivity 27
gender distinctions: streaming services 51–2
gender gap 113
generative AI: application 302; business
applications **303**; and creative professionals
305; graphic 302; interactivity 304; IP issues
304–5; in MEI 302, 304–5; personalization
304; potential uses 304–5
gig workers 253
Giovagnoli, Max 43
"glass ceiling" phenomenon 113
global scanning 95
global teams: communication 112; composition
112; conflict management 112; cultural
differences 112; informal connections 112;
managing 112; structure 112
globalization 80–1
goals 93–4, 127–9; characteristics 128;
characteristics of good goals *94*; purpose 128;

Index **381**

SMART 128–9, *128*; *see also* corporate vision
Google Analytics 246
Google Pay 262
groups *see* teams
guarantees: and differentiation strategy 144

Hachette Livre 15
Hamel, Gary 129
Harley Owners Group (HOG) 193
HarperCollins 15
Harry Potter 23, 41, 53, 177
Hearst Magazines 15
Hebdige, Dick: *Subculture: The Meaning of Style* 52
hedonic consumption 56; decision-making criteria for 36–7, **37**; definition 35; marketing 38; unique characteristics 36; utilitarian consumption, comparison **37**
Hello Kitty 41
Henderson, Bruce D. 142
high-risk: high-return 43–4, 44–6, *44*, *45*, 56
hit marketing: and branding strategy 177–8, *178*; viral campaigns 177
hit paradigm: MEI 177; vs branding paradigm 177, **177**
Honor of Kings 18
human resource management (HRM):and corporate culture 99
human resources (HR) development 338
HYBE: case study 346; portfolio 6

identity: and Gen Z 26
Iger, Bob: profile 116
Indiegogo platform 26, 289
Industrial Revolution: digital revolution, comparison 242
influencers 187, 271, 281, 282, 290, 291
information: definition 244, *244*
information systems: concept *245*; *see also* enterprise resource planning
information technology and information systems 245, *245*; business value of 246, 248–50, *248*, *249*; productivity frontier 249, *249*
innovation: and entrepreneurship 356; and online platforms 250; Schumpeter's definition 283; *see also* open innovation
integration: vertical vs horizontal 150
intellectual property (IP) rights 12, 77; and blockchain technology 311; creative industries 353; and generative AI 304–5; and open innovation 285
intended learning outcomes (ILOs) *xi*; definition x–xi; tasks xii
interactivity: generative AI 304; metaverse 319; Netflix 273; platform business model 342

Internet of Things 241, 296
Isenberg, Daniel 360
iTunes 25, 242

Jacobson, David 40
Jobs, Steve 100

K-pop 53; cultural familiarity 54
Kart Rider 18
key business disciplines x
Kickstarter platform 26, 289
Kindle Direct Publishing 243
knowledge: definition 244, *244*

leaders: key characteristics 101–2, *101*
leadership: entrepreneurship 357; path-goal theory 102–3, *102*; styles 101, 116; traits 100, 117
League of Legends 18–19, 56
lecturers: role xii
The Legend of Zelda 18
LEGO: case study 84
LEGO Digital Designer 288
linear pipeline model: platform business model, comparison 341, *341*
The Lion King 195
Live Nation 16
long tail: e-commerce 257, *257*, *258*; vs blockbusters 258–9
loyalty programs: customer retention 219–20, **220**; examples 220; importance 220; mistakes to avoid 220–1; Starbucks 230

m-commerce: apps 263; services 262
machine learning (ML) 299, *299*; applications 299
Macmillan 15
Madden NFL 18
management: concept 64; definitions 64, 85; Fayol on 64–6; functions 64–6, *65*; history of 66–9; Industrial Revolution era 67; MEI, traditional management, comparison 78–80, **79**; modern era 68–9; music 77–8; overview 63–4; pre-Industrial Revolution 66–7; scientific era 68; skills 75–7, *76*; styles 75; *see also* artist management; event management; music management
Management by Objectives (MBO) 68–9
management team: and business model 338; tasks 339; *see also* leaders; leadership
managers: definition 69; developing people 70, 71; devising measurement systems 70–1, *70*; different levels 74–5, *74*; low-level 74; middle-level 74–5; motivating the team 70, *70*; objectives setting 70, *70*; organizing 70, *70*; primary functions *70*; roles 71–3, *72*; senior-level 75

382 Index

MapleStory 18
market: orientation 164
market failure: MEI 49–51
market opportunities 335–6
market strategy: development 337–8
marketing analysis 167–71; 3C analysis 170–1;
    corporation analysis 170–1; customer
    analysis 170; macroenvironment factors 167;
    microenvironment factors 168, 170;
    PEST(LE) framework 167–8, **169**;
    see also segmentation-targeting-
    positioning (STP)
marketing channels 174, 182–3, *183*;
    comparison 184–5, *184*, **184**; digital 185–6,
    186; direct 183–4, **184**; indirect 184, **184**;
    internet 185
marketing management: overview 161–2
marketing mix 166, 173–88; 4Cs 174–5, *174*; 4Ps
    166, *174*; communication *174*, 175;
    components 162; convenience *174*, 175; cost
    174, 175; customer needs 174, *174*; definition
    162; distributors 183; hedonic consumption
    38; objectives *162*, 163; price 174; product
    174; promotion 174; questions 165; sales,
    difference 164, **164**, 165, *165*; and value
    163–4; *see also* marketing channels;
    promotional mix
marketing planning process 166, *167*
marketing promotion 186–7; advertising 187;
    expectations 187
marketing segmentation 166
marketing strategy 166
marketing trends 25–6; *see also* digital
    marketing
Marvel Cinematic Universe (MCU) 41
media *see* digital media; print media
Media and Entertainment Industry (MEI):
    categorization 12; characteristics vii, 34, *35*;
    consumer demand 23–4; convergent
    segments *13*; economic traits viii; emerging
    trends 22–8; external drivers 24; history 8–12;
    management in 77–80; management style viii;
    market failure 49–51; media impact 46–7;
    new business models 46; overview 19, 28–9;
    production aspects 22–4, *22*; projected
    growth vii; representative companies 4;
    revenues vii; roles in society 7–8; scope
    12–19; and social media 24; societal values
    50; star systems 47; statistics 19; uniqueness
    viii
media franchise 40–1; benefits 41–2, *42*; brand
    recognition 41–2, *42*; cross-promotion 42, *42*;
    diversification 42, *42*; examples 41; fan
    engagement 42, *42*; *Star Wars* case study 55;
    sustainability 42–3, *42*
media impact: MEI 46–7
mergers and acquisitions (M&As) 7

metaverse: business applications 318; challenges
    318; concept 12, 315; functionality layers
    316–17, *317*; growth rate 316; interactivity
    319; market value 316; and MEI 319;
    monetization 319; and NFTs 315; origins
    316; *Roblox* 320
Microsoft Azure 246
Miller, Madeline: *The Song of Achilles* 282
Minecraft 316; case study 320
Mintzberg, Henry 69, 71
MMORPG (multiplayer online role-playing
    game) 11
mobile applications: native apps 262, *263*;
    web apps 263
mobile business: concept 260
mobile entertainment: drivers 271–2;
    interactivity 272; personalized content 272
mobile gaming 17, 22; user-generated
    content 273
mobile marketing 261
mobile networks 260–1
mobile technology 260–1
monetization: metaverse 319; and social media 279
movie theaters: and COVID-19 281; customer
    share map *217*; upselling 224–5
movie tickets: price discrimination 182
music composition: AI use 301–2
music industry 16–17; digital transformation 21,
    242; distribution 25; growth 20–1; streaming
    services 242; *see also* streaming services
music management 77–8
music sales: influence of TikTok 282

Napster 242
National Public Radio (NPR):COPE 40
natural language processing (NLP): and AI 300
NBA Top Shot 12
Net Promoter Score (NPS): calculation *208*;
    customer loyalty 206–7; top performers 208
Netflix 24, 243, 342; case study 84, 264;
    interactivity 273; streaming revenue 5
networks *see* cellular networks; WiFi networks
New York Times: case study 290; digital
    subscriptions 273
News Corp.: case study 153; diversification 153
Nexon 18
Nintendo 18
Nintendo 64 18
Nintendo Entertainment System 18
Nintendo Switch 18
non-fungible tokens (NFTs) 12; advantages 314;
    applications 313; case study 319–20; and
    digital artworks 313; gaming industry 313;
    risks 314, 315
non-market environment *152*

Oculus Studios 319

Ohmae, Kenichi 170
one source, multi-use (OSMU): *Mickey Mouse* 38; *Star Wars* 38, **39**
online platforms 13–14; benefits 251; concept 250; and COVID-19 253; ecosystem driver 251; effects on employment 252–3; hybrid 251; and innovation 250; innovation 250; and MEI 253; modular producer model 251; omni-Channel 251; R&D investment 250; risks 252; supplier model 251; transaction 250; types 250–1; *see also* platform business model
open innovation: closed innovation, comparison 283–4, **284**; concept 283; and IP rights 285; obstacles 285–6; purpose 284; system dynamics *285*
open-source software 288
organization and organizing 96–8
organizational behavior (OB): elements 117; overview 89–90
organizational change: change agents 111; drivers 111; role models 111; success factors 111
organizational communication: comprehensive plan for 109–10; directional 108; downward 108; formal vs informal 107–8, **107**; functions 107; horizontally 108; importance 107, 117; internal vs external 108–9; multiple channels 110; oral vs written 109; process 105–6, *106*; tools for 109; training programs 110; upward 108
organizational control: importance 103; and organizational performance 104; processes 104, 117; tasks 103; *see also* planning
organizational coordination 103
organizational creativity: definition 110; managing 110–11; originality 110; processes 110; usefulness 110
organizational culture 111, 338
organizational design: adaptive 98–9; divisional structure 98; functional structure 98; key elements *97*, 117; matrix structure 98; project structure 98; traditional 98; virtual 98
organizational development: key elements 338
organizational performance: balanced scorecard 104–5, *105*; and organizational control 104
outcome-based education (OBE) x
outcome-based teaching and learning (OBTL) x; overview *xi*
Over-the-top (OTT) services 270
Overwatch 18

packaging: and differentiation strategy 144
Paramount Global: portfolio 6
Patagonia company 99
Patreon: case study 372
pay-cable services 51

pay-per-view services 51
Penguin Random House 15
personalization: AI 301; blockchain technology 310; digital marketing 26; digital transformation 273–4; generative AI 304; and MEI 273; value proposition 334
PEST(LE) framework: economic factors 168, **169**; environmental factors **169**; legal factors **169**; marketing analysis 167–8; political factors 167–8, **169**; social factors 168, **169**; technological factors 168, **169**
piracy: recording industry 16, 25
planning: collaborative 94; definition 92–3; externally oriented 124; financial 124; forecast-based 124; foundation 93–4; techniques/skills 94–6, 116–17; top-down 94; *see also* business model planning
platform business model: disintermediation 342; interactivity 342; linear pipeline model, comparison 341, *341*; in MEI 341–2; personalization 342; scalability 342; value creation 342; *see also* online platforms
Pokémon 18, 41
Porter, Michael 69
Porter's Five Forces Model 130–2, *130*; key success factors 132, *133*; MEI 132, 133
prejudice 112–13
price 136; customers' perceptions 178; and value 178
price discrimination 181, *181*; airline industry 181; movie tickets 182; success factors 181–2
pricing: competition-based 179; cost-based 179; golden rule *178*; mistakes in 179–80; new product 180; penetration 180, **180**; penetration vs skimming pricing **180**; skimming **180**, 181; value-based 179; virtual reality headsets 181; *see also* subscription pricing
print industry 14–15
print media: history of 8–9
print and publishing industry: growth 20
product lifecycle: stages 176, *176*
product orientation 163–4
product types: experiential 175, *175*; functional 175, *175*; symbolic 175–6, *175*
production orientation 163
profitability: and customer acquisition 213; and customer expansion 223, *223*; and customer loyalty *207*; key factors 135–6
promotion: awareness building 187; brand reinforcement 187; creating interest 187; providing information 187; stimulating demand 187; *see also* promotional mix
promotional mix: advertising 187; direct marketing 188; personal selling 187–8; public relations 187; sales promotions 188
PUBG Mobile 18

384 Index

public goods 56; definition 48; free-rider
   problem 48–9; MEI products 49
public service broadcasters 14
publishing industry: digitalization 243; key
   roles 15

R&D investment: online platforms 250
radio: history of 9
radio broadcasting industry 14
recording industry: piracy 16, 25
Red Bull: case study 197
resourcefulness: and entrepreneurship 356
resources 133
responsibility concept 97
retail stores 185
revenue model *333*, 334–5; advertising 334;
   development *334*; "freemium" 335; MEI 334;
   subscription 335
Riot Games 18–19, 56
risks: cost leadership strategy 140; creative
   industries 352; online platforms 252
Roblox 316; case study 320; metaverse 320
role models: organizational change 111

Sahlman, William 329–30
salesforces 184–5
scheduling 96
Schumpeter, Joseph: on entrepreneurship
   355–6; on innovation 283
Scott, Travis 12
Scriptbook software 301
search goods: examples 46; *see also* experience
   goods
Second Life game 316
segmentation-targeting-positioning (STP) 162,
   171–3; positioning 172–3, *172*; segmentation
   171, *171*; strategy *173*; targeting 172
selling orientation 164
Simon & Schuster 15
The Sims 18
social media 271; benefits 276–7, **277**; and
   celebrity 279; and creator economy 282–3;
   democratization 280; disadvantages 277, **277**;
   examples 275; and MEI 24, 278–80, *279*, 281;
   and monetization 279; as primary platform
   281; reasons for using *275*, 276; strategy,
   "4Ms" 278, *278*
social responsibility: elements 114–15
societal values: MEI **50**
sociocultural values: creative
   entrepreneurship 368
Sony: portfolio 7
Sony Music Entertainment 16
span of control 97
Spotify 16, 25, 242, 243, 258–9, 272; case study
   289–90

star systems: MEI 47
Star Wars 23, 38, **39**, 177
Starbucks: case study 230; diversification 148,
   149; loyalty program 230
Stephenson, Neal: *Snow Crash* 316
stereotyping 113
Stevenson, Howard 356
Stranger Things 53
strategic business units (SBUs) 124
strategic management 124; and competitive
   advantage 123; components 122, *122*;
   concept 122–3; importance of 123; process
   125–6, *125*; theory development 124–5;
   see also business strategy; corporate strategy;
   cost leadership strategy; differentiation
   strategy; focus strategy
strategic thinking: examples of failure 123; need
   for 123
strategy: nonmarket 151
strategy implementation 152–3; success
   factors 153
streaming services 16, 25, 270; gender
   distinctions 51–2; growth 21; music industry
   242; and traditional media 281
stress reduction 111–12
students: expectations xi
subcultural groups 51–2
subculture: definition 51
subscription pricing: advertising, comparison
   50–1, 272–3
Super Mario 18
sustainability: critical issue in MEI 83;
   economic 81, *82*; environmental 81, *82*;
   examples 84; social 81, *82*; and UN
   Sustainable Development Goals (SDG) 82–3
SWOT analysis: elements 136; external factors
   136–7, **137**; internal factors 136, **137**;
   potential questions **137**

target audience: customer acquisition 213
Taylor, Frederick: and output measurement 68
teaching and learning activities (TLAs) *xi*;
   definition x
teams: conflict management 100; decision-
   making 100; and external conditions 100;
   formation 99–100; norms 100; resources 100;
   roles 100; status system 100; structure 100;
   see also global teams
technology: exponential growth 80
telecommuting 99
television: history of 10
television and radio broadcasting: growth 20
television station: structure 14
Tencent: case study 264; portfolio 6–7
Tencent Games 18
theme parks: Walt Disney Company 27

Threadless 288; case study 290; crowdsourcing 290
TikTok 14, 272; case study 28; influence on music sales 282
Time Inc. 15
TKTS Theater Centers: case study 197
transmedia storytelling 43

UN: environmental, social and governance (ESG) criteria 82, 83; Sustainable Development Goals (SDG) 82–3
Universal Music Group 16
upselling: cross-selling, comparison 226, **227**; customer expansion 224; examples *225*; movie theaters 224–5
utilitarian consumption: hedonic consumption, comparison **37**

value: definition 135; equation 163; and marketing 163–4; and price 178; subjectivity 163
value creation: platform business model 342
value proposition: business model 329; characteristics 334; definition 334; personalization 334
value-added partners 185
value-price-cost framework *135*; and business strategy 139–40, **139**
ViacomCBS 84
videogames 17–19; development 17; growth 22; publishing 17; *see also* mobile gaming

Virgin Group: case study 153–4; diversification 148, 153–4
virtual production 24
virtual reality headsets: pricing 181
virtual reality (VR) 241
Vivendi: case study 28

Walt Disney Company: case study 27; portfolio 4; theme parks 27
Warner Music Group 16
Web 3.0 315
WeChat Mini Programs (MPs) 263
WiFi networks 260
Wii 18
window effect 38–43, 56
Winfrey, Oprah: profile 116
word of mouth 47–8
Wordle 17
work specialization 97
work-life balance: and creative entrepreneurship 368
World of Warcraft 18

Xbox 320

young customer groups: characteristics 26; consumption patterns 27
YouTube 13–14, 24, 342

Zappos: case study 230–1

Threadless 288; case study 290; crowdsourcing 290
TikTok 14, 272; case study 28; influence on music sales 282
Time Inc. 15
TKTS Theater Centers: case study 197
transmedia storytelling 43

UN: environmental, social and governance (ESG) criteria 82, 83; Sustainable Development Goals (SDG) 82–3
Universal Music Group 16
upselling: cross-selling, comparison 226, **227**; customer expansion 224; examples *225*; movie theaters 224–5
utilitarian consumption: hedonic consumption, comparison **37**

value: definition 135; equation 163; and marketing 163–4; and price 178; subjectivity 163
value creation: platform business model 342
value proposition: business model 329; characteristics 334; definition 334; personalization 334
value-added partners 185
value-price-cost framework *135*; and business strategy 139–40, **139**
ViacomCBS 84
videogames 17–19; development 17; growth 22; publishing 17; *see also* mobile gaming

Virgin Group: case study 153–4; diversification 148, 153–4
virtual production 24
virtual reality headsets: pricing 181
virtual reality (VR) 241
Vivendi: case study 28

Walt Disney Company: case study 27; portfolio 4; theme parks 27
Warner Music Group 16
Web 3.0 315
WeChat Mini Programs (MPs) 263
WiFi networks 260
Wii 18
window effect 38–43, 56
Winfrey, Oprah: profile 116
word of mouth 47–8
Wordle 17
work specialization 97
work-life balance: and creative entrepreneurship 368
World of Warcraft 18

Xbox 320

young customer groups: characteristics 26; consumption patterns 27
YouTube 13–14, 24, 342

Zappos: case study 230–1

Printed in the United States
by Baker & Taylor Publisher Services